SALA

The Portrait of an Eminent Victorian

By

RALPH STRAUS

*With a frontispiece in colour,
sixteen plates of
illustrations
and others in the text*

CONSTABLE AND COMPANY LTD
LONDON

PUBLISHED BY

Constable and Company Ltd.

LONDON

·

*The Macmillan Company
of Canada, Limited*

TORONTO

First published in 1942

Printed in Great Britain by T. and A. CONSTABLE LTD,
at the University Press, Edinburgh

To

EDWARD HOWELL

WITH GRATEFUL ACKNOWLEDGMENT OF HIS
ASSISTANCE, GIVEN OVER A NUMBER OF YEARS,
AND A COMPLETE UNDERSTANDING OF HIS
REASONS FOR REGARDING THE NAME OF

SALA

WITH THE UTMOST DETESTATION

CONTENTS

BOOK ONE: THE SETTING OF THE STAGE

LIST OF PLATES

NOTE

I WISH to record my particular thanks to Mr. A. T. Butler (*Windsor Herald*), Mr. William Andrews, Editor of the *Yorkshire Post*, Mr. Michael Sadleir, and Mr. Hugh Wheeler, for the help they have given me; to Sir Max Beerbohm for permitting me to include so admirable a frontispiece; and also to Captain F. L. Pleadwell, C.B.E., M.C., of Honolulu, Mr. de V. Payen-Payne, Mr. A. H. Cleaver, and the Hon. Sec. of the London Press Club for allowing me to see and make use of letters written by Sala and now in their possession.

BOOK ONE: THE SETTING OF THE STAGE

CHAPTER ONE

OVERTURE: MAINLY THEATRICAL

I

THIS is the story of an Eminent Victorian about whom, I regret to note, most modern interpreters of the period have nothing whatever to say. Admittedly he was no genius. Perhaps he was not even what generally passes for a great man. He died less than fifty years ago and today he is almost forgotten. Almost, but not quite; and if there can be no pedestal for him, at least there is a niche, and the niche, I like to think, is not without its interest. His story, moreover, is in some slight measure a reflection of the story of his times. In almost every part of the civilised world his name was well known, on more than one occasion he showed himself to be a pioneer of importance, and he played his part in guiding public opinion. So much, of course, does not excuse yet another full-length memoir. Nor, indeed, can the multiplicity of his interests be put forward in extenuation. Novelist and essayist, special correspondent and leader-writer, draughtsman and engraver, dramatist and scene-painter, critic and lecturer, a *bon viveur* who could cook an admirable dinner and round it off with a speech even better: in his manysidedness George Augustus Sala certainly did not stand alone. He was not the only writer whose work was mistaken for Dickens's or came in for Matthew Arnold's displeasure. He was not the only man of his time who could discourse upon anything under the sun and give to his writings an individual touch, a polish, something of a sparkle. Even the fact—I dare to call it a fact—that no man ever wrote more words than he did hardly entitles him to special treatment. But he was much more than a mere scribe: he was, definitely, a Figure.

All his life odd and unexpected things continued to happen to him, from the day when his nurse nearly killed him to the day when a Prime Minister of England came to his rescue. He was a man of many friends but almost as many enemies; a man who was half-blind and in almost constant ill-health yet took but little care of himself and lived to be nearly seventy; a man who earned the princeliest sums by his pen, but was generally in debt and died in the greatest poverty; a hot-tempered, blustering, but always picturesque personality who, as I shall attempt to show, swaggered his way through those decorous Victorian days and came to occupy a position which may fairly be called unique.

A

He wrote his own *Life and Adventures*, and the book is entertaining enough, but it fails to reveal the man himself. It was the work of a tired old champion, bowed down with domestic worries and in desperate need of money: a "full-dress" affair of the kind that was so popular in those days, amiable, easy-going, amusingly discursive, and, in spite of its numerous inaccuracies, of some value to students of nineteenth-century social history, but oddly impersonal and, above all, of an almost monumental respectability. Nothing which could possibly give offence was included. Whitewash was freely applied to everybody, including the author himself. Old quarrels and misunderstandings were conveniently forgotten, and there was nothing to show that in the course of a long and arduous life there had been some episodes not as happy, nor, indeed, as seemly, as others. And without some knowledge of these it is impossible to understand the fiery, unstable, but not unlovable man whose career built itself up into a queer kind of angry romance.

2

We may as well begin with another eccentric: a Florentine ballet-dancer who, jauntily but improperly, assumed the rank and title of a British knight, and, because at the time he was a popular figure in London, persuaded the public to believe that the dignity which he claimed was rightly his.

A gallant and modish fellow, this Giovanni Andrea Battista Gallini, and something more than a clever dancer blessed with unusual good looks: a shrewd man of business, with ideas, and not afraid to take risks; an enthusiast with the loftiest opinion of his own abilities, but not without tact and with several languages and a veneer of scholarship to help him; a gay and amusing chatterer, equally at home in the box-office of a theatre or in a nobleman's drawing-room. In a word, a man almost bound to succeed.

Succeed he did, though in which European capital he first made his reputation is uncertain. Not much, indeed, is known about his earlier life, but he was born in 1728 and trained for the ballet in Florence. During the late 'fifties he was dancing in Paris, where, we may believe, he enjoyed something in the nature of a triumph, for when in 1759 he came, on a sudden and, according to Doran, "unannounced," to London, "he had hardly entered his lodgings when he was engaged on his own terms." It was at the Opera House in the Haymarket, then usually called the King's Theatre, that he made his English début, and his success was immediate. Within a few months' time he had become

the principal male dancer at the theatre, and all London came to see the
man who, it was said, was not only a superb exponent of classical dancing
but was introducing attractive innovations of his own.

In due course he became manager of the theatre, thus following in
the footsteps of Congreve and Vanbrugh, and for several years was
"despotic master of the ballet." But he was equally successful off the
stage and was soon earning large sums of money as London's most
fashionable dancing-master. It was said that more than one member
of the Royal Family was amongst his pupils. He even produced a book :
The Art of Dancing. True, this was taken largely and almost without
acknowledgment from a French treatise issued a few years before, but
not many of his adoring pupils could be expected to be aware of the fact.
Fame and riches had come to the Signor Gallini, and both, no doubt,
were well deserved.

This, however, was not all. Amongst his pupils was the Lady
Elizabeth Bertie, a daughter of the Earl of Abingdon, and she not only
fell in love with the handsome Italian, but married him, and in 1766 bore
him twin sons. Their marriage was a nine days' wonder, though it was
far from being the first of its kind, and the story goes that on hearing
some people discussing it the dancer with a courtly bow announced that
his proper designation henceforth would be the Signor Giovanni Gallini,
Esquire.

It was not a success, that marriage, but at least husband and wife
seem to have parted amicably, and on her death he inherited some of her
property. And then, while on a tour through his native country, he
danced before the Pope, who, we are told, was so delighted with his
skill that he conferred on him a knighthood of the Order of the Golden
Spur.

A knighthood! True, the honour had not been accorded him by
His Majesty King George III. True, he was not an Englishman by birth.
But had he not married an earl's daughter and so, in his own view at
any rate, become entitled to be called Esquire? Was he not British by
adoption? Had he not amassed a considerable fortune? Cavaliere del
Sperone d'Oro might be his rightful appellation, but to his friends in
London what would that signify? Very little. Nothing at all. There
was only one way by which a knight could be recognised. And so the
Signor Giovanni Gallini, Esquire, disappeared: in his place there
emerged the even more enterprising Sir John Gallini, who not only
managed the King's Theatre but was also the proprietor of the Assembly
Rooms in Hanover Square which were patronised by the King himself.

Now it may well be the fact that the Pope was delighted with the

Florentine's dancing, and what more appropriate reward than golden spurs for so clever a pair of heels? But it is more likely that His Holiness was aware of Gallini's generosity to his countrymen in England and of the numerous engagements of artistes, singers, and musicians, as well as dancers, for which he was responsible during his Italian tour. More than one Roman dancer at any rate owed his introduction to appreciative London audiences to Gallini's good offices, and amongst these was one Claudio Sebastiano Sala, who, it seems, was not only dancing for some years in the ballet in London but became associated with "Sir John" in the management of the King's Theatre.

About this Sala little enough is known. His grandson made some enquiries into the family tree, but was cured, he tells us, of all desire to learn more about his forebears on being gravely assured by an old gentleman named More that he, More, was a direct descendant of the More of More Hall who had succeeded in killing the famed Dragon of Wantley. For several centuries, I believe, Sala has been a fairly common name in three or four European countries, and if Turkey has had her Count Sala (for whose diplomatic shortcomings, by the way, at the time of the Russo-Turkish War, George Augustus was frequently blamed in Balkan newspapers and elsewhere) there are Salas today in Italy, Spain, and Portugal in the humblest positions. In England, too, Claudio's was not the only branch of the clan to acquire a new home and a measure of fame. In the eighteen-eighties, I find, one J. G. Sala is amongst the professional billiard-players—champion of Scotland in 1885—and more than one other of the name, unrelated to George Augustus, has appeared on the concert platform during the last sixty years.

It is probably just as well that George Augustus himself stopped his genealogical researches where he did, for I can hardly think that he would have discovered very much. Yet his particular clan could boast of at least one celebrity at the end of the eighteenth century, and if Claudio himself, who was born in Rome about 1750, never achieved much fame he had a brother, Giuseppe, who after being domestic prelate to Pope Pius VI. became a Cardinal and a historian of some note. A sister, too, Nina, seemed likely at one time to make a name for herself as a tight-rope dancer, but she married a Trieste merchant and sank into respectability. And that is about the extent of our knowledge of his generation.

He seems to have arrived in London about 1776, and his name appears at intervals in the Haymarket programmes until 1788, though never in a prominent position. Probably he was a more useful man behind the scenes as instructor than on the stage itself. His greatest success was achieved after his retirement from the theatre, for it was then that he opened his dancing academy which speedily attracted more than local attention. It seems to have catered more particularly for the professionals, and those of his pupils who afterwards opened their own schools were careful to advertise the fact that they had graduated under the tuition of the renowned Signor Sala. He certainly achieved a modest fortune by his teaching—a fraction of it ultimately came to his best-known grandson—and, like Gallini, who remained his good friend and stood godson to one of his sons, he showed no desire to return in his old age to the country of his birth.

The name of the lady whom he married I have not been able to discover, but she cannot have been an Englishwoman. "In my own poor veins," George Augustus once confessed, "I have not the honour to possess a single drop of Anglo-Saxon blood." But, whatever her nationality, she was careful to give all her children English names. In her widowhood she kept a small school in Lisson Grove, Marylebone, not then the urban slum it was to become; but where her husband lived or where he died I do not know, though the fact that he possessed freehold property in Camden Town suggests that he may have spent his last years in that then rustic retreat.

About three of his six children little or nothing is known. There was a Frederick who had his own house at 12 New Street, Dorset Square —the birthplace of George Augustus—and there were two daughters called Susanna and Ann who almost certainly died young. About the other three a word or two may be said. Sophia, apparently the eldest of them, kept on the school in Lisson Grove for some years and died unmarried in 1837, shortly after a broken romance, and this romance has its interest inasmuch as it provides the first of many links, some of them admittedly rather thin, between the Sala family and Dickens.

It will be remembered that Dickens's first publisher was the enterprising if not always judicious John Macrone, a handsome young Irishman who, arriving in London almost penniless, managed to raise enough money to embark on a business of his own, and, with Ainsworth at the top of his list of authors, made his way rapidly to the front. Additional capital, however, was required to pay the author of *Sketches by Boz*, and £500 was lent him by Miss Sophia Sala, with whom at the time he seems to have had an understanding, though there may have been no actual engagement. Poor Sophia! She must have been considerably older than her Irish admirer, but that was no excuse for the treatment she received. For, hardly had the money been paid over before Macrone was finding a lady whom he liked better. That was bad enough, but there was worse to come. There was a moment when he could easily have repaid her: instead, he entered into new commitments, over-reached himself, and died, within a year or two, in the wretchedest poverty. Dickens came to the rescue of his widow, but neither Miss Sala nor her heirs received a penny of the money advanced.

The younger sister, Eliza, was luckier. She, too, had her admirer, but he proved to be a more faithful swain. He was a fashionable tailor in St. James's Street named Crellin, and although two of his nephews afterwards professed to be shocked at such a mésalliance—they showed their feelings by running up very large bills at the St. James's Street establishment without the means, I imagine, to pay—she lived on happily enough until her death in 1850, when the remains of her small fortune came to her younger brother's four surviving children.

About that brother, Augustus John James Sala (1790-1829), the information is meagre. There is hardly a mention of him in all his youngest son's voluminous writings. True, he died less than a year after George Augustus's birth, but that hardly explains so complete a silence. But we know that he stepped into his father's neat shoes as a dancing-master, and that although presumably English he preferred to be called Monsieur Sala. (A majority of the most fashionable Professors of Dancing and Deportment seem to have been French at the time.) On his father's death he must have succeeded to a snug little fortune—at the time of his marriage he certainly had money advantageously invested—but for one reason or another his money dribbled away, and for some years before his death he was in a money-lender's hands. Probably his poor health had something to do with the matter, and it is difficult to avoid the conclusion that he was a victim of the consumption which carried off so many of his children in infancy. I figure him as a courtly, painstaking, amiable man, without his father's business ability.

In his marriage he was fortunate. I have mentioned his mother's school, but perhaps school is hardly the right word. What Claudio's widow seems to have done was to play the double role of guardian and governess to a few children whose parents lived out of England. They would live in her house and be treated as one of the family, staying sometimes until they were of marriageable age, and amongst her charges during the last years of the eighteenth century was a girl from Demerara in Guiana, the Henriette Catherina Florentina Simon whom, on June 22nd, 1812, her son Augustus married.

3

Now Madame Sala was a very remarkable woman.

She seems to have been the queerest mixture of *grande dame* and second-rate artiste: as much at home in a Royal Palace or a duchess's salon as in a provincial green-room or humble seaside lodgings. She could be imperious—a Boadicea—in her family circle and temperamental on the stage or concert-platform. Like her son George Augustus she had a temper and made enemies, and, like him, she had her loyal and admiring friends, in almost every class, who rarely failed her at moments—they were frequent enough—of crisis. She must certainly arouse our admiration. Her earlier upbringing had hardly prepared her for the domestic and financial troubles which dogged her for the greater part of her life, yet at a time when she might reasonably have been looking forward to a life of elegant ease she prepared herself for a strenuous career and worked, with varying success but always most energetically, almost to her seventieth year. One thinks inevitably of her better-known contemporary, Mrs. Trollope, Anthony's mother. In their general character the two women may have had little in common, but both embarked on a public career which in their youth they had never contemplated, in order to bring up their children, both achieved a certain position in their chosen profession—if Madame Sala rarely shone as an actress she was a most pleasing singer—and both had the satisfaction of seeing at least one of their sons achieve fame.

Her ancestry was curiously mixed. George Augustus is content to describe her father as "a wealthy planter owning hundreds of slaves." An earlier account speaks of him as a Prussian nobleman, born in Dantzig, who was "induced by family misfortunes and political quarrels" to leave his own country. A slightly different version is to be found in a character-sketch of his grandson printed in *The Drawing Room Portrait Gallery* for 1861. Here he is described as a Polish Colonel—a first cousin to the unfortunate King Stanislaus Lezczynski—who migrated to Guiana and there married a lady with Red Indian blood in her veins. In any case the planter, whether Colonel or not, was undoubtedly flourishing during the last years of the eighteenth century, and, following the custom of many of his wealthy neighbours, he sent his daughter, escorted by two negresses, to England to be educated. This was about 1796 when the little Henriette was four years old. She never returned to her native Demerara nor saw her father again.

Her official guardian was a Mr. M'Garell, a rich London merchant, who must have heard good accounts of old Mrs. (or Signora) Sala and placed the girl under her care. There was no lack of money at the time, and the Salas, no doubt, were delighted to receive so profitable a pupil. So the years passed, and the drafts continued to arrive regularly from Guiana, and nobody anticipated disaster. In due course the young heiress, as she was considered to be, was sent to a fashionable establishment in Kensington which catered almost exclusively for the daughters of rich residents in the East and West Indies. The proprietress very properly put the acquirement of good manners and a genteel deportment in the forefront of her curriculum. An old French émigré marquis was in permanent attendance to provide the pupils with a Parisian accent, and—of greater importance than he, it would seem—an ancient yellow chariot was kept in a courtyard and used, not to carry the young ladies to and from their guardians' houses, but solely for the purpose of instructing them how to enter and dismount from a carriage with dignity and grace. You might suppose that even in the most elaborate costume a girl would hardly require prolonged tuition in the matter, but apparently there was an art in the business not easily to be acquired. At any rate the chariot was in regular use amongst the senior pupils, and Henriette, I presume, became as proficient a carriage-enterer as she was singer and pianist. She seems to have been happy enough at the school and long afterwards recalled to her son the pleasant friendships she had made and the abundant food she had enjoyed there. The British climate, however, she found not altogether to her taste. Chilblains, no doubt unknown in Guiana, appeared on her feet, and every week she paid a small sum to one of the younger children to crawl under the table during evening lessons for the purpose of rubbing her toes.

And then on a sudden and at a time, I imagine, when the "heiress" was proposing either to return to the Indies or take her place in London society, came the unexpected news. There had been a succession of bad crops and severe commercial losses. Mr. Simon had been forced to sell his land, his slaves, everything. Hitherto, he wrote in a Prussian-like letter which confirmed this melancholy intelligence, he had been most liberal in conferring on her every advantage and means of improvement in his power: henceforth she must depend on her own abilities and conduct for any future provision. In other words, there would be no further drafts, and he had no particular desire to see her again.

What was to be done? The situation was bad, but not so bad as it might have been. She was about eighteen at the time, a highly talented and vivacious creature, and Augustus John James was attracted. It was inconceivable after the long years during which she had lived with the Salas that she should cease to regard their house as her home merely because there were to be no further drafts from ~~Guinea~~, ~~this~~ was the moment for her to become one of the family in a more ~~intimate~~ sense?

He proposed and was accepted, and in 1812 they were married.

The young Madame Sala, however, seems to have looked ahead. Even at that time, I fancy, she was entertaining doubts about her husband's commercial abilities. Excellent gentleman and admirable dancing-master he might be, but he was no Gallini ready to advertise himself in every possible way, and there was also the question of his health. Would it not therefore be as well if she herself were to take steps whereby the family exchequer, if need be, could be materially increased?

It was lucky for the children who were to come that almost immediately she made preparations to continue her musical education.

She left little to chance. She studied under the well-known Dr. Timothy Essex, whose interests ranged from voice-production to the proper management of eight or nine instruments. She studied under Thomas Welsh, the ex-chorister from Wells who was now at the height of his fame as a professor of singing. From his studio she was passed on in the usual way to various Italian masters, and she finished under the celebrated Velluti who in due course engaged her to preside at the pianoforte in his own academy.

By this time, however, she was earning other money elsewhere. Pupils had been obtained, chiefly in the families of the nobility, and she appeared now and then on semi-private concert-platforms. Unfortunately at the same time she was experiencing a series of the cruellest domestic tragedies. In 1814 a girl, Henrietta, had been born, a poor little consumptive who managed to keep alive just four years. She was luckier than the seven who followed her. One after the other they were either born dead or survived but a few days. It must have been a heartrending procession. Nevertheless, at a time when it seemed difficult to believe that Monsieur Sala would ever continue the family name, nature relented, and between 1820 and 1826 four more children were born who refused to join the procession. True, one of them, the only girl, Augusta Sophia, died of the dreaded consumption in her twenty-sixth year, but the three boys, Frederick Augustus, Charles Kerrison, and Albert, lived on, though none carved out much of a career for himself.

Their arrival must have been welcome, but the family exchequer felt the additional strain. It was now that Monsieur Sala's remaining investments were finding their way into the market, and there were numerous references in a note-book of his to interviews with Mr. Luscombe, the moneylender. By that time he must have been forced relinquish much of his work, and more than once, I fancy, his brother was obliged to come to his assistance. (Periodically, it seems, the family stayed at Frederick's house in New Street, Dorset Square.) And it was then that Madame Sala "was induced to appear on the English stage."

Her decision was not easily taken. "Ladies" in those days did not appear on the stage, and, as one of her admirers was to point out shortly afterwards in the genteel columns of *The Ladies' Museum*, she was wholly ignorant of the various "arts and schemes" by which, unfortunately, popularity was too often obtained. Money, however, was badly needed, and "sacrifices" had to be made.

So it happened that on December 14th, 1827, Madame Sala made her "first appearance on any stage," and at once discovered that life behind the scenes could be acutely uncomfortable.

4

The chief attraction at Covent Garden Theatre on that memorable Friday night was *The Marriage of Figaro* : not, however, Mozart's Opera as it had been written, but a revival of what George Augustus was years later to describe quite accurately as the "fearfully mutilated, patched and cobbled version" which Henry Bishop had prepared eight years before.

In electing to make her bow in this particular Opera Madame Sala showed a discreet understanding of her own talents. In the character of the Countess Almaviva she had a neat and not too prominent though not obscure part which was well within her powers. "A passive character, mild and unassuming," wrote one of the critics, and one "less calculated," Madame Sala herself declared, "to excite agitation." What exactly these words of hers meant is not quite clear, but there can be no doubt that her decision to become a professional actress had not been received in all quarters with acclamation. I can imagine some of the comments which were being made in stage-circles. Another of these interfering amateurs! And not even a young woman. A matron of thirty-five, if you please, with four children! A talented lady, no doubt, but would Mr. Kemble—then manager of Covent Garden Theatre—have engaged her if she had not happened to possess a host of aristocratic and powerful friends? And, no doubt, more than one of the great ladies and influential peers who came to the theatre that Friday night had gone out of their way to smooth the newcomer's path.

Yet on the whole, and in spite of unseemly squabbles both before and behind the curtain, the evening may be counted a success. The theatre was packed, though for this fact Madame Sala cannot have been altogether responsible. Madame Vestris, then at the height of her fame, was the great "draw," and, as it happened, the rival houses were offering nothing new in the way of a programme. Kemble, too, had assembled a good cast. Besides Vestris herself as Susanna, Wrench was the Count, Penson Figaro, Fawcett Antonio, and Mrs. Chatterley, whose reputation was no mean one, the Page.

Affairs, however, began badly. The temperamental Vestris does not seem to have hidden her displeasure at being asked to appear with "a lady" without experience; but, during the half-hour before the curtain rose, she made a discovery which added considerably to her indignation and pique. I do not know what the conventional costume for the Countess Almaviva may have been in those days, but it does not seem to me that Madame Sala erred very greatly in appearing in a magnificent satin dress with a stomacher of jewels, a necklace of diamonds and pearls, and in her abundant dark hair a tasteful tiara. After all, she was supposed to be a countess. Unfortunately for her the jewels were real. They had been lent to her for the occasion by a distinguished admiral's wife, a certain Lady Pole whose daughter had been amongst her pupils. They were doubtless very beautiful gems, but in Vestris's view there was only one woman on the stage that night who should rightly have worn them. The "amateur" calling attention to herself in this illegitimate way? It was not to be thought of, and in the wings the incensed actress, who for all her amiable qualities could on occasion behave like a spoilt child in its naughtiest mood, seems to have threatened not to appear unless the offensive jewels, many of which had been sewn on to the dress, were removed. With difficulty she was persuaded not to persist in her refusal, and the curtain rose.

For a while all seemed well. "The reception of Madame Sala," wrote a critic in the *Times*, "was most flattering." Her first solo was encored. So, too, was her letter-duet with Vestris. Unhappily this seems to have added to the leading lady's irritation, and in the middle of the demanded encore she abruptly left the stage. Immediately there was an uproar in the house. Angry shouts came from the gallery, and so menacing did they become that after the stage had been cleared Vestris returned alone, and with her usual Puckish sense of humour restored, grinned at her audience and gave them "I've been Roaming" which happened to be a favourite song of hers. For all its applicability at the moment it was hardly the kind of song to be interpolated in a Mozart

Opera, and she was sharply reprimanded by the Press for introducing so incongruous a "turn." The audience accepted the implied apology, but the *Times* did not hesitate to say that she had received a lesson on the subject which, it was to be hoped, she would not forget.

With the best will in the world, however, it was impossible to acclaim the newcomer as a great actress. All, on the other hand, praised her gentility and considered that her voice if one of rather confined compass could be full and sweet. "Madame Sala," wrote one critic, "is truly a lady in manners; and her theatrical style is of that sweet, delicate, graceful and feeling kind which is calculated to please rather than astonish." Another penned a shrewder comment when he confessed his inability to divest himself of the idea that he was listening to a gentlewoman singing in her own drawing-room.

What Madame Sala herself thought of her reception we do not know. She appeared as the Countess for a second time, and with the same cast, at Covent Garden on the first day of the New Year, and was doubtless considering other parts when domestic ties once again claimed her. For the thirteenth time she found herself about to become a mother, and on the 24th of November, 1828, her last child was born: the George Augustus Henry Fairfield Sala who just managed to survive, to add lustre to his mother's name.

CHAPTER TWO

A SMALL BOY IN BOHEMIA

I

Less than nine months later Monsieur Sala was dead.

At the time the family were in lodgings at 10 Upper Montagu Street, but almost immediately after the funeral they left London for Brighton. For some years now it had been their custom to spend several months in Brighton, less, however, for its good sea air than for the number of Madame Sala's patrons who either had houses there or were amongst its regular visitors. George IV. no longer drove down to his grotesque pavilion, and a little of the old glamour was temporarily gone, but Brighton itself was flourishing—it proudly claimed forty thousand citizens in 1830—and Madame could reasonably be sure of finding enough pupils (at a guinea a lesson) in its fashionable crescents and squares to stave off disaster.

For disaster was near. There were now five small children to be looked after—the eldest was only eight—and no funds in reserve. It was hardly surprising, moreover, that theatrical managers were showing no great eagerness to engage so mediocre a performer. There was only one thing to be done: more pupils would have to be found, and in the usual way benefit concerts once or twice a year would have to be instituted. And for the next four or five years Madame Sala did not spare herself. She was a clever teacher of singing—in one instance, it is recorded, she was able to cure a girl who from birth had been practically dumb—and the dowagers were well satisfied to put their daughters into the hands of so genteel an instructress. But she was also an admirable woman of business. In those days the publicity agent had not yet made his appearance, but there were ways and means of thrusting yourself forward without seeming to do so, and Madame Sala made good use of them. Indefatigably she moved her family as fashion directed, from London to Brighton, from Brighton to London. She was to be seen at many of the functions which today would quaintly be described as "exclusive." At concerts given for charity her services might be obtained almost for the asking. She was, moreover, a witty and vivacious talker —the Duke of Wellington was amongst those who liked to listen to her shrewd comments—and received many invitations to stay at the country mansions of the Great. Her friends and patrons, indeed, were exceedingly kind and went out of their way to help. Chief amongst them was the Duchess of Clarence, so soon to become Queen Adelaide, but I fancy that her most useful ally at this time was the sprightly Harriet Mellon, the ex-actress who had been left a colossal fortune by one of her husbands, the banker Coutts, and was now the Duchess of St. Albans. At the Duchess's Brighton house more than one new pupil must have been obtained, and it was this kind-hearted old lady who saw to it that so many prominent and not particularly musical folk supported the benefit concerts. But there were others, of course, and, as we shall see, it was not only Royalty and the peerage who showed their sympathy for the widow in a practical way: the most famous singers of the day appeared at her concerts and did not always demand their usual fee.

Yet there were occasional troubles and setbacks. With her fashionable friends Madame Sala remained on the most cordial terms, but with some of those who regarded her as their rival, she was not always as amiable as she might have been. Just as her appearance on the London stage had caused jealousy in "the profession," so the undoubted success of her benefit concerts though fully deserved—their preparation entailed an immense amount of not very easy work—was not always well received by those less fortunate in the matter of powerful patrons. On one occasion, indeed, a concert of the kind was abandoned altogether owing to an anonymous attack of a very mean, if slightly ludicrous, nature. This was at Brighton in 1834. A placard, it seems, announcing the concert had been placed in one of the fashionable "circulating libraries." Some ill-disposed person managed to scratch out a few letters from Madame Sala's name without being discovered, with the unfortunate result that MAD SAL was advertised as about to take her benefit at the Town Hall. It is said that her patrons took steps to recompense her, but she could never forget the insult.

Even with a sufficiency of pupils, however, to say nothing of the benefit concerts which, with this one exception, were held with the greatest regularity for many years to come, affairs with the Salas were not too easy, and, as George Augustus was to show, all unwittingly, in his earliest known contribution to letters, financial difficulties of the acutest kind were frequently presenting themselves. For the children were growing up, and all were levying an increasing toll on the family exchequer, not least the youngest who no long time after he had arrived in the world came perilously near to bidding it good-bye; always an expensive business.

2

They had done their best for him at his christening. True, it is nowhere recorded that any of those most intimately connected with the ceremony in the Church of St. Mary, Wyndham Place, ever did anything to assist him in after life, but at least his two godmothers bore highly distinguished names. One of them was the Hon. Mrs. Villiers, a daughter of Admiral Viscount Keith and a grand-daughter of the celebrated Hester Thrale, and the other was Lady Augusta Fitzclarence, a daughter of the then Duke of Clarence and Mrs. Jordan. About his godfather, a Captain Henry Fairfield, I can discover nothing of much interest, but there is, incidentally, an odd little mystery connected with his name. In mid-Victorian days, and, indeed, right on to the end of the century, there was but one "George Augustus" of any great renown; but until 1849 Madame Sala's youngest son signed himself either "George Sala" or "George F. Sala." Then for some reason the Fairfield was suddenly dropped, never to be reassumed, and so important was this very slight alteration held to be by some of his friends that they could speak of it as "a change of name."

George F. Sala

16 July. 1849

4 Carlisle Street Soho Sq

In the early 'thirties, however, the small George seems to have been battling with only one problem: how to keep alive.

What exactly the trouble may have been is not very clear, but in addition to great physical debility there were apparently some disquieting mental symptoms. Afterwards he claimed to have a distinct remembrance of the death of George IV., though he was less than two at the time, and he recalled in some detail an incident in the cholera epidemic of 1832. His mother had taken rooms in North Audley Street for the London season. Opposite them was the town house of Lord Clarendon, one of whose footmen had died of cholera. A rumour had spread that the unfortunate man's body had been placed in its coffin without being washed, a crowd had collected, and its demeanour had become so menacing that a company of Guards was necessary to disperse it. But apart from these isolated events, and in spite of a memory which, if occasionally inaccurate, could be astonishingly vivid, George Augustus could remember nothing whatever that happened to him during the first three or four years of his life. Indeed, he hints that for some little time before he was struck down even more cruelly, the heaviest curtain had fallen about him.

In the usual way he had been put out to nurse, and most part of the year was spent in a cottage at Edgware, in the charge of a "strong-minded" woman who, I imagine, cared less for the ailing infant than for the money he brought her. The story goes that when the time came for him to be restored permanently to his family she did not hesitate to adopt the most drastic measures to prevent his departure. It was a bitterly cold March, and he was recovering from an attack of measles. Ogreishly she determined to retard his convalescence to the last possible moment. To this end she opened all the windows and allowed them to remain open. The result was not precisely what she expected. The poor little victim nearly died of the shock. There was a "horrid attack of inflammation," he tells us, after which he lost his hearing, and soon enough his sight was also being affected.

He was fetched away by a distracted mother as soon as he was well enough to be moved, and at once there began that long but losing battle against total blindness which remained vividly before him until the end of his life. "I shudder now, sometimes," he wrote more than sixty years later, "when I think of the tortures that I underwent through the kind endeavours of those who loved me to make me see." "The kind endeavours!" What a ghastly experience for a sickly and sensitive child! Every day the world becoming dimmer and darker, and nothing to look forward to except more "tortures!" And they knew how to hurt you in those pre-anaesthetic days. Madame Sala, moreover, was not satisfied with two or three opinions: almost the entire medical profession was bombarded. There was hardly a distinguished oculist who was not consulted during the next few months, and hardly a surgeon of Madame Sala's acquaintance whose advice was not sought. The unfortunate child—he cannot have been more than five at the time —was dragged hither and thither, and almost everything was done to his eyes except their entire removal.

Nobody, however, seemed able to discover the real cause of the trouble. In London the elder Guthrie and William Lawrence, kings of their profession, were no more successful than were Sir Wathen Waller and Sir Matthew Tierney at Brighton. Visits were paid to fashionable physicians like Sir James Clark, who would accept no fee, but they, too, could do nothing. Slowly the eyes grew worse. In despair Madame Sala had recourse to the quacks. In place of the cuppings, the scrapings, and the fortifying drops, there came the application of Somebody's Golden Ointment (of which the advertisements spoke so well) and Somebody Else's Infallible Eye Snuff. On the lamentable failure of these remedies the wretched child was taken to a jeweller's shop in the Regent Street Quadrant, where the lobes of his ears were pierced. The eyes failed to respond, and they shaved his head. The result was not pleasing, and they wrapped his head in a black handkerchief. And matters were hardly made easier for the boy when he chanced to hear his mother's maid speak of him as "that miserable little object." The words, no doubt, were apt, but you can imagine their effect on a helpless child, unable to read or write and hardly able to distinguish one toy from another. It was almost a relief, he was inclined to think in after years, "when the twilight deepened into night."

It is difficult to say for what length of time he remained totally blind. Probably it was not much more than a year, though to the little George it seemed endless. Yet there were consolations. All his life he was to suffer from a variety of the least fashionable but most painful ailments, but the nervous troubles of his infancy, whatever they may have been, now disappeared, and during these black days he found in his sister Augusta the perfect companion.

Gussy, as they called her, was only ten or eleven at the time, and already, I imagine, in the throes of the disease which was to bring her life to so early a close, but she was a lively and intelligent girl and she set herself out to play a little mother's part. For hours every day she would read to her small brother—the Bible, fairy-tales, history, books of travel, even extracts from the newspapers. Games would be invented for two people which needed only one pair of eyes, and stories of surprising, and, if we may judge from the boy's earliest literary efforts, most lurid adventure, would be interchanged. Afterwards, indeed, George Augustus rarely lost an opportunity to pay the warmest tribute to his sister's devotion. His mother, no doubt, did her best, but she had little enough time to give him, and the three elder boys were now at school. There was only little Gussy to make life bearable, and it is she more than anybody else who must be given the credit for instilling into her brother's ugly and shaven head that love of books and eagerness to acquire knowledge about everything under the sun which he was never to lose.

Luckily help was not far off, in the person of a French homeopathist. Madame Sala had never given up hope that the day would come when somebody or other would be found with an entirely new treatment to suggest. Dr. Curée, a pupil of the great Hahnemann himself, appeared, examined the useless eyes, and laughed at the idea of anything permanently wrong. An acute inflammation of the mucous membrane of the eye, he maintained, was the cause of the trouble. And the treatment? A very carefully-selected diet, some "globules," and, of course, the inevitable ointment. I must confess that Dr. Curée's menu which included such unlikely dishes as oysters in abundance, macaroni, and sweet curds, reads rather strangely today, but it and the globules between them undoubtedly brought about an improvement, and the day came when the long-promised "vine green shade" was placed over his eyes, and "like a gentlemans" he once again Saw.

It was not a complete cure, and one of his eyes remained "a duffer" as long as he lived. It stared at you blankly, considerably larger than its fellow, but with it he could do little more than distinguish between light and darkness or, if an object were held sufficiently close to him, have some vague idea about its general outline. The other, however, behaved extraordinarily well, as his etchings on copper and minute calligraphy testify. Moreover, it was not until his fiftieth year that he found any necessity to use glasses.

3

Many boys might well have envied the small George during the three or four years that followed. He was not exactly allowed to run wild—if his mother happened to be in a poor temper and George, as was often the case, chose to be naughty, harsh words would be used and ears boxed hard; there were even times when his eldest brother followed her example—but in general he lived the life of a tiny Bohemian. No school, though there were lessons of a sort at home; no "regular" hours of the kind which all normal boys detest; all kinds of parties, and not all of them confined to small folk; and almost daily meetings with interesting and celebrated "grown-ups" who seem to have made much of the queer little fellow who had so recently been blind and was so old for his age.

Queer and queerly adult he undoubtedly was. Already, indeed, he was showing signs of that astonishing industry and insatiable curiosity which continued throughout his life. It was Gussy who now taught him to read, but, as he tells us, he taught himself to write, characteristically by a pictorial method of his own, and when his mother attempted to instil into his mind more orthodox precepts he would have none of them. The family solicitor had given him a book of calligraphic engravings, "and I used to sit," he records, "on a little low stool with *The Universal Penman* propped up easelwise against some other book on the carpet; and on my drawing-board, which I held on my knee, I imitated not only the different styles of writing, but also, as well as I could, the emblematic sculptures at the top of the pages, and especially the flourishes between the different paragraphs." In his reading, too, he progressed with such remarkable celerity that he was soon playing tutor to his less brilliant sister, a fact which in after years she was always very ready to admit.

Meanwhile Madame Sala was moving from place to place, paying visits to her aristocratic friends, ever searching for the necessary new pupils, and as the time drew near for her annual, or semi-annual, benefits, working tremendously hard to make sure of a financial success. Occasionally she would take her youngest boy with her when she went to some pupil's house—he would be left, rather like an umbrella, in the hall—and she would exhibit his childish drawings and already fine calligraphy to those who attended her afternoon receptions: very popular gatherings these, he tells us, in spite of the fact that no refreshments whatever were offered to the guests.

We have isolated glimpses of him in Brighton at the time. He was taken to his first pantomime. There was a policeman in the harlequinade who was thrown into an immense cauldron labelled HOT WATER, from which he emerged a few minutes later no longer decently blue but the brightest of reds. The nurse explained that a veil of crimson gauze had been thrown over his uniform, but the boy could not at first be persuaded to believe that the unfortunate man had not been boiled and, lobster-like, changed colour in the process. He was taken to a Twelfth Night party at the Duchess of St. Albans's house, and there for the first time met the youthful Angela Burdett whom he was to know so well years later as the Baroness Burdett-Coutts. He was not as lucky as she on that occasion, for the slice of cake which fell to her lot contained a diamond ring, whereas he obtained no more than a sugared figure. And because he was a precocious and sharp-tongued child, he would often be "lent out" to a neighbour, Madame Michau the celebrated dancing-mistress, when she had guests to be entertained after dinner. The little George did not always enjoy himself on these occasions even when a sumptuous supper was served at midnight—he would have preferred a supper without singing for it—but he fought down his shyness and seems to have well satisfied his hostess. In those days such youthful performances were common enough. The young Dickens, you may remember, was frequently stood on a table and made to recite for his father's admiring friends.

On one memorable day, too, he was the means of adding considerably and at a most unexpected moment to the family exchequer. In 1834, as

I have said, the Brighton benefit concert had been abandoned. In the following year Madame Sala determined at all costs to give her patrons such a musical treat as they would not easily forget. The most famous artistes were to be engaged and everything possible done to prevent a repetition of last year's deplorable affair. Who, then, would prove to be the greatest "draw"? Well, in the first place, there was the great Paganini, that strangely saturnine figure round about whom so many legends had long been accumulating. At the time he was the most famous violinist in all the world: a wizard whose name was sufficient to fill the largest hall ever built. Obviously he must be approached, though it was known that the fees which he could command were enormous. But there must also be a vocalist, and who, unquestionably, was the reigning Queen of Song? The peerless Malibran, Garcia's daughter, who was so soon to be struck down. Would Madame Sala's purse, however, run to the two of them? Or would they, perhaps, like so many of the lesser artistes who had helped her before, take pity on the poor widowed gentlewoman with five children, "all clamouring," as somebody said, "for large slices of roast mutton," and forgo their fees? Boldly she determined to take the risk, and both artistes accepted her invitation.

I cannot be sure whether Malibran agreed to sing for nothing at all or demanded her customary fee—long afterwards Sala wrote two accounts of the incident which did not always agree with one another—but Paganini, notorious for his avarice, insisted on his twenty-five guineas, a large enough sum for those days.

Undoubtedly the presence of these two "stars" drew the crowds, and the concert was a brilliant success. Madame Sala was delighted—until the moment came for her artistes to receive their remuneration. As had been expected, several of them refused to take a penny; they were only too pleased, they said, to have been of assistance; but what of Paganini?

A friend of hers made a shrewd suggestion. "Take your little boy with you," said he, "when you pay Pag. Perhaps *that* will soften him a little."

The idea was adopted, and the small George was washed and combed and carefully dressed, and taken to the Old Ship where the violinist was staying.

"We were ushered in," he wrote in 1877, "not without much fear and trembling on my part, into the presence of the mighty musician, who was at breakfast, and was gnawing a large and terribly underdone mutton chop. I say that he gnawed it; for he held the chop in the fingers of one hand and by the shank of the bone, and he devoured it in a manner so fierce as at once to call up in my mind the most disagreeable associations connected with the story of Little Red Riding Hood. Then my mother, alluding so far as she in delicacy could to her large family and her small means, proceeded to count out, sovereign by sovereign, and shilling by shilling, Paganini's fee of five-and-twenty guineas. I can see, with the eye of memory, the whole man before me now; his gaunt, angular form; his black elf-locks falling in weird confusion over his neck and shoulders; his cadaverous face and shaggy brows; his long, bony hands, with the veins standing out like cordage; his amazingly large feet; and especially his neck, disproportionately long, scraggy, and corrugated. I can see the glare—so it seemed to me—which, when he raised his pent-house brows, darted upon the pile of money, and the spasmodic avidity with which he extended his bony digits, and swept the pile towards him.

"And I remember," he went on, "that when he had pocketed the money, he concluded the consumption of his chop, drained a large cupful of black coffee, and wiped his lips on the table-cloth.

"''E a very nice little boy,' he was good enough to say, alluding to myself; 'but time is bad, and there is no monish in de vorld; no, no monish at all.'

"My mother rose, with a heavy heart, to depart.

"'Stop, little boy,' cried the great violinist, and he beckoned to me with a skinny finger, which any one of the witches in *Macbeth* would have been proud to own. 'Stop, take dis; it will buy you a cake.'

"He thrust a crumpled piece of paper into my hand; rose from his chair; and without more ado, 'bolted'—that is the only word suited to the action—into his bedroom.

"He had given me a bank-note for fifty pounds."

Even so, however, the financial position remained fairly acute, and in the early autumn of 1836 when an opportunity was given Madame Sala to return to the stage she was glad to take it.

In the previous year an old friend of hers, John Braham, the well-known tenor who had made a fortune by his voice, had added himself to the number of those optimists who believed that London would support a theatre devoted to English Opera. At the cost of half his fortune he had built the St. James's Theatre, and with the usual trumpets it had opened its handsome doors. As he had been warned, London was only mildly interested—it is recorded that on one early occasion no more than seventeen people were to be found in the pit of which Braham always professed to be so proud—and in due course, no doubt

to the amusement of rival managers, recourse was had to the usual
burlettas and musical farces. Braham persevered for a year or two, but
his losses continued, and in less than three years' time he had finished
with management. Yet during that period he had made one or two
interesting experiments. Amongst his company were the popular
comedian, John Pritt Harley, Mrs. Keeley who was to survive until the
last year of the century, and the "Mr. Sidney" who was afterwards to
become so well known as Alfred Wigan, his real name. But there were
also several ladies and gentlemen, like John Parry the Younger, the
singer who was also a harpist, and Miss Rainforth, the soprano, who
had hitherto been better known on the concert-platform than they were
on the stage; and when the suggestion was made that Madame Sala
should join their numbers she could not refuse. She was no longer a
young woman and could not hope to be given any of the principal
parts; but Braham's experiment had its appeal, and the salary offered
was a regular one. She brought her family to some rooms in King
Street, opposite the theatre—Parry was living on the floor above—and
was lucky to be given, almost at once, a part well suited to her powers,
in a farce written by no less a person than Charles Dickens himself.

The Strange Gentleman, first produced at the end of September, was
no masterpiece, but it enjoyed a great success. In part, no doubt, this
was due to Harley's amusing performance in the title-role, but I imagine
that many people came to the St. James's because just at this time the
name of Boz was on everybody's lips. Mr. Pickwick had taken a few
months to make friends with his countrymen, but now, with Sam
Weller to help him, he was conquering the civilised world. Madame
Sala created the part of Julia Dobbs, a lady very keen to find a husband
for herself, played it on nearly sixty occasions, and for the next eighteen
months was seldom omitted from the cast, even though in some of the
burlettas and burlesques which were produced she was required to utter
no more than a sentence or two.

Now, too, the nine-year-old George was introduced to the exciting
world of the theatre, and while his brothers were at college or school—
Fred at the Royal Academy of Music and afterwards in Paris, Charles
at Christ's Hospital in his blue coat and yellow stockings, and the less
astute Albert at Clapham—he was being given the freedom of the Green
Room at the St. James's. Truly a thrilling time! To be taken "behind
the scenes" at a real theatre was by itself a joyous excitement for a boy
who had already been busy with theatricals at home; but at the St.
James's there was always the chance of seeing Boz himself, the hero of
every youngster who could read, and that was a delight to be shared

by very few boys indeed. He never forgot his first introduction to the
young man who had "thought of Mr. Pickwick." It was at the conclusion of the first performance of *The Village Coquettes*, the operetta
written by Dickens and composed by John Hullah—Mr. Hullabaloo,
they called him at the theatre—that he was taken to the Green Room
to find his mother talking to Boz with his long hair and ultra-fashionable
clothes. Madame Sala was merely understudying some part in the play,
but already she and Dickens had become good friends. Years later
G. A. S. was to be known as one of Dickens's Young Men on *Household
Words*. That night, perhaps, there was born in him the desire to become
a writer himself. At the moment, however, it was the theatre rather
than books which captured his imagination, and his admiration for the
author of *Pickwick* took the form of dramatic versions of his work,
acted by Augusta, Albert, and himself to an audience of two or three
in the King Street rooms. And then in the spring of 1837 he had his
first taste of more professional duties : he was allowed to play prompter
to his mother. A third play by Dickens—*Is She His Wife?*—was about
to be put into rehearsal; Madame Sala had been chosen for the part
of Mrs. Peter Limbury; and, day after day, George with the script in
his hands, though he was soon able to declaim the whole play from
memory, would "hear" her and no doubt experience a pleasurable
thrill when she failed to respond to a cue.

So the months passed, and a new era for Great Britain dawned.
William IV. died, and the youthful Victoria came to lend a new lustre
to the throne. New railroads were opened where the landowners had
sworn they should never be built, and the pillory was abolished. There
was civil war in Spain, and somebody was experimenting with the
Electric Telegraph. The old Duchess of St. Albans died, and the Royal
Exchange was burnt to the ground. In Parliament a Mr. Disraeli made
his maiden speech and was howled down. There was great poverty
about, but there was also a comfortable suggestion of prosperity to
come. At the St. James's, however, no great success came to reward
Braham for his efforts in the cause of high art, and some of his company,
Madame Sala amongst them, were invited to appear in a kind of music-
hall show at the huge Colosseum in Regent's Park.

Here in the past Londoners had been able to admire a panorama of
their own city as well as various minor exhibitions and side-shows. An
elaborate grotto, sham but grandiose ruins, an apiary, a Hall of Mirrors,
or some new invention like the "Ascending Room," the first lift to be
seen in London : for such attractions as these the Colosseum had opened
its doors some thirteen years before. But all novelty had gone, and

Braham's part-purchase of the building in 1831 had been only another instance of his misplaced enthusiasm. He now tried to tempt a London which would have none of his English Operas to enjoy an entertainment of a distinctly less "refined" character. A variety show was staged which did not differ very greatly from those which were to prove so successful thirty years later at the Tivoli and elsewhere: playlets, comic songs, circus turns—with waiters moving freely about soliciting your orders. I cannot suppose that Madame Sala was too pleased to be seen and heard in such surroundings, though the extra money must have been a godsend, but to the young George just then discovering that there were less classical but rather more exciting writers than Milton or Johnson—in other words the "Newgate" novels and "bloods" of the day—the Colosseum was a celestial place.

It was fine, no doubt, to be allowed to see the great Boz and be petted by distinguished men and women at the St. James's. It was sometimes amusing to be taken to patrician palaces where his mother still found pupils. It was something to boast about, too, that at Gore House (where some fourteen years later he was to be employed by Alexis Soyer, the chef) he had met Lady Blessington and Count D'Orsay. But it was only at the Colosseum that he could listen to the "funny men" with their vulgar but easily-memorised choruses, watch acrobats performing miraculous feats, or—chief attraction of all—make friends with a troupe of Arab boys who on the stage built themselves up into a human pagoda and in their own stuffy lodgings on the Surrey side of the river were such fascinatingly unusual playmates. Gala days, in fact: but they were to be rudely cut short. In the spring of 1838 Braham found himself unable to continue. For a while it was possible to stave off disaster. At the Haymarket Theatre, where at the time Benjamin Webster was manager, one of the chief actresses, Mrs. Glover, was taken ill, and Madame Sala was engaged in her place. Mrs. Glover was soon back again, but an understudy was required, and Madame Sala remained with the company until May or June. Then she herself was cruelly struck down. The family doctor arrived and took a grave view. Her old friend, Sir James Clark, hurried round and was no better pleased: the patient was suffering from small-pox.

The poor woman was dreadfully ill. She lost her good looks and, like her youngest son, became temporarily blind. More than a year passed before she had fully recovered, and then, of course, it was only to find herself in a worse financial position than ever before. Of her children only Charles was as yet earning any money at all—he had been given a desk in a City office—and although kind nurses and maids had taken charge of the younger ones for little or no wages, and the doctors and surgeons would not hear of a fee, such little savings as there were had been completely exhausted. Her friends, however, Dickens amongst them—he wrote a letter assuring her that both Forster and himself were eager to help—had not been idle, and when plans were made for a grand benefit performance at the Haymarket (where, it is interesting to note, the first meeting for the purpose of establishing an association for the relief of aged and infirm actors had recently been held) there was the readiest response alike from the public and the theatrical profession.

The Queen gave her patronage, all the great ladies in London came to the theatre, and Macready himself headed the list of actors, none of whom demanded a fee for his services. An unexpectedly large sum of money was obtained, and all seemed to be well again.

4

All, however, was not well with the young George.

He was eleven at the time, shy and nervous, for all his social ventures, though in some ways curiously adult. He had read far more widely than most boys of his age, and was already making experiments in the matter—of such paramount importance to him in later years—of tabulating the knowledge so gained. (There is in existence a folio exercise-book belonging to this time which is filled with long and generally well-chosen excerpts from the best essayists and historians in his extraordinarily neat handwriting.) His brother Charles was teaching him the rudiments of Latin, and from his mother who, incidentally, was now insisting that all her children should learn how to cook their own meals, he had managed to obtain rather more than a smattering of French. Nor had his studies been seriously interrupted by Madame Sala's long illness. The curriculum might have become less regular than before, but at least he was finding plenty to do. It was certainly not a question of mere boredom. Much of his leisure was being given to pen-and-ink drawing, and he had recently been trying his skill at water-colour painting. He was the unmusical member of the family, but even he showed a quick ear and would often be heard cheerfully humming the latest popular air. He had also become the devoted admirer of a cousin of his, Miss Sarah Ashley, a young woman of some means who had recently arrived with a sister from the West Indies and who seemed able to understand his juvenile problems better than anybody else. And with these two cousins and his adored Gussy he would amuse himself with private theatricals, games of his own invention, even a monthly illustrated magazine, of which, of course, he was the principal contributor and Editor-in-Chief.

What, then, was wrong? Why, when Madame Sala, restored to health, with a considerable sum of money in the bank and eager to pick up the threads which had been dropped, brought her family to comfortable apartments in the Regent Street Quadrant, did her youngest son almost at once sink into a state of apathy, brooding sulkily in a chair for hours at a time, ignoring his painting-block, hardly uttering a word at meals?

In *Twice Round the Clock*, perhaps the best of all his books, he gives an interesting glimpse of himself at the time, though it burkes the real cause of his trouble.

"I am again in Regent Street, but at another window, and in another house. There is no nurse now, but a genteel young woman, aged about thirty—she asked me once, for fun, how old she was, and I guessed, in all youthful seriousness, fifty, whereupon she slapped me—to take care of me. Her name is Sprackmore, and she has long corkscrew ringlets, and is very pious, and beneath her auspices I first study the 'Loss of the *Kent* East Indiaman,' and the 'Dairyman's Daughter.' She has fits, too, occasionally. I am just of that age to be a hollow-eyed little boy in a tunic, with a frill and a belt, and to be dreadfully afraid of the parent I used a year before to love and caress with such fearless confidence. They say I am a clever child, and my cleverness is encouraged by being told that I am not to ask questions, and that I had much better go and play with my toys than mope over that big volume of Lyttelton's *History of England*, lent to me by Mr. Somebody, the lawyer—I see him now, very stout and gray, at the funeral whenever any of us dies: of which volume—it is in very shabby condition—I break the top-cover off by letting it fall from the chair, which is my reading-desk. I suffer agonies of terror and remorse for months, lest the fracture should be discovered, though I have temporarily repaired it by means of a gimlet and a piece of twine. Then, one bright day, my cousin Sarah gives me a bright five-shilling piece—I take her to the opera now, but she always remembers my childish dependence upon her, and insists upon paying the cab home—and take Lyttelton's *History*, still with great fear and trembling, to a bookbinder's in Broad Street, Golden Square, who tells me that the 'hends is jagged,' and that there must be a new back, lettering, and gilding to the book. He works his will with it, and charges me four shillings and sixpence out of the five-shilling piece for working it; but to tell of the joyful relief I feel when I bring Lyttelton's *History* back safe and sound! I do not get rid of my perturbation entirely, however, till I have rubbed the back against the carpet a little to soil it, in order that it may not look too new.

"Oh! the agonies," he continues, "the Laocoon-like conscience windings, the Promethean tortures, that children suffer through these accidental breakages! Oh! the unreasoning cruelty of parents, who punish children for such mischances! So I am a little boy in a tunic; and I dare say that, with my inquisitiveness, and my moping over books, I am an intolerable little nuisance."

Nuisance, however, was hardly the right word. Nor was a mere breakage the real cause of his moping. The truth was simple. The boy was fond enough of his mother, but he had undoubtedly enjoyed his temporary freedom from maternal restraint. Madame Sala was probably no stricter than were most parents in those early Victorian days, but her temper could be short and, as a slave-owner's daughter, she believed in the rod. This had not been applied to her youngest son on more than one or two occasions, but he could never forget its effect on himself.

Now to most boys, I suppose, a beating at home means little enough: an unfortunate and, no doubt, most painful business but one which will soon be forgotten. To George, then as later, it held an importance which to many people will seem strange if not inexplicable. All his life, indeed, the question of corporal punishment was to remain vividly before him. Time and again he was to take up his pen in support of those who were advocating its abolition in schools, in the Services, and, except for the grossest crimes, in the prisons. As so often happens, however, his very horror of flagellation proved to be for him its greatest attraction, and, as his private correspondence shows, he could never banish an eager interest in its practice. Even as a small boy he had viewed the matter from an unusual point of view. It was not the actual pain which mattered so much as the resulting degradation, on which he would allow his mind to dwell long afterwards, deeply ashamed of himself for so doing and yet powerless to dismiss such "wicked" thoughts. At this time, with his mother back in the house and exerting all her old-time authority, he was longing for some such freedom as his elder brothers enjoyed. Unfortunately the one possible remedy—school—held out no hope whatever of avoiding further "degradations." From the books, and from what his brothers had told him, enjoying, no doubt, the effect of their picturesque exaggerations, he had gathered that life at an English school meant one dreadful round of "rods, canes, and straps" from the masters and the coarsest bullying from the boys. It was a frightening prospect, and matters were hardly mended when, after a worse exhibition of "sulks" than usual, his mother threatened to send him to the strictest school she could find. A *maladie de langueur* in a boy of eleven? It was not to be permitted.

The threat had such serious consequences that a doctor was summoned. The boy could not bring himself to blurt out the "shameful" truth, and the doctor could make nothing of him. Whereupon Madame Sala convened a Family Council. Aunt Eliza arrived, and prescribed an immediate visit to a Devonshire farm where a diet of eggs and cream might be expected to work wonders. The elder boys, no doubt, were in favour of a "good" school and no more nonsense. But Miss Sarah Ashley was also present, and by this time she had some inkling of the truth. School, yes, she said; but why in England? Already George had shown himself to be a bit of a linguist. She knew a Frenchwoman who would assuredly know of the right kind of school in Paris. The schools there, she had heard, were exceedingly good. A little more freedom might be given to the boys than was the custom in England, but they were none the worse, she believed, on that account. Incidentally, too, they managed without corporal punishment.

"An immense load of agony and terror," Sala records, "was removed from my mind when these words were uttered," and in a little while Madame Sala had given her consent to the proposal.

So it happened that in the autumn of that year she with Gussy and the youngest boy set sail from London Bridge for France.

CHAPTER THREE

FROM PARIS VIA DOVER TO TURNHAM GREEN

I

WHEN towards the end of the century the *Daily Mail* inaugurated a new era in popular journalism in this country some not always good-tempered fun was poked at its "sensational" methods. The news which it printed, declared its critics, was always being dramatised, its contributors were writing in a language which might be understandable but was certainly not English, and in general there was a lack of dignity about its "halfpenny" columns which was not only pitiable in itself but might have the most regrettable effects on the public mind. It was all very well to appeal to "the man in the street"—presumably a gentleman who had hitherto been unwilling, or unable, to give much attention to the daily press—but these screaming passages, in which as often as not the truth was held to be of less importance than "a good story," were dragging a noble profession down to the depths.

That was the kind of thing that was being freely said in households which continued to subscribe to the "respectable" journals. It is to be noticed, however, that amongst such "respectable" periodicals was the *Daily Telegraph*, and, hardly more than a generation before, this then youthful newspaper had been the object of similar attacks. Its great popularity had never been denied, but its vilifiers accused it of pandering to the lowest tastes by giving undue prominence to scandal and crime, and of being repeatedly guilty of the grossest errors of fact. Its self-complacency and implied omniscience were widely lampooned, and its very name was cunningly perverted in ways best calculated to suggest its insistence on the seamier side of things and its general unworthiness as an organ of public opinion. (Actually at the time it wielded an influence in home affairs second only to that of the *Times*.) But the most damning, because the most justifiable, attacks had come from those who, like Matthew Arnold, were deploring the singularly florid language—journalese, it came to be called—in which so many of its columns were being couched. It might not always be advisable to call a spade a spade, but even a bloody shovel would be preferable to some such monstrosity as a ferruginous utensil of the more sanguinary pattern. Yet day after day there appeared a queer jungle of unusual and generally long words, all, or nearly all, "English," but by no means all necessary to convey the writer's meaning.

In other words, it was the day of a verbosity which was truly exuberant. Your smart reporter did not speak of coffee, for instance, but of the fragrant berry of Mocha. Blood, of course, was the crimson stream of life, a dog's tail his caudal appendage, and the oyster had been temporarily banished in favour of the succulent bivalve. And for this unfortunate change one member of the *Daily Telegraph's* staff of "young lions" was largely if not wholly responsible: Sala himself.

He could be the most brilliant of recorders and the liveliest of commentators, but he was rarely able to resist the lure of curious words, redundant epithets, and, because one thing would always be reminding him of something else, unnecessary, if picturesque, clauses. It was as though he enjoyed forcing his way through an almost impenetrable forest of words. That by itself would not have mattered so much, but the circumstances in which he did so much of his work did not always permit him to choose his vocabulary with the nicest care, and so there came about those heavily-laden, cliché-ridden sentences which so often aroused unfriendly or contemptuous comment.

I mention the fact here because Sala himself, who was well aware of the eccentricities of his style, rightly or wrongly attributed them to his lack of an *English* education. "In my childhood," he wrote in 1859, "I browsed on a salad of languages, which I would willingly exchange now for a plain English lettuce or potato . . . I was pitchforked into a French college before I had been through Pinnock in English, and I declare that to this day I do not know one rule out of five in Lindley Murray's grammar." He did, however, know his French grammar. Indeed, he had made such good use of his eighteen months spent as a boy in Paris that on his return to London he not only spoke French like a native but for some little time found it difficult even to think in English.

It would be easy to make too much of this linguistic point, for he could on occasion write as good and virile English prose as any of his contemporaries, but all his life, and largely as a result of his Paris sojourn, a polyglot touch clung to his writings, and he could rarely indict a private letter of any length without breaking into French, German, Italian, or Greek.

So we come to those early days in the Paris which he was afterwards to know so well. He arrived by *diligence*—from his description about the most cumbersome machine ever seen on the public road: four separate vehicles, he thought, squeezed longitudinally together, must have gone to its making—and within a few days' time had become a

member of the Pension Hénon, a large boarding-house in the Rue de
Courcelles which was affiliated to a well-known day-school, the College
Bourbon.   There were about fifty boarders—the younger Dumas
amongst them—at the establishment, and they do not seem to have been
always friendly towards the newcomer.   (But English people were not
too popular in Paris just then.)   Yet, as he tells us himself, he was not
unhappy, finding the lessons interesting and the masters for all their
little eccentricities helpful and understanding, and in "Monsieur Gogo's,"
one of those embroidered slices of autobiography which he was to write
for Dickens's *Household Words*, he could speak of the Pension Hénon
and in particular of its staff with an amused affection.   Nor had Miss
Ashley given him a mistaken impression of life in a French school.
There was discipline which on occasion could be stern, but there was
freedom as well.   The curriculum was sufficiently elastic to include
such delights as official visits to the Opera or playhouse, there was no
compulsion in the matter of organised games, and in general M. Hénon's
pupils could spend their leisure hours much as they pleased, a fact of
which the young George, already immensely curious about almost
everything in the world, was not slow to take advantage.   His week-ends
at first were invariably spent with his mother and sister who were in
rooms no great distance away; but at other times he would wander
off with a companion or two, to explore: wondering at the untidiness
of the streets but enjoying the gaiety of the people, rushing from gallery
or museum to military spectacle or gypsy-run fair, and gaining the while
an astonishing insight into Parisian manners and, incidentally, Parisian
slang.   When, moreover, in the spring of 1840 his mother returned to
London to continue her singing-classes he must have felt that now at
last he was following in his brothers' footsteps and being allowed to
see life.

You are not to suppose that already he was beginning to run rather
wild.   Five or six years later that was certainly the case.   If, however,
during those eighteen months in Paris he managed to explore more
of the outside world than most English boys of his age would have
been in a position to see, he was never in any serious trouble with
M. Hénon or his staff, and in school hours worked tremendously hard.
Music and dancing, as taught by a dapper gentleman who, we learn,
invariably wore orange-coloured pantaloons, had no interest for him, and
in the English classes, conducted by a master who, though British himself,
had lived so long in France that he had forgotten much of his native
language, his attention generally strayed; but at history, geography,
and Greek he made remarkable progress and obtained prizes in all three

subjects. Whether the Hénons of those days were accustomed to send "reports" to parents at the end of term I do not know, but if they did so it is not difficult to imagine the kind of document which Madame Sala would have received. An exceptionally clever boy, *le petit George*, eager to learn once his interest had been aroused, and gifted with an unusually retentive memory. Excellent in history and composition. General behaviour good. Another year or two at the Pension Hénon, and he would be a scholar likely to bring the greatest credit to his school.

But there were to be no other years at the Pension Hénon.

In the early autumn of 1840 Madame Sala returned to Paris—singing pupils in London unfortunately remained shy or were finding teachers with more modern methods—and, with her eldest son, now a youthful composer of some promise, to help her, she staged a grand concert at the Salon Frascati. The wife of the British Ambassador, Lady Granville, was present, and such international favourites as Grisi, Lablache, and Tamburini sang. And even though the French authorities unkindly insisted on impounding an appreciable portion of the receipts, all seemed to be financially and socially well.

Parisian society, indeed, was pleased to accept Madame Sala, who during that autumn was to be found, sometimes with one or other of her sons, in many of the great houses. In the previous August, however, there had occurred that rather ludicrous and ill-fated attempt at Boulogne. Louis Bonaparte had landed, from an English ship, and with his fifty-eight followers proposed to follow in his illustrious uncle's footsteps. The adventurer had speedily been arrested, duly tried, and sentenced to "perpetual" imprisonment; and the matter seemed to be more or less at an end. To the ordinary Frenchman, as well as to most Englishmen, he seemed to be little more than a half-crazy fellow, and incredulous laughter would have greeted any prophecy that he would ever occupy the French Imperial throne. As it was, Parisians seem to have shown a much greater interest in the trial of a Madame Laffarge on a charge of poisoning her husband than in any Bonaparte escapade. But as the day drew near for another Napoleonic ceremony—the second burial of the great Emperor at the Invalides: it took place in December, and Sala, like the Thackeray who was to become his friend, was one of those who witnessed the processions—there came a curious change of view. It was now that the Boulogne attempt began to be spoken of as "the London plot." It was now, too, that French dissatisfaction with British policy in Egypt and Syria became unpleasantly audible. England, Russia, Austria, and Prussia had undertaken to expel Mehemet's son Ibrahim from the Syrian strongholds which he had seized. In October

Sir Charles Napier had bombarded Beyrout, and when at the beginning of November the Allied Fleet under the British Admiral Stopford captured St. Jean d'Acre there began an almost nightly series of disturbances in Paris outside the British Embassy. Madame Sala, living in the near neighbourhood, became alarmed, and when, just before Christmas, her friend Tamburini prophesied an almost immediate declaration of war, she took fright. The position, no doubt, of the British colony in Paris was decidedly uncomfortable, and she may perhaps be excused for making the hastiest preparations for departure. Gussy was removed from the convent to which she had been sent, Fred charged to order the fastest vehicle for Boulogne, and George, sorely against his inclination, required to bid an abrupt good-bye to the Pension Hénon and join the fleeing party.

2

Why, he must have wondered, was it necessary to drag him away in this feverish manner? What would happen to him in England? He could hardly hope that an English school would be found for him in the least like the one where he had been so happy. In all probability he would be sent to an institution where they would use the dreaded rod, and where those who worked hardest were not always, or even often, the most popular. Even if he escaped school for a while and was left to study, as before, more or less by himself, his mother once again would be "in charge" instead of being the gracious lady whom he had been delighted to visit at week-ends. In other words, he would be forced under petticoat government again—the one eventuality which he had been hoping would never recur. It was a dreary prospect for a "Frenchified" boy of twelve who had almost forgotten how to talk English, and it was a rebellious and possibly tearful youngster who took his seat in the swift, and most expensive, *berline de voyage*.

But there was a larger question than her youngest boy's future for Madame Sala to consider. What was she going to do next? Whither were they to go? For years now she had had no settled home, and had rarely been in a position to know what her financial resources might be six months hence. Crises had come, and in one way or another they had been safely passed, but only by the most carefully-laid plans. True, there was no actual crisis at the moment, but in all probability another would shortly be upon them. Her second boy, Charles, was now earning a meagre salary in a Tithes Commissioner's office (where he was not in the least happy), but Fred—"an expensive young man," according to his brother—was doing nothing very much, and there were Albert's fees to be found. She could, of course, find rooms in the Quadrant again and seek for work on the London stage. And yet, I imagine her thinking, was this the best moment to return to the Quadrant? Might it not be better to try Brighton? Brighton, or some other watering-place less fashionable perhaps, but where the living was cheaper?

The *berline* brought them to Boulogne, whence they crossed to Dover. *Dover!* It was no Brighton, but it was a town of growing importance, it had its well-to-do visitors, and smart regiments were occasionally quartered in its Castle. Moreover there was the Duke of Wellington who as Lord Warden of the Cinque Ports was often in residence at Walmer Castle, a few miles away. More than once the Duke had shown her the greatest kindness, and if she were to see him now he might have the most useful suggestions to make. And was not another good friend of hers living in Dover: Henry Wallack, a brother of the better-known James and himself an actor of some little standing in the provinces? Surely he was managing that curious little Theatre Royal in Snargate Street? In which case might he not also have some useful suggestions to make? There was money enough to last for some months, during which she would have time to look round, and living in Dover was cheap. She decided to stay there for a little while.

She stayed there for a year (though she was in London in June while preparations were being made for the annual Benefit Concert—a more than usually anxious time, as it happened, for the Haymarket Theatre had been leased and Mr. Macready's services engaged for the evening: an outlay, we learn, of £130), and it was a year during which for the second time young George found himself in a theatrical Bohemia, shabbier than that which he had discovered in King Street, St. James's, but in its way even more exciting, for, temporarily, it seemed, Madame Sala was ready to forget that he was only a little boy.

Furnished rooms were found in Snargate Street itself, "and I can recollect with minute fidelity," wrote Sala some twenty years later, "the little first floor . . . we occupied; the good old widow-woman who kept the lodgings, who used to tell my little sister and myself heart-rending stories about the missionaries in Quashibungo, also soliciting small pecuniary aid from us towards the funds of the Anti-Slavery Society, but who, at the same time, would bestow upon us those appetising but too luscious delicacies known as 'Fleet-cakes'—thin, brown, crisp parallelopipeds, into the composition of which hog's lard enters somewhat too largely." On visiting the Theatre Royal, however, his mother found that her friend Mr. Wallack had recently departed

from Dover—for a reason which was immediately apparent. The
theatre was in a very bad way; for the last few years it had been in a
very bad way; at the moment it was facing the worst crisis of its
existence.

The new manageress, an indifferent comedy-actress who called herself
Miss Darling, had sacrificed her small savings in a valiant effort to turn
the tide, but the Dovorians would not come, and her company minus
their salaries were threatening to leave her, and unless somebody—
somebody well known to the great world of London, somebody, for
instance, like the distinguished Madame Sala—were to come to her
immediate aid, the Theatre Royal would have to be closed.

Now, whether it was that news arrived just then that H.M.'s Fifty-
Fourth Regiment of Infantry were due to arrive at Dover, or that a
chance meeting—in Snargate Street itself—with the Duke of Wellington,
who patted the small George on the head, had its effect, or that during
her stay in Paris Madame Sala had witnessed a comedy, *La Rose Jaune*,
which could be "adapted" for the English stage and was just the kind
of entertainment for a provincial audience, or whether it was that her
sympathies had been thoroughly aroused for a woman even less lucky
than herself, I do not know; but before many days had passed she had
not only offered her professional but also her financial assistance. By
February, moreover, the Sala family, temporarily increased by the
arrival of the second boy Charles who now talked of going on the
professional stage, were to be found every day at the theatre. And when
the Fifty-Fourth Regiment actually arrived, and Madame Sala found
herself in the kind of society where her particular gifts were most
appreciated, business began to improve. It continued to improve, and
she remembered the French comedy. Miss Darling, presumably, thought
well of the project, whereupon the entire family set to work to produce
an English version. George's services as calligrapher-in-chief were
naturally requisitioned, but he, too, helped with the translation and may
well have suggested some of its "lines."

For, young though he was, he had acquired more than a smattering
of stage-technique, and already he had begun to "write." The exercise-
books continued to be filled with long extracts from the classics, and his
Latin and Greek were not being neglected. Almost every day, too, saw
its fresh batch of little sketches and caricatures. Now, however, he was
discovering the delights of bloodthirsty thrillers, sugary romances of
high life, and tales of astonishingly improbable adventure: the Penny
Dreadfuls of the period. Voraciously he devoured all that Dover could
provide, and conceived the notion that he could write just as exciting

stories himself. One, indeed, entitled *Jemmy Jenkins; Or, the Adventures of a Sweep*, was finished within a few weeks, and in the oddest manner the manuscript found its way to New York amongst James Wallack's luggage. His knowledge of sweepery cannot have been great, but it is something for a boy of thirteen to complete a "novel," even if it contain no more than ten thousand words. Nor was this all, for already he was the author of a "fearsome" five-act tragedy, written in French and called *Frédégonde*. "There was a murder in almost every scene," he recalled long afterwards. "Somebody was poisoned, or burnt, or put to the torture *coram publico* at the end of every act; and I think that, as a *dénouement*, the wicked French Queen was to be torn to pieces by wild horses (from Mr. Ducrow's stud at Astley's), or devoured by wild dogs." *Frédégonde* was despatched to Alfred Wigan—the Mr. Sidney whom the young author had met so often in the St. James's days—and the choice of manager was shrewd, for Wigan was now making his name and he spoke French almost as well as he spoke English. What the actor thought of this ambitious but sanguinary drama I do not know, but he had not forgotten it when, a generation later, he became lessee and manager of the St. James's and Sala wrote for a private box. I hope that at the time of its composition his family were duly impressed. In any case they did not disdain his assistance in preparing the script of *The Yellow Rose*, and so, even if *Frédégonde* found no producer, he did have the satisfaction at a surprisingly early age of hearing his own words spoken by "real actors on a real stage."

There are no details of that performance, or, indeed, of the comedy itself, but, alas, the Dovorians failed to respond.

"The officers of the new regiment," records George Augustus, "mustered in force in the dress-circle. The stage-manager, indeed, had the courage to come before the curtain at the conclusion of the play, and to announce that it would be repeated until further notice; whereupon one of the nine occupants of the gallery called out in a resonant, but scarcely friendly, voice, 'Not by no means.' Exit *The Yellow Rose*."

Exit, too, it would seem, the unfortunate Miss Darling.

Her successor, Mr. William Copeland, did not fare much better. In later years as manager of the Theatre Royal, Liverpool, he did unusually well, but at Dover he was hardly a success, and, to be frank, one is not surprised. To stage *Hamlet* in a fashionable London theatre with famous players in the principal parts and elaborate scenic effects is one thing, but to stage it in a third-rate provincial house without proper scenery or costumes, and with an unknown youngster playing the Prince, is another. It may be magnificent, but it is not good business,

Yet this is what Mr. Copeland did. He had his reasons, of course. In the first place, his wife, a sister of Douglas Jerrold, was an actress who at the time seems to have held the belief, singularly common amongst the ladies of her profession, that Nature had always intended her for the perfect Ophelia. In the second place, there was Madame Sala with her name and her useful military connection, and Madame Sala seemed eager to appear in the tragedy. In the third place, young Charles Kerrison Sala, who had now definitely cut himself off from an office-bound life, seemed to Mr. Copeland to be a more than usually promising actor, particularly in the matter of reciting verse, and so well suited for the Prince. (And here the manager showed perspicacity, for in after years Charles under his stage-name of Wynn made some little reputation for himself on the London stage.)

So, for the second time that year the Sala family prepared themselves to astonish Dover. New costumes were devised by Fred, and George, no doubt, was kept busy copying out the parts and "hearing" the new Hamlet his words. But Dover unkindly refused to be astonished. It refused to show any interest whatever in the theatrical treat prepared for it. The Copelands, disgusted, left the town almost at once, and took their company with them. The Salas, one supposes, shrugged their shoulders: by this time they must have been well used to such temporary set-backs. Nothing, however, could discourage Madame Sala. If these Dovorians declined to enjoy great drama they must be offered something else. A concert? No; not in Snargate Street. But why not one of those masquerades which were so popular in London? Even Dover would have heard of them. True, there were those who spoke of masquerades as immoral exhibitions which all respectable citizens must shun like the plague, but under proper supervision they could be singularly delightful and, what was of greater importance, most profitable to their organisers. A masquerade was duly given, and on this occasion, at any rate, the theatre was full. It proved so successful, indeed, that Madame Sala felt justified in following it with a Grand Ball. This was something outside her usual line, but with her wonted energy she set out to obtain the right kind of patronesses and when the great night arrived had the satisfaction of seeing Snargate Street blocked with the fine carriages of half the County.

Once again there was money in the Sala coffers, and, no doubt rightly, the head of the family decided that the time had now come to move on. So they moved on to London, and found apartments in Silver Street, Golden Square. And while Madame Sala looked about her for new pupils and Fred and Charles in their charmingly light-hearted way played at

being young gentlemen about town, George, left temporarily to his own
devices, turned author again.

3

The juvenile scribblings of a writer are rarely anything more than
diverting curiosities, and Sala's earliest surviving story is no exception.
It is full of childish pomposities and laughable mistakes. Yet it is not
without its biographical interest. It is lurid melodrama of the usual
Penny Dreadful type—so much was to be expected—and there are
delicious "gaps" in its plot. Its vocabulary, however, is considerably
more extensive than that to be found in most boyish effusions, and there
is a real attempt at portraiture. It suggests the kind of play which its
writer had been seeing at the Theatre Royal, Dover, and the queer
mixture of good and bad books which he was reading at the time.
With its rather pathetic insistence, moreover, on financial details, it
allows us to understand just what the extra shilling could mean to a
household like the Salas', where the exchequer was liable at any moment
to play the most alarming tricks.

Sala's widow once publicly expressed the hope that she would one
day be able to print *Gerald Moreland; Or, the Forged Will* in full, if only,
said she, with a curious lack of humour, "by way of encouraging some
of our schoolboys of fourteen to take up their pens in their Christmas
holidays, and try to write stirring stories during wet days instead of
teasing and pinching their sisters."

It was certainly a stirring story: more than 12,000 words in length,

George Augustus Henry Fairfield Sala.

Tuesday March 22nd A.D. 1842.

*29 Silver Street Regent Street
London*

AUTHOR'S SIGNATURE (AET. 14) FACING PAGE ONE OF MS. OF
" GERALD MORELAND "

finished, as the neatly-written manuscript informs us, on "Teusday
March 22nd 1842," and very properly dedicated with all affection to

Cousin Sarah Ashley. The scene is Ireland (where the young author had recently spent a short Christmas holiday), and it will be enough, perhaps, if I say that its villains, all of whom are inordinately fond of " prime havannahs " and strong drink, include a lawyer dubbed "a pettifogging, insignificant, low, cunning 6s. 8d.", a false heir, and one Lorenzo Scrubbs, a coal-merchant's son—apparently the lowest possible social rank—while the hero and heroine, long parted, of course, by the forces of evil, undergo all manner of distressing hardships before they have the satisfaction of hearing that the lawyer has poisoned the false heir and gone mad in prison and that Lorenzo has died miserably of cholera abroad.

Gerald Moreland, I fancy, did not have any immediate successor. Authorship could be an attractive pastime, but there were too many easier excitements. At this time, indeed, as George was to admit, he was "running intellectually to seed." The family was splitting up, and there were frequent "moves." In London he made particular friends with the two daughters of Balfe, the composer, and was often to be found at their Conduit Street home; but he had also renewed his acquaintance with some of the St. James's players who had been amused by his adult ways, and in general he was being left too much to his own devices. Madame Sala was now finding pupils more elusive than ever and feverishly looking for theatrical engagements—she was not successful until the late autumn when the Princess's Theatre in Oxford Street came under new management—and she had little time to give to her son. Gussy was not now in a position to supervise his studies, for she had begun to earn her own living as a governess, and his brothers were no longer at home. Money had been scraped together to purchase for Fred a piano-teaching connection in High Wycombe, and all his leisure time was now being given to composition. Charles in his new name had obtained an engagement at the Theatre Royal, Dublin, and the rather mysterious Albert, whose subsequent career was peculiar, was preparing to leave England for ever. No doubt there were hours still given to desultory study, but George was doing little enough, and during the autumn it became obvious that some very definite step would have to be taken. He was hardly old enough to be expected to earn his own living—at this time, it seems, he supposed that he would become some kind of "an artist"—and I imagine that Miss Ashley once again came to the rescue. There was a small boarding-school at Turnham Green, then a charmingly rural hamlet, where "Pestalozzian" methods were adopted and the rod was unknown. Its principal was a Mr. John Godfrey Dyne, and Mr. Dyne believed in bringing out the best in his boys by a kindly interest in their youthful enthusiasms. And so to this Bolton House School George was sent.

Here, during the Afghan troubles and while at home the Chartists were beginning to alarm peaceful folk, income-tax proposals were disturbing the sleep of the rich, and maniacs attempted to assassinate the Queen, he spent a happy enough year. At first boys and masters seem to have laughed at his Frenchified ways, but he rapidly made himself at home. Luckily for him, too, at Bolton House artistic leanings were not, as so frequently happens, discouraged. On the contrary, out-of-school hobbies were officially recognised, and interest was expressed in young Sala's powers as calligrapher and draughtsman. They taught him to model in clay—the figures for a new Grecian portico at Bolton House were his work—and they took advantage of his theatrical experiences. Mr. Dyne believed in his boys acting rather than "doing" their Shake-speare and other dramatists sufficiently "classical" to be included in the school curriculum. Twice a week, indeed, stage plays were acted, and there were daily rehearsals. And it was here that he achieved his greatest school triumph. Amongst the plays chosen for the midsummer "Examination," or Speech Day, was *Julius Caesar*. It happened that on May 1st one of the Drury Lane actors, the James Anderson who, I fancy, was to outlive Sala himself, was taking his benefit at that theatre and in the same play. Macready was Brutus, Phelps Cassius, Helen Faucit Portia, and Anderson himself Mark Antony. George had been chosen to play Brutus—no mean compliment, for he can hardly have been one of the senior boys—and with the rest of the youthful cast he was taken by omnibus to Drury Lane, in order to see how the parts should rightly be sustained. And it is interesting to find that the Examination itself was held at the Hanover Square Rooms, built by Gallini, where Madame Sala had so often appeared.

It must have been a peculiar Examination, enacted as it was before a crowded audience of parents, guardians, and friends. In addition to the plays there was an exhibition of mass-fiddling by more than half the school, and oral demonstrations with a blackboard on mathematical subjects. Incidentally, Madame Sala does not seem to have been too well pleased at the idea of her youngest son "playing at play-acting," and warned Mr. Dyne that she had no intention of paying for the hire of any costume from Nathan's. But the difficulty was successfully surmounted, and George's performance surpassed everybody's expecta-tions. It was an arduous part for a boy to play, and it was not the only one which he was called on to play on that occasion; but "there was such hearty applause from the audience," he records, "that the delighted

Mr. Dyne caught me up in his arms and carried me away to the refreshment room to regale me with sponge-cake and a glass of sherry." And it may well have occurred to the boy that night that providence had intended him not for painting or authorship but for the professional stage.

If, however, any such thought crossed his mind just then it was speedily banished. A few months later, during the Christmas holidays and apparently without warning, Madame Sala announced that he would not be returning to Bolton House.

He was now fifteen: the time had come for him to settle down to some remunerative work. Obviously the stage held no opening for a boy of his age: he must seek some other employment. She had been showing some of his drawings and caricatures to friends of hers who thought well of them. There was a growing market, she had been told, for such things, and not only in the book-world. The illustrated newspaper and the illustrated comic weekly had come, and come, apparently, to stay. There was the *Illustrated London News*, for instance, and that clever *Punch*. With the right kind of introduction, she thought, there was no reason why he should not find immediate work.

What the boy thought of this sudden change of plan or what opinion he had at the time of his own drawings it is a little difficult to say; but he must have been pleased and excited when his mother put into his hands a letter of introduction from a musical friend of hers to the great George Cruikshank himself. The most famous living draughtsman, and a hero of heroes to the boy from the days when he had made his first rude scratches on paper! Eagerly he chose out a number of his best drawings, and on the appointed morning set out by himself for Cruikshank's Pentonville house. The artist, then in his fifty-third year, received him with the greatest kindness, and in spite of the difference in their ages there was born that day a friendship which lasted unbroken until the fiery old man's death. But it was hardly a helpful interview. "George," wrote Sala long afterwards, "looked carefully over the large pile of pen-and-ink drawings which I had brought him; advised me to turn my attention to etching and drawing on wood, and told me to come to him again when I had made some mastery of those processes." This, he admitted, was encouraging, but it was not an immediate help towards obtaining a livelihood.

Madame Sala, however, was not discouraged. She had been looking at *Punch*, and to her it seemed that even Leech's graphic humour was not vastly superior to her son's. And she had been making enquiries. The editor of *Punch* was the ex-brewer, Mark Lemon, who had had so

many recent successes as a dramatist. She did not know him herself,
but she believed that he was one of Dickens's particular friends, and that
was good enough. Boz would assuredly do what was necessary. Nor
was she mistaken, for he was good enough to see mother and son at the
Euston Hotel, as he passed through London, examined the drawings,
and "thought they would do." "So the next day we called upon
Mr. Lemon," Sala was remembering fifty years later, "with a letter of
introduction from the author of *Pickwick*. The genial editor of *Punch*
greeted us with effusive, I may say with unctuous kindness and a whole
cascade of smiles. . . . He smiled at my mother; he smiled at me; he
smiled at the drawings, and promised to look over them with a view
to their favourable consideration; and then he smiled us down a very
rickety flight of stairs into Bouverie Street; but I am afraid that when
we got into the open, both my mother and myself were in doubt as to
whether we should smile, ourselves, or have a good cry. As it was,
that dreadful portfolio came back to us in about a week with a polite
intimation—he could scarcely smile in pot-hooks and hangers—from
Mr. Mark Lemon that he was unfeignedly sorry for his inability to make
use of my very promising, but, as yet, immature productions."

He can hardly be blamed, but Sala could not easily forget the
"unctuousness" with which his ill-fated sketches had been declined—
a fact which was to have its sequel before any long time had elapsed.
As for Madame Sala, even she must have realised that if her son was
to live by the sale of his drawings there would have to be some form
of professional tuition.

So it was that in the spring of 1844 George Sala signed his first articles,
and within a few months' time was, unexpectedly, facing life on his
own.

CHAPTER FOUR

SEARCH FOR A PROFESSION

I

AT the beginning of 1839 Mr. Fox Talbot, the Squire of Lacock, possibly Wiltshire's most beautiful village, had described to the Royal Society certain experiments which he had been making on paper rendered sensitive to light. A few months later Monsieur Daguerre's "new invention for taking pictures" had been publicly exhibited in Paris. By 1844 the commercial possibilities of photography had been but imperfectly realised, but even at that date one type of artist was fearing lest, for him, the good old days had gone for ever. This was the miniature-painter. The Humphrys and the Cosways were dead: their successors were complaining that commissions were becoming ever rarer, and that if this new-fangled machine continued to improve with any rapidity, as seemed more than probable, they would soon be put out of business altogether. One or two men, like Sir William Ross, R.A., continued to prosper, but a number of his less fortunate colleagues were feeling the pinch; and amongst them was a near neighbour of his—the German-born but almost completely anglicised Carl Schiller.

Mr. Schiller lived opposite to Sir William in a large house in Charlotte Street, Fitzroy Square, then a much more fashionable district than it is today. He possessed a good art library and a large collection of casts, relics of the days when he had been the Principal of an Academy of Art. He was no genius, but he had enjoyed the patronage of many well-known and wealthy men. At this time, however, he was finding it exceedingly difficult to secure new clients, and, oddly enough, it was this unfortunate fact which in a large measure was responsible for the astonishing variety of trades and professions to which, during the next four or five years, young George Sala apprenticed himself.

It had been arranged that he should be articled to Mr. Schiller for three years: actually he stayed with him for no more than four or five months. No doubt during that time he learnt much, though he was never to be anything more than a mediocre draughtsman. For three hours in the morning he would be kept "steadily and seriously drawing from the round," and for three hours in the afternoon he would be allowed to browse amongst Mr. Schiller's books or make drawings "out of his own head." "And," he adds, "my evenings were alternately devoted to the study of artistic anatomy and of perspective."

This last, I am afraid, is a slightly misleading statement, for on most evenings his studies of artistic anatomy seem to have been conducted not at the house in Charlotte Street, but either behind the scenes at the Princess's Theatre where his mother was now regularly engaged in a not too prominent and probably not too well-paid position, or, more frequently, in other less reputable and rowdier haunts. The boy, in fact, was growing up fast : rather too fast. Schooling was finished and done with. In his own eyes he was already a man, and in truth there was some reason for the belief. He was entirely at home in the lighthearted world of the theatre, by no means shy, ready-witted, and ever eager for new experiences : a personable youngster, too, in spite of his "duffer" eye. Now, moreover, he was making friends not only with the doubtlessly clever and amusing but undisciplined and not always sober gentlemen who were connected in one way or another with the theatre but also with various young ladies belonging to the same profession who had not yet emerged from the chorus. It was all very innocent, no doubt, but there were too many late nights in questionable company. His mother expostulated ; George, now developing that savage temper which in later years was to alienate so many of his friends, and envious of the freedom which his brothers were enjoying, angrily retorted that he was of an age to choose his own way. And when Mr. Schiller's financial position became suddenly acute and there was a hurried departure from the big house in Charlotte Street, matters came to a head.

(Poor Schiller ! In after years he was lucky to obtain work in a fashionable photographer's studio, engaged to convert photographs into "miniatures"—Sala's, as it happened, amongst them.)

Madame Sala, no doubt, suggested another drawing-master, but her son refused to listen. Here, surely, was the opportunity to follow his brothers' example : henceforth he would be his own master.

Was his kind-hearted Cousin Sarah consulted first ? Did she understand how "difficult" Madame Sala could be at times and agree to provide a scanty allowance while he was finding his feet ? I do not know, but some time in the autumn of 1844 Master George packed up his few belongings, and although he remained on good terms with his mother, never again lived under her roof.

What to do ?   2

Such artistic qualifications as he possessed were hardly, it seemed, of much commercial value. He knew a few men in the newspaper world,

a number of actors, even an author or two who had made his name :
none of them could be of much assistance. He had, however, made the
acquaintance of various tradesmen in the West End, and for a while he
managed to earn a little money by making up their books. He cannot
have been too comfortable at the time—afterwards he was very ready to
admit that again and again he had been obliged to go supperless to bed
—but he was "on his own," in an attic somewhere in Soho, uncertain as
to *what* he wanted to do, but confident that in due course he would find
his own niche. Making up tradesmen's books was certainly no job for
an ambitious youngster, even if it had meant regular employment. He
did remain for some time in this capacity at the fashionable St. James's
Street establishment of Crellin, the tailor, his Aunt Eliza's husband, but
otherwise no job lasted for more than a week or two, and by the beginning
of 1845 he had had enough of counting-houses and was looking elsewhere
for work.

He found it in a copyist's office, and in that extraordinarily neat handwriting of his transcribed numerous legal documents. The voluminous
Will of a recently-deceased peer with its twenty-four codicils "boarded
and lodged me," he records, "for at least three weeks."

About the same time there came that curious railroad "mania" which
at one moment almost threatened to become a second South Sea Bubble.
Then it was that George Hudson, the "Railway King," reached the
highest point in his chequered career, and there was the maddest scramble
for shares in any undertaking with which he was known to be associated.
Then, too, there arose a hundred lesser promoters with railway schemes
which, had all of them been carried out, could hardly have left a single
acre in all Britain uncrossed. For all these schemes it was necessary to
prepare the most careful maps and plans, and in not a few cases these
were required to be lithographed. In the course of his studies—not all
of them, by the way, conducted by himself with help from a manual, for
by some means money had been found for him to attend evening classes
at "Dagger" Leigh's art school—Sala had taught himself to draw upon
stone, and he now found work of a more congenial kind. The "mania"
was short-lived, but he made the most of it, and at least he ended his
cartographic career in a blaze of financial triumph. "By a certain hour
in a certain afternoon," he tells us, "all the maps and sections of the
almost innumerable lines which had been projected had to be deposited
at the Offices of the Board of Trade." Most of the work had been
entrusted to one of the best-known firms in London, and Sala was one
of a score of assistants called in to help. Luckily for him these assistants
were paid according to their capacity and endurance. Sala received

fifteen shillings an hour, and remained at his table for two days and most of the intervening night.

It was princely pay for a boy of seventeen, and of course too good to last. But the railway mania was directly responsible for yet another attempt on Sala's part to decide on a profession. It gave him the idea for a satirical story. In a Chinese disguise he recounted the rise of Hudson and prophesied his speedy fall. It was not much of a story, this *Choo-Lew-Kwang; or, the Stages of Pekin*, but it was sent off to the recently established and now successful *Family Herald*, and to its author's astonishment and delight it was duly printed. "But I was so raw," he records, "so 'green' I may say, at the time, that I never asked to be paid for it; and when at Christmas time I sent in another story which was called *Barnard Braddlescrogs*, and which I know was a shameless imitation of Dickens's *Christmas Carol*, the little contribution was neither published nor returned to me."

But he was "in print" for the first time, and that, as any author will admit, is a very great moment. At the time of the story's appearance Madame Sala had retired from the Princess's, and was proposing to resume her singing-lessons. She had taken rooms in Brighton, and George was staying with her over Christmas. Many copies of the *Family Herald* had been purchased and were now given to some of his mother's friends, amongst them the well-known Miss Costello, whose latest story he had recently been reading in the *Illustrated London News*. She was asked for her opinion: should the boy persevere with his writing? Miss Costello's reply was blunt. In attempting authorship, she considered, he had entirely mistaken his vocation. One or two others agreed with her, which was not altogether surprising, for apart from its occasionally amusing vocabulary, the burlesque showed little enough promise.

Whereupon the boy who was afterwards to be called the Prince of Special Correspondents and the First Journalist of Europe regretfully decided that newspaper work was not for him.

3

There followed a dismal month or two. Shillings continued to dribble in from the transcription of Wills and the like or from the casual sale of a drawing; but what the disappointed young author was now looking for was a regular job, and this was not too easily found. Luckily for him his brother Charles—always his favourite in the family—had just then been engaged at the Princess's Theatre, and, in a distinctly curious way, he became indirectly responsible for the next step in George's career.

Until a year or two ago, if you had stepped a few yards to the north-east of Oxford Circus, you would have found, standing by itself on an island, a square shabby building known as Oxford Mansion. Here were bachelor chambers, not unlike, though more modest than, the better-known suites in Albany. In the 'forties, however, Oxford Mansion had not yet arisen, and its site was occupied by a collection of irregular buildings and wooden sheds known as Oxford Market. To the south of this market there stood an old tavern, the White Hart, kept by the well-known pantomimist George Wieland. At this time he was no more than thirty-five, and there was probably nobody on the London stage who could play the part of a sprite or a monkey—any role calling for droll antics—better than he. His health, however, would not permit him to act—within two years he was to die of consumption—and so he had purchased the White Hart. Naturally this was a resort much patronised by theatrical folk, and more particularly by those who were employed at the Princess's only a few yards away. Charles Sala took his brother there one day and introduced him to the proprietor. Wieland liked the boy, and on learning what he could do with his pencil and brush forthwith commissioned him to paint a series of lithographic portraits of himself in his various characters. They were to be used as labels on his bottles.

It was a task which interested the boy and he did his work well, so well that Wieland proposed a more important commission. It happened that a Lodge of the Ancient Order of Foresters held its meetings in one of the rooms in the White Hart, and in his grandiose way the actor wanted some novelty which would mark off *his* Lodge from all the others. He finally decided on a large picture which would illustrate some of the principal scenes in the history of the Order and be embroidered with reproductions of its regalia. The picture was to be painted in oils and on linen, stretched over a large frame, and at the appointed times exhibited just within the front door, with a light behind it. In this way the Brethren on arrival would be amazed and delighted with the magic-lantern effect and so of course heap congratulations on the clever inn-keeper.

Gaily the young artist set to work. There were scores of sketches to be made, and there was the embroidered design to be carefully built up. All went well until the actual painting was begun. Then, however, he found himself in a dilemma. "It was the first time that I had essayed painting in oil," he wrote afterwards; "I did not know what was the best medium to use; the surface I was painting on being intended for a transparency I could not, obviously, 'prime' it, and my colours ran." It became necessary to seek expert advice, but from whom? Brother

Charles was consulted, and at once suggested that the chief scene-painter at the Princess's would be the very man to decide the problem : a delightfully friendly person, it seemed, and in his own way a genius. And so the half-finished picture was taken to the painting-room at the theatre— with unexpected results.

Now at this time the lessee and manager of the Princess's Theatre was a Jew whose real name was Medex. He, I fancy, had some years before been in partnership with his brother Sam who was still the proprietor of a flourishing cigar "emporium" almost opposite the theatre ; but the stage had always attracted him, and as a young man he had wandered off, toured the provinces with second-rate companies in various capacities, written melodramas himself, tried management, and in the early 'forties become known to Londoners as the Mr. John Medex Maddox who was proposing to re-open the hitherto ill-starred Princess's as yet another home for English Opera. How he obtained the money to do so remained an unsolved mystery, though rumour had it that a Brunswick Royal Highness then living, not too reputably, in London could have explained, but obtain it he did, and almost at once showed that he was a man with ideas. In the usual way the projected programme of English Opera was speedily widened to include almost every form of entertainment, though a certain standard was maintained. He became notorious for his "closeness" with money, but knew well enough when an unusually heavy expenditure might be advisable. So it was that he secured the services of both Macready and Madame Vestris, and introduced more than one European or American with big reputations in their own country to the London stage. He believed in lavish decoration and cunningly contrived publicity, and was always on the search for some novelty with which to startle his patrons. In a word, though he occasionally made bad mistakes, as, for instance, when he engaged "General" Tom Thumb at a moment when the public were rather tired of the American dwarf's antics, he was an exceedingly clever showman.

It was he who had taken Madame Sala into his company, and he who in the autumn of 1844 had secured the services of the one man then alive who seemed at all likely to revolutionise stage-production : the William Roxby Beverley, real inventor of the transformation scene as the Victorians knew it, who was delighted to see his good friend Charles Wynn's brother in his painting-room and gave him the benefit of his advice.

Turpentine, it seemed, was the required medium for Mr. Wieland's great picture, and turpentine was duly applied ; but that was not the end of the matter. It happened that the manager of the theatre strolled into

SALA AT NINETEEN.

From an oil painting by himself, 1847.

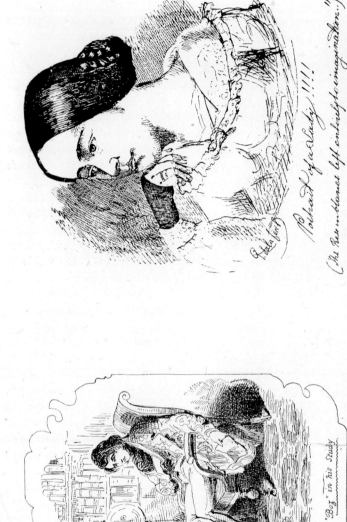

"Boz" in his Study

(a) From *The Battle of London Life*, 1849.

Robert of yesterday!!!!

(*His Pen in hand left entirely to imagination.*)

(b) The beloved "Gussy" sketched by her Brother in 1842.

TWO EARLY DRAWINGS.

the painting-room while the merits of the Forester picture were being
discussed. Maddox had met the young artist on several previous occasions,
and had, as it happened, accompanied him and his mother in the train to
Brighton only a few weeks before. Now, after examining his work and
discovering that the boy was still looking for regular employment, he
"good-naturedly" asked Beverley if he would take him on as an assistant
scene-painter, which "the even better-tempered artist" at once agreed
to do. A salary was suggested and accepted, and the thing was done.
It was not a large salary—fifteen shillings a week—but the offer came at
a moment when it was most welcome, and it was all the more acceptable
because Beverley's most junior assistant, so far from receiving any
remuneration at all, was an articled pupil required to pay a substantial
premium.

And so in the early months of 1846 George Sala became a regular
employee at the Princess's, and he stayed there, well content in spite of
the wretched pay, for more than a year, learning the mysteries of "sinks"
and "slides," mixing the colours and assisting with the "sets," modelling
masks for the pantomime and inventing "effects" for the ballet, and,
incidentally, making sketches and caricatures of everybody connected
with the theatre. He learnt his job very well indeed, and rarely lost an
opportunity in after years to pay tribute to Beverley for his kindness and
consideration.

Mr. Maddox, however, soon discovered that his scene-painter's new
assistant could be quite as useful outside the painting-room as within it,
and for those fifteen weekly shillings he came to require a multiplicity of
services which included "translating comedies and farces from the French,
copying out the parts, drawing up the advertisements for the newspapers,
taking stock of the wardrobe, occasionally holding the prompt book at
the wing, and helping the treasurer to make out his accounts": everything, in fact, except appearances on the stage itself. Truly a young man
who gave good value for his money! Yet he managed to enjoy himself
—the glamour of the theatre was not easily fading—and did not seem to
worry overmuch at the fact that his brother was receiving five times as
much money as himself for considerably less work.

Incidentally, at this time, he narrowly missed being the adapter of a
play which was to become one of the dramatic successes of the century.

At the Princess's, as at every other London theatre, a "stock" author,
in this case one Reynoldson, was regularly employed on such work.
Maddox, as it happened, had had his attention drawn to a French farce
which, he thought, would be well suited to the English stage. Reynoldson was away ill at the time, and the script of *Une Chambre de Deux Lits*

was given to the only other employee in the theatre with a good knowledge of French—young George Sala, who, working like six Trojans (as
he always could when driven), managed to complete his adaptation within
a day or two. It was handed to the reigning low comedian for his
opinion. This gentleman remained unimpressed, and that, so far as the
Princess's was concerned, was the end of the matter. Others besides
Maddox, however, had seen possibilities in *Une Chambre de Deux Lits*,
amongst them Maddison Morton, who already had several farces to his
credit, and he, after grafting on to it portions of another piece of French
drollery, produced his *Box and Cox* at the Lyceum with Harley and
Buckstone in the principal parts, and so achieved the success of his life.
No doubt Sala's version was less sprightly, but one cannot help wondering
whether its production might not have materially altered his career.

As it was, for all the interest he took in his work for Maddox, he was
forced soon enough to realise the fact that Nature had never intended
him for a scene-painter, and when in the early spring of 1847 Beverley
received a good offer from Madame Vestris to go to the Lyceum and
packed up his brushes and paints, Sala decided that he, too, had had
enough of the Princess's, though another six months were to pass before
he definitely said good-bye to scene-painting.

For a little while he remained (at double the salary which Maddox
had been paying) with Beverley at the Lyceum. Then came a somewhat
different commission. This was the time when the huge panoramas of
great cities or world-famous "sights" were beginning to be popular with
Londoners, and more than one building was being used exclusively for
their exhibition. This year there was trouble in Mexico, and Beverley's
chief assistant at the Princess's had been engaged to paint an immense
canvas giving a general view of the capital city. He invited Sala's assistance, and the young man executed all the figures required in the foreground. Finally, he was engaged at the recently-opened Standard
Theatre in Shoreditch.

No doubt it was satisfactory to be more or less his own master, and
I dare say that the two scenes for which he was responsible at the Standard
were no worse than the majority of such things, but the pay was poor,
and he was selling few enough of his drawings and caricatures. He was
still living in his Soho attic, and his two cousins, he tells us, would occasionally send him parcels of food; but was it worth while to continue
in this way? Was there any likelihood of his ever being able to make
any new or vital contribution to the art of scene-painting? No; Beverley
had taught him its technique, and no doubt he might be able to eke out
some sort of a living by its practice, but he would never make a name for

himself in a theatrical studio. He would have to look elsewhere for that successful career which, he was determined, should sooner or later be his. He looked about him, and his eyes remained fixed upon Fleet Street. He was not proposing to write: they had told him that he could not write. He was not proposing to submit further drawings to *Punch*. But there were other publications of the kind on the market now. He might not be a "pen-and-pencil" man like that very tall and most entertaining Mr. Thackeray whom he had been so pleased to meet at a Soho club to which his brother had recently taken him; but were not his drawings and his neat caricatures at least as amusing as many of those thought worthy of reproduction? And so, for the second time, armed with a letter of introduction and carrying a portfolio under his arm, he paid a visit to a London editor, and was received with smiles.

This time, however, there was no "unctuous" rejection.

4

At this time *Punch* itself was in the sixth year of its existence: a flourishing youngster. Its success, of course, had brought rivals into the field, but with one exception these were negligible and rarely lasted for more than a few numbers. Its domestic troubles had been satisfactorily resolved, and, with Mark Lemon in the editorial chair and Thackeray and Douglas Jerrold amongst its regular contributors, it was enjoying an enviable reputation. Enemies it had, and with some justice they accused it of malice and errors of taste. On more than one occasion, too, they were able to show that Mr. Punch had not been the first to print a particular joke. But in general all such attacks could safely be ignored. The shortly-to-be-great Middle Classes had taken it to their respectable bosoms, and all was well.

Yet in this same year *Punch* not only found itself unmercifully attacked by a powerful and what at one moment seemed to be a most dangerous rival, but suffered a signal defeat at the hands of one of its private victims. And, as luck would have it, the youth whose drawings Mark Lemon had declined three years before, not only became a member of this rival's staff, but took an active part in administering the private victim's victorious counter-attack.

In the previous January there had appeared the first number of a sixpenny "comic monthly" which had at once caught the public taste. In its outward appearance it was unlike any other comic periodical. It was a dumpy quarto, so small that without being folded it could be slipped into any normal-sized pocket. It resembled, in fact, nothing so much as one of the admirable Mr. Bradshaw's Railway Time Tables, and this had been deliberately intended, for the *Man in the Moon*, as it was called, facetiously professed to be "an Act for the Amalgamation of the Broad Gauge of Fancy, with the Narrow Gauge of Fact, into the Grand General Amusement Junction." Nor was its success undeserved. It was a topical and witty *mélange*, illustrated with perky little cuts. If it gave rather more attention to theatrical and rather less to political matters than did most of its contemporaries, its burlesques were as good as anything that was being printed at the time, some of its parodies were exceedingly droll, and at first it was not noticeably malicious. It was financed by the proprietor of the very successful *Illustrated London News*, and its moving spirit was a man who, though he is now almost forgotten, was in his own day a considerable figure.

Mention the name of Albert Smith today, and what would it recall? Little enough, I suppose, to most people. A novel or two, perhaps—*The Adventures of Mr. Ledbury* and *Christopher Tadpole* still find their readers— and something vaguely connected with Mont Blanc. But what else? Nothing, assuredly, about the man himself. Yet in the course of his short career—he died in 1860 in his forty-fifth year—he touched success at half a dozen different points, and as a private person he left the most contradictory impressions on his contemporaries. Some loved the man; others detested him. Some thought him a genius; others a humbug. Actually he was neither: merely a man who worked tremendously hard and made the most of his opportunities. But to Sala, with whom, by the way, he had much in common, he was always a hero, and if for no other reason he must have his niche in this chronicle.

His father was a not very successful surgeon in practice at Chertsey. He himself had obtained a medical qualification, and for a while practised in a more or less desultory way. Chertsey, however, does not seem to have done what was required of it in the matter of broken limbs or disease, and in the early 'forties he had settled down with his family in Percy Street, off Tottenham Court Road, and put up his plate. He called himself a surgeon-dentist, and no doubt at first intended to remain in practice, but already the pen was proving to be a more attractive weapon than the scalpel or tweezers, and although the plate remained in position, visitors to the Percy Street house rarely came for professional advice. Working, moreover, all day and most of the night, he soon made his mark, in the dramatic as well as the literary world. His energy seemed to be inexhaustible. Original dramas, adaptations, burlesques: to the theatrical managers all were welcome. Novels, stories, lyrics, parodies, satirical essays and gossipy "columns" illustrated by himself: all were eagerly purchased by editors. And when the *Man in the Moon* first appeared his name by itself was a considerable asset. Within a month or two, moreover, he had published the first of his so-called "Natural Histories"—sociological satires—and although today their humour seems decidedly thin, they enjoyed an astonishing success. In the 'fifties, too, he was to appear by himself on the stage in what nowadays would be called travelogues—entertainments cleverly compounded of fact and fancy—and one of these, *Mont Blanc*, was generally considered to be the most popular exhibition of the kind ever known, and only surpassed, in point of public interest, by Dickens's Readings.

Something of a celebrity, then, this big-bodied, ruddy-haired, laughing fellow who dressed so carelessly and worked so hard ; and a man with friends in every walk of life who would speak of him in terms of the warmest affection. A devoted son, they said—his parents, a sister, and an aunt all had rooms in his house and for some years were almost wholly dependent upon him—and ever ready to do somebody a kindness. Not a man without his dislikes, capable even at moments of a show of bad temper, but in general the best of companions, and half literary and artistic London delighted to come to those untidy, ground-floor rooms of his in the Percy Street house and listen to his quips and jests. Yet, as I have said, there were those, Thackeray among them, who had little love for one whom they regarded as a loud-mouthed vulgarian ever on the look-out for some fresh opportunity to advertise himself. And it was true that at a time when anonymity was considered to be the first essential of dignified journalism, Albert Smith invariably insisted on his name being prominently displayed wherever possible. It was also true that his manners could be rough. He was not what polite circles called "a gentleman." "Altogether too familiar," complained some, "and a little too keen for the main chance." "A bit of a mountebank," said others, and in various ways showed their feelings towards him.

Probably his bitterest enemy at this time was Douglas Jerrold. Three or four years before they had been colleagues on *Punch*, but Albert Smith had never been happy there, and if his withdrawal was not primarily due to Jerrold's unmerciful jibes, they certainly did not help to retard his departure. Since that time, however, the jibes had continued, and in *Punch* itself and in Jerrold's own magazine nothing amiable was printed about the author of *Mr. Ledbury*. When, therefore, the *Man in the Moon* appeared in obvious rivalry to the older journal, it was only to be expected that *Punch* and Jerrold would come in for some hard knocks. And hard knocks there were. Rewards were offered for a laugh produced by one of *Punch's* jokes. Accusations of plagiarism, difficult to refute, were repeatedly made. Clever cartoons, too, appeared, culminating in one of a down-at-heel and Hebraic Mr. Punch carrying a large sack on his shoulders and crying out : "Any jo'; any old jo'?" Finally one of Albert Smith's most versatile contributors, Shirley Brooks, then a young man who had recently deserted the Law for journalism and was destined to make no small name for himself, wrote a set of verses called "Our Flight with Punch" which were about the most scathing of their kind ever printed. After a sarcastic reference to *Punch's* diminishing sales, its loathsome cant, and its "blind scorn" of so much that all good Englishmen cherished, "Back! foolish Hunchback," he thundered,

> "to the course that whilom made thy fame.
> Back! to thy lawful quarry, to thy Jove-appointed game.
> Shoot folly as it flies, but shoot it with the arrowy joke—
> Not with the brazen blunderbuss, all bellow and black smoke."

It was said at the time that on reading these verses Mark Lemon uttered a warning to his colleagues. "That young man," he is reported to have said, "is formidable. He must be sought as an ally." And ally he became, ending a successful career as Mark Lemon's successor in *Punch's* editorial chair.

There were other good men, however, besides Albert Smith and Shirley Brooks on the staff of the *Man in the Moon*. Its co-editor was Angus Reach, one of the cleverest journalists of the day and the author of several novels, and on the "art" side there were "Phiz," the Frenchman "Cham," H. G. Hine (whose large folding plates were a very popular feature), and Kenny Meadows. A merry little group, in fact, and just the men to receive with open arms any clever youngster who showed himself to be clubbable, unsnobbish, and able to appreciate a joke.

To such a company came Sala some time in the course of the summer. It was Shirley Brooks who had given him his letter of introduction—the two men had recently met and made friends—and Albert Smith had at once put him at his ease. Surely they had met before? Yes, that old scoundrel Maddox had produced a burlesque of his at the Princess's and paid him nothing much for it : he must have seen his visitor then, somewhere behind the scenes. And now what about his work? No "unctuous" smiles here and a promise to give favourable consideration to any drawings he might care to submit. Then and there, in the Percy Street study with its queerly-huddled collection of curious objects, its books, and its litter of papers, the caricatures were examined—luckily there was an adroit one of Maddox amongst them—and pronounced good enough. More, there was an immediate commission to make some comic cuts on wood, and the visitor was despatched to the Strand alley where Angus Reach was then living, so that he might make the other editor's acquaintance without delay. And within a week or two he was being generally accepted as a junior member of the staff.

At last, then, it seemed that George Sala had discovered his real vocation. He was on the staff of a popular magazine, accepted as a friend by men who had already made their names, a youngster of nineteen with a foot, as he himself might have said a few years later, on the lowest rung of the ladder of success. In the September number his caricature of Maddox was duly reproduced, and in the next issue there appeared for the first time in any publication a drawing which bore his name.

The *Man in the Moon* continued its monthly career until June, 1849, and Sala remained a fairly regular contributor, possibly assisting Smith and Reach editorially, enjoying his new status as an artist who was "published," making new friends in London's Bohemia, and, incidentally, spending rather more time and money than was advisable in the various taverns and cigar-divans where they were wont to assemble. One or two drawings

SALA'S CARICATURE OF JOHN MEDEX MADDOX

a month, however, even with some extra work which Albert Smith was able to give him, hardly sufficed to pay the rent of his attic, and it became necessary to find other employment. Luckily for him, Ebenezer Landells, the man who was responsible for the cuts in the *Man in the Moon*, was no ordinary craftsman. He had learnt his art from Bewick himself and had come to occupy a premier position amongst the engravers of the day, but he had also interested himself in newspaper enterprises, and at the beginning of the year had launched the *Lady's Newspaper*—a journal intended chiefly for women, and the first of its kind, I believe, on the market. Landells had a vacancy on his staff, and Sala was glad to accept a commission to design some of the "patterns" and fashion-plates which were a feature of the paper. Work, too, of a less monotonous though hardly more dignified character came his way about this time from an introduction to another engraver. This Mr.

Calvert—not to be confused with the Edward Calvert who produced some very beautiful woodcuts at a little later date—was a very poor artist, and he rarely if ever signed his work, yet it was widely appreciated and is occasionally reproduced even today in articles devoted to the cheap literature of the 'forties. Mr. Calvert, in fact, spent his time making blocks for those queerly stiff and unnatural cuts which you will find in the Penny Dreadfuls and less reputable newspapers of the period. Many of the romances came out in penny weekly numbers—sometimes they

"THERE MUST BE MORE BLOOD"
One of Sala's illustrations for *The Heads of the Headless*

"ran" for more than a year—and each number was required to contain at least one illustration. The most successful publisher of these things at the time was the Edward Lloyd who founded the newspaper bearing his name, and it was for him that Mr. Calvert worked, he himself doing the actual cutting on wood—chopping would be the better word—and employing draughtsmen to draw the design on the block. He was glad to find somebody like Sala who had a considerable knowledge, gained from his theatrical experiences, of costume, and for the best part of a year he employed him on several of Mr. Lloyd's publications.

A number of these gory romances were issued from the office of the *Penny Sunday Times,* and on this not noticeably sabbatarian journal, one of Lloyd's earlier ventures, Sala was also occasionally employed, if the previous week had witnessed a more luscious murder than usual. It was the "gothic" tales, however, which engaged most of his attention— Lloyd seems to have issued between thirty and forty of them during 1847 —and although it is almost impossible to identify his work it is known that he was responsible for the cuts in *The Heads of the Headless* by "Faucit Saville Esquire"—the Saville Faucit whose daughter was Helen Faucit (Lady Martin) the well-known actress—and for those in another "horror" with the appropriate title of *Murder Castle.*

The young man seems to have given general satisfaction, although on one occasion Mr. Lloyd, who knew his public, complained that one or two recent drawings had lacked the necessary vigour. "The eyes must be larger," he wrote, "and there must be more blood—much more blood:" instructions, no doubt, which presented no particular difficulty.

5

Soon enough, of course, all such "marrow-freezing" cuts were forgotten, alike by their designer and by the public; but there was another commission executed by Sala at this time the effects of which he was to feel for more than thirty years.

I have mentioned the "private" attack on *Punch.* It was probably the most successful attack of the kind ever engineered. Immense pains were taken with its preparation, and it called forth no reply from its victim. None, indeed, was possible which would have turned the scales. The blow was dealt, and accepted in silence. All London laughed, and henceforth *Punch* ceased to worry the man who from its commencement had been one of its principal butts.

Now I dare say that in many ways this Alfred Bunn, for so many years the manager of Drury Lane and Covent Garden Theatres, "asked for" what he got. His position in the theatrical world was admittedly no easy one, but he was a florid, bumptious, quarrelsome person with too good an opinion of himself and a regrettable habit of airing that opinion in long-winded sentences. Nevertheless, for all his mountebank antics, he was an excellent showman who worked remarkably hard and could on occasion compose a passable lyric, and he came in for rather more than his fair share of contemptuous attack on the part of *Punch*. Its contributors, in particular Jerrold and Gilbert à Beckett, would seldom leave him alone. In their eyes he could do nothing right: a humbug of the most pestilential kind and therefore fair game for Jerrold's most waspish wit and Leech's cruellest pencil. So, for instance, when some Opera with libretti by him was produced, he would be dubbed, ironically, the Poet Bunn or the bardikin, and his translations described as "undone into English." Neither his theatrical quarrels—the most notorious of them was with Jenny Lind—nor his financial misfortunes were allowed to pass without malicious reference to Signor Bombastes Bunnerini, the Hot Cross Bunn, or His Dramatic Majesty Alfred, with a mock Speech from the Throne. For six years, indeed, there had been a "persistent cannonade," to use the words of *Punch*'s own historian, and Bunn had done nothing.

Then in the number for October 2nd, 1847, there appeared an article called "Bunn's Prose" which roused him to fury. He had lately taken over the management of the Surrey Theatre (which was not precisely the "promotion" that *Punch*, of course, had called it), and an advertisement of his intentions had given his tormentors a good opportunity for further baiting. As an advertisement, no doubt, it did all that was required of it, and if some of its writing was careless, Bunn was not the only offender in that respect, even supposing that he had written every word of it himself. In *Punch*'s hands, however, it was transformed into "an important state document." Bunn's prose, it was now declared, was "if anything, better than his poetry," equal to anything which Moses & Sons (a well-known tailoring-firm of the day which couched its advertisements in doggerel verse) had written, and so on, and so on. It was no more virulent than any previous attacks, but for some reason it brought matters to a head.

Exactly how he went to work, or who was responsible for the form which his philippic ultimately assumed, he does not tell us. After seeing his solicitor, who was not a little useful in disinterring some items of information about his intended victims which they must have hoped had long been forgotten, he seems to have gone to Albert Smith, as the editor of *Punch*'s chief rival. Albert Smith almost certainly made valuable suggestions—he may even have supervised Bunn's manuscript—introduced him to Landells, who had no reason to love a publication which he had helped to found only to be thrown overboard, and mentioned Sala as a possible illustrator. At any rate, Bunn, Landells, and Sala were

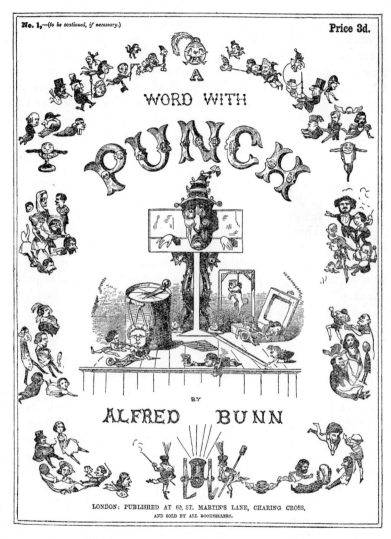

soon at work together, judiciously mysterious advertisements were inserted in the newspapers, and in the second week in November there appeared *A Word with Punch*. By Alfred Bunn. No. 1. (to be continued, if necessary). Price 3d.

At a casual glance you might well have supposed that here was an extra number of *Punch* itself. The design on the front page, the printing and general arrangement of the pages, even the advertisements : all were a colourable imitation of those to be found in *Punch*. The resemblance, however, was only superficial. Sala's design for the first page, one of the cleverest he ever drew, followed in its general lines Richard Doyle's first cover for *Punch*; but on examination it could be seen that both Mr. Punch and his principal contributors were being shown in anything but a favourable light. A lugubrious hunchback stood in the pillory, Toby was hanging from his master's gallows, à Beckett lay face-down on the floor, Jerrold as a wasp stared mournfully at a dropped baton, and Mark Lemon, dressed as a potboy, was trying vainly to reach a pewter-pot. Even Thackeray seemed unable to support himself and was obliged to lean against a broken drum. Bunn's text, moreover, was just as cruelly amusing. With Thackeray and Leech he had no quarrel, and there was no mention of them, but Jerrold (dubbed Wronghead, though like the others he was mentioned by name), à Beckett (Sleekhead), and Mark Lemon (Thickhead) received no quarter, and Sala's caricatures of them did not lack the necessary touch of vitriol.

Who, asked Bunn, were these three "puppets" who dared to deliver malicious attacks on people merely on the ground that they were "public characters"? Not, perhaps, the distinguished literary figures they considered themselves to be. Jealous, no doubt, of other dramatists whose work, unlike theirs, had been successfully produced at Drury Lane. But "public characters" for all that—had not Lemon graduated in a tavern? —and so, according to *Punch's* own ruling, fit to be pelted with abuse. And how easy, continued Bunn in mock-respectful fashion, to pull these "puppets" to pieces! Jerrold, for instance (shown by Sala as a snake), who had been hissed off the stage, could write verses which meant nothing at all—examples were given—and had even attempted to act himself: the most awful exhibition ever seen. Then Mr. Gilbert à Beckett : the *gentleman* who was so fond of making fun of other people's literary work and other people's financial misfortunes : was he quite the right person to throw mud? A former proprietor of such edifying publications as the *Penny Trumpet*, the *Thief*, the *Terrific Penny Magazine*, the *Lover*, and the *Gallery of Terrors!* And had he been so financially successful himself? There followed some damning details of his appearance in the Insolvent Debtors' Court in 1834, though the actual figures (which Bunn knew) were not given. And as for Mark Lemon, the literary potboy, what was one to say of some of the stuff which poured from his beery pen?

"I mingle with thee, lovely river,
   Drinking thy soul!
Thou art my own, Oh, Rhine! for ever,
   My beautiful!

"There's harmony for you, Punch —SOUL and FUL—isn't it lovely ?"

So it went on, ever more savage, ending up with some mock advertisements no less trenchantly inimical, and a hint that should No. 1 prove
insufficient to put the puppets in their places, kind correspondents had
provided Mr. Bunn with enough material for further issues.

A Word with Punch caught the town's taste. Bunn is supposed to
have made £100 from its sales. The *Punch* people bought up as many
copies as they could, but they were able to do little to stop its circulation.
Wisely they suffered in silence and left the Poet Bunn alone.

In after years Sala often regretted the part he had played in its production, and this was not because he was to remain on *Punch's* Index
Expurgatorius until his friend Burnand became editor in 1880, but because
he realised that he had had no real quarrel with the "puppets" themselves,
only one of whom he knew personally at the time.

6

And then, more or less accidentally, there came a change of occupation.

At the beginning of 1848 the work for Calvert and Edward Lloyd
was beginning to pall. A few commissions from other less bloodily-
minded publishers came his way, and this was the time when he taught
himself to etch upon copper; but even with his contributions to the
Man in the Moon he was not receiving any regular salary, and until that
had been obtained he was in no position to congratulate himself.

He had much in his favour. His mother was in retirement at Brighton,
and very definitely he was his own master : a fact of importance to a
young man of his particular temperament. All the old nervous troubles
were gone. His brother Charles was a popular figure in literary as well
as theatrical circles and was now introducing him to clubs and coteries
where he speedily made good friends on his own account. Already, in
fact, he was showing himself to be a clubbable youth equally ready to
join in earnest discussion or light-hearted spree. And people liked him
and were very willing to do him a kindness if they could. Unfortunately
there were too many sprees and not all of them of too reputable a kind.
Young though he was, that love of strong drink from which he was
never able wholly to free himself was beginning to be noticed. He had
little enough money to spend on himself, but these new friends of his,

careless, good-hearted fellows who would stay up drinking half the night did an opportunity present itself, saw to it that young Sala was not left out in the cold. Undoubtedly he was running rather wild, and even at this time, and badly as money was needed, not all the commissions that were offered him received too punctual an attention. He was ardent and full-blooded, delighted to have arrived at manhood, but he was also undisciplined and erratic : interested in too many things. Here he was, barely twenty, yet accepted in the gay world of artists, pressmen, and the fascinating creatures of the chorus, and—why worry? Now, however, a new self-assertiveness was making its appearance. This, ordinarily, did him no harm, but if he had imbibed a little too much brandy-and-water that sharp temper, inherited from his mother, would blaze up, and sometimes there would be trouble. A prickly fellow, they found him at such times, very ready to take offence, even ready for physical violence. "I was a pugnacious youth," he admits, "with a great capacity for quarrelling and getting my head punched." And, oddly enough, it was a fight during which his head was punched remarkably hard that was responsible for the next step in his career.

That year there were riots and revolutions in more than one European capital. In February there had come the abdication and flight of Louis-Philippe. There had been risings in Berlin, Munich, and Prague, and serious trouble in Russia, Denmark, and Spain. Ireland was in a state of something like open rebellion, and at home the Chartists had called their National Convention. (Sala was amongst those who were enrolled as Special Constables at the time and joyfully prepared for a fight.) On April 10th the Great Demonstration had taken place on Kennington Common and led to nothing very much, but two months later precautions against further disturbances were still being taken in London. On June 11th the *Times* felt justified in announcing that all real danger was over, but there was still considerable tension about, and only the next day one of the most disgraceful riots in the history of the theatre was witnessed at Drury Lane.

Amongst other results of the latest French Revolution had been the expulsion of an appreciable number of English people who had been earning a living in France. At the same time many French refugees had crossed the Channel and were endeavouring to find work in this country. There were the usual outbursts in the less responsible newspapers, and even the Government were obliged to take measures to restrict alien immigration. And it was at a moment when anti-French feeling in London (already rendered nervous enough by Chartist activities) was at its height that M. Jullien, Bunn's successor at Drury Lane, announced the forthcoming appearance of a French company from Dumas's theatre in Paris in his drama of *Monte Cristo*.

It was not in the circumstances a wise move. No sooner had Jullien's announcement been made public than rumours arose that steps would be taken to prevent the French players from obtaining a hearing. In the Clubs several distinguished gentlemen did not hesitate to say that they themselves were prepared to take an active part in any anti-French demonstration. Whereupon other distinguished gentlemen, Albert Smith amongst them, declared their intention of being present at the performance in support of the players.

The theatre authorities were in a dilemma, but decided that contracts must be kept and contented themselves with distributing small handbills, appealing for fair play, throughout the house. These proved to be entirely useless. "The house," wrote the dramatic critic of the *Illustrated London News*, "was very full soon after the doors opened, but there was that preponderance of coats and hats, and restless movement of the audience, which usually foretells a theatrical row. 'God Save the Queen,' played by the band, and lustily encored by the audience, was received with loud cheering; but immediately this was finished, before the first bars of the overture had been played, the hooting, whistling and shrieking began, and lasted without interruption for three hours, the whole of the drama— for it was played through to the end—passing in dumb show. M. Jullien appeared in the course of the second act; but after vainly attempting to gain a hearing for ten or fifteen minutes, was compelled to retire, after informing the malcontents, as well as he was able by pantomime, that their money should be returned. After that several persons started up to address the house, but could not get a chance of being heard." He might have added that several other persons, Sala amongst them, in the pit, began to throw potatoes and cabbage-stalks not only at the unfortunate performers but also at their supporters who were massed in the dress-circle. The refuse from Covent Garden Market, however, was soon exhausted, and as the din grew and tempers became frayed, a series of sanguinary encounters took place, in which, according to the police reports, certain Frenchwomen were involved. Peaceable citizens who had merely come to see the drama had angrily departed, but during the third act, when fists were being freely used and some of the seats were in danger of being broken up, the police arrived and there was additional confusion.

Although some of his friends, Sam Cowell, a well-known comedian from the Princess's among them, were not so lucky, Sala himself escaped arrest. Hoarse with shouting and the sorriest sight, for his clothes were in rags, one eye was closed, and his lips had swollen to double their normal size, he was smuggled away, no doubt very pleased with himself and willing enough to attend again if, as actually happened, M. Jullien made a second attempt to repeat the performance.

But he was not present when *Monte Cristo* was given again at Drury Lane two nights later. How much nursing his various wounds needed I do not know, but he seems to have stayed in his Soho room, pondering over the battle, reading the newspaper accounts, and finally deciding that his own pen must be utilised to record its full bloodthirstiness and grandeur.

There and then he composed a set of mock-heroic verses entitled "The Battle of Monte Cristo." For obvious reasons there would be little use in offering his work to the *Man in the Moon* : at the moment, he knew, Albert Smith was furious with him. But there was a halfpenny weekly called *Chat* which had been running for the last twelve months, and *Chat* had had something amusing to say about *A Word with Punch*. So boldly he walked round to the offices of this journal, saw the editor, and sold him the verses for a sovereign.

What followed sounds entirely fantastic, but it is true. Straightway he became a regular contributor to *Chat*, and that might have happened to anybody. But in less than two months' time George Sala had done much more than that : he had succeeded to the editorship itself!

CHAPTER FIVE

PENCIL AND PEN: WITH A BALLOON INTERVENING

I

"CHAT—Facts, Fun, Fiction, and On-Dit, for Rail, Boat, Bus, and Cab. Out every Wednesday, at Twelve o'Clock. Full of Original and Surpassing Wit. . . . Price, One Halfpenny—worth One Shilling."

So runs an early advertisement of the journal in whose pages was printed "The Battle of Monte Cristo." Its first number had appeared in May, 1847, and created no great stir. The wit displayed, indeed, had been neither surpassing nor noticeably original. Yet it was not merely another would-be rival to *Punch*: it did endeavour to blaze a trail of its own, and found a ready sale in London amongst those who liked to think themselves "in the know" with regard to matters of social, literary, and theatrical interest. It must have been about the first of the weeklies to make a particular feature of the intimate personal paragraph which

Chat Office

304 Strand.

Edmund Yates and others were to popularise in the near future. Occasionally, too, it would be first in the field with some item of real news, for outside contributors, like Edward Leman Blanchard, the writer of pantomimes and dramatic critic, would send in short paragraphs (and not always be paid for their trouble). Its writing-paper was beautifully engraved, and its address—No. 304 Strand—was impressive: for all that, its staff of four or five were obliged to squeeze themselves into a single room which did duty as editorial sanctum, counting-house, and publishing offices.

Had its proprietor possessed a little more capital at the time, he might have made a success of his venture. Unfortunately capital was the one thing which for some years now had consistently and, in his own view, most unfairly refused to come his way. A curious figure, this Frederick Marriott who was to give George Sala his first chance as a journalist: a would-be financial magnate with a persuasive tongue and an astonishing belief in himself; a man, too, of ideas, some of them undeniably sound; but an ill-balanced optimist always eager to rush wildly ahead, and one who would rarely listen to advice which he did not wish to hear. Not exactly a humbug—in the end he was to build up a solid reputation for himself in California where he founded the successful *San Francisco News-Letter*—but at this time an unstable, careless, and, incidentally, quarrelsome person whom few people wholly trusted.

His father had owned the *Taunton Courier*, and he himself for a while had conducted a staid paper-making business. Then he had married a woman with money and almost at once embarked on various newspaper speculations. One after another had failed, and it was no surprise to his friends when Mrs. Marriott refused to make further advances of money. Undaunted, her husband looked elsewhere for the necessary backers, and on two or three occasions managed to find them, though without adding much thereby to journalistic history. Then he had become associated with Herbert Ingram at the time when the *Illustrated London News* was being planned, only to quarrel with and part from him before the first number had been printed. Subsequently he had been connected with the *Morning Chronicle*, and caused its proprietor—a new-comer to journalism—to lose thousands of pounds in one of his grandiose schemes for its improvement. On his own once again he looked about for another idea and another backer. What kind of journal, he asked himself, was most likely to prove a popular weekly? Not a rival to *Punch* or Ingram's *Illustrated London News*, but something which would be assured of an even wider public than theirs? Mr. Marriott did not long remain in doubt. What type of news was it which invariably roused up the greatest excitement? Nothing could beat a really "good" murder. Then why not a journal entirely devoted to serious crime?

So there had been born the *Death Warrant*, with a skull and cross-bones for its heading and a deep mourning border to its pages. Luscious details of the previous week's horrors, old murder trials furbished up as gorily as might be, and a fine array of historical instruments of torture: of such delights were its pages composed. Unaccountably the *Death Warrant* failed to please. Marriott removed the cross-bones and borders, added a few lighter touches, and transformed his weekly into the *Guide to Life*. But nobody sought his guidance, and for a year or two he seems to have lived, unspeculatively, on pocket-money doled out by his wife. Then the railway mania came, and while Sala had been drawing his maps and plans Marriott was launching the *Railway Bell*. It rang for a few times before dying from very natural causes. There had been one or two minor projects after that, but backers were becoming wary these days, and when *Chat* was born its proprietor, financially speaking, was in very low water indeed.

It was one of his sounder projects, but luck was against him. For some time, too, luck had been against his editor, Thomas Littleton Holt, another remarkable figure in the journalistic world of the day. Holt, unlike Marriott, came of an old landed family—many believed him to be a baronet who had never assumed his title—and he was an accomplished Greek scholar. Like Marriott he was for ever projecting some new publication—according to Sala he was "the direct means of putting more money into the pockets of the compositors of London than any other journalist of the period"—but few of them enjoyed a long life. Like Marriott, too, he had had his railway newspaper during the '45 boom, but whereas the *Railway Bell* had hardly rung at all, the *Iron Times* with its advertisements of all the scores of projected new lines had done well and at one moment had been an exceedingly valuable property. Then the bubble burst, and from that time Holt had flitted from this paper to that, working sometimes for himself and sometimes for others. He was not a great journalist, but he had a neat sense of humour and was to write at least one work of fiction, possessed a host of friends, and, unlike his present proprietor, was superlatively honest.

It was these two gentlemen who received Sala when he called at No. 304, Strand, with his poem. Marriott, he records, "was sitting behind the counter by the side of the editor . . . while the publisher . . . discreetly occupied a stool at a high desk in the background. Mr. Marriott very civilly read my poem, giving at the same time, from the till, change for a shilling to a small boy who had come to buy four copies of *Chat*. Then he handed the verses to the editor, Mr. Holt, a middle-aged gentleman, with very bushy whiskers, and—a rarity in those days—moustaches. Mr. Holt wagged his head approvingly; and Mr. Marriott informed me that he should be very glad to publish my poem; and he handed me a sovereign, saying that there was no need for me to have a proof of it, as the editor could touch it up and make it, if it was thought advisable, a 'little spicier.'"

So the poem appeared in *Chat*—I do not know whether it was made "spicier" or not—and, as I have said, it was only the first of a series of regular contributions. And then this young man who was not yet twenty-one received the surprise of his life. Mr. Holt, it seemed, was proposing to launch yet another journal on his own account and would shortly be leaving *Chat*. If Sala cared to take his place the editorship could be his.

"I knew as much about editing as I did about driving a locomotive

engine," he admits; but of course the offer was accepted. The salary
was small—about twenty-five shillings a week, and this modest sum
was intended to include payment for all contributions from his pen—
but what did that matter? He was a London editor and so a privileged
person. Obviously *Chat* was not exactly in a flourishing condition,
and equally obviously Mr. Marriott had little enough money to spend
on it, but again what did that matter? It behoved the new editor to
make the most of an opportunity which he could never have expected
to come his way. And at once he applied all his energies to the task
before him. If there was no available cash for outside contributors,
well, he would do without them, and for the next few months he wrote
almost the entire paper himself.

Luckily at least one series of his called "The Australian Nights
Entertainment" caught the public taste and took the sales well past
the danger point. As their title implied they were stories and sketches
of convict-life and bushranging activities: no fanciful inventions, but
compiled after much study in the British Museum Reading Room, where
he now became an almost daily visitor. Another series of little essays
was almost as successful. In his editorial capacity he had the run of the
London theatres, and with youthful audacity he proceeded to compose
"A Hundred Faults of a Hundred Different Actors." One or two
managers closed their doors to so impudent a critic, but the others were
prepared to laugh with him.

It was a busy time. There were his editorial duties; there were
his studies at the British Museum, conducted in real earnest at this period,
for he was beginning to realise how serious were the gaps in his education;
and, three or four evenings each week, he was required to be at the
theatre. There were also the drawings to be made for the *Man in the Moon*,
and now and then a commission was forthcoming to illustrate a volume
of stories or a new satirical pamphlet. (One such pamphlet may be
briefly mentioned, for it still rouses curiosity amongst bibliographers.
It was entitled *The Battle of London Life; or, Boz and his Secretary*, by
"Morna," the pseudonym of a brokendown "swell" by name Thomas
O'Keefe whom Sala had met at the theatre in his scene-painting days.
The little book is entirely without literary merit, but has an interest for
its ludicrous travesty of Dickens and, more especially, for Sala's etching
of Boz in his study.) He was still wretchedly poor, but he managed to
buy a few good books for himself and moved to a more comfortable
attic in Carlisle Street, Soho.

By the beginning of 1849, however, he must have become aware
that a crisis was near. For some weeks there had been difficulties in

finding enough cash even to pay the editor of *Chat* and his tiny staff. Then, without warning, Marriott disappeared. Sala arrived at the office one morning to find a group of angry creditors demanding instant satisfaction from a frightened office-boy. The till was empty, Marriott could not be found, and what was to be done? There followed a scene which might well have been taken from a contemporary farce. "A meeting was promptly held," wrote Henry Vizetelly, who had known Marriott well and was soon to be Sala's chief employer, "for the division of the spoil, when one creditor satisfied his claims by appropriating the shaky office table, a second contented himself with the counter, and a third had to put up with two or three rickety chairs. The office partition, the shelving, and the gas fittings were in turn speedily laid claim to, and nothing whatever seemed left for one timid individual who had certainly been most backward in pressing his claims. Suddenly a thought seized him and stooping down he scraped the dirty flooring with his pocket-knife. 'Lead, by jingo!' shouted he. 'I collar this;' and he was delighted to discover, when the broker was called in to value the lot and clear the place, that this find of his, when taken up, proved to be worth nearly as much as all the rest of the office sticks together."

That was not quite the end of *Chat*. One of its staff who had been responsible for obtaining its advertisements (at sixpence a line) was a cheerful young man named Richard Pond. He had a wide acquaintance alike in Bohemian circles and amongst well-to-do London tradesmen. He proposed that Sala, Benjamin Clayton, an engraver who was also on the staff, and himself should see Marriott's solicitor with a view to carrying on the weekly by themselves. Somehow the few guineas demanded for the copyright and good-will were forthcoming, and the three proprietors found a new office in Brydges Street. Sala's own position was not thereby improved. In place of a salary he was to be given a share of the profits, but the profits failed to materialise, and so, he records, "we were constrained to appropriate the gross proceeds. Unfortunately my co-proprietors were as poverty-stricken as I was; and on more than one occasion we were under the unpleasant necessity of fighting for the small change in the till." And it was then that in desperation he turned, for the first and last time in his life, to commercial speculation.

Some American had a new pill to put on the market. Sala accepted the British agency, and forthwith made the most valiant efforts to foist on an unappreciative public the merits of the Shaking Quaker's Herbal Pill.

Unfortunately the cartoon which he designed for his boxes was hardly of a kind to attract any potential pill-taker. Rightly, no doubt, it showed a number of Shakers dancing in their Meeting House; but the Shakers themselves, instead of being shown in the rosiest health, were grotesquely emaciated creatures who obviously had derived no benefit from any pill whatsoever.

Nobody wanted his pills, and few people, it seemed, now wanted *Chat*. Disgusted with "the entire concern," Sala sold his share in the weekly to his two partners for ten pounds, and left the pills to look after themselves. They had told him that he could not write, and now for the second time it seemed that journalism was not for him. So he withdrew from Brydges Street, and, he adds, "I did not write a line for the press for three whole years."

2

Here, however, his memory was at fault.

He had lost his editorship, and nobody would pay very much for his drawings. Nobody had a bench for him in his office, and nobody wanted an assistant in a theatrical painting-room. Now, indeed, when the ten pounds had been spent and a supperless evening was no rarity, he came to know what it was to be really poor. Afterwards he could never forget those days in 1849, made additionally miserable by the death of his much-loved sister, when it seemed as if he were ever to remain the most wretched of failures. Pathetically he recalls his anguish as he would walk past the clubs in Pall Mall, see well-fed members sipping their wine, and contrast their pleasant lot with his own. "I know that I have often turned half-sick when I went into a tavern for half-a-pint of porter, to see a swaggering customer throw down a sovereign and rattle in his hand the shining change which the barmaid handed him." Even the solace of tobacco would be denied him, and "often," he records, "I have taken a wretched pleasure in walking the streets behind a gentleman who was smoking a good cigar."

Yet little commissions continued to come his way, and not all of them were artistic. Littleton Holt had launched his new illustrated weekly and invited Sala's co-operation. What the journal was called I cannot be certain—it did not enjoy a long life—but it seems to have specialised, like the *Death Warrant*, in violent crime, and Sala was given the job of making sketches of the criminals, either at their trial or, more horribly, at their last moment on earth. When, moreover, some provincial town was flashed into the news by reason of a more than usually gruesome murder, he would be required to furnish an account of the Court proceedings as well as the customary sketches. And, as it happened, he was present that year, in a professional capacity, at the trial and execution of three of the most notorious criminals of the century: James Blomfield Rush, the Norfolk Monster, and the even more ghoulish Mannings.

Rush's case reads like one of the Penny Dreadfuls for which Sala had so recently been providing the illustrations. It was an essentially bloody business which had not been forgotten ninety years later, when the criminal's figure was still to be seen prominently exhibited in Madame Tussaud's Chamber of Horrors. Rush was hanged for two murders, but he was widely believed to have been guilty of killing two members of his own family as well. There was nothing whatever in his favour—he was a violent bully in whose presence no man or woman was safe—but there was a picturesque side to, as well as a touch of mystery about, his final crime, and at the time it roused up all England to a fury.

The story, which Sala himself was fond of telling and once thought of making the basis of a novel—again and again he was to mention it in his *Daily Telegraph* leaders—begins in 1838, when the then Recorder of Norwich, Mr. Isaac Preston, afterwards Jermy, succeeded to the family property at Stanfield Hall, an old moated mansion near Wymondham in Norfolk. Almost at once more than one claimant appeared to dispute his rights, and a rabble took forcible possession of the Hall. They were expelled by troops, and more than eighty of the rioters were sent to prison as a result. For ten years the Recorder was permitted to enjoy his inheritance in comparative peace. Then, one evening towards the end of November, 1848, there came the ghastliest tragedy. In the porch of his house Mr. Jermy encountered a man wrapped in a cloak and wearing a mask. The intruder raised a blunderbuss and shot him dead. He then rushed into the house by the servants' entrance, forced the butler into his pantry, and, making his way into the hall, killed the dead man's son, shot at his son's wife as she lay weeping beside her husband's body—she was badly injured—and seriously wounded one of the maids who, less fearful than the others, had rushed to her mistress's assistance. The rest of the servants in a state of panic hid themselves in attics or cupboards, but a groom managed to evade the murderer's notice, swam across the moat, and gave the alarm at Wymondham. When the police arrived from Norwich the murderer had gone, but suspicion pointed to one of the tenants of the estate—a farmer and auctioneer named Blomfield Rush, who had not only been amongst the rioters of ten years before but was known to be a violent fellow with whom the Recorder had had frequent trouble—and he was immediately arrested.

It would be difficult to exaggerate the excitement and indignation that followed, more particularly when the full melodramatic story with its details of a rich property in dispute, an ambitious farmer's real or fancied wrongs, a deserted mistress, and the like, became known. For the next few weeks Norwich was the centre of England. Sala was but one of a score of London newspaper men who hurried to the city. He arrived in time to hear Rush's message from the Castle gaol with regard to food on the day of his first appearance before the Justices. "Pig today, and plenty of plum sauce," ran this missive, and forty-four years later Sala was to recall it for Madame Tussaud's catalogue.

There was little doubt in anybody's mind about Rush's guilt, though the failure of the police to find any weapon was a point in his favour. He defended himself at his trial—it lasted six days and disorganised the entire city—but the evidence against him was overwhelming, and his bullying treatment of the chief witness, one of his many mistresses, deprived him of the least spark of sympathy. Sala was not present at the actual trial, but he saw the mask—"an arrangement of a fringe of black glossy hair, a beard, and moustaches combined"—and he returned to Norwich at the end of March for the hanging, when he made sketches of the murderer, hangman, and chaplain, and saw the huge black banner unfurled by the Sheriff "to mark the extraordinary guilt of the criminal."

He tells us specifically that on this occasion he sent "an account of the dismal tragedy" to his newspaper as well as the sketches, and in all probability he was engaged in the same dual capacity later that year at the trial and execution of the Mannings.

About the crime of this truly wretched pair it is unnecessary to say very much: the whole sordid story has been told so often before. It is, perhaps, chiefly memorable for the two letters from Dickens, printed in the *Times*, which described in unforgettable language the appalling scenes at the execution of the criminals in front of Horsemonger-lane Gaol: letters which undoubtedly played their part in the growing agitation to put an end for all time to public hangings, though twenty years were to pass before the last of such revolting spectacles was witnessed. The facts were simple. A husband and wife brutally murdered a man in their Bermondsey kitchen and threw his body into a hole there already dug. The victim was missed, a search was made, and the body was found. Where were the murderers? There were all the elements needed for a first-class sensation. In point of fact no long time elapsed before the wife, an alien, had been arrested in Edinburgh and the husband in Jersey, and on October 25th their trial opened at the Old Bailey. By this time Holt's journal was defunct, but Sala found occasional work on the *Weekly News*, and as the accredited representative of that newspaper he managed to find a place for himself in the overcrowded court. Forty-six years later the memory of the closing scenes at that trial and at its dreadful aftermath had not been dimmed, and his account of the pair as they stood on the platform—the man in a black frock coat, the woman in a gown of black satin with white lace : it was said, but I know not with what truth, that as the result of her choice of dress the sale of black satin ceased for some years—was almost as poignant and vivid as Dickens's own.

Truly macabre commissions! But he was hardly in a position to refuse any work which came his way. Indeed, at this time it was only an inconvenient police-court charge which prevented his leaving his drawings altogether for a while and turning biographer; and I dare say that he would have made a fair amount of money by the change, for the subject of the proposed biography was none other than the notorious dancer who called herself Lola Montez.

An astonishing woman! Her career reads like a fairy-tale. Her real name was Marie Eliza Gilbert. She was born in Limerick in 1818. Her father, a military officer, died in India seven years later. Her mother married again, and came to live in Bath. They wanted the girl to marry Sir Abraham Lumley who was rich, but ugly and old. Marie ran away with a man named James, and married him in Ireland. The domesticities did not suit her particular temperament, and in due course Captain James obtained an order for divorce. This was in 1842. The stage suggested itself to her as a profitable career, and for a while she studied under the well-known Miss Kelly, but it was as a dancer that she made her début in London in the following year, and was not too pleased when some members of the audience recognised in "Lola Montez, the Spanish dancer" their old acquaintance Betty James. She had better success on the Continent, and on coming to Munich in 1847 completely enslaved the old King Ludwig. He created her Comtesse de Landsfeld, and within a few months she was virtually the ruler of Bavaria. More, she seems to have ruled it with considerable ability. Public opinion, however, at last turned against her for more than one reason, and on the King's abdication she fled. In the early months of 1849 she was in London, and in the most casual way met Sala in a cigar-divan. He is discreet about their relations, but one wonders a little.

Now, so far her career had been picturesque enough, but it did not altogether satisfy the dancer. She liked to think of herself as a semi-royal personage related not only to famous matadors but to half the grandees of Spain as well—it was true that her mother had Spanish blood in her veins—and she had built up a magnificent legend about herself which she had told so often that she had come to believe in its authenticity. It was a story, she thought, which ought to be given to the world, and—would Sala write it for her?

It occurs to one to ask why she should have invited this unknown youngster to undertake the task, but Sala seems to have shown no hesitation. Unfortunately for his purse it was just at this time that another youngster named Heald, a handsome cornet in the Life Guards with £7000 a year of his own, appeared on the scene. Injudiciously he and the dancer married. A lady who had been the boy's guardian caused enquiries to be made, and it was discovered that the sentence of the Consistorial Court in 1842 had prohibited Captain or Mrs. James from re-marrying during the lifetime of the other. The Captain was alive, and there was a police-court summons. After one or two appearances in court the dancer, who was on bail, deemed it wise to disappear. She fled to Spain with her Guardsman, and Sala's *Life of Lola Montez* remained unwritten.

3

There followed what for him was a pleasantly exciting time, during which he published his first book of sketches, made elaborate preparations for a flight across Europe in a balloon, and came in for a small fortune.

In that November he came of age, and under the will of his Aunt Sophia became entitled to a tiny legacy. It was no more than £20, but it was something like riches to Sala who at once decided that a holiday was long overdue.

For the last ten years he had been wanting to revisit Paris: here was his opportunity. But who was to be his companion? Brother Charles was the obvious person, but Charles as usual was playing one of his small parts at the Princess's, now under Charles Kean's management. Shirley Brooks? No, he was too busy putting the finishing touches to a drama. Richard Pond? No, there was the question of expense. But Pond had recently introduced him to a curious person, Dr. Gustav Strauss, a Canadian-born cosmopolitan who liked to describe himself as a Prussian, and Strauss, a considerably older man who was at home (though not invariably welcome) in almost every European capital, was delighted with the idea of playing guide. He was one of those adventurously-minded people who never make a success of their lives because they must always be having half-a-dozen irons in the fire. He had brains and a sense of fun. Men enjoyed being in his company. With the old boy, they said—he was not yet fifty, but generally consorted with younger folk—with the old boy in one of his over-sanguine moods, you never knew *what* might not happen. And, indeed, his career had been unusual enough. He had taken one doctorate (philosophy) in Berlin and another (medicine) at Montpellier. He had been a French army surgeon. He had mixed himself up in revolutionary politics, and at different times had been banished from both Germany and France. In England he had made a living as a teacher of languages, a translator, a medical man, a private tutor, a lecturer, and once, I fancy, as a cook. Of late years, however, he had devoted himself to journalism of a more or less technical nature, and at this time he was conducting the *Chemical Times*. He generally had some magnificent scheme whereby a fortune was to be made, but so far none had led to anything much. Sala and he suited one another, and gaily they set out together.

The holiday in Paris was not a success. It began as it ended—only a few days later—badly. As they walked into their hotel a coffin was being carried out. Sala found the city shabby, the "sights" disappointing, except the Morgue, where he made the ghastliest sketch of a "handsome" corpse, and his £20 curiously insufficient. Strauss seems to have felt the necessity for evolving another of his magnificent schemes and suggested a mild gamble. Somebody, he had discovered, was promoting a lottery with a large nugget of gold as the prize. Sala took a ticket with what was left of his aunt's legacy, and of course drew a blank. There was nothing to do but to return home.

So they returned home, penniless, but not without ideas for the future. Of Strauss's grandiose scheme I shall speak in a minute. Sala's was less ambitious. He had been amused at the antics of people travelling on the railway, both at home and abroad: why not a series of sketches to illustrate them—a comic guide-book of traveller's "Don'ts"?

He took his proposition to Adolphus Ackermann, one of the partners in the well-known firm of that name, and Ackermann was not only interested in the idea, but offered him other work. More, he arranged for him to be articled to a professional engraver and advanced the money required. And for the next four or five months, with one brief interval, Sala was working as he had never worked before: by day in the engraver's studio, and at night in his own room on the various commissions for Ackermann. Valentines of all sorts and sizes, fashion-plates, including "a series of elaborately lithographed designs, illustrating the newly-introduced 'Bloomer' costume," and etchings for the gift-books of the day: one followed the other, and he worked so hard that even his good eye showed an inclination to go on strike.

At the same time he completed the sketches for his original idea, and in due course there appeared the *Hail, Rain, Steam & Speed*, by an Old Stoker, which must be ranked as his first book.

It was not, it may be admitted, particularly funny, and its little sketches were no more than mediocre. Yet it "took off" the usual foibles of travellers neatly enough, and its advice to people paying cabmen, losing their luggage, eating at railway-stations, making friends in trains, staying in strange hotels, or returning home from foreign countries, was amusingly terse. The little jest, however, sold well— a shilling plain, half-a-crown coloured—and it paved the way for more elaborate panoramas.

Meanwhile there was Strauss's new scheme, and his proposal was nothing less than a journey to Asia in a balloon: the precursor of a regular trans-continental service by air. The science of aeronautics, he thought, was only in its infancy, but there was a glorious future before it. They must become pioneers, and fame and fortune would be theirs.

Now whether Sala was genuinely interested in the subject or merely hypnotised by the Doctor into believing that there was money to be made, I do not know. It is even a little difficult to determine in what way or exactly when their plans began to take shape. In his role as the "Old Bohemian" Strauss in 1882 published his *Reminiscences*, and they were certainly *founded* on fact, but either his memory was frequently at fault, or, anticipating Mr. Harold Nicolson, he deliberately served up a dish skilfully compounded of fiction and fact. Sala, moreover, in this case is not too clear. What did happen was that some time during that winter of 1849-50 he made a careful study of the whole question of aerial navigation and agreed to play his part in the Doctor's scheme.

It was not, perhaps, so wild a project as it might seem to be. At this time there was much talk about aeronautics, and a balloon ascent was as popular a form of entertainment with the man in the street as an aeroplane flight was to become in the years immediately preceding the first world-war. Just now, too, aeronauts were finding it profitable to invent new tricks or "stunts." They would ascend by night and let off fireworks from the skies. They would even suspend a horse or a pony from the basket of the balloon and ascend on the frightened animal's back. Curiously-shaped balloons, fitted with devices for steering, were making their appearance, and if none of these was successful, their inventors never seemed to be discouraged. Models of flying-machines would be exhibited and draw the crowds. Learned mathematicians would write newspaper articles to prove that in no circumstances whatever would man be able to raise himself up in the air without the aid of gas; but they would be at once contradicted by other distinguished gentlemen who proved that, given the right type of apparatus, there was nothing whatever to prevent man's speedy conquest of the skies. All of which stimulated the general interest. And so balloons of all sorts and sizes continued to make their appearance, people gathered to watch them, and Dr. Strauss was not the only man to dream at the time of a regular service in the air.

As it happened, one of his many friends was a man who for some years had been making a precarious living—he had a wife and eight children to support—by giving public exhibitions of the kind. Twenty years before, this George Gale had been a small-part actor in London. He had gone to New York, done well there, and returned with a troupe of Red Indians. In due course London had had enough of these braves, and Gale had been glad to accept a post in Ireland as coast blockade inspector. The stage, however, still called, and seven years later he was trying to return to it. The attempt was not successful, and in 1848 he turned to ballooning. On the strength of his blockade job he announced himself as Lieutenant Gale, R.N., and soon became a popular figure with the Cremorne crowds. Fireworks from the air, ascents on horseback, races with a rival "professor": such had been his programme, and he had shown himself to be not only a good showman but a very brave man.

It was to Gale that the Doctor went with his latest scheme. Would the Lieutenant care to consider the matter? Naturally there would have to be a grand preliminary campaign, but he had worked out most of the necessary details with his young friend Sala. It was suggested that the three of them should tour all the principal towns in the kingdom, himself as manager, Sala to prepare all the diagrams which would be needed, and Gale to deliver a series of lectures, "scientific," of course, but at the same time light and entertaining. In this way a great deal of money would be forthcoming, enough at any rate to reimburse them for their work and to finance the Great Flight to the East.

Gale, it seemed, was delighted with the idea, more particularly as his own balloon was in pawn at the time and he himself in very low water: anything in the nature of an engagement was welcome. Whereupon Sala set about preparing his diagrams of the immense new balloon which would be required for their venture, and composed a suitably entertaining lecture for the Lieutenant to deliver. Gale himself, who was not without ideas of his own about heavier-than-air machines, constructed a model with "wide, waving wings" which with the aid of two wires and some clockwork could "fly" across the largest hall. Enough money was scraped together to hire a hall and pay for the necessary advertisements, and all was ready for the grand campaign to be opened. At Gale's suggestion it was agreed that their tour should begin at Hull—he apparently thought that Hull would be peculiarly susceptible to his naval title—and the Assembly Rooms there were engaged for three nights. At the last moment the Doctor found himself unable to go—a piece of translation was urgently required, and he was in no position to refuse any commission just then—and Sala and Gale set out by themselves.

They arrived in Hull in the best of spirits. Their hotel was comfortable, the Assembly Rooms were spacious, the bills had been posted, and a confectioner arrived who agreed to pay twenty-five shillings a night for the privilege of serving refreshments after the lecture. The appointed hour came, the doors were flung open, the Lieutenant in his best clothes gallantly prepared to face his audience, and Sala in the box-office had his piles of tickets ready.

Alas, no more than a score of them were required! Nervously they waited for late arrivals, but none put in an appearance. The Lieutenant was obliged to deliver his, or, rather, Sala's disquisition to a hall which was almost empty, and was received in no friendly spirit. No interest whatever was shown in the proposed "service" across Europe, or in the new balloon, or even in the model which did flap its way over the wires, but caused only jeers. Then the confectioner angrily demanded his money back, and Sala thought it best to lock himself in until the man had retired in disgust. The whole affair, indeed, was so lamentable a failure that it was there and then decided not to repeat the performance. But that was not all, for if Strauss is to be believed, there was an unpleasant scene that evening with the landlord of their comfortable hotel, another with the proprietor of the Assembly Rooms who was demanding his rent, and the two pioneers were unable to leave Hull until the Doctor managed to obtain the necessary cash.

And that was the ignominious end of the Great Flight to the East.

Sala's interest, however, in aerial navigation survived this setback. In the spring of 1850 there was much talk of sending aeronautical expeditions in search of Sir John Franklin, and the Lieutenant was eager to gain official support for a scheme of his own. Sala helped him to bombard the Admiralty with detailed plans for the explorer's rescue, and, when these were coldly rejected and it became necessary to resume the old exhibition flights, advanced £100 towards the purchase of a new balloon.

Poor Gale! Sala's money did not help him very much. At the beginning of September he accepted an engagement to make a series of ascents on horseback in France, and a blunder on the part of some peasants near Bordeaux brought about his death. He had descended in safety, and the animal had been freed; but the aeronaut's instructions from the basket were not fully understood, and the ropes were let go when they should have been held. The balloon rose suddenly with an upturned car, and, after hanging on for a considerable distance, the unfortunate man fell.

4

The £100, as you will have guessed, was part of the small fortune which had just come Sala's way. Eliza Crellin, the tailor's wife, had died. She had been enjoying a life interest in her sister's property, and this with her own money—a matter of a few thousand pounds and the house property in Camden Town—was now divided between her four nephews. Of these the eldest, Frederick, had married and was settled in Southampton as a teacher of music. Albert at the moment was in the East India Company's service, but he was soon to go even further afield, and was never to return to England. Charles's health was not good, and already, I fancy, he was thinking of retiring from the stage. His portion, at any rate, enabled him to take a much-needed rest. And George? Well, there is no need to dispute his assertion that in the course of the next few months he made a complete fool of himself. To say truth, indeed, it was only the first of many occasions when he made a complete fool of himself. For the next thirty years he was regularly to receive large sums of money, yet there was rarely a moment when he was wholly free from financial embarrassments.

What should he do? A University career? That was what Littleton Holt suggested. He was rather old, perhaps, to put on an undergraduate's gown, but Holt, who had a high opinion of Sala's general abilities and sufficient critical powers to know that he was unlikely to make any great success as a draughtsman, believed that he might do well at the Bar. And for a while Sala seems to have played with the idea of entering his name at one of the Inns of Court. But it was not to be. Any such career would have meant a long and wearisome preparation, and with money in the bank for the first time in his life—no, he could not face the prospect. He would be a young man about town and leave the future to take care of itself.

He said good-bye to his Soho attic, to share more fashionable apartments with his brother in Mornington Crescent. He bought smart new clothes. He went to the Derby, and entertained his friends. There were parties in his rooms, and parties in Thames-side inns. Now, too, he began to think of marriage, and from his private letters and papers one may gather vaguely what happened. During the last year or two he had been paying visits to Lancaster. On one occasion he had stayed at a particular house there for a considerable time, and fallen in love with his host's daughter. Now he rushed north again with the news of his legacy. The young lady, however, remained shy, and he returned to London with no more than a locket which, as we shall see, was to be taken from him in the most curious circumstances. But they remained good friends, and four or five years later when she was asking for his help in some domestic affair, he put everything aside to hasten to her assistance.

Three or four months passed, and Sala awoke to the not very remarkable fact that his capital was rapidly disappearing, with nothing to show for it. Something would have to be done, and done quickly. "After considerable deliberation," he says, "I made up my mind to turn to substantially profitable account the few hundreds which yet remained to me. My brief career as part proprietor of a weekly periodical had certainly not been of a nature to offer any bright encouragement as to my chances of success in other journalistic adventures. But a passing breeze of literary ambition fanned my normally rather sluggish nature; and I resolved to start a monthly magazine at the patrician price of half-a-crown."

Truly a magnificent gesture! A high-class monthly journal of politics, literature, and science, which would rival the most dignified quarterlies in existence! Unfortunately as soon as Sala, in his new lordly way, had taken the lease of a house in Upper Wellington Street, Strand, installed Littleton Holt as his editor, and appointed Richard Pond as his publisher, one bad blunder followed another. There was insufficient and too-hurried preparation, and a lack of clear policy. No well-known writer was approached, and such public announcements as were made were wholly inadequate. Indeed, the Wellington Street staff seem to have sacrificed everything to speed, once a title for the journal had been chosen. Rightly, no doubt, it had been decided that one or other of the two great political Parties must be supported, but which of them was to be thus favoured? In his later years Sala was to become an ardent Liberal, and on more than one occasion his name was mentioned as a possible Gladstonian candidate for Parliament; but at this time, as he admits, he had no political views. Free Trade or Protection: he had hardly considered the question, and his choice of a political title was a mere bid for popularity. In the previous June Sir Robert Peel had been thrown from his horse on Constitution Hill. He had lingered for a few days in the greatest pain, and died on July 2nd. Never before, in all probability, had the death of a public man caused such general and genuine sorrow. The whole country was mourning his loss, and even some of those who had disagreed with his views were now minded to revise their opinions. The Conservatism for which he had stood was "in the air." What better title, then, for a new Review, than *The Conservative Magazine*, if, that is to say, it could be produced while Peel's name remained on everybody's lips?

The trouble was that Sala showed such small inclination to advocate any Conservative principles at all. True, there was an article in the first number to which even the most orthodox Tory could not have taken exception, but the rest of the contributions either avoided party politics altogether or cheerfully adopted an attitude of critical independence. Obviously the proprietor's chief interests were literary, and it is hardly surprising to learn that no official interest, much less support, was shown.

Today, it is unlikely that many copies of *The Conservative Magazine* will be found. Only one number was issued (August, 1850), and its sales were microscopic. Yet, except to the party-politician, it had not a little to recommend it. Its general appearance was good: it *looked* important. If, moreover, some of its hundred two-columned pages were rather heavy, one or two of the contributions were not only informative and graciously written but nicely provocative. Sala's own "Historic Doubts Relating to the Existence of Mr. George Hudson," supposed to be the work of one Jeremiah Brown, Leather-Seller, was not perhaps too judicious—the Railway King was unmercifully flayed—but it was certainly lively, and his "What's Come of It?", an attack on the newly-formed French Republic and a plea for Bonapartism, had its piquancy. But the usually efficient and persuasive Mr. Pond seems to have had little luck with the advertisers, and when the accounts for that first number came to be examined, it was at once seen that a second number was out of the question.

It was, no doubt, a bitter disappointment, but hardly an excuse for what followed. Sala's capital had now dwindled to such an extent that if he were to avoid an immediate return to poverty in a Soho attic some drastic measure was essential. What next, then? Another, and rather less ambitious periodical? No. Dr. Strauss, of course, had one of his magnificent schemes only waiting for the right man to adopt it. He had a young friend, a remarkable young man who after innumerable experiments had really succeeded in inventing an "infallible" system for use at the gambling-tables. With it, it was mathematically impossible to lose. And Sala agreed to risk his last hundred pounds at Aix-la-Chapelle. Did he really believe in the young man, or was this just another gesture, the gambler's last throw? I do not know, but the three fools set out to break the bank, and, as usually happens, "nearly" succeeded. Within a day or two of their arrival at Aix they had won between them nearly a thousand pounds. A few days later they were telegraphing for money sufficient to pay their fares home. It was Ackermann who sent the money: he wanted another panorama or two.

And that autumn a sadder and possibly wiser Sala settled down as best he could to his etching work. Luckily for him a good opportunity for his pencil almost at once presented itself, for it was now that the Pope divided England into Roman dioceses, and there was an immense outcry throughout the country. Within a couple of months several hundred anti-papal pamphlets, polemical, satirical, or merely comic, were issued. Sala engraved a series of sketches called *No Popery !* which had an agreeably large sale, and he followed it with another called *Grand Procession Against Papal Aggression*. This, too, sold well and brought him other commissions of a similar nature. And once again it seemed that journalism and he had parted company for all time.

CHAPTER SIX

IN THE YEAR OF THE GREAT EXHIBITION

I

MEANWHILE the entire civilised world was preparing for the Great Exhibition of the Works of All the Nations.

As long ago as June, 1849, Prince Albert—not yet created Prince Consort—had first put his proposals for a universal Exhibition before a large gathering at Buckingham Palace, and from that time he had been almost ceaselessly working at his project. He had met with and surmounted numerous obstacles, and by January, 1850, his plans were taking shape. At home the public were beginning to be interested, and abroad the nations were promising their co-operation. Naturally the most diverse opinions were being expressed—there were those who did not disguise their misgivings about the whole scheme—and amongst the points which raised up the greatest controversy was the site upon which the Exhibition buildings should be erected.

It was here that Sala saw his opportunity. As we have seen, he was now working diligently for Ackermann, and it occurred to him that a comic forecast of the Exhibition in panoramic form might well catch the public taste. Ackermann agreed, and he set to work. The Hyde Park site had definitely been chosen before any of his sketches were made, and the work was interrupted more than once, but that did not matter: the idea was a good one, and Sala was able to give full rein to his whimsical invention.

And so in due course there appeared *The Great Exhibition Wot is to Be,* one of the most successful skits of the kind to be issued at the time. Sala himself was to design at least two other panoramas of the Exhibition and he was to etch a third from designs by Alfred Forrester (Crowquill), but none sold as well as the first, which brought him in more than a hundred pounds and added considerably to his reputation as a clever caricaturist. In its finished form it was a series of folding plates which extended to more than eighteen feet and contained hundreds of sketches, each with its neatly-written letterpress. The author announced himself to be "Vates Secundus (who can see thro' a stone wall as well as his neighbours)," but inconspicuously in a corner of the cover-design was his real name, and now for the first time the soon-to-be-familiar "Aug:" appeared between the "George" and the "Sala."

In later years he was to describe the little squib as "a farrago of juvenile impertinence," and yet it was a genuinely amusing publication which deserved its success. A site in Hyde Park might already have been chosen, but Sala, still thinking aeronautically, preferred the Isle of Skye, while in place of Joseph Paxton's Glass House he boldly housed the world's exhibits in a little cluster of buildings erected in the carriage of a colossal balloon. Almost every nation was represented, impudently enough, no doubt, but in just that manner which the man in the street (who imagined that all Americans beat their slaves and that all Russians were bearlike in appearance) would best appreciate, and good-humoured satire was directed alike against Parliament, the Press, and the more fashionable foibles of the day.

The panorama, of course, had its rivals, and from the purely artistic point of view many of these were vastly superior, but *The Great Exhibition Wot is to Be* was not only a good joke in itself but gave expression to many of the wilder surmises which were current at the time.

Now, amongst the sketches in the French section of the exhibits, and in the closest juxtaposition to those of Louis Bonaparte, the elder Dumas, and Victor Hugo, was one of a chef. But he was no ordinary chef: he was the one and only Alexis Soyer, until recently in charge of the Reform Club's magnificent kitchens where he had earned his thousand pounds a year, and famous throughout England as the author of two cookery books without which no housewife's kitchen was properly furnished. He was a widower, vain and erratic, but kindly and amusing : *persona grata* with men in almost every class. A personage, in fact, and one who thoroughly enjoyed being a personage. A man who was childishly pleased to see his name in the newspapers and saw to it that it regularly appeared. A man with an air and a sweep, both theatrical and yet in their way not unimpressive. A man of no taste whatever outside his kitchens, yet one who liked to pose as an authority on innumerable matters—the arts, for instance, and the ballet—wholly unconnected with cooking. A man of ideas, some of them of real importance—he was the inventor of more than one useful contrivance—but none of these could be given to the public without a fanfare of trumpets. A bit of a showman, to say truth, who loved high-sounding words—only a title like *The Gastronomic Regenerator* would satisfy him—and dressed himself in clothes which on anybody else would have seemed merely grotesque. In a word, a grandiose eccentric whom London had taken to its heart.

At this time people were still wondering why he had resigned from the Reform Club—the mystery was never fully solved—and he was,

SOYER, THE GOOD SAMARITAN,

GOING ASHORE IN THE CRIMEA.

PUNCHINELLO, No 53.]   [PRICE ONE PENNY.

ALEXIS SOYER.

From the cartoon in *Punchinello*, March 3rd, 1855.

(a) The Right-handed Lady.   (b) The Left-handed Lady.

(c) Grotesque.

THREE SKETCHES.

as it were, free-lancing: living comfortably on the proceeds of his books and occasionally staging some immense banquet in the provinces. Sala had but recently made his acquaintance. He was with his brother Charles one afternoon in Hungerford Market (soon to give place to Charing Cross Station), when his attention, he tells us, was drawn to "a stoutish, tallish gentleman, a little past middle age, with closely cropped grey hair and a stubbly grey moustache," who, he thought, "might well have been mistaken for the riding master of a foreign circus, who had originally been in the army. He wore a kind of paletot of light camlet cloth, with voluminous lappels and deep cuffs of lavender watered silk; very baggy trousers, with a lavender stripe down the seams," a costume made odder by the fact that every article had been cut out on a "bias." He was bargaining for lobsters, and "evidently knew all about shell-fish." Who was he? Charles was amused at such ignorance. Who *could* he be but Alexis Soyer? Forthwith George was introduced to the great man and invited to supper that very evening. The two men made friends at once, and in a little while Soyer, delighted, no doubt, with his appearance in *The Great Exhibition Wot is to Be,* was seeking his young friend's co-operation in a new scheme of his, also connected with the Exhibition: the most ambitious scheme that he had yet attempted.

The question of the refreshments to be served in the Glass House in Hyde Park had already been fully discussed by the Exhibition Committee. Tenders had been invited, and Soyer amongst others had examined the position; but there were too many restrictions for his liking—it had been proposed that no stronger drink than ginger-beer should be permitted!—and he had refused to tender even after the Committee, fearful lest they were adopting too puritanical an attitude, had written to say that if he were to do so they would be glad to know what he thought of the idea of allowing *single* glasses of wine to be served.

By that time, however, he was developing a scheme of his own. If the Committee were going to make it so difficult for visitors to obtain decent food and drink inside the Exhibition, would not a fully licensed restaurant, run by himself, in its immediate neighbourhood be assured of success? A friend of his was willing to provide the necessary capital, and at the beginning of 1851 he was able to announce that he had taken a six months' lease—it cost him £100 a month—of Gore House, Lady Blessington's old home, which, although on the "wrong" side of the Exhibition, was no more than two hundred yards away.

Once his decision had been taken he set to work to make this restaurant of his as magnificent and as startling as anything to be seen in the Glass House itself. It was to be called The Gastronomic Symposium of All the Nations, and was to be not only a place where superlatively good food and wine could be obtained, but also a pleasure resort as beautiful and gay as Cremorne itself had ever been. He called in Sala to hear of all the splendid features which this wonder-house would possess, and invited his help. Naturally he was proposing to be his own architect and decorator, even his own landscape-gardener—the grounds of Gore House were to be transformed into a fairy-like paradise —but he needed somebody to assist him, somebody as artistic as himself: a flag-captain, as it were, to be on regular duty until the ship was steaming ahead, and who better qualified for the post than George Augustus? There was so much to be done which he and he alone could do. The Grand Staircase, for instance, at Gore House: George would remember the great expanse of wall-space, now horribly bare. Well, *The Great Exhibition Wot is to Be* had given him an idea. Why not a panorama, large enough to fill that blank space, of all the world's celebrities? George could do it, and it would assuredly make his name. It was a superb idea. Moreover, there were to be so many surprising innovations in the house and its grounds that a catalogue would have to be prepared—a splendid catalogue which, of course, would leave nobody in any doubt as to who was the genius bold enough to have conceived and brought into being The Gastronomic Symposium of All the Nations.

And Sala, catching a little of the great man's enthusiasm, one imagines, interested and amused, with no particular plans in his head, pleased, too, with the idea of a regular salary for a while, and wholly ignorant to what freakish, what monstrous scheme he was committing himself, lightheartedly agreed to do whatever Soyer wanted.

For the next two or three months he lived in the house where once on a time he had seen and spoken to Lady Blessington and D'Orsay and the man who was so soon to be declared Emperor of France. There were ghosts about, he thought at first, as, after wandering about the empty and dismantled rooms, he retired to the attic which had hurriedly been furnished for him; but any ghosts there might be must have been driven out very soon, for within a day or two of his arrival there began the strangest invasion.

A whole army of tradesmen, scene-painters, plumbers, drapers, gardeners, and odd-job men descended upon the old house and held high carnival. Then, because the newspapers were beginning to talk and *Punch* was hinting at a Rival Wonder to the Exhibition, Society began to take notice. Dukes and duchesses, warriors and statesmen, distinguished foreigners and fashionable journalists arrived to enjoy a kind of prolonged "private view," and "I remember one Sunday during that strange time," wrote Sala, "seeing Mr. Disraeli, Madame Doche, the author of *Vanity Fair*, a privy councillor, a Sardinian attaché, the Marquis of Normanby, Flexmore the clown, the editor of *Punch*, and the Wizard of the North, all pressing to enter the whilom boudoir of the Blessington."

What these important folk may have thought of the alleged international and certainly bizarre decorations upon which Soyer insisted I cannot say, but Sala himself did not hesitate to speak of the Symposium as the most pretentious sham that ever was. House and grounds alike he considered appalling. As for his own work by the Grand Staircase, "I painted its walls," he records, "with a grotesque nightmare of portraits of people I had never seen, and hundreds more upon whom I had never set eyes save in the print-shops, till I saw the originals grinning, or scowling, or planted in blank amazement before the pictorial libels on the wall." Outside, too, no better taste was exhibited. There was a huge barrack of wood, glass, and iron which was filled with pictures and adorned with calico of all the colours in the spectrum : this was the Baronial Hall. A grazing-meadow at the back of the garden was hired, another barrack was erected, and there was the Pré D'Orsay. The Middlesex magistrates were approached, and, after considerable trouble, were coaxed into granting a licence not only to sell wine and spirits but also for dancing. "We sprinkled tents and alcoves all over the gardens," Sala tells us, "and built a gypsies' caravan, and a stalactite pagoda with double windows, in which gold and silver fish floated. And finally, having engaged an army of pages, cooks, scullions, waiters, barmaids, and clerks of the kitchen, we opened this monstrous place on the first of May 1851, and bade all the world come and dine at SOYER'S SYMPOSIUM."

2

He could write in that way in 1860, when Soyer, worn out by his exertions in the Crimea, was dead, but a very different style was required for *The Book of the Symposium; or Soyer at Gore House*, which he wrote at the time. There was no mention of bizarre taste, calico, or nightmares in that slim quarto of fifty pages: nothing but the almost inconceivable marvels which the magic wand of Soyer, "the Macaulay of *l'art culinaire*," had brought so miraculously into being. Never before can so many superlatives have been gathered together within the confines of a single essay, which today reads almost as amusingly as its author's *Gerald Moreland*. It was one long paean of praise, and long afterwards Sala wondered how he could ever have lent his pen (not, as we shall see, by any means innocent of commercial "puffs") to so extravagant a compilation. He had an honest affection for Soyer as a man, and a sincere admiration for some of his gifts; but he must have smiled rather wryly to himself as he was called on to transmute this or that meretricious façade into an amazing architectural wonder or a celestial triumph of the decorator's art. Even the paintings of the late Madame Soyer, an indifferent artist, now hung in the Baronial Hall, became world-masterpieces, and the lady herself was compared to Murillo, Morland, and Van Dyck. As was meet, of course, his own contribution on the walls of the Grand Staircase received a less dazzling treatment in the catalogue, but even here he was required to be absurdly grandiloquent. To his horror he found that Soyer was insisting on one of his preposterous designations for the huge cartoon which covered nearly seventy feet of wall-space. It was to be

THE GRAND MACEDOINE OF ALL NATIONS

BEING A DEMISEMIMIMITRAGICOMIPANODIOCOSMOPOLYOFANOFUNNIOSYMPOSIORAMA:

OR, SUCHAGETTINGUPSTAIRSTOTHEGREATEXHIBITION OF 1851.

"I groaned," he wrote, "as I interpolated this hideous rubbish in my manuscript." But what could he do? He had contracted to work under Soyer's directions.

And yet, when all was ready and he had returned to the house in Upper Wellington Street, he was probably almost as sanguine as Soyer himself about the Symposium's success. Everything in it might be vulgar and in the worst possible taste, but, apart altogether from the good food that was promised, it set out to astonish and probably would. Even the immense table-cloth, over a hundred yards long and specially manufactured at a cost of more than £60, might by itself attract many

THE

BOOK OF THE SYMPOSIUM;

OR

SOYER AT GORE HOUSE.

Catalogue Raisonné,

ARTISTIC, HISTORIC, TOPOGRAPHIC, AND PICTURESQUE

OF

THAT UNIQUE AND GIGANTIC ESTABLISHMENT.

~~~~~~~~~~~~~~~~~~~~~

"Rien ne dispose mieux l'esprit humain à des transactions amicales qu'un, dîner bien conçu et artistiquement preparé."

SOYER'S GASTRONOMIC REGENERATOR, 1846.

women to Gore House, and it was only one of a score of novelties which could in fairness be called unique. Sala, indeed, need not have found much difficulty in believing his own words when he described, in the broadly comic manner of the day, the cosmopolitan guests who might be expected to attend. "The lightning-winged locomotive, the heavy vetturino, the clumsier diligence, the steamboat, the caique, the junk, and the felucca," all would bring their myriads. "Lively Frenchmen, expatiating over their potages and fricandeaux; phlegmatic Turks, discussing pillaf and hachis; mercurial Persians, enjoying their sherbet; sententious Spaniards, luxuriating over olla podrida; wide-awake Americans, consuming johnny cakes and canvas-backed ducks; pigtailed Chinese, devouring their favourite stewed dog; metaphysical Germans, washing down prodigious quantities of sauerkraut with oceans of rheinwein; swarthy Russians, up to their eyes in caviar; Cossacks, calling for more train oil; Tartars, swallowing quarts of mare's milk," everybody, in fact, except the New Zealand natives (who would probably call for Baked Young Woman for two and a Cold Boiled Missionary to follow) must assuredly find their way to Soyer's incomparable palace.

For a while it seemed as if this indeed might be so. The Symposium at first did well. The newspapers sent their representatives, who seemed well satisfied with the food and apparently impressed by some of the decorations. They spoke of "M. Sala's grotesque pencil"—taking him for a Frenchman—and had much to say of the gardens. The distinguished people, moreover, who had come to the private views now came again and, allowing Soyer to choose a menu for them, were delighted with the result. There were semi-public banquets, too, held at the Symposium, at which famous men spoke—Dickens was amongst them—and Soyer had no cause to be dissatisfied with the additional publicity which he thereby received. Yet the venture was far from being a financial success. There had been too lavish an expenditure, and too many people came once out of curiosity and were not seen again. In an endeavour to add to its attractiveness Soyer engaged musicians and singers to perform in the grounds, arranged for balloon ascents from the Pré D'Orsay, and in the evenings provided fireworks in addition to the usual illuminations. Even so his debts mounted up, and it only needed a complaint from some interfering magistrate about the manner in which these *fêtes de nuit* were being conducted, to turn his disappointment to fury and cause him to close down the establishment with dramatic abruptness.

And so the great cartoon on the staircase disappeared from public view and the elaborate catalogue was no longer in circulation. Sala, however, did not mind very much: he had something else to think about just then.

3

Had an inquisitive foreign visitor to the Exhibition met George Sala during the earlier part of that July and asked him what his business might be, the answer would assuredly have been: a commercial engraver, with offices in Upper Wellington Street, Strand. Had it been suggested, moreover, that within a month or two his engraver's workshop would show signs of transformation into a writer's study, he would merely have uttered an incredulous snort. Write? Not he; he had tried authorship too often. With his work for Soyer finished and done with, and nine-tenths of his little fortune swept away, he was a staid man of business now, like his friend Pond, the advertising agent who rented his first floor. They might call him an artist, but he was settling down at last to commercial pursuits. That, I have no doubt, is what he would have said, and, indeed, at the beginning of the summer it did really seem as if he were forgetting his old ambitions to be somebody or something and resigning himself to a humdrum business career. There was no lack of small commissions coming from Ackermann, and he was adding to his income by sharing with Pond in some of his advertising ventures. For a short while the two partners even combined this work with an insurance agency.

It was then that there came a ludicrous mishap.

Now although there were several unoccupied rooms in the Wellington Street house, nobody slept in it these days except Sala himself. He refused to take a lodger, Pond lived with his family in the suburbs, and the old woman who attended to the necessary chores would arrive with the milk and depart when her work was done. One evening Sala was working very late. About eleven o'clock he decided to take a stroll before going to bed, turned off the gas, and went out. For a while he watched the Opera disgorge its fashionable audience, smoked a cigar, and then walked back to Wellington Street, only to find that he had left his latch-key, his watch, and, except for a few coppers, his money on the workshop-table. A ridiculous business: what was he to do? He did not know where the old woman lived—she had the only other latch-key—and where was he to sleep? Walk boldly into a hotel, and explain his little difficulty in the morning? No; hotel-keepers were not always amiable in the mornings. Demand a bed and breakfast at the house of a friend? That was what many people would not hesitate to do, but he—no, he could not do it. Yet the only alternative was hardly attractive : a seven-hours' tramp. Nobody could reasonably be asked to wander about for that length of time after a hard day's work. Besides, *where* did one tramp ? And then on a sudden he realised that there must be thousands of men in London in a similar situation, but men who, unlike himself, possessed no latch-key to be left stupidly on a table : men with no homes at all. Well, he had known poverty himself, and once or twice when everything pawnable had gone had not dared to go back to his attic, but what sort of men would these others be ? He must have brushed past hundreds and never troubled his head about them. All his natural inquisitiveness was aroused. He would tramp the streets, and keep his eyes open. The night was warm ; it would be a novel and educative experience ; he might even meet with an exciting adventure.

Thus it was that in a half-serious, half-jocular mood Sala began his journey of nocturnal discovery, and nothing very startling or dramatic happened. On the other hand he saw much that night which excited his imagination and much which moved and depressed him. He listened to more than one tale of distress, and found that sympathy was the last thing that was required. He spoke to one or two "roughs" at a coffee-stall, and their answers to his questions ceased to be polite when it became clear that at the moment his purse was no heavier than theirs. There was a fire, and on joining the gathering crowds, he observed that most of those who were pressing about him were less interested in the flames than in the contents of their neighbours' pockets. When a policeman who must have noticed a vagrant air about him asked questions, he found a difficulty in framing an "innocent" reply. He became very tired, and on noticing a common lodging-house, made up his mind to spend his few remaining coppers on a bed. The stench in the dormitory, however, to say nothing of the state of the beds, was too much for him, and without asking for the return of his coppers, he bolted. He spent an instructive hour in Covent Garden market, he watched London wake up, and at seven o'clock, physically weary but mentally alert, vaguely indignant with a Government which could permit anybody to be homeless night after night and eager to discuss his experiences with Pond, he was standing on his Wellington Street doorstep.

Pond was amused. Casually he suggested that an account of the "evening out" ought to be written and sent to one of the magazines. Sala shrugged his shoulders. What editor was likely to accept anything of *his* ? Whereupon Pond reminded him of the now very popular

Household Words which Dickens had launched the year before. Had he not known the great man in the old days?

"Ah! I thought, but it was such a very long time ago. What chance was there for the great Charles Dickens even condescending to cast his eyes on a manuscript penned by a necessitous engraver, three parts of whose time was passed in digging tools of steel into metal plates, laying etching grounds, smoking them and biting the needle-work in with aquafortis?" Thus Sala himself. And yet perhaps he *had* something to say. The horrors of that lodging-house, the stories of distress, the feeling of utter helplessness when penniless and hungry: yes, it might be that he could make something of it.

There and then he sat down, and, using a large lithographic stone which had just arrived from Ackermann's as a desk, he managed within four hours to finish an article which was not only to excite the warmest admiration of both Dickens and Thackeray but was definitely to shape his future career.

BOOK TWO: IN THE LIMELIGHT

CHAPTER SEVEN

ONE OF DICKENS'S YOUNG MEN

I

In January, 1846, the *Daily News* had been launched, with Charles Dickens in the editorial chair. Within three weeks he had resigned, and none of his friends can have been greatly surprised, for he had undertaken duties which were wholly unsuited to a man of his particular temperament. Yet in a little over four years he was to prove himself to be one of the shrewdest of nineteenth-century editors. Under his close supervision *Household Words*, a weekly journal of general literature, issued at two-pence, rapidly gained the public's affection. Indeed, this miscellany, with its judicious mixture of entertainment and instruction, had no real rival at all: it sold in its tens of thousands. For this, of course, Dickens's name as Conductor was in part responsible, but a standard was maintained which was remarkably high. Dickens's judgment was rarely at fault; he had a peculiar flair for discovering new talent; and his sub-editor and manager, W. H. Wills, was the perfect second-in-command. Within a year or two of its inception the journal had become a valuable property, and although all its contributors with the exception of the Conductor himself remained anonymous, it was considered an honour to be included in their number.

Today, I imagine, few people take the trouble to read through any of the nineteen volumes into which *Household Words* was collected, yet they make very good reading, and the social historian will find much that is valuable to him in their dignified but often sprightly pages. Un-provided, moreover, with a copy of the Office Book, he may find a difficulty at times in deciding who the author of this or that essay or story may have been, for so many of them have a distinctly Dickensian flavour. So much, no doubt, was to be expected, and some curious bibliographical mistakes were made at the time; but there was a particular reason for supposing that certain contributions were Dickens's own work. He did not hesitate to make frequent use of his editorial prerogative by "touching up," and sometimes adding materially to, his contributors' proofs. Naturally enough nobody objected. Until the appearance of their work in *Household Words* many of these writers had met with no recognition at all—they owed everything, in fact, to Dickens—and those of them who were lucky enough to become regular contributors were proud to form the little band which was generally known as Dickens's Young Men. Gradually the public came to pierce their identity, and when in due course their essays were republished in volume form they reaped their full reward. And, wrote Forster in his *Life of Charles Dickens*, "I may say at once that of all the writers, before unknown, whom his journal helped to make familiar to a wide circle of readers, he had the strongest possible interest in Mr. Sala, and placed at once in the highest rank his capabilities of help in such an enterprise." That was high praise from Forster, but it was no more than the truth.

Now it must have been some time during the first week of August, 1851, that Sala wrote "The Key of the Street." Pond read it, approved, and offered to take it himself to the *Household Words* office a few doors away. Sala penned a short note to go with it, reminding Dickens that he had known him as a boy, and waited with what patience he could for a reply.

It was soon forthcoming.

Within another four hours he was enchanted to receive a letter from Dickens himself, congratulating him on the article and promising speedy publication. One or two passages, he thought, might be softened with advantage, but he would attend to the matter himself. And a bank-note for five pounds was enclosed. It was by far the largest sum of money that Sala had ever received for a piece of literary work. Nor was this all. Within a few days Wills had written to say how glad he would be to receive further articles, and Dickens had invited him to step round to the office.

It may be a little difficult today to understand the unusual enthusiasm which greeted "The Key of the Street" on its first appearance (Sept. 10th). It is certainly interesting, it has a spice of novelty, and it rouses one's pity and indignation; but it is hardly a work of genius, and there is little in it which lingers on in one's memory. In 1851, however, it created what in these days would be called a minor sensation, and within a day or two people were asking who the author might be. Dickens's own opinion may be judged from a letter he wrote to Wills in the second week of August. "It is a very remarkable piece of description, and (although there is little fancy in it) exceedingly superior to the usual run of such writing. I have delicately altered it myself, so as to leave no offence in it whatever. If the young man can write, generally, as well as that, he will be an acquisition to us. I think it," he added, "quite good enough for a first article,—but we will not put him first, for fear we should spoil him in the beginning." As for Thackeray, he could not forget it. "One of the best things I ever read," he told George Hodder a few years later.

"I couldn't have written it. I wish I could." Hodder "ventured to suggest that although there could be no doubt that the article in question possessed great merit, and that it had been talked about in the literary world as amongst the most attractive features in the publication, he was scarcely doing justice to his own powers by the observation he had made. 'No, No,' he repeated, with increased earnestness, 'I couldn't have written that article, and as I shall have a periodical of my own shortly, I shall hope for this man's co-operation!'"

He did not forget, for when the *Cornhill Magazine* was about to be launched Sala was amongst the first of those who were approached for contributions.

2

It is easy to imagine the "commercial engraver's" state of mind during that week-end. By itself, and however successful, a single article in print might not amount to very much—after all it was far from being his first —and at the moment it does not seem to have occurred to him that a new career might be dawning. He was still a man of business, possibly an artist, and one who might add to his income by writing; but that was all. Yet he must have been pleased and excited at his unexpected success, eager to listen to the congratulations of friends, and disinclined for work. A great deal of liquor, I have no doubt, was consumed, and on the Monday he was still in holiday mood. And it was then that he drove out in the afternoon with his brother Charles to the Symposium, and had not a notion of what was in store for him.

Soyer was no longer his employer, but they had remained good friends, and he may have gone to Kensington that day merely to pay his respects and enjoy a good dinner. Perhaps, too, he wished to have another look at his huge cartoon and receive more congratulations as he stood on the Grand Staircase. It may be, however, that he had seen advertisements of a balloon-ascent—Soyer's latest novelty—due to take place that afternoon from the Pré D'Orsay. I have said that he retained his interest in aerial navigation after his unfortunate experience at Hull, and, according to the public announcements, there were novel features about this balloon which may have aroused his curiosity. At any rate the brothers arrived at the Symposium and found the balloon in process of inflation.

Actually it differed from most machines only in its shape. "It was cylindrical rather than spheroidal in form; that is to say it resembled a huge horizontally-sailing sausage, instead of a vertically-directed pear with the stalk undermost." Basket, valves, and ropes did not seem to differ from the usual run of such things, and the rumoured apparatus for steering was non-existent. Sala did not disguise his disappointment, but stayed on with Soyer and a party of friends to watch.

There was a crowd of spectators surrounding the balloon, but none of them seemed eager to make an ascent. Perhaps it was that the five guineas demanded was too high a price. Perhaps they were dissuaded by the fact that the inventor, who was present and full of admiration for his sausage, had announced that on *this* occasion he did not propose to be a passenger. It was rumoured that a distinguished nobleman had promised to make the ascent, but he failed to appear. Two Guards officers had paid their passage money but at the last moment had sent word to say that military duties were detaining them. An elderly aeronaut named Chambers had been put in charge, with his son as assistant, and there was room for two others. Who would be brave enough to go? An hour or two passed, and no hero presented himself. By six o'clock, at which hour the balloon was fully inflated, a large crowd had collected both inside and outside the gates of the Symposium and was becoming impatient. Soyer asked Sala if he would like to go up, and on the spur of the moment he agreed. Ordinarily he would have refused. He was no coward, but he had never yet ascended, even in a captive balloon, he knew little or nothing about Chambers, and it was an untried machine. The occasion, however, was exceptional, the spirit of successful adventure was upon him, and so he stepped into the breach. A Mr. Gardiner followed his example, and ten minutes later the two of them took their places in the basket with Chambers and his son.

The balloon rose easily, and there were the usual cheers as Chambers cut away a quantity of toy balloons which had been attached to the side of the car. As it happened, these were to be indirectly responsible for the disaster that followed. They were, wrote Sala a few years later in one of his contributions to *Belgravia*, "mere inflated linen-bags, fashioned as lions, dragons, fish and other preposterous forms, and all emblazoned with the cognisance of the Symposium. . . . The aeronaut had instructions to cut the windbags adrift when he had ascended a short distance, in order that they might amuse the *gobemouches* of Brompton and the Fulham-road, and scatter advertisements of the Symposium far and wide." Unfortunately the old man was so busily engaged with his pocket-knife that he forgot to take the necessary precaution of slipping off the handkerchief which in those days was almost invariably used to close the neck of a balloon while on the ground, in order to prevent the entrance of air. (At a certain height it would be loosened, so that the gas, expanding owing to diminished air pressure on the envelope, could escape.) The assistant either did not notice the omission or was unaware of what ought to be done: he seems to have been chiefly interested in estimating the height they had reached. "He cried out gleefully that we had risen to the altitude of one mile, that we were just over Fulham Church, and that we were about to cross the Thames." And at that moment Sala was startled to hear "a sharp cracking report, precisely like a musket-shot" above his head.

The balloon had burst, and "we fell, as a stone falls, half a mile."

What followed reflected the greatest credit on Chambers, who was quick to realise what had happened. As they dropped, "staring death in the face," he climbed up into the netting, shouting the while to his passengers to throw out ballast, and managed to cut the cords which attached the neck of the balloon to the hoop. It was a courageous act, and it saved four lives, for, as he had hoped, the silk envelope immediately flew up to the top of the netting, forming an inverted saucer which acted as a parachute. "We were then steady for a moment," Sala was inform- ing the world a day or two later in the *Times*, "then oscillated (a proof of comparative safety), then went down again with frightful force. Certain death was now before us," he continued, and in the circumstances the phrase may perhaps be excused, "but not one of us lost presence of mind, though I had not the slightest hope of escape; Mr. Chambers was entirely calm and collected. We cut away the grapnel, threw out more ballast (bags and all on my part) and descended with a concussion not nearly so severe as I expected in a market-gardener's field. I fell on Mr. Gardiner, Mr. Chambers jun. on me, three bags of ballast on him, and the car over us all; while 'the pilot who had weathered the storm' was thrown with considerable violence from amongst the cordage round the hoop, where he had been standing."

They were bruised and bleeding, but they were safe. Unluckily for them, a number of gardeners at work amongst the cabbages seem to have resented the damage to their master's property, and the half-dazed men were rudely hustled and robbed before they were permitted to depart. When Sala arrived back at Gore House, it was to find that his precious locket as well as his money had been taken from him.

He was badly shocked, and that must be his excuse for the ill-considered letter which he sent to the *Times* on the following day. He was justified in contradicting the absurd rumours to which the accident had given rise, but it was a stupid move on his part to denounce the folly of balloon- ascents undertaken for the mere amusement of idlers, more particularly as he excused his own ascent on the grounds that he was "an artist."

The *Times* not only published his letter but another which endorsed his views, but the *Morning Post* unmercifully attacked him in a leading article which he never wholly forgot. He an artist, forsooth! What had he done to justify the title? He was probably one of those conceited creatures who wore their hair long, dressed in velvet jackets, and deluded themselves into the belief that they could paint. An artist! Was every Tom, Dick, or Harry so to describe himself on the score of a few mediocre scrawls?

The holiday mood passed quickly, to be followed by one of black anger. He, George Sala, not an artist? The man whose panoramas had sold in their thousands! The cartoonist of the Grand Staircase! It was a monstrous impertinence on the *Morning Post*'s part. Such an insult was not to be borne. He would take a horsewhip to the editor. And then he began to wonder a little, and to remember a little. . . . For years he had worked hard enough, but had he so much to show for it? Not very much that was good. He was only a mediocre draughtsman. That, indeed, was why he had been resigning himself to a commercial career. No, he would never do anything much with his drawings. The *Morning Post*, confound it, was right: he was hardly an artist at all. But something else had happened. He had begun to write for the magazines, and Dickens, like his own Oliver, was asking for more. Wills was even hinting that if he continued as he had begun, there would be room for an article from his pen every week, and at £5 a time he would be "made" —practically on the staff of the most successful weekly in the world! For a while it might be advisable to continue his engraving work—there were still commissions awaiting his attention—but he was a writer now, acclaimed and applauded. Very well, then, "beshrew art!"

It was as a writer that he would make his name.

3

The work which Sala executed for Dickens during the next four or five years definitely made his reputation as a lively essayist almost without a rival in his own line. It did not seem to matter very much what subject he chose: always he had something piquant or oddly moving or "not generally known" to say. Indeed, he owed not a little of his success to his ability to invest even the most commonplace affair with a novel excitement. Again and again that one good eye of his would rest, shrewdly and inquisitively, on this or that object or occurrence which, it seemed, previous authors had unaccountably ignored. An empty house in a Whitechapel slum, a lost shilling, old clothes, everyday superstitions, a cup of coffee : the little things of life, perhaps, predominated, but in his hands they were transmuted into something which, if not of the first importance, would open out the most unexpected but most welcome vistas in the reader's mind. His style might be florid (though such a good writer as E. V. Lucas could set out to model his own upon it), and his vocabulary could be heavy and sometimes eccentric, but his vignettes, if not always learned, were vivid, and if they often showed a touch of crude sentimentality, so much was expected at the time. Week followed week, and it was a rare event for a number of *Household Words* to be without a contribution from his pen. Afterwards the great majority of these essays, sketches, and stories were gathered into one or other of the five volumes—*Gaslight and Daylight* (1859), *Looking at Life* (1860), *Dutch Pictures* (1861), *Accepted Addresses* (1862), and *After Breakfast* (1864)— which made his name so well known on both sides of the Atlantic ; and, if read today, they will be found to build up, collectively, a picture of mid-Victorian life only surpassed in intimacy and variegated colour by Sala's own *Twice Round the Clock*.

You would naturally suppose that for the man himself these four or five years must have been a period of growing enchantment. Here he was, in regular and well-paid work, acclaimed as a writer with an individual touch, "gleefully" accepting Dickens's frequent invitations to his *Household Words* dinners where he met such considerable figures as Leigh Hunt and "Farthing" Horne, elected to this or that Bohemian club which attracted the celebrities of the theatrical and literary worlds, and in general regarded as the coming man. Everything seemed to be in his favour. He could work fast, no article of his was refused, and if new ideas were sometimes slow to present themselves, there were friends, Dickens himself prominently amongst them, who were regularly providing him with useful suggestions. Now, surely, there was nothing to prevent him from speedily realising his ambition to become a great writer.

Yet his very success proved to be temporarily his undoing, and it was his work for *Household Words* which was chiefly responsible for converting him into "one of the idlest young dogs that ever rambled between London and Paris, London and Lancashire, and Lancashire and Ireland, that ever—to all appearances, at least—wasted his precious time in a seemingly reckless and wholly indefensible manner." The knowledge, in fact, that a few hours' not very difficult writing could produce a fair number of guineas seems to have gone to his head.

"I became a loafer," he confesses, "a slovenly, careless young ne'er-do-well."

It was essential, of course, that he should travel about, making wide explorations, for it was as a *reporter*, first and foremost, that he had distinguished himself, but after years of drudgery he had found that it was possible to live in some comfort without working long hours every day, and the discovery was fatal. "I rose and retired to rest when I liked; and I worked when I chose—which was rarely. I was very much like the miller who lived on the banks of the river Dee. Apart from my very few relatives 'I cared for nobody' in particular, 'and nobody cared for me.'" This, however, was not all. In pre-Wellington Street days he had shown a curious unwillingness to allow even his intimate friends to know precisely where he was living: now that a workshop was no longer required, he gave up his house and ceased to have what the police like to call a fixed place of residence. He became little better than a vagabond, generally hard up and borrowing from friends when he could get no further advances from the long-suffering Wills. He was unpunctual with his work, drinking heavily, finding pretty ladies to entertain, and, worst of all, very seriously undermining his health. A brilliant young man, you would have been told at the time, and a delightful companion —if he happened to be sober; but an unreliable, erratic, short-tempered fellow who, if he did not pull himself together, would speedily sink down to the depths.

Was there any particular reason for this "bad dream" of a time, as Sala afterwards spoke of it? From his letters it is difficult to be sure, but I fancy that the anonymous young lady of Lancaster was not unconnected with it. Again and again he would rush up North and not be seen for a week or two in his usual London haunts, and then, to quote from his own *Gerald Moreland*, "plunge in every species of dissipation." He must have been fully aware of the fine things that he could do; he cannot have failed to see how others of his own generation, writers with some but not all of his gifts, were settling down to enjoy a quiet success. That he was genuinely unhappy we know, and so much Dickens, who was viewing with alarm a growing carelessness on his part, probably realised, for he went out of his way to be kind. About the young woman there are no details whatsoever. She may have found a difficulty in making up her mind; he may have been an unsatisfactory lover. I can only suppose that after a series of doubts and misunderstandings, quarrels and reconciliations, he recognised the hopelessness of his quest and went to Lancaster no more.

Loafer he may have been during those years but that is not to say that he was always satisfied with a weekly article for Dickens, or that his visits to Paris, which at this time were frequent enough, were always undertaken for mere pleasure. When, for instance, the news of the *coup*

d'état of December, 1851, reached London, Sala constituted himself a
Special Correspondent and rushed over for "copy," and his "Liberty,
Equality, Fraternity, and Musketry," printed on his return, probably
gave Londoners a clearer idea of what had been happening in the besieged
city than was to be found in any of the daily newspapers. Afterwards,
too, he had some lantern slides prepared, and delivered a lecture on his
experiences. At the same time he was engaged on another piece of work,
of a very different kind, with his brother.

His contemporaries are generally agreed that if Charles Kerrison Sala
was not a great actor, he was a very remarkable man. Even Macready,
who was not usually too courteous towards his subordinates behind the
scenes, treated him with marked consideration, and in spite of a pretended
detestation—he would invariably address him as Beast—admitted him
to something like intimacy. Charles, indeed, was in many ways his
brother's superior. He was by far the better scholar, equally witty in
his conversation, and a fastidious man of taste who, had he cared to write
something more ambitious than a few sets of satirical verses, might well
have made a big name for himself. He was of the greatest assistance to
his brother in the preparation of the *Household Words* articles, and it was
he who persuaded him to write the pantomime which George Ellis, then
stage-manager at the Princess's, was requiring for Christmas. If George,
he said, would write the "words" he himself would be responsible for
the lyrics and Ellis could be trusted to provide the "effects." George
agreed, Dickens seems to have been interested in the venture, and
Harlequin Billy Taylor; or, the Flying Dutchman and the King of Raritongo
was the result.

Now to read the "book" of this Grand Operatico, Tragico, Serio-
pastoralic, Nautico, Demoniaco, Cabalistico, Original Christmas Pantomime in cold blood today is something of an ordeal. Its rhyming dialogue
is rarely funny and its wit for the most part is puerile. An examination
of the programme, however, is enough to show that the well-known
story of the tailor, torn from his beloved, "pressed" into the Navy,
wrecked on an island, and narrowly escaping compulsory marriage with
the blackest of black princesses, had been neatly adapted to the stage and
as neatly joined on to the all-important harlequinade, which in this case
was divided into no less than six scenes. The effects, moreover, were
novel—they included the deck of a man-of-war and realistic waves—and
the cast was exceptionally good. Flexmore, the cleverest clown of his
day, was in it, and although on this occasion he was accused in some
quarters of coarseness, he seems to have enjoyed a triumph. Carlotta
Leclerc played Columbine, and when the man-of-war's figurehead came

to life in the person of a tiny Britannia it was the little Kate Terry who pirouetted across the stage. The pantomime was the greatest success, even though it did not produce much money for its authors, but, as it happened, it was to have for Sala a rather more profitable sequel.

On Boxing Night, 1851, Charles Sala appeared in the character of Paulina, Billy Taylor's dearly-beloved, but by the end of the following week his place had been taken by a Mr. Daly. For some little while his relations with the stage-manager had been strained—for what precise reason is not known—and after the second or third performance the two men came to blows. Attempts were made by Dion Boucicault, at that time the Princess's "stock" author, to compose their differences, but without avail. Charles Kean felt obliged to take his manager's part, and to the general regret of the company "Mr. Wynn" resigned from the theatre. Now Kean at that time was rehearsing a new play, adapted from the French, which was destined, in one or other of its many forms, to enjoy a lasting success. This was Boucicault's version of *The Corsican Brothers*, in which Charles Sala had been cast for the small part of the woodcutter. Both the brothers were greatly taken with the play's possibilities, and, after Charles's resignation, and remembering that he had some few grievances of his own to redress, "I took," records Sala, "what I thought to be a very legitimate revenge by writing on my own account another version of *Les Frères Corses*."

It was all delightfully simple : no worrying questions of copyright; no fear of legal injunctions. "Without compunction," he tells us, "—so comically are one's notions of ethics influenced by circumstances—I proceeded to purchase a copy of the French drama and turn it into English. I set to work at eight o'clock ... and the adaptation was finished by ten the next morning. Then I went to bed, to sleep the sleep of the just—well, the questionably just—but the grass was not allowed to grow under our feet. My brother took the drama to which we had given the title of *The Corsicans*, over to the Surrey Theatre, which was then under the management of my old friend Mr. Creswick, the tragedian, and Mr. Richard Shepherd, a transpontine actor of considerable ability. My brother returned at three in the afternoon ; he had lunched with Creswick and Shepherd ; those worthy managers at once accepted *The Corsicans* ; and, moreover, they had offered my brother a twelvemonth's engagement at a handsome salary. *The Corsicans* was within seven days produced at the Surrey, and ran for more than a hundred nights. I had associated my brother's name with my own as joint-author ; but he had nothing to do with turning the French dramatist's prose into English. Our remuneration was not splendid; but it was sufficient. We received twenty-five shillings a night: a sum considered in those days to be prodigious for authors' rights at a minor theatre."

Incidentally, one other visit to Paris was thoroughly well "earned," after a lengthy and difficult piece of work, the last of its kind that Sala was to execute, had been brought to a conclusion.

On September 14th, 1852, the Duke of Wellington died, and the most elaborate preparations for his funeral were immediately put in hand. London was to witness a pageant such as it had rarely if ever seen before, even at a Coronation, and Ackermann proposed to issue several publications fitly commemorating the event. The most ambitious of these was to be a grand panorama of the entire procession: a series of steel plates, etched and aquatinted. In view of the fact that the procession would be largely equestrian, he approached in the first place Henry Alken, the son of the well-known animal painter and himself a sporting artist of high repute. Alken agreed to engrave the horses, but suggested a collaborator for the carriages and figures, and the commission was offered to and accepted by Sala.

The work took several weeks to complete. There were thousands of figures to be etched—the finished panorama extended to more than sixty-six feet and was sold at the very considerable price of two guineas —and the greatest care was required to ensure that every uniform and state carriage was correctly limned. The authorities—the City Corporation, Horse Guards, and the Dean of St. Paul's—all gave the artists every assistance, and on the day of the funeral the Chief Commissioner of the Metropolitan Police, the newly-knighted Sir Richard Mayne, gave Sala a special pass "to walk between the lines." He saw the pageant from three different points on the route, and was inside St. Paul's for the service itself.

"We had finished aquatinting the plates about Christmas," he recounts, "when, utterly worn out with hard work, I took a trip to Paris. I was suffering from something else, more serious than fatigue. The fumes of the acids used in biting-in the plates, and the glare of the bright metal itself, when the varnish was removed, had played, as I feared, almost irrevocable havoc with my only valid optic; and for the second time in my life, I was within measurable distance of blindness. Happily, this affliction was spared me, and my sight grew strong enough for me to cover, during the next thirty years or so, very many thousands of pages with a small and more or less legible handwriting. I never, however, touched an etching needle or graver again."

4

An improvident and often drunken loafer, yes; "wrecked in Bohemia," to use a contemporary novelist's words, yes: Sala had little cause to be pleased with himself at the time. Yet he did periodically make endeavours to pull himself together. The vagabond's cloak was not doffed, and his work was not yet to be systematised; but he was shrewd enough to realise that if the high standard demanded by Dickens and Wills was to be maintained, and if journalism were really to be his chosen profession, there would have to be some very serious study. Several years were to pass before he created those astonishingly comprehensive commonplace books of his which enabled him, with a minimum of research, to write his ten or more leading articles each week for the *Daily Telegraph*, but already in 1853 he was familiarising himself with the work of the great journalists, and read from cover to cover many volumes of the *Examiner* and other dignified journals of the past. Now, too, he was prepared to undertake rather more literary work than a weekly article or two for *Household Words* entailed. At intervals he contributed to its not very long-lived rival, the *Illustrated London Magazine*, and in the late autumn of this year he launched a weekly periodical of his own—this time, of necessity, with somebody else's money.

Amongst his new friends was a man named Peter Morrison—a bland, well-spoken gentleman who liked to call himself a banker. And at this time, I suppose, he had some right to the title, for he was the head of an establishment widely advertised as the Bank of Deposit. There was to come a time—it was not far distant—when Mr. Morrison's various financial transactions were to be regarded with extreme disfavour by the authorities and when Mr. Morrison himself, successfully avoiding those who claimed to be his creditors, unobtrusively and for all time, was to leave the country of his birth; but at the moment, like his Bank of Deposit and its allied National Assurance and Investment Association, he was flourishing. More, he liked to be seen in literary and Bohemian circles, and like other unorthodox financiers who looked forward to the days when a country seat and even a knighthood might be theirs, he was willing enough to play Maecenas, more particularly if there seemed to be a reasonable chance that his money would be returned to him with an appreciable bonus. And when Sala approached him with his latest idea, he at once agreed to provide capital enough for the initial expenses.

The idea was a good one. For his *Household Words* articles Sala had gone hither and thither in London, and found within its limits an almost inexhaustible fund of material. London, in fact, had become his particular province. Who better qualified, then, than himself, a genuine Cockney even if he could boast of no British blood, to give to the City its own particular weekly? A serio-comic, illustrated journal, it should be, a little like *Punch*, but, of course, its superior in wit, a little like *Chat*, but perhaps spicier in tone, and containing—its special feature—a series of London "scenes," written by himself, of the kind that readers of *Household Words* were finding so much to their taste. There would be a political cartoon—Keeley Halswelle, whom he had recently met, would be just the man to design it—and theatrical news and popular science would not be neglected. And for a title what more satisfactory than *LONDON* itself?

He set to work. An office was found in the Strand, and a dour Scot named Archibald Jack engaged as publisher. Pond was brought in, and if Littleton Holt and Dr. Strauss were not official members of the staff they were certainly hovering about. Charles Sala, too, who had now retired from the stage and was becoming tired of doing nothing in particular with his mother at Brighton, returned to London to give what assistance he could. Sala himself drew a reversed design for the cover, with Gog and Magog prominently displayed, but, no doubt to mark his altered status, left others to execute the actual etching. And on December 24th, No. 1 of *London*—Literature, The Drama, Music, Science, Art, with Contributions by the First Authors of the Day—was duly published, price 3d.

It may be admitted that the new journal in its general appearance hardly differed from *Punch*. Perhaps, too, the wit that it showed was not singularly brilliant. The cartoons, however, were apt, and the editor's contributions were not below *Household Words* standards. There were "Growls and Grunts" about London sufficiently provocative, one would imagine, to have piqued the citizens of the day, its "Curiosities" were picturesquely presented, and in the fifth number a serial story entitled *The Mysteries of Moonshine* was begun, a fact which at any rate suggests that at the time the bantling had no intention of dying. Nor did the two following numbers show the least sign of what their editor would assuredly have called moribundity. But when Saturday, February 11th, 1854, dawned there was no No. 8 of *London* to be distributed, and, in fact, no further number was printed.

This sudden demise can hardly have followed on the political situation, bad as it was. In the previous November Russia had declared war on Turkey, and for some weeks now it had been generally accepted that Great Britain and France must give active support to the Ottoman

Government. We were not yet at war, but as Lord Clarendon said then and Neville Chamberlain was to say eighty-five years later, we were hardly at peace. True, earlier this week, the Russian Ambassador had left London, and nobody believed that the deputation from the Society of Friends who were received by the Czar on the Friday could alter the course of events. No, it was not the threat of immediate war that killed *London*, and I can hardly suppose that Sala's attempt at "spice"—"I was a little in advance of my age," he was saying in 1880—or his troubles with his staff—the theatrical critic seems to have been curiously unwilling to witness any plays—had much to do with it.

It was chiefly, I imagine, the price. The citizens of London, to be frank, obtained little enough for their threepence, and little enough that they could not obtain elsewhere. And that was not all. Exactly how much of *London* was written by Sala it is difficult to say for the simple reason that almost every article, if not his own, seems to have been modelled on his style. A delicate compliment, possibly, but hardly a wise one, for even the liveliest note, if sustained for too long a time, is apt to pall. The "spice," too, was hardly pungent enough. The truth was that by himself Sala was not big enough to "carry" any journal. Had he obtained help from Albert Smith or Shirley Brooks, or had he known Edmund Yates, just then emerging from his post-office labours with ideas which really were a little in advance of his age, all might have been well. By this time, however, *Punch* was too firmly ensconced in the public's affections to be disturbed by such a midget, and so *London* died.

Yet, phoenix-like, it was to rise again exactly four weeks later, in a slightly altered form. Precisely what happened it is impossible to say. One imagines that there were hurried meetings at 291, Strand, in which Holt took a leading part. At the moment he was about to launch yet another new weekly newspaper of his own, also, it would seem, to be financed by Morrison. *Holt's Army and Navy Gazette* was to deal exclusively with the forthcoming war. His publisher, a Mr. Strange, seemed interested in *London*, and thought that it could be turned into a success if the price were to be changed. Would Sala and his staff care to try again? It was perhaps a little unfortunate that less than three years ago Mr. Strange had been through the Bankruptcy Court, but he was flourishing now, and with a *Police Gazette* (also edited by the industrious Holt) and a circulating library on his hands, he would be in a favourable position to launch a new *London*. The suggestion was adopted, although Sala himself resigned from the editorial chair, a new title was chosen for the weekly, and on March 11th, 1854, No. 1 of *Punchinello*, price 1d.—"the Cheapest Periodical of the Day"—made its appearance as a thin folio.

We have Sala's own word for it that *Punchinello* never rose beyond
the status of a weakling; but it managed to drag out a meagre existence
for eighteen months, and to the end he contributed with some regularity
to its pages, though his serial *Charley in the Guards; a Tale of Military
Life*, begun in the third number when patriotic fervour was high, did
not run through more than some eight or nine numbers.

Strange found it convenient to retire before many months, and Mr.
Morrison followed his example, but "the proprietors"—Pond, Clayton,
the two Salas, and possibly Holt—decided to continue. For a while
Archibald Jack acted as publisher, but in March, 1855, there was a serious
dispute, apparently about the price which in point of fact was altered
more than once, and he left. His place was taken successively by Clayton,
Charles Sala, and Charles Pond, Richard's brother. The size of the
weekly was altered, a new office was found at No. 1, Exeter Change, and
a room over it became Sala's home, so far as he could be said to have
any, for the next two or three years.

5

He was to assume editorial duties more than once again in the course
of his career, but at the moment he preferred to remain what was so
soon to be known as a free-lance. His *Household Words* articles were still
appearing almost every week, and his reputation, more particularly after
the appearance of a story called "The Conversion of Colonel Quagg"
which was to be reprinted with some regularity on both sides of the
Atlantic until the end of the century, was now sufficiently high for his
name to be suggested as a possible contributor when any new periodical
of a popular kind was being projected. As it happened, too, this was the
time when a memorable reform in the newspaper world was about to
be effected. For some years there had been a growing agitation against
the so-called "tax on knowledge," in other words the Act which required
all newspapers to be stamped. This agitation was now very near to
success. A Bill was before Parliament, and although opposition was
expected from Die-hard peers, not a few projects for cheaper journals
were afoot, even before it passed its third reading in the House of
Commons.

Amongst the most important of these was one for a rival to the
Illustrated London News, until this time in a seemingly unassailable
position. Its originator was the publisher David Bogue, who had money
to risk. It would be a risk, of course, for the *Illustrated London News*, if
now set a little deeply in its dignified lines, was an admirably-conducted

newspaper. But its price was high—with the almost inevitable supplement it was generally sold at sixpence—and it occurred to Bogue that there would be an immense public for a weekly of a similar, though livelier, type issued, unstamped, at twopence. He took his idea to Henry Vizetelly, who by this time had made his mark in the publishing world: would he join in the venture as part-proprietor and editor with an entirely free hand? Vizetelly was willing, and soon showed himself to be a man of courage and vision. He gathered about him a curiously-chosen but most excellent staff. For his artists he engaged such old favourites as Birket Foster, Kenny Meadows, and "Phiz," but he also gave work to Gustave Doré, then hardly known in England, and commissioned wholly untried men like his old pupil, Julian Portch, whose Crimean sketches were amongst the best of their kind to be reproduced in any newspaper, and William M'Connell, who was to illustrate more than one of Sala's books in the future. On the literary side he was no less bold an innovator. Dignity there must be, but for the most part it was to be the dignity of youth, and so there came Dickens's Young Men, Sala, of course, amongst them, with a kind of roving commission: vignettes of public men, accounts of unusual events and art exhibitions, occasional leading articles on non-political subjects. There was Robert Brough, one of two clever brothers already well known for their stage-burlesques: a hard-working man whom Sala had known since *Man in the Moon* days. There were Frederick Greenwood, afterwards founder of the *Pall Mall Gazette*, and Augustus Mayhew, the youngest of seven more or less celebrated brothers. But there were also others who had yet to make their reputation: Edward Draper, a solicitor who discovered a pleasantly novel way of reporting police news; Mr. White, a former Bedford bookseller and now door-keeper at the House of Commons, who proved himself to be a vivacious guide to Parliamentary customs and an unconventional recorder of its proceedings; and, last but not least, Edmund Yates, whose gossipy column entitled "The Lounger at the Clubs," with its slightly impertinent and intimate asides, was something entirely new and took London by storm.

There was never a doubt about the success of the *Illustrated Times*, as it was called. More than two hundred thousand copies of the first number were issued—rather rashly, as it happened, for they bore no stamp, and the Royal Assent to the Stamp Repeal Bill was not given until a week later—and there was little falling off in numbers as the weeks passed. Nor was this surprising, for apart from the difference in price the new weekly in variety, general liveliness, and clever illustration, easily outdistanced its rival. Augustus Mayhew proved to be an excellent special correspondent at home, and Sala's first despatches in the same capacity abroad—he described the Paris Exhibition of 1855 in an amusingly personal way which at the time must have startled readers accustomed to more rounded periods—enhanced his growing reputation. And then, early in 1856, there came Vizetelly's greatest triumph.

In the previous November a Rugeley surgeon by name William Palmer, who was well known on most of the race-courses as a heavy gambler, had been arrested for murder, and such were the circumstances that within a few days the words "Palmer" and "Rugeley" were on everybody's lips. Not since the days of the Rush and Manning cases had the country been whipped up into a state of such tense excitement.

Palmer's arrest had followed on the inquest held on the body of one John Parsons Cook, a Lutterworth solicitor whose friend he was supposed to be. The jury found that Cook had died of poison wilfully administered by Palmer. On enquiries being made it was discovered that a number of the surgeon's friends and acquaintances as well as more than one member of his own family had died in a more or less mysterious manner, and he was also accused of poisoning his wife and brother. Such was the feeling against him in Staffordshire (though in Rugeley itself they had at first spoken warmly in his favour) that the authorities arranged for his trial to be held at the Old Bailey. It is hardly credible, and, indeed, Vizetelly himself afterwards expressed astonishment that he and his staff had not been prosecuted for the most outrageous contempt of court, but three months before the trial was due to take place a special Rugeley Number of the *Illustrated Times* was produced, which, with its cunning mixture of ascertained fact and local rumours, its interviews with everybody in any way connected with the case, its articles on poisoners of the past who had been hanged for their crimes, and its cool assumption that if anybody remained alive in Rugeley and the district it was not Palmer's fault, was about the most remarkable piece of journalistic impertinence for which a reputable newspaper had ever been responsible. Yet nobody seems to have raised a single word of protest at the time. It was certainly most picturesquely done. Vizetelly had sent half his staff up to Rugeley to gather every item of information, however trivial, which could possibly be used for a Life of Palmer, vignettes of his neighbours, or accounts of those of his family who were no longer in a position to speak for themselves. Augustus Mayhew explored Rugeley with all the thoroughness of an experienced archeologist. His colleague, C. H. Bennett, whose shadow-pictures and caricatures had brought him something like fame, made sketches of every nook and corner of the town and dozens of clever pencil-portraits of those who had played any part in the preliminary investigations. Even the potboy at Palmer's favourite house of call was not neglected. Nothing like the Rugeley Number had ever appeared before, and more than 400,000 copies were sold.

Conspicuously absent, however, from the list of contributors was Sala. Afterwards he had much to say of the Rugeley murders and the strange man who had been responsible for them, but at the time he was silent. His graphic pen could have found much which would have delighted Vizetelly's vast public, but when he was wanted—during December and January—he could not be found.

As it happened, at least one other London editor was frantically searching for him at the time. This was Edmund Yates, always to be a good friend of his, though even now under no illusions about his careless and intemperate habits. In the previous summer Yates had launched yet another rival to *Punch*: the *Comic Times*. This had been sponsored by Herbert Ingram of the *Illustrated London News*—he had recently quarrelled with the proprietors of *Punch*—and there had been a moment when it seemed likely to achieve a lasting success. Yates had had the benefit of Albert Smith's advice, though the author of *Mont Blanc* was too busy at this time with his daily performances to write very much, and the Brough brothers and Sala were among his regular contributors. From a mathematical lecturer at Oxford, moreover, he had received a few sets of verses which went a peculiar way of their own. They were printed without a signature, but one of them at any rate was to achieve immortality when, in an altered form, it was to be recited by the White Rabbit in *Alice's Adventures in Wonderland*. Even then Sala's contributions—two series of essays: soliloquies, respectively, of a stage-doorkeeper and an elderly landlady (with illustrations by himself)—had led to one or two good-humoured protests in the periodical itself. Matters, however, had become more serious when, after its sixteenth number, the *Comic Times* was sold to another proprietor who with a new staff of his own choosing killed it within a month or two. It had been Yates's first experience of editorship, but he was not discouraged. Meetings of the dismissed staff were held, and Yates and several of his contributors, Sala among them, decided to launch a high-class monthly magazine on their own account. So was the *Train* born, and Sala himself not only produced for it a vivacious essay but also accepted an invitation to try his hand at a long novel to be serialised in its pages. The plot of *Fripanelli's Daughter*, as it was to be called, was outlined and approved, and William M'Connell was commissioned to illustrate it. But when the time came for the first number to be printed, there was no Chapter I. of the novel, and no Sala to explain its delay.

"We held a conclave," Yates relates in his entertaining *Recollections*; "we drew up an advertisement couched in mysterious terms, intelligible only to the initiated, and inserted it in the *Times*. It commenced, I recollect, 'Bohemian, where art thou?' and I saw it the other day, to my infinite amusement, reproduced in a volume compiled from the 'Agony Column.'" But even this elicited no reply, and had not Robert Brough thrown himself into the breach and begun to write in the form of a novel a thinly-disguised account of his own life called *Marston Lynch*, the first number of the *Train* would have been decidedly thin.

Luck, moreover, was with Yates. His magazine ran for a considerable period, and its five volumes are eagerly sought for by collectors today, not, I must admit, for the Sala or Brough contributions, but because there were more verses from the mathematical lecturer at Oxford, this time signed Lewis Carroll. Yet at the outset he was faced with a powerful rival in the *Idler*, another monthly magazine very similar in its outward appearance to his own, which had managed to be first in the field and had announced its intention to castigate the follies of society and the absurd pretensions of various "minor literary lights." Its moving spirit was James Hannay, a young man whose powers of sarcastic invective were considerable, and, indeed, his polemics against such "eminent modern writers" as Cuthbert Bede (the Rev. Edward Bradley) author of *Verdant Green*, Peter Cunningham the antiquarian, and Gerald Massey the poet, were little short of devastating. Yates in an endeavour to show that the "Train Band" were quite as capable as any of the "Idlers" launched an attack on his rival at the end of the first number. In a dialogue entitled "Nights at the Round Table" he and his staff were shown in conclave. "Who," asks somebody, "are the people on the 'Idler'?" Sala, under the guise of "Quarll" is made to reply: "Hannay and Co. University-and-water (with a dash of—no, not gin, but a little cheap claret in it). Fellows who, if you once get into their pillory, will pelt you with Greek roots, like so many cabbage-stumps." Hannay was at no loss for a reply, and in his second number included amongst his "Kicks and Halfpence" the following (and often-quoted) attack on the supposed "Bohemian" leanings of Sala and Brough:

> Easy to see why S. and B.
> Must hate the University.
> Easy to guess why B. and S.
> Must hate cold water little less.
> While by their works we know their creed
> That men who write should never read,
> Their faces show they think it bosh
> That men who write should ever wash.

And in a later number Sala was again, with equal unfairness, castigated:

> S. steals from ev'ry modern author's page:
> Yet in some circles S. is quite the rage.
> "A man of talent, S.," they all agree;
> "A man of letters;" yes—a man of three.

It might have been expected that so pugnacious a fellow as Sala would have immediately retorted in kind, but there came no riposte. None of his friends thought fit to offer a reply. As for the victim himself, he seemed to have disappeared off the face of the earth.

6

He was, to be frank, in a bad way.

A letter reached Yates from Paris in the second week of January. He had been ill, he wrote, utterly incapable of work, and, although better, was still suffering from "an incessant horrible pain in my head that nearly drives me mad." He had seen Dickens (who was making Paris his headquarters for the winter), and Dickens, he thought, "would do anything" for him. And there would be an essay ready for the *Train* at an early date. But the letter to Yates did not tell the whole story.

He was dreadfully unhappy and for the last few months had been drinking very heavily indeed. Now, too, like his father before him he was in the moneylenders' hands. Reading between the lines of the essays which he wrote at this time—he would speak of himself as unmarried and poor and without real friends—one is almost forced to conclude that he could not forget the old Lancaster days. Now, however, there were new worries. He was worried about his brother Charles who had gone to live in seclusion in the village of Erith (the Dumbledowndeary, by the way, so frequently mentioned in the *Household Words* essays): his health had taken a turn for the worse. He was worried about his mother at Brighton, now half-paralysed (though surprisingly enough in her seventieth year she was to make one more public appearance in London) and living on the minutest income. Above all, he was worried about himself. For all his growing reputation in literary circles he was almost unknown to the man in the street. He could make a bare living easily enough as a journalist, and once again words of his were to be heard on the London stage—he was the author of the "book" of the forthcoming pantomime at Covent Garden Theatre—but that security for which he had so long been pining remained curiously elusive. It was his own fault, no doubt, but if he was aware of the fact it only added

H

to his troubles. He wanted to take his place amongst the established writers of the day, and there seemed to be no immediate way of doing so.

It says much for him that at a time when he seemed to be sinking down so fast both Dickens and Thackeray went out of their way to be kind. For Sala Thackeray was to retain a warm regard until the day of his death. As we have seen, he thought highly of his writings, but he also enjoyed the younger man's conversation, and the fact that both of them could wield a clever pencil was an additional bond. They had met again at the Fielding Club, to which Sala had been brought as a guest one evening by Albert Smith, and Thackeray must have noticed that something was wrong, for he took the guest's arm, piloted him into an empty room, and there after talking gaily of the coming men and the work they were doing asked Sala to speak about himself. And "I have not forgotten, I hope," Sala wrote nearly forty years later, "one word of the wise and gentle counsel which Thackeray gave me that night, and how he bade me 'buckle my belt tight,' 'hang out my sign,' and ask him to come and take a chop with me." For a while a new ambition was fired : he would embark on some more serious piece of work. He would, he must, write *a book*. At once the ideal subject presented itself. From childhood he had been a keen student of Hogarth's work : he would write a Life of the great painter. A few mornings later he called on Thackeray to seek his advice. A Life of Hogarth ? The very thing! And on Sala's admission that he knew no publisher who would be likely to commission any such work, Thackeray sat down at his desk and wrote a letter of introduction to George Smith, head of the firm of Smith and Elder who published his own books. After which he walked with his visitor from Brompton to Piccadilly. It was a happy morning which Sala never forgot.

George Smith thought well of the project, and once again Sala went daily to the British Museum. But that for the moment was all, and when at the end of the year, ill and pursued by his creditors, he sought sanctuary once again in his beloved Paris, not a line of the book had been written.

We get the sorriest glimpse of him at this time from Dickens.

The novelist had lost none of his admiration for Sala's work, but it was becoming difficult to close his eyes to Wills's repeated complaints of unpunctuality and ever more frequent demands for payment in advance. Two years before, he had been able to write : "Sala is very good. Don't run him too close in the money way. I can't bear the thought of making anything like a hard bargain with him." And there had been nothing like a hard bargain. On the contrary, there had been a steadily rising debit account. For the last two months nothing of Sala's had reached the Wellington Street office, and Wills was now insisting that until this debt had been cleared off no further advances should be made. Dickens was loath to agree, but was obliged to admit that all was far from being well.

"Sala came here at 12 o'clock on Tuesday," he wrote on January 10th, "by appointment, at his solicitation. It was the second appointment. On the first occasion he was 20 minutes behind his time (but I really believe by accident), and of course I had gone out. He sat here *two hours*, telling me about his reputable friends at Erith, and so forth. I had no suspicion that he was postponing a request for money and couldn't make up his mind to make it, until at last he stammered out a petition for £5. I gave it him. Please place that sum to his debit and my credit. He told me he had sent two articles to you. I derived the idea," he went on, "that he was living very queerly here and not doing himself much good. He knew nothing, I observed, about the pieces at the Theatres, and suggested a strong flavour of the wine shop and the billiard table." Four days later he was writing again. "If Sala really has not sent those papers, it is a very, very bad business. But he described one of them to me, and I still hope that they may turn out to have been on the road while we have been communicating about them."

The two articles in question did ultimately arrive, and although Dickens continued to "distrust Sala's affairs" he managed to get him to work regularly again. "Albert Smith," he was telling Wills on January 19th, "has sent me a proof of his pamphlet about hotels. I, in my turn, have sent it to Sala, and suggested to him that he may write an article on the subject. I have *begged him* to send it to me here, thinking that may expedite him." He was right. Sala pulled himself together, and wrote four separate essays on the Great Hotel Question in reply to Albert Smith's pamphlet. Other articles followed, until Wills had a reserve enough for two months or more. It seemed, indeed, as if Sala, in common with most other Europeans, was now waking up from a very bad dream. At the beginning of February an armistice had been arranged between the Allied Powers and Russia, and a Conference fixed to take place in Paris. By the end of March the Treaty of Peace was signed, the new Czar had made a speech at Moscow inviting his late enemies to visit his country, and Sala saw a new chance for himself.

That speech, as he admitted himself, proved to be a turning-point in his career. Russia under its new Czar! That strange, slave-ridden country about which so few Englishmen knew anything at all: what a place to explore! He might have gone to the Crimea with his friend Soyer; he might have joined the small army of war correspondents:

something had kept him back. But nothing should keep him back now, and he would write such a book as never was. Dickens would help him : he had promised to help.

A long letter was written. Would Dickens agree to send him to St. Petersburg and Moscow in order that he might write "a series of descriptive essays touching Muscovy and the Muscovites, in the pages of *Household Words*" ? A reply came by return of post, "fully and very warmly and gladly" accepting the proposal, and a new, earnest, and enthusiastic Sala rushed to London to make his preparations.

CHAPTER EIGHT

THREE BOOKS—AND A HALF

I

THERE were a thousand things to be done, and Sala was eager not to lose a moment. A letter of his written from his old rooms in Exeter Change and sent to Wills with rough estimates of what he expected his expenses to be, shows very well his state of mind at the time.

"I should wish to press upon you," he declared, "most respectfully but most earnestly the necessity of my leaving London, at least, immediately. I *cannot* do good on route . . . I am surrounded here by dangers, temptations and ties, the only cure for which is a quick and sharp severance; and I am so deeply and seriously impressed with the importance of what I have attempted to do, that I would sooner cut my right hand off than incur the danger of relapse from the course of self-discipline and honourable conduct which I have prescribed for myself." In other words, there were to be no more Bohemian extravagances, no more expensive ladies, and no more drinking bouts. As for the estimates of expenses which he had "endeavoured to keep . . . within all margins of prudence and moderation," it would, he thought, "be false delicacy to Mr. Dickens and yourself to conceal the fact that I am not in a position to start in anything like respectability" without a separate grant for the necessary kit and his immediate requirements: £20 for his outfit, £15 to "leave at home" (either to pay his rent or for his mother's use), and £10 for living expenses. He was careful, however, to make no suggestion about the price to be paid for the Russian articles themselves. He had, he said, drawn up "the cost of fitting out the ship"—with £18 for his fare this came to £63—and, he added, "it is for you to estimate the value of the cargo."

His figures were not considered excessive, and the remuneration offered—£10 a week for a minimum of five months: on his next visit to Russia, it is interesting to note, he was paid at the rate of £100 a week—fully satisfied a Sala determined to practise the most rigid economy. At the same time, neither Dickens nor Wills was altogether easy in his mind. Much time would necessarily elapse before any Russian "copy" could be expected to arrive, and they had no guarantee that Sala's good intentions would hold. Obviously he was eager to avoid his creditors, and, no doubt, away from London he would be in a state more conducive to work, but there had been good resolutions before, and the debt to *Household Words* had not yet been cleared off. Wills as a good business man took all possible precautions with regard to the sums to be advanced, and even Dickens was minded to safeguard himself—in a way, as it happened, which, though quite legitimate, was to have unfortunate consequences for Sala. "I have no suggestion to offer," he wrote to Wills on April 20th, "on the subject of the credits, which seem to be well and carefully arranged. But I think that before he goes, you should draw up, and have legibly copied out, a memorandum of all the arrangements made and all the understandings entered into, and should attach your signature on my behalf, and make him attach his. In that memorandum you can state that the question of the partition of the copyright of the completed book, between Sala and H. W. is reserved until the book shall be producible." Sala, no doubt, was in a mood to sign anything which might help to expedite his departure from England, and so was sown the seed of that quarrel between Dickens and himself which was not only magnified absurdly at the time but was to lead to many, often grossly unfair, attacks upon him.

Meanwhile the preparations were being hurried on. A passport was procured for which the Russian *visa* was to be obtained in Berlin, there were visits to the tailors and shirt-makers—it was a little unfortunate that no dress-suit was ordered, for in St. Petersburg Sala found that this hitherto unworn garment was a necessity, and the Russian tailors proved to be hideously expensive—useful letters of introduction were forthcoming, and in the first week of May the young man who was to become about the best-known European traveller of his time crossed from Dover to Calais, stayed a few days in Berlin, and in due course reached Stettin, the Baltic seaport from which he proposed to proceed by boat.

At Stettin there was some delay. No steamer was due to start for Cronstadt for at least a week, and he crossed to Copenhagen in the hope of finding an earlier ship. He enjoyed his first sight of Denmark, but found no boat, and it was from Stettin that his friends in London had their first news of him. Already, it seemed, he was not too happy about the financial arrangements made for him. He had taken a berth, he told Wills, on the first available steamer, first class, for a sum of rather more than £9. "The second-class berths," he explained, "besides being intolerably nasty, are all taken up—the rush of Jews and Gentiles from here and Berlin being enormous." It was a lot of money, he was afraid, and he had thought of travelling post overland, but this would have meant a six days' journey through the most "abominable" country, and in order to secure a place in the mail-coach it would be necessary to give at least a fortnight's notice. So the fare to St. Petersburg had swallowed up the first week's salary, and—one can imagine Wills's feelings on reading the next sentence—"I am much afraid that I shall be three or four pounds short, and as a measure of safety I am unwillingly obliged to ask you to remit me Five pounds more." The letter contains some interesting particulars about the proposed series of articles. Their general title, for instance: what did Wills think of "Due North," "The Russians at Home," or "A Pocket Book in Russia Leather"? There would be no difficulty, he thought, about the transmission of the articles if he wrote them in the form of private letters, though if the Russian authorities gave trouble he was prepared to face it. "I am not afraid of anything short of the knout and Siberia," he concluded, "and if Lord Clarendon's passport and the 'Civis Romanus sum' won't save me from that peril I shall give in at once, solicit employment as a spy, change my name to Salakoff and embrace the orthodox Greek religion."

It was from Stettin, too, that he sent home to Edmund Yates his amusing set of verses entitled "Caviar and Rudesheimer" which were considered good enough to be printed in the *Train*. The last verse is often to be found, without its author's name, in the unlikeliest volumes:

> The King of Prussia drinks champagne;
>   Old Porson drank whate'er was handy;
> Maginn drank gin; Judge Blackstone, port,
>   And many famous wits drink brandy.
> Stern William Romer drinketh beer,
>   And so does Tennyson the rhymer;
> But I'll renounce all liquors for
>   My CAVIAR and RUDESHEIMER.

There was further news of him from St. Petersburg. The crossing had taken eighty hours, it had been bitterly cold, he had been "only provided with the ordinary amount of great coats," and by consequence he had nearly perished. As for the Russians, so far he had received at their hands the greatest politeness; he had found a clean hotel under German management; the strange sights and the costumes of the people had "dazed" him; and everything except vodka and beer was fabulously dear. The new dress-suit had cost him £6, and (for all his praise of Rudesheimer) he had been as sober as a judge from the moment he had left England. Cigars were sixpence apiece, which was a monstrous price; he sent his love to the ladies; and he intended to make £500 from his journey.

So far so good. True, the police had taken charge of his passport, but so much was to be expected. True, he was alone in a strange country, on a slender allowance, and unable to speak a word of the language, but he had met some charming Americans named Ward—the daughter was to end a distinguished career on the stage as Dame Geneviève—and their Minister had invited him to a Ball. Already he had gathered enough material for half a dozen articles, and a full-sized book was taking shape in his mind. In a little while, however, he was beginning to revise his views about the Russian police: they remained polite, but they were subjecting him to every kind of annoyance. They seem, in fact, to have become not a little suspicious of this Englishman who, without being either a wealthy mad lord or an official representative of any kind, was not apparently trying to *sell* anything. Why, then, had he come? More than once the question was asked, but, acting on advice, Sala made no mention of his work: he was merely a traveller from England. Soon enough, too, he discovered that his letters home were being opened. He was able to pass on this information to Wills (in a letter which no Russian could have been expected to understand), and it was agreed between them that nothing should be written for *Household Words* until he had stepped off Russian soil.

It was this decision which led to the numerous rumours circulating in London and elsewhere during that autumn. The "London Correspondent" of one of the provincial dailies was first in the field. Anxiety was being felt, he recorded, amongst Mr. Sala's friends: for some time now no news of him had reached them, and it was feared that he was in serious trouble with the Russian police. Within a week or so there were paragraphs in a score of newspapers, and the vaguest of rumours crystallised out into definite and alarming statements. The unfortunate gentleman had been expelled from St. Petersburg. He had been caught spying, and a bundle of incriminating papers had been found in his rooms. Worse, he had been secretly tried and sent to Siberia, where presumably the knout would be freely applied unless the British authorities were to take instant action. After which, of course, it was only to be expected that he had succumbed to the hardships of prison routine. There could be no doubt about it: Mr. George Augustus Sala was dead.

Even when it was authoritatively stated, in the last week in September, that he had safely passed the frontiers and was at the moment in Brussels, preparing an account of his experiences, there were many who refused to believe the news. Nor did the appearance of his first Russian article

in *Household Words*, early in October, succeed in altogether stamping
out the rumour.

And then, amusingly enough, that rumour was succeeded by another.
Good stuff, no doubt, this *Journey Due North*, but, of course, Sala had
never really been to Russia at all. The police would have stopped him
at the frontier. But he was a deuced clever fellow. He had bought
a lot of books about Russia, and spent an agreeable summer with them
in Brussels!

2

The earlier chapters of *A Journey Due North*, as printed in *Household
Words*, proved to be an undoubted success. They were vivid and lively
and delightfully intimate. Above all, they were almost strikingly
different from previous "travellers' tales." Here were no long and
learned disquisitions on Russia's politics or her geographical peculiarities
or her past history, of the kind which had hitherto been considered an
essential feature of any such book. There was no scientific interpretation
of the Russian character. Even the Czar himself was hardly mentioned,
and for Sala his palaces with their astonishing treasures might almost
never have existed. But he had not gone to Russia in order to elaborate
or correct earlier descriptions: he had gone as an ordinary sight-seer.
"I am incorrigible," he confessed. "If you want a man to explore
the interior of Australia, or to discover the North-West Passage, or
the sources of the Niger, don't send me. I should come back with a
sketch of Victoria Street, Sydney, or the journal of a residence in Cape
Coast Castle, or notes of the peculiarities of the skipper of a Hull whaler.
If ever I write a biography it will be the Life of John Smith; and the
great historical work which is to gild, I hope, the evening of my days,
will be a Defence of Queen Elizabeth from the scandal unwarrantably
cast upon her, or an Account of the Death of Queen Anne. Lo! I have
spent a summer in Russia; and I have nothing to tell you of the Altai
mountains, the Kirghese tribes, Chinese Tartary, the Steppes, Kamtschatka,
or even the Czar's coronation." But he had plenty to say about matters,
the smaller domestic matters, which during the past year or two had
been puzzling Englishmen so much. The man in the street, indeed,
was now given the answers to all the questions which it would naturally
have occurred to him to ask. What the streets and the houses and the
women were like; how people dressed, and what they ate and drank;
what goods were to be seen in the shop-windows and the prices asked;
the status of the moujik, and whether the slaves were knouted every
day for the pettiest offences; and, of course, the truth about the alleged

savagery of the police : it was to satisfy curiosity upon such points as
these that the Journey Due North had been undertaken, and the result
more than fulfilled the expectations of those who had made it possible.
Criticism there was. Interesting trivialities, thought the starchier
type of critic, but these rambling speculations "all about nothing"—
Russia ? "Too much Sala and too little Russia," said the wits. "Bugs,
boots, and beatings," they might have added, in reference to three of
the "speculations" which received lengthy treatment. As always, too,
with Sala when he became particularly interested in some little point,
it would remind him of some other little point, as likely as not nothing
to do with the Russians at all, and all thoughts of his journey would
be forgotten. Yet it is hardly an exaggeration to say that his chapter
on the police, whether as a piece of accurate description or as an essay
in restrained satire, has rarely been surpassed, and to this day *A Journey
Due North* provides as entertaining a personal record of travel as is to
be found elsewhere in contemporary literature. As such, indeed, it
was generally recognised at the time. Its appearance in *Household
Words* was anonymous, but everybody except the very few who
continued to believe that any article in the periodical which greatly
appealed to them *must* be Dickens's own work, now knew the name
of its author. When, moreover, some time in November and after
another spell of illness (which he erroneously thought must be due to
a diseased heart) Sala returned to London, it was to find himself not
yet, it is true, a celebrity, but an interesting literary figure described
more than once in the press as "the most picturesque essayist of the day."

For a little while he enjoyed the novelty of being somebody. True,
he was so far from having made the prophesied £500 from his travels
that he had been obliged to write to Wills for the money for his fare
home from Brussels and was once again endeavouring to raise loans
from one or two particular friends ; but three-quarters of the Russian
book had been written, and Vizetelly had welcomed him back to the
Illustrated Times, which had lost none of its popularity, and both Dickens
and Thackeray expressed the greatest interest in the articles and were
strongly urging him to make immediate arrangements for their
republication in book-form.

Their words were all the more welcome because Sala in his ignorance
had supposed that once he had received his weekly payments for the
articles he would cease to be "interested commercially" in their reappear-
ance. But if Dickens earlier in the year had wisely safeguarded himself,
he had no intention of being a hard taskmaster, provided that the full
series of articles were forthcoming, and so Sala found himself in the

pleasant position of having something of value to sell. He sought his brother's advice. Charles came up from his Kentish retreat, saw an old acquaintance of his who was now a successful publisher of cheap books, and within a few hours' time was able to announce that the firm of George Routledge and Sons was prepared to pay £250 for the book-rights.

It was a small fortune, and a fortune which would come to him for very little more work. Half a dozen further articles to write, perhaps a dozen or so which needed revision, and the money would have been earned. Assuredly the tide seemed to have turned. Vizetelly was giving him as much work as he could conveniently undertake, and, if all continued to go well, in the course of the next few months the *Illustrated Times* would be introducing him in a new role to the public. For some little time an idea for a novel had been simmering in his mind, and it was now beginning to take shape. Vizetelly was interested and agreed to begin its serial publication so soon as *A Journey Due North* should be completed in *Household Words*. If, moreover, the story in book-form were to produce any such "extra" sum as that promised by Routledge, it was more than probable that within a twelvemonth or so he would be able to free himself entirely from all his financial liabilities.

The £250, however, never came his way. Idiotically and inexcusably he chose this moment to quarrel with Dickens.

It is difficult to understand the exact course of that sorry affair. Sala himself gives an account which seems to be fairly clear, but only until such letters relating to the affair as have survived come to be examined. The one indisputable fact is that the Russian series in *Household Words* ended with marked abruptness after the twenty-second instalment.

It was freely said at the time that Dickens had stopped the articles on purely literary grounds. Percy Fitzgerald, another of his Young Men and almost as prolific a writer as Sala himself, maintained that *Household Words* had been "greatly injured" by the vagaries in some of the later chapters. Readers, he thought, had had far too much about cab-drivers and the like, and Sala, he was sure, had become tired of a piece of work which he would fain have finished in Russia itself. There was probably some truth in this last statement, but no letter of Dickens supports the contention that he was dissatisfied with the work. On the other hand there is no doubt that he was becoming increasingly anxious about the unpunctual delivery of the chapters—a definite number had been promised—and it was just here that Sala, as he afterwards admitted, put himself in the wrong.

The later chapters, to use his own words, were hanging fire, there was other work which he was eager to do, and for that work he was being well paid. True, he had been paid for his Russian articles, but had not a good portion of that £240 gone in legitimate expenses? Ought he not to receive further sums on that account? Wills was approached on the matter and very rightly reminded him of the fact that in addition to the agreed weekly stipend he had also received a sum of money to enable him to prepare for the journey. Whereupon Sala, deciding that "the most picturesque essayist of the day" was not a man to be dictated to in this fashion, bluntly declined to write any further Russian chapters without additional payment.

He was not prepared for what followed.

Dickens, naturally, was angry. He refused to see Sala, and referred him to his solicitor who, it would seem, was instructed to say that after the Russian articles already written had been printed, *Household Words* would have no further use for his services.

This, for Sala, was a rude shock, and he seems to have realised that he had gone too far. An unfinished book would hardly meet Routledge's requirements. There was probably some sort of an apology; he agreed to provide the full number of articles; and Dickens, though maintaining his decision to accept no further work from his pen after the Russian series, generously allowed him to draw upon Wills for money while his articles continued to appear.

One or two of the new chapters seem to have been delivered on time, but there were further delays, and in March Dickens's patience came to an end. He had done his best, but his kindness had not been rewarded: very well, then, this must be the end. On Sala's behalf only one point can be raised. For some time now Charles Sala had been complaining of his heart, and it was in a darkened room at his Erith home that his brother toiled at the last of his Russian articles and began to write his first novel. For a while the doctor's reports had been reassuring, but in the second week of February there was a sudden turn for the worse, and he died in his brother's arms. An inquest was considered necessary—the actual cause of death was apoplexy —and Sala, rushing frantically between Erith, London, and Brighton, had little time and less inclination for work. He was genuinely devoted to his brother, and the shock was great. Even so, however, he was hardly justified in beginning his novel before completing his Russian task. There came a second and final visit to Dickens's solicitor. No further chapters would now be required, and there would be no further payments. So be it, said Sala, and prepared to go. But there was worse to come. According to the memorandum signed by both parties before the Russian journey had been undertaken, it had been agreed that all questions of copyright were to be reserved until the completed book should be producible, and in the circumstances, he was told, Mr. Dickens felt unable to grant permission for the reproduction of any of his essays which had appeared in *Household Words*.

Today, this unexpected embargo may seem a little harsh, but Dickens was fully within his rights, and it is not difficult to understand his annoyance. But if Dickens was annoyed, Sala was furious, and now perhaps for the first time those who were his admiring friends must have realised what a wild and prickly fellow he could be when affairs did not go to his liking. There would be an initial burst of anger, and then, as somebody said, the volcano would be in continuous eruption. A torrent of abuse would be poured out which it was not always easy to forget or forgive even though the humblest apology might be forthcoming when his passion had spent itself. Just now, too, the torrent was all the fiercer because, to be frank, Sala was suffering from swollen head. He seems to have rushed round London attacking Dickens and Wills and making a general nuisance of himself. Dickens of all people, the man widely lauded as a warm-hearted friend of the poor, the social reformer, the pillar of Victorian rectitude, to rob a hard-working wretch of £250! It was monstrous, the meanest trick, an insult which he would never forget.

Luckily for him, he had not yet quarrelled with Vizetelly, and the week after *A Journey Due North* ceased to appear in *Household Words,* the first chapters of his novel *The Baddington Peerage* were printed in the columns of the *Illustrated Times*.

3

It may be admitted that as a novelist Sala was definitely poor and sometimes almost laughably bad. His powers of invention were meagre and his men and women seldom other than puppets. His plots were of the conventional order, and often it would seem as if he had temporarily forgotten the necessity for their orderly development. As in his essays he would become interested in some out-of-the-way morsel of information or oddity of human behaviour, be reminded of other curious affairs not wholly dissimilar, and ramble on, agreeably enough and buttonholing the reader in his intimate way, until with a jerk he would wake up to the fact that he was supposed to be telling a story. But, as he once told Wills, "I am not Wilkie Collins, or Mrs. Gaskell, or

Charles Reade: I depend entirely on pictures of manner, sketches of character, and general maunderings thereupon, and my plots are merely pegs on which to hang the old clothes of world experience which I have gathered up in my bag." And so it is that you can take up any of his novels and, choosing a page at random, be almost certain of finding entertainment of some kind or another, even though it may have little or no connection with any of the people whose story is being unfolded. Indeed, it may well be that these rather whimsical digressions —their one original feature—were largely responsible for such success as his earlier novels obtained. All four of them were reprinted more than once and were still finding a market more than thirty years after their first appearance in print.

It is amusing today to read the mid-Victorian second-raters and to observe with what care they upheld the recognised canons of literary taste. Dickens might continue to write about "low" people (and still be abused for it in the *Saturday Review* and other polite quarters), but your lesser men felt obliged to introduce Mr. Mudie's subscribers to social circles at least as high as their own, and preferably higher. Unconscionable villains there might be, some of them nobly born— now, indeed, was the hey-day of the black-moustached and evil-minded Sir Jasper—but it was rare for a hero to belong to the working-classes, and a novel without at least one peer of the realm or a Dowager Duchess was hardly a novel at all. It is interesting, too, to note the number of novels which were written round the theme of the missing or unknown or false or rightful heir. Readers, it would seem, in the 'fifties and 'sixties could not have enough of him, together with his inevitable companions, the family lawyer, the handsome scapegrace, and the cruelly ill-used and impossibly virtuous young woman whose marriage-lines (or, alternatively, locket and ring which the faithful old retainer might be expected to recognise at the right moment) would remain lost or hidden away by interested parties until the penultimate chapter. Naive and artificial such stories may seem to us, though none, surely, was stranger or less probable than that which was to be unfolded in the Law Courts a decade or so later—I shall have more to say of the Tichborne case in a little while—but at the time they exactly suited the public taste, and no doubt Sala was well advised to begin his career as a novelist with yet another story of a missing heir.

The Baddington Peerage, instantly dubbed by the wits "The Paddington Beerage" or "The Badly Done Peerage," in its original form was described as "Being the Lives of Their Lordships: a Story of the Best and the Worst Society," and it began well enough. There were illustrations by Phiz, and curiosity was aroused by the intimate method adopted; but it soon became clear that its author was being content to furbish up the merest potpourri of previous "romances of the peerage." True, there was a villain who dared to be jocose, and there were picturesque scenes which Dickens himself might have written; but otherwise the story had little to recommend it, and even after it had been altered and revised for publication as a three-volume novel, it remained the stagiest of melodramas, interesting only to the historian eager to discover new sidelights on the social customs and eccentricities of the day. "The worst novel ever written." That was Sala's own verdict in later years, and he was not being mock-modest. He had soon realised his own limitations and could afford to laugh at his earlier mistakes. Even at the time he was conscious that this first novel of his was not the work which he had envisaged, and there is a typical personal passage in one of the later chapters which is not without its touch of genuine pathos :

"Throughout these hazy pages—these sheets written in danger and distress, in sickness and contumely—commenced in a darkened room surrounded by the shadows of death, and drawing rapidly to a limping termination now in a strange land, far away from the friends I love and the kinsfolk who love me not—I have never dared to decide *myself* what were the real motives, the thoughts in the holy of holies of the hearts of the people whose shadowy likenesses I have drawn. I have endeavoured, so far as my lights will permit me, to tell you what they thought and felt; but there are secrets in their souls I cannot fathom. For all shadowy as they are, and rudely and clumsily depicted, I Believe in my people. They are not puppets, they are not marionettes; they are not sticks and stones. They exist. They do. They would walk and talk, they would live and breathe, if a more cunning hand than mine could lift the curtain that veils them."

The wonder is that the story was ever completed at all. "I don't think," he wrote in 1860, "there was ever a book written in such a desultory and shiftless manner. The beginning differed very much from the commencement I had originally planned; the end was hastened, blurred and truncated; and I am afraid that the middle was wanting altogether. The chapters of *The Baddington Peerage* had to struggle and take their chance with leading articles, criticisms on picture exhibitions, theatrical notices and descriptive essays on woodcuts." As he tells us in the passage quoted above, he was, for part of the time, out of England—apparently in order to avoid his creditors who had not become less persistent since his name had come prominently before the public—but there was another reason why the "middle" seemed occasionally to be "wanting altogether," for work of another kind had unexpectedly come his way, and it was work, as he was soon to find, which was far better suited to his powers than fiction.

4

Two years previously journalistic history had been made. At the end of June, 1855, a new twopenny daily newspaper had been founded by a Colonel Sleigh. The *Daily Telegraph and Courier* did not prosper, and the Colonel soon found himself in financial difficulties. His largest creditor was Mr. Joseph Moses Levy, the head of a firm of printers who had recently become chief proprietor of the *Sunday Times*. Levy, a man of vision with ideas ahead of his day, agreed to take over the struggling journal in settlement of his claims, and on September 17th of the same year he startled London by issuing the *Daily Telegraph* at a penny, an innovation in price which at the time was considered suicidal. How, people asked, could anything good be expected of a newspaper which was "practically given away"? Assuredly it would be nothing but the cheapest trash. From the beginning, however, Levy's paper was most ably edited, it appealed to the man in the street inasmuch as it steered a cunning course between the highly-starched dignity of the *Times* and the *Morning Post* and the sensationalism of lesser publications, and soon enough it began to make its presence felt. Nor was this surprising, for not only was the *Daily Telegraph* up-to-date with its news, but it was, I suppose, the first responsible daily to contain what came to be called a "magazine element." Its news, that is to say, was presented, when possible, in the way of a story, and the scope of its leading articles was broadened to include a novel survey of the more intimate affairs of life. More, expressions of opinion on current topics were welcomed not only from prominent people accustomed to see their names in print, but also and more particularly from unknown members of the public; and if more space than was considered seemly in some quarters was devoted to crime, support was also forthcoming in no uncertain measure for what were known as "good causes." The newspaper, in fact, was something different, one destined to appeal to men and women of average intelligence but especially aimed to reach those who had not hitherto provided themselves regularly with a daily digest of the news. Today one may wonder at the feeling roused against it, but at the time and for a considerable period it was very generally regarded as a bumptious upstart, and privileges freely accorded to older-established newspapers were almost contemptuously withheld from those on its staff.

By the beginning of 1857 the *Daily Telegraph* was doing very well. The time had not yet come when it could boast of its ten or twelve pages, its wonderful printing-machines capable of producing so many thousands of sheets every hour, or its "largest circulation in the world," but its readers were steadily increasing in numbers, and Levy was now prepared to risk almost his entire fortune in the venture. Already he had engaged the services of some good men, Leigh Hunt's son and Edmund Yates among them, and in his eldest son Edward, afterwards Sir Edward Levy-Lawson and first Lord Burnham, he had an altogether exceptional assistant who in his room in the Peterborough Court offices was even then dreaming of gigantic strides and was soon to be the virtual head of the entire organisation. But more good men were required on the staff, and Edward Levy was eagerly searching for them. In common with many other shrewd judges he had been favourably impressed by the second or "inner" leading articles to be found in the *Illustrated Times*. One in particular had delighted him, and he had enquired of Yates who its author might be. Sala's name was given him. And where, he asked, was the author of *The Baddington Peerage* living? He would like to communicate with him. But this budding novelist, it seemed, was very shy when it came to the point of revealing his address. Very well then, would Yates arrange a meeting?

The meeting was arranged, at the *Daily Telegraph* offices, and, some time in the spring of 1857, Sala paid his first visit to the building where so much of his best work was to be done, and met the man who for so many years was to be his principal employer. He must have realised the importance of the occasion, for he went to the greatest trouble to array himself in fine garments. As usual there was little available cash for new clothes, but with the aid of two brothers who were anticipating the activities of the Moss Bros. of a later generation, he succeeded in making what was certainly an impressive appearance. There was, first of all, a chocolate-coloured frock coat, and this, being his own property, fitted him rather better than did the trousers "of uncertain hue" which had been hired for the day. The blucher boots which went with them suggested any profession rather than a journalist's, but no doubt they were finely polished and exuded a pleasant hint of affluence. It was the waistcoat, however, which seems to have attracted Edward Levy's particular attention, even though as the years passed his memories of its glories became dimmed. In a short while Sala was to adopt as a kind of uniform without which in the day-time he hardly cared to be seen, a waistcoat of wondrous whiteness and a tie of flaming crimson, but for this momentous interview he had chosen, also out of the costumier's stock, "a black camlet vest, profusely embroidered with beads and bugles of jet." This, it seems, was his idea of the "exceptionally smart waistcoat" which, he felt, would be proper to the occasion. What part it may have played in their subsequent discussions does not appear, but Edward Levy forthwith engaged his gaily-dressed visitor to write occasional articles, and Sala returned to his Exeter Change rooms in a pardonably excited state.

There was no written contract—there never was to be a written contract, and, strictly speaking, Sala was never "on the staff" at all—but it was understood that for the time being any work which he might submit would be favourably considered, and in the event of its proving to be what was required, he might expect in due course to be commissioned to write one or more leading articles for every number. Which is more or less what happened. At first there were no editorial conferences to decide upon subjects : at irregular intervals Sala submitted articles on current topics—home politics alone excepted—and, so far as I know, none was declined. On the contrary, Levy was soon in a position to know that he had found the right man. These lively little essays might be florid, they might lack "importance," but they had their appeal : they were precisely what he and his growing public wanted in the way of critical commentary. Gradually Sala's contributions became more frequent, and within a year or two, though unsalaried and expected to submit a weekly account, he had become not only a valuable member of the "outside" staff but also a journalist whose novel methods were beginning to be imitated in more than one quarter. Nor was this all, for soon enough he was much more than one of a small team of "leader-writers" : he had become the *Daily Telegraph's* art critic and, what was of far greater importance, the chief of its special correspondents.

And so it was that at the age of twenty-nine he found that regular and permanent job for which he had been hoping since his scene-painting days. Thirty years or more were to pass, and still the *Daily Telegraph* had first call on his services. There might be a new novel or volume of essays to be written, an editorial chair to be filled, or a weekly article to be provided for some other periodical : always the *Daily Telegraph* came first, and more than once he was obliged to leave all his London work to depart, at little more than a moment's notice, for some distant country on its behalf.

This new work meant an appreciable increase in his income—he must have been earning more than £15 a week—but it did not mean that he had become any less impecunious. His creditors refused to leave him alone, and try as he would he could never manage to satisfy all their claims and so make a fresh start. He was not, at this time, unduly extravagant, though he was beginning to form a library of books and could rarely resist a fine Hogarth print, but I fancy that he was making his mother a small allowance, and already he was discovering the delights of playing host to friends. But he was working hard, and not only at his writing, for, as a note-book of his shows, he was zealously pursuing his studies of Latin and Greek, and even now was continuing to copy out in a fine copperplate passages from the older historians and essayists which particularly appealed to him. There were friends of his, indeed, who were never able to understand how he managed to do so much. A case of burning the midnight oil? No, for of an evening he was almost certainly to be found in one of the three or four taverns in the neighbourhood of Drury Lane. Now, too, by day he was frequently to be seen in less Bohemian quarters, for his American friends, the Wards, had come to London and insisted on his joining their little circle. Then *when*, people wondered, did he do his work? A mysterious fellow. But what good company he could be—as long as he remained sober! A little too fond, perhaps, of relating his Russian experiences and too easily inclined to take offence, but how knowledgeable and how witty! How amusing to listen to his arguing with the Broughs or the Mayhews, teasing old Dr. Strauss, or composing some ribald rhyme! Obviously one of the coming men and very generally liked. And it was now that he played his part—a rather larger part than has been realised even by its accredited historians—in the founding of the Savage Club.

Whose idea it was that an inexpensive Bohemian club should be founded by the little group of authors, journalists, and artists who were accustomed to forgather at a particular tavern, or who suggested the name adopted, are questions which may continue to be debated, for there are contradictory accounts all of which probably contain a germ of the truth; but it was Sala, I find, who played the chief part in arranging the preliminary meetings and he who acted as honorary secretary until the original members formally banded themselves together. His letter summoning the first meeting was sent to a score or more of his friends, most of them men who wrote regularly in the *Illustrated Times,* some of Yates's contributors to the *Train,* now in its fourth volume, and others like Henry J. Byron, the playwright, and Landells, the engraver:

"Thursday, eighth October, 1857.

"DEAR SIR,

"The favour of your presence is requested at a meeting of gentlemen connected with literature and the fine arts, and warmly interested in the promotion of Christian knowledge and the sale of exciseable liquors, to be held at the 'Crown' Tavern, Vinegar Yard, Drury Lane, on Monday the 12th. Instant at five o'clock : p.m. ; there and then to confer upon the expediency of forming a social society or club, hereafter to receive a suitable designation, and to have its *habitat* at the 'Crown' Tavern aforesaid.

"I am, Dear Sir,
"yours very faithfully
"GEORGE: AUG: SALA:
"Hon: Sec: pro: tem:"

He might have been considerably surprised had he lived to see into what palatial quarters his Brother Savages were to remove, some eighty years later.

5

So that year drew to its close. From rebellious India came the welcome news of the Relief of Lucknow, and Parliament was recalled, to deal, amongst other minor crises, with the widespread alarm occasioned by recent commercial failures in the City. In December Sala slipped away to Paris in time to witness Orsini's attempt to assassinate the Emperor and Empress, but he was home again for the wedding of the Princess Royal and Prince Frederick William of Prussia. And while Vizetelly was thinking of a new magazine to rival *Household Words*, Sala himself was planning a new literary scheme which was destined to make his name with the general public. For him, indeed, 1858 was to be *annus mirabilis* : a year of happy surprises and surprising successes ; a year when even some of the shrewdest judges believed—mistakenly— that a new literary star of the first magnitude had arisen.

When at the beginning of May Vizetelly with a flourish of trumpets launched the *Welcome Guest*, an illustrated weekly quarto issued at a penny, he was not yet assured that in Sala he had found his most valuable contributor. Pride of place was given to a translation of a novel by a then popular German author, Gustav Freytag, and amongst his hundred and twenty thousand readers there were many who were delighted with the rather conventional excitements of the story called, in its English dress, *Debit and Credit*. It very soon became clear, however, that the chief attraction was Sala's *Twice Round the Clock*—a series of papers which attempted to describe "the London of our day as we have seen it and as we know it."

Now, this vivid panorama is, to my mind, by far the best book that Sala ever wrote and one which may be read today with the greatest pleasure alike for its mass of curious information and for the lively entertainment it affords. I admit its faults, as Sala did himself. The idea was not original—it came to him from an old volume called *Low Life* issued precisely a hundred years before, which had been lent to him by Dickens, and "I confess," he wrote in the following year, "that I thought as little of *Twice Round the Clock* in the earlier hours of its publication as the critics of the *Saturday Review*—who, because I had contributed to another periodical whose Conductor they hold in hatred, have been pleased to pursue me with an *acharnement* quite exciting to experience—may think of it now. I looked upon the articles as mere ephemeral essays, of a description of which I had thrown off hundreds during a desultory, albeit industrious, literary career. But I found ere long that I had committed myself to a task whose items were to form an Entirety in the end; that I had begun the first act of a Drama which imperatively demanded working out to its catastrophe. I grew more interested in the thing; I took more pains; I felt myself spurred on to accuracy by the conscientious zeal of the admirable artist, Mr. William M'Connell, whose graphic and truthful designs"—nearly fifty in number —"embellished my halting text." Yet halting or verbose, pretentious or superficial though it might be—I use Sala's own words—there was real feeling in the work, and even those not usually prone to enthusiasm were both touched and excited, and wrote to the editor of the *Welcome Guest* to say so. There was, in fact, a steady stream of letters. Who, exactly, was this Mr. Augustus Sala? An Englishman? How ought his name to be pronounced? (Sarla, said the editor.) Was it true that he had written *A Journey Due North* as well as scores of other articles in *Household Words*? It was. Then would the editor (who, by the way, was generally believed to be Sala himself, though this was not so) be kind enough to give a list of the best of them? He did so, and the letters took an even more gratifying turn. On a sudden, it seemed, Mr. Augustus Sala had become a popular favourite. As we have seen, the *Saturday Review* could find no good word to say, but apart from its attack, a curious allusion from an anonymous correspondent to Sala's "vile Spanish blood and weak hair," and the *Islington Gazette's* ill-tempered notice of what it called his "flippant, ungentleman-like, unchristian fanfaronade," hardly a critical voice was raised.

And it was while Sala was basking in this new-found popularity during the early summer that his quarrel with Dickens was most unexpectedly and happily brought to an end : a fact which was incidentally responsible for introducing him to an even larger public.

At the time Dickens was at the parting of the ways. In an ill-advised statement which he asked, and, indeed, expected, all London editors to print, he announced to the world his own domestic crisis : he and his wife had agreed to live apart. Many newspapers, including the *Daily Telegraph*, printed the statement without comment ; a few, the *Liverpool Mercury* in their van, printed it with a more or less stinging commentary ; one or two, like *Punch*, ignored it altogether. The public, of course, was eager to lap up so juicy a morsel of scandal. Everywhere the affair was being discussed. Dickens of all people in the world, the man who had come to stand for what was most solidly respectable in English life, the man who in all his work had been the staunchest upholder of family integrity and had pleaded so earnestly for a kindlier and more generous understanding of others : *Dickens* involved in a vulgar and rather disgraceful business of this kind ! People took sides, and in a majority of cases, I fancy, were strong supporters of his wife. Only the very few, however, had any knowledge of the real facts of the case—facts which go to show that while there were faults on both sides Dickens was certainly no saint—and amongst these few was Sala. He was never to be numbered amongst Dickens's most intimate friends, but like Mark Lemon, Forster, Wilkie Collins, and Edmund Yates, he knew the whole rather miserable story and could easily have rivalled the *Liverpool Mercury* in blunt speaking. He chose to say nothing, except by implication. In one of his leading articles in the *Daily Telegraph* there was a passage which, though guarded, could not be misunderstood by those who were minded to gloat at a famous man's private misfortunes. More than once Sala himself had suffered from "poisonous" rumours, and his words were sincere. He was still angry with Dickens, but he shared the novelist's hatred of hypocrisy, and could not bring himself to remain wholly silent. Dickens, it seems, saw the passage, enquired who the writer might be, and at once in his happy, impulsive way, extended a hand. There must be no further misunderstandings and no more talk of legal rights. The *Journey Due North* was now Sala's again, and with it was to go the copyright in any other essay of his in *Household Words* which he cared to reprint.

It was a great day for Sala when that hand was extended to him again, though those which followed it brought their disappointments. Unfortunately for him public interest in Russian affairs had by this time considerably abated, and Mr. Routledge felt unable to renew his handsome offer of eighteen months ago. Other publishers seemed equally chary. Finally, however, Richard Bentley agreed to pay £75, with a further £75 should a second edition be called for, and almost at the same time Sala was able to arrange for the publication of two separate volumes of his *Household Words* essays. As, moreover, he had just completed for the *Welcome Guest* a short humorous story called *How I Tamed Mrs. Cruiser*, he felt that he was now fully entitled to a few weeks' holiday.

So there came that lively if not wholly successful visit to Homburg with Vizetelly and Augustus Mayhew, which led, indirectly, to yet another indecorous quarrel, an exceedingly serious "accident," and— Sala's marriage.

6

It happened that big, bluff Gus Mayhew, who in the previous year had published his very successful *Paved with Gold*, had just received a modest legacy. It happened that Vizetelly in his leisure moments had invented what seemed to him to be an infallible system whereby the fortune of a Monte Cristo could be acquired at the roulette table. It will be remembered, also, that Sala had lost the remains of his Aunt Eliza's legacy in a continental gambling-saloon. He had not forgotten that calamity, and had frequently announced his intention of leaving "no stone unturned to recover it." When, therefore, the three of them decided to enjoy a holiday together little argument was needed over the matter of their destination: they would go to Homburg, "then the Monte Carlo of Germany," and proceed, very coolly and methodically, to break the bank.

The details of their pilgrimage need not be given here: they are to be found in a nicely-embroidered but fairly truthful if bowdlerised account of their adventures which Sala was soon to publish under the title of *Make Your Game*. It will be enough to say that although they thoroughly enjoyed themselves and there was not the slightest hint of an impending quarrel, the holiday ended in financial disaster. At first, of course, the system worked. Within a day or two Vizetelly had won more than £1000 and the other two almost as much between them. And then, and equally of course, the system unaccountably broke down. In desperation all three devised new systems of their own, and at the end of a fortnight were penniless. There was even some awkwardness with the hotel proprietor while Vizetelly was waiting for the money, sufficient to pay their fares home, for which he had telegraphed. At

Dover too, Sala, who was now considerably in his editor's debt, was dismayed to read in the *Times* a forthright attack on his just-published *Journey Due North*. This, at the time, seemed to him to be the last straw, and it was in a very poor temper that he returned to London.

It would seem, however, that the notice in the *Times* roused public curiosity, and other more favourable reviews followed. Within a few weeks Bentley was informing him that the first edition of his book had been exhausted, and that a second was required at once. Yet the book's success was not to prove an unmixed blessing, for now in addition to private creditors the Inland Revenue authorities were pressing for moneys due, and, to use his own words, he was "forced to lie very low indeed." It was at this time that Shirley Brooks, who had recently been appointed editor of the *Literary Gazette*, wrote to him suggesting contributions. "I should be glad, I am sure," was the reply, "to do anything for the L.G. 'on the quiet.' I mention tranquillity as the infernal Income tax people and other miscreants who believe I am making a thousand a year watch me like a cat a mouse and pounce on me for 'more' directly they detect me in print." Vizetelly, too, was no longer the gay holiday-maker that he had been, but inclined to be "difficult." For all its large circulation the *Welcome Guest* had been losing money, Sala had not paid his Homburg debts, and, like the Inland Revenue authorities, was asking for "more," and on more than one occasion there had been trouble about the unpunctual delivery of "copy."

It is a little difficult to understand the exact position of affairs during those winter months, but there is no doubt that Sala was in a curiously excited state and at one time seriously ill. He was working feverishly when the mood was upon him, but for days at a time he would disappear altogether. His mother's health was now giving him cause for alarm and he was often at Brighton, but it was the growing craving for drink which generally took him away, usually at moments when "copy" was most urgently required. It may be that in his endeavours to be clear of his debts he had engaged himself to do too much. In addition to his leading articles for the *Daily Telegraph*, there was his work for the *Illustrated Times* (including several long essays on Carlyle's new book *Frederick the Great*), a special Christmas number of the *Welcome Guest* with several sketches and stories of his own, a careful revision of the Russian book, and the opening chapters of *Make Your Game*, which had been widely advertised to appear in the first week of January. Even so, however, he had only himself to thank for the legal proceedings in which he became involved when the clearest promises remained unfulfilled, and, indeed, for the "accident" which might easily have cost him his life. Neither could have been wholly unexpected by those who knew him best. He might be in poor health, he might be miserably unhappy, and that unfortunate love-affair about which so little is known might have been responsible in the first place for his ever more frequent drinking-bouts; but how could any dependence be placed on a man liable to be found any day in a drunken stupor? Vizetelly was not the kind of man who would ordinarily have had recourse to the law against a personal friend, but, like Wills, he realised that with Sala in one of his most unsatisfactory moods only one course of action was likely to prove efficacious: supplies must be cut off and their place taken by a solicitor's letter.

As a result the serial publication of *Make Your Game* was rudely interrupted, and for several months it seemed that this time the public would have to be satisfied with half a book.

CHAPTER NINE

INTERLUDE: NASAL AND MATRIMONIAL

I

In his youth and in spite of that "duffer" eye Sala was not ill-looking; in his middle and later years his appearance was hardly attractive. He was a heavy man, short and stoutish, and his face was blotched and coarse-featured: distinctly a florid person. Not unlike his own literary style, said Hain Friswell in an essay which, as we shall see, was to bring him to the Law Courts, and, he added maliciously, a *coloured* photograph would best illustrate the truth of that remark. This had reference to a feature which, alike for its size, its peculiar contours, and its fiery hues, was destined to become, as another journalist once facetiously observed, "Fleet Street's most prominent landmark." Sala's nose, indeed, was like nothing else in the civilised world. It was a potato of a nose, a bludgeon of a nose, a very gargoyle of a nose; an angry and blustering nose which at moments would seem to be gathering purple patches into its expanse of crimson; a nose which, as strangers at first sight must instinctively have felt, would never permit the slightest sign of amused curiosity: a warning beacon of a nose, in fact. Yet curiously enough and luckily for all concerned, Sala himself, usually so ready to take offence, was rarely disturbed by any reference to his "olfactory organ," and on more than one occasion made fun of it in his own writings. Once, it is true, he administered a sharp and not very delicate though witty rebuke to a young Guardee who had spoken disrespectfully of it—"you must be the snot that ran down my nose," said he, on being introduced to the culprit at a Mess dinner—but in general he never allowed its peculiarities to disturb him. Even in his late twenties it was to him an object for chuckles and in his account of the Homburg trip, though in reference to an enormous box which contained all his luggage he usually spoke of himself as the Man with the Iron Chest, he frequently described himself as the Man with the Nose—a nose, he wrote, which was *such* a red one that when its owner was comfortably replete it would "shine like a fog signal."

That, however, was before it had been punched and battered and broken into its final and most unnatural shape—a never-to-be-forgotten and indecorous event which occurred in the first days of 1859.

Relations at the time with Vizetelly were distinctly strained. A few weeks before there had been trouble over the Christmas number of the

Welcome Guest—at the last moment part of the work which Sala had agreed, and been paid, to do had had to be given to other contributors—and there had been delay with the opening chapters of *Make Your Game*. Copy had also been promised for the *Illustrated Times*, but was not forthcoming. There were almost daily demands from Vizetelly, but from his rooms in Salisbury Street—another address which was known only to a very few people—Sala continued to be evasive. He was in his most difficult mood, alternately petulant and abusive, ill perhaps, though more probably half-drunk, willing to work but only at moments convenient to himself. Why, he complained, couldn't they leave him alone? In due course the promised chapters would be forthcoming, but would editors *never* understand that something more than pens, ink, and paper were required for the production of literary work? Peace of mind, for one thing, and how was any man expected to work when he was being hourly dunned and hunted from pillar to post? Perhaps Vizetelly did not realise that he was not the only taskmaster in the field? All in good time. . . . Then on January 7th, a Friday, Vizetelly wrote another letter which seems to have roused his dilatory contributor to fury. The second chapter of *Make Your Game* had been completed and delivered—Sala had sat up all the previous night for the purpose—but some alterations were required at once and with them the much-overdue Chapter III. And there was a veiled hint that any further delay might have consequences which would be particularly distasteful.

It was too much. Angrily Sala scribbled a reply. "You seem to take a delight in working me into a frenzy of excitement . . . every time you want copy. . . . I cannot stand this continual strain on my brain: it is more than Angus Reach ever stood who went mad through it, and as soon as I am out of your debt I shall give up journalism altogether and take to book-work. I wonder," he added in a burst of self-pity, "how many of the people who see my portrait this week [in the *Welcome Guest*] know what a hunted devil I am." But he would no longer allow himself to be hunted, and not another word would he write: he must have laughter and gaiety, amusing companions and champagne.

It was late when he sauntered forth to seek them, but in those days there was no lack of "night houses" and most of them kept open until daylight. Somewhere he found friends of his to share an uproarious supper, and then slipped away, apparently by himself, to a Panton Street establishment where, as it happened, he was wholly unknown.

Except in one particular it seems to have differed little from the majority of such places. There were beautiful ladies, music of a kind, and comfortable chairs for those who were not dancing. Also there

was champagne. Unfortunately the price demanded for the champagne
was even higher than that which most night-house proprietors dared to
ask. Sala, now in his most bellicose mood, sent for the proprietor's wife,
and there was an angry dispute. It was an unheard-of imposition: he
had not the slightest intention of paying any such price. The proprietor,
a Jew, appeared on the scene, and he was not polite. Whereupon Sala,
whose language on occasion could be forthright, shouted out genealogical
and racial insults. On a sudden the dispute turned into a brawl. Sala
raised his fists, but unfortunately for him his opponent was well
accustomed to deal with troublesome clients. Even more unfortunately
he was wearing, as so many of his race like to do, several diamond rings,
and diamond rings on the fingers can be used as weapons of a particularly
savage nature. Sala fought as best he could, but in a few moments he
"took the floor," with the now infuriated Hebrew astride his chest
raining un-Queensberrylike blows on his luckless nose. One of these
blows succeeded in splitting it open "throughout its entire length."
After which, the half-insensible man, streaming with blood, was "dexter-
ously rolled into the street."

In those days Panton Street, with the Haymarket and other near
neighbours, was no very reputable quarter. Ironically enough Sala himself had already called attention to its dangers, and in the *Daily Telegraph*
was repeatedly to attack the authorities for their refusal to put an end to
"so vicious a cesspool." By night the police were rarely to be found
there, and the goriest of private battles could be waged without official
interference. And Sala, no doubt,
might have lain where he was, on
the pavement, until sufficiently recovered to stagger away, had not
the proprietor of another night-house
next door, a man named Coney who
knew him, hurried out to see what
was amiss. Coney picked him up
and administered first aid, and an
hour later the wretched and now
sobered man was in Charing Cross
Hospital, where a surgeon stitched
up his nose.

He remained in bed for a fortnight
or more. Work was almost impossible, but with help from George
Hodder and one of the Kenneys—his companions at supper before th

SALA'S SKETCH OF HIMSELF AFTER THE
" ACCIDENT "

"accident"—he managed to complete a leading article or two, though no attempt was made to continue *Make Your Game*. Vizetelly at first seems to have been sympathetic, though he inserted a cool enough notice in the *Welcome Guest* explaining the delay; but when, after another fortnight, no further copy was forthcoming he insisted on a medical certificate. This was duly printed, and Sala's admirers were no doubt interested to hear that he had been "very near to losing his life through the consequences of a murderous attack made upon him . . . in circumstances of the most cowardly ferocity." It was hoped, however, that means would "soon be found of bringing the perpetrator of the outrage to justice." For good enough reasons such means were not found, and a chastened Sala managed to write a little more of his book. But there came further delays, and the quarrel with Vizetelly took a serious turn.

From that quarrel, I am afraid, Sala did not emerge with much credit. It is just possible, of course, that for some curious psychological reason not unconnected with the Panton Street affair, he really could not bring himself to recall the frivolous days of the Homburg trip: he was certainly not feeling light-hearted at the time, and the artistic temperament was not, I dare say, unknown in Victorian days. I imagine, moreover, that Vizetelly, with his almost hourly demands for further chapters, must have been an irritating correspondent. True, he had paid for these chapters, had advertised them, and had a personal interest in their appearance, but, judging from Sala's written replies, his letters cannot have been couched in very tactful terms. Yet that hardly excused Sala's behaviour in giving promise after promise to complete his book and then seeking refuge in the most pitiful evasions or vulgar abuse. It was not as if he were still in great pain and confined to his bedroom. The doctor might have ordered complete rest for a little while, but the nose had healed quickly enough, and by the beginning of February he had been out and about. On the 11th he had even spoken at a deputation of literary men to the Prime Minister, Lord Derby, praying for the repeal of the duty on paper. It was not as if a brilliant idea for a new novel had presented itself and was demanding his whole attention: his work was appearing with some regularity in the *Daily Telegraph*. Yet although he continued for some weeks to profess all possible eagerness to complete his book "within the next few days," no further instalment was received, and at the most critical moment he chose to make use of the flimsiest pretext in an endeavour to render his agreement with Vizetelly "utterly null and void."

The *Welcome Guest* for March 12th contained no chapter of *Make*

Your Game and no explanation of its absence. A week later, however, the editor inserted a note to the effect that its writer had "not thought proper" to furnish the continuation of his narrative, and Sala could not ignore such unwelcome publicity. "I am half crazy," he admitted, "at not having written one line for anybody since Wednesday last. Give me till midday tomorrow, Wednesday, before you go to press, and you shall see what I can do. This is the last chance, and if I fail you may call me all the D——d rascals in the W.G. that you like." The Wednesday came and went, but no copy arrived, and a sharper rebuke was inserted. That was not all, however, for Vizetelly printed much the same announcement in his advertisements in various daily newspapers. Sala was informed, flew into one of his rages, and declared his intention of having nothing whatever to do with a man who could issue such a statement "with the sole and deliberate intention" of doing him an injury.

Not for long was he able to sustain his role of aggrieved party. The law stepped in, and only a few days later, a letter of his, while not without its note of truculence, shows that he recognised he had only himself to blame. "Copy not being forthcoming on Thursday," he informed Vizetelly, "I received a letter from your solicitor stating that in default of security being given, his instructions were to proceed against me for an amount (not stated) alleged to be due from me to yourself. I beg, now, to state that I am not in a position to offer any security whatsoever, and that you are at liberty to proceed against me, and in whatsoever manner you please. I am not to be coerced into writing copy by threat of imprisonment; and, though sweating taskmasters are no novelty, must confess it is the first time I have heard of means of pressure being brought to bear on an author of the nature you have availed yourself of." At the end of his letter, however, he showed clearly enough that he was by no means sure of himself. Was their private friendship as well as their professional connection to be at an end? Might it not be best, even though such connection were to cease, if the final chapters of *Make Your Game* were to be printed? And once again came the usual offer: he was ready to provide them immediately.

What happened then I can only guess, for the Sala-Vizetelly correspondence breaks off abruptly. Were there any further legal proceedings? There probably were, though it is doubtful whether the Court were ever troubled. Possibly Sala agreed to make a "token" payment; he may even have settled his Homburg debts. The threat of imprisonment need not be taken very seriously. Vizetelly may have been exceedingly angry—he had good cause to be—but he was not a vindictive man

He seems to have bowed to the inevitable, and the *Welcome Guest* ceased to speak cuttingly of the missing chapters. It ceased to speak of them at all. Its editor had had enough of delays and unkept promises. Sala was informed that his services would no longer be required.

2

That he was soon to feel deeply ashamed of himself there is ample proof, but at the moment he seems to have been able to dismiss very lightly all thoughts of his unfinished book and the quarrel with Vizetelly. His dismissal meant an appreciable loss of income, but on the other hand Edward Levy was now giving him additional work on the *Daily Telegraph*, and Frederic Chapman, of the firm of Chapman and Hall, had paid him a good sum of money for a collection of his *Household Words* essays. This was published under the title of *Gaslight and Daylight* and sold very well indeed. About the same time, too, there appeared a revised edition of his *Journey Due North*, agreements were signed with other publishers for further collections of essays, and he accepted a commission to write a short series of articles for the *London Journal*, one of the *Welcome Guest's* new rivals. He was seen at this and that banquet, and there were numerous paragraphs in the newspapers about himself and his work : the successful young littérateur.

Yet the Panton Street affair had not been forgotten. There was no pain now, and he had soon resigned himself to the fact that his nose was even less an object of beauty than it had been. He had not on a sudden renounced his intemperate habits nor cut himself off from his flashier friends. (I dare say he renewed his acquaintance with Lola Montez, who was just now lecturing to amused audiences in London on her own most peculiar experiences.) He was still in the moneylenders' hands, and not always to be found at the Salisbury Street rooms. But the memory of that "murderous attack," which might so easily have had far more serious consequences than it actually had, could not be effaced. He had, indeed, been badly shocked. It had been his own fault, of course : he must have been disgracefully drunk. But he was often disgracefully drunk, and—was it not about time for him to think of "saying good-bye to Bohemia" and settling down ? I think that he must have asked himself the question many times during that summer of 1859, and indulged in little orgy of self-pity as he recalled the old Lancaster days, before making up his mind. It is just possible, too, that his mother unwittingly helped him to his decision.

She was a very frail old lady these days, living in seclusion in her

Brighton lodgings, but early that May she not only managed to come up to London for what was to be the last of her annual concerts, but sang herself. The hall at Willis's Rooms was well filled and the audience as fashionable as she could have wished. Distinguished artistes as usual had given their services, and a novel note of splendour had been introduced by the band of the Coldstream Guards. When, moreover, the *bénéficiaire* herself appeared on the platform and sang that favourite old ballad "Fading Away" she received an ovation. What a day it must have been for her! Frederick Sala, I am sure, had come up from Southampton, and perhaps brought his wife and Edward, his eleven-year-old son who was so soon to pay a prolonged visit to his uncle; and George was there, anxiously watching to see that the excitement was not too much for his mother. They had not always been the best of friends, but Charles's death had helped to bring them together, and in her old age she was no longer minded to play stern and masterful parent. Already he had made a name for himself, and she proudly acknowledged his success. How long she remained in London after the concert I do not know, but he must have noticed how tired she was, for he took her home, and, if I am right in my supposition, it was in those quiet rooms of hers by the sea that he made up his mind.

It is unlikely that Madame Sala herself urged him to marry. She may not have been ignorant of the details of that unlucky fracas at the nighthouse, and I cannot suppose that she was altogether ignorant of his irregular habits. She must have guessed, too, the nature of his interest in Lancaster and its neighbourhood. Of such things, however, a wise mother seldom speaks. No, I think that it was her pitiful frailty and the realisation that she could not hope to live very much longer which decided him. Within a few months' time she was to die of the dreaded paralysis, and already the signs were clear. Charles was gone, and Albert away in the East was as good as dead, and he saw little enough of Frederick. When his mother died he would be even more miserably alone. Many times he must have played with the idea of marriage and rejected it. Why? Because his love would not have him. But she had gone her own way. A tragedy, of course, but it happened every day of the year. And he was earning good money: he could support a wife now. But was there anybody whom he would be willing to make his wife?

As it happened, there was.

It is just here that a little mystery presents itself which, so far, has obstinately refused to allow itself to be solved.

3

According to Sir Sidney Lee in the *Dictionary of National Biography* George Augustus Sala was married in September, 1859.

Where that piece of information was obtained I cannot discover. Search amongst the registers of Somerset House has yielded nothing, and the Vicar General's Office, the Faculty Office, the Bishop of London's Office, and the Commissary of Surrey have likewise nothing to tell us. All that I feel disposed to say is that some time in 1859, probably in July, Sala was married to a young woman who had been born in London in 1833 and whose Christian names were Harriett (or Harriette) Elizabeth.

At the same time I am bound to record the fact that most of those accustomed to deal with genealogical matters who have examined the question incline to the view that no such marriage ever took place. This I cannot bring myself to believe. In view of Sala's own account and the complete absence of the least suspicion, then or afterwards, that Harriett Sala was not his lawfully-wedded wife, I prefer to think that she was. Unless, indeed, he had married in his early youth, discovered his mistake and separated from his wife, what possible reason was there why he should not, to use his own words, "marry the girl of my heart"? I admit that a woman who had to be kept in the background might help to explain the recurring financial crises which came his way, but in that case the registers at Somerset House for the twelve years preceding 1859 would surely have something to reveal.

Who, then, was this Harriett Elizabeth?

I give, first of all, Sala's own account of his marriage in his *Life and Adventures*:

"So, after a few days' holiday with my mother at Brighton, I went and married the girl of my heart. I had known her ever since she was a child; and I think that when I asked her to name the wedding-day, she called me 'Sir' when she expressed her opinion that the following Monday would be quite a nice time for the wedding. It took a little longer than that; as I had to purchase a license, and she had to reside for a certain number of days on the other side of the river—a whimsical fancy having possessed me that I would not be married in the county of Middlesex.

"Of the whereabouts in Southwark or Lambeth we were eventually united, I have not the slightest remembrance; but I know that when the ceremony was at an end, shortly before noon, the beadle gave the bride away, and the pew-opener was her bridesmaid. I put her in a hansom, and bade her engage some nice, quiet, furnished apartments at Brompton.

Then I walked over Southwark Bridge to my work at the *Daily Tele-graph*; and on my way, at a second-hand bookseller's I bought for six-pence a copy of the first edition of Mrs. Glasse's Cookery-book, of which scarcely half-a-dozen copies are known to be in existence. So you see I secured two treasures in one happy afternoon."

Now, in speaking of her as a treasure he was certainly justified. Never was a man blessed with a wife so loving, so forbearing, and so helpful. Again and again at moments of crisis which few women would have had the courage to face more than once, she stood by him, hiding her own feelings from the world, ever loyal and devoted and uncom-plaining. And when, after more than twenty-five years of marriage she died, in the saddest circumstances, it was small wonder that her husband for long months was an utterly broken man. His first marriage, indeed, was the wisest act of his life, and, had Harriett Sala survived him, his last years would not, I think, have been the rather pitiful tragedy they were destined to become.

It is difficult, however, to accept without question all the details given in Sala's account of his marriage. On one point he flatly contradicts himself even in the autobiography itself. To speak of Harriett as "the girl of my heart" was no doubt very right and proper, but it is hard to reconcile the statement that he had known her "ever since she was a child" with a story he gives, in an earlier chapter, of his single appearance on the professional stage.

Some time in 1855, it seems, an actor, one Benjamin Barnett, a brother of the better-known Morris Barnett, was playing at the Lyceum Theatre. He was given a "benefit," and the play he chose for the occasion was *Monsieur Jacques*, an old favourite in which his brother, its adapter, I fancy, from the French, had made his first big success. For some curious reason he invited Sala, whom he had known since the old Princess's days, to take one of the minor parts, and Sala, amused at the idea, agreed to do so provided Barnett would announce him on the bills as "Mr. William Watling: his first and last appearance on any stage"—Mr. Watling being an eminent pork-pie manufacturer of the day. And so Mr. "Watling" attended rehearsals, in the course of which, he tells us, he noticed the leading lady, Miss Murray, more than once in earnest con-versation with a woman friend at the back of the stage. "But it was so dark," he adds, "that I could not discern who the lady was or what she was like. Some five years afterwards, to my great comfort and joy, I entered into the state of matrimony; and shortly after our honeymoon my wife told me, laughingly, that she had seen and heard me speak years before I had been formally introduced to her. 'Where?' I asked her in amazement. 'Well,' she replied, 'it was at the Lyceum Theatre when they were rehearsing *Monsieur Jacques*. I was at the back of the stage and was watching you flirt with Miss Murray, who was a great friend of mine.' " From which, one must deduce, their "formal introduction" was of very recent occurrence.

Which is the truth? I know not. Unfortunately from other sources only the most meagre fragments of information about Harriett Sala are to be obtained. William Tinsley, so soon to become her husband's publisher, is the only man, so far as I know, who speaks of her in any detail. They became good friends, and "a charming little woman, she was," he writes in his *Random Recollections of an Old Publisher*, "one of the sweetest and most patient wives that ever graced a man's home. She never professed to be learned or witty, and at her husband's table, as I have seen her, surrounded by a goodly company of men and women of wit and learning, not one of them could have imagined that she had worked hard in her young days." Worked hard at what? It has been suggested in more than one quarter that she had been in domestic service. Possibly she had been, and it may well be that she was a daughter or niece of one of Madame Sala's old maids or nurses, "family friends" who were to receive mention more than once in her son's autobiography. "I think she called me 'Sir '," he tells us, and it may be that he intended to write: "I had known *of* her since she was a child." It has also been suggested that although Sala was no snob, the fact that his wife came from a very humble home may explain the secrecy surrounding his wedding. Not a single friend or relation invited to the ceremony! Not a day's holiday from his *Daily Telegraph* work! Why? Because where his most private affairs were concerned he was always inclined to be mysterious? It may be so, but I fancy that there may have been some other reason as well.

But whoever she was, and whatever her previous history, Harriett Sala was a wholly exceptional woman. She was not successful in putting an end to those sad periods when he would sink down to the depths, but without her it is difficult to see how he would ever have obtained the eminence in his own profession which was so shortly to be his. "For some years," wrote Tinsley, "Sala's excellent wife had ample cause to have abandoned him altogether, but she loved her lord too well to resort to such measures. Besides, she knew he was a good and loving husband when he was in his right mind. She would not follow him when he went away on his drinking bouts, but as a rule went to her parents or some relations at or near Greenwich, and so highly was she respected by Mr. Joseph Levy and his son Edward . . . that they always advanced her all the money she required for pressing claims and personal comforts."

For the moment, however, there were no drinking bouts, and life for the young couple was shining and gay. Furnished rooms had been found in Brompton Row, and in a little while Sala was introducing his wife to his friends. One of the first to meet and admire her was Thackeray —a near neighbour—and another genius who became a very welcome visitor was Dante Gabriel Rossetti. Nor did any long time elapse before the quarrel with Vizetelly was brought to an end. The copyright of *Twice Round the Clock* was no longer Sala's. Vizetelly wrote formally to say that a proposal had been made to reissue the papers in volume form, and Sala seized the opportunity to offer a belated apology. He would be very glad, he said, to make some corrections in the work and also to write a preface for it. And "is there no way," he added, "in which I can compensate for my disgraceful disasters on the Welcome Guest? Cannot anything be done in completing 'Make Your Game' with my other W.G. articles in a volume? Cannot I do you a tale? My pen is at your service, and I feel the loss and annoyance to which I have subjected you far more than you give me credit for."

Vizetelly, who knew very well that at least two other editors were endeavouring to obtain his services, was by no means loath to forget and forgive, and within a week or two the remaining chapters of *Make Your Game* were in his hands.

The short note of explanation which prefaced Sala's return to the fold was considered sufficiently piquant to be reprinted in more than one of the newspapers. It did not explain much, but its wording is not without its interest.

"When Harry the Eighth visited Boulogne," he wrote, "the batteries of that town—or rather the officers in command there—omitted to salute him with the number of guns customarily used in saluting Royal personages. The Mayor of Boulogne, who happened to be the responsible party in the matter of salutes, was summoned before the irate monarch, and, under peril of his neck, enjoined to explain the cause of the absence of the required salvoes of artillery. 'May it please your Grace,' answered the municipal functionary, in no wise abashed, 'I have four-and-twenty good reasons for not firing the salute.' 'Name them,' thundered the husband of six wives. 'In the first place,' continued the mayor, 'I had no gunpowder.' Now Henry the Eighth, albeit a tremendous tyrant and polygamist, possessed a considerable amount of natural sagacity, and he forthwith consented to forgo the remaining twenty-three reasons for the worthy mayor, and didn't hang him; nay, I believe, knighted him eventually.

"The editor of this long-interrupted series of papers has at least four-and-twenty good reasons for not having finished 'Make Your Game'; yet he hopes to experience the leniency and forbearance of his readers when he assures them that the first and most imperative reason for the non-performance of an implied contract with the public, and the continuation of a—to him—delightful task, was ill-health. He has been quite well, though, for some months past; and the readers of the 'Welcome Guest' may wish to become acquainted with the balance of his reasons. But he hesitates to enumerate them all. There was love, there was law, and there was physic. There might have been some quarrelling; there might have been (perhaps) a little matrimony; and he is certain there was a good deal of misunderstanding. However, here at least is the continuation of 'Make Your Game.' The public must not be too angry with an old servant, and one who has worked not unfaithfully—nor always unfruitfully, he hopes—since he was a little lad, to amuse them. It is good to take the will for the deed sometimes; and it is earnestly hoped that it will be so taken in this instance."

And so far as *Make Your Game* was concerned, all at last was well. Those, however, who were beginning to know their Sala were hardly surprised when, a year or two later, a much more important book of his in process of serialisation was left incomplete. On that occasion, as it happened, a solicitor's letter would have been useless, but the editor was Dickens, and Dickens, as we shall see, had his own way of dealing with an unfortunate situation.

CHAPTER TEN
A POPULAR AUTHOR
I

PUBLIC attention that summer was largely directed to political matters. At home there was a change of government—the Derby Administration resigned in June—and abroad there was the war in Italy between France and the Austrians. But in July there was an armistice, and the man in the street was able to turn happily to a question which, while of no national importance whatever, was rousing in his breast considerably greater excitement than any ministerial defeats or European wars could create : was Dr. Smethurst guilty or not ? This medical gentleman was accused of poisoning a woman whom he had bigamously married and at whose death he would inherit a comfortable fortune. In August he was found guilty of murder and duly sentenced to death. An outcry followed, and the doctor was not only reprieved but granted a free pardon, though only for the crime of which he had been found guilty. There was, however, another impending excitement just then and one with more legitimate claims to nation-wide interest : the largest ship in the world was about to proceed on her trial trip.

For some months past the public had been given details of the *Great Eastern*, that colossal floating hotel, nearly 700 feet in length, which could accommodate 4000 passengers and had cost close upon three-quarters of a million pounds to construct. There had been those, of course, who prophesied disaster. No such unwieldy mammoth, it was said, could survive an Atlantic gale. Would she even be able to reach the open sea in safety from her Deptford moorings ? On this point neither her designer, Isambard Brunel, nor Scott Russell, the head of the Millwall firm which had built her, seems to have had many qualms. On the other hand, in many responsible quarters doubts had been freely expressed about her commercial success. She might be a miracle of engineering, she might be more luxurious than any royal or imperial yacht, but—would she pay ? This and a hundred other questions were being asked, and all helped to increase public curiosity, so much so that before ever her tugs towed her out into mid-stream many thousands of visitors from all parts of the country had paid their shillings to see her manifold wonders for themselves.

She was due to leave her moorings on September 7th for Portland

Broads, and a large party of distinguished gentlemen and press representatives had been invited to accompany her down the Thames and
through the Channel. Amongst these was Sala, and for him the short
voyage was to be doubly memorable. It was his despatches on that
occasion to the *Daily Telegraph* which confirmed its proprietors in
their belief that they had found a prince of special correspondents,
and henceforth his status in their office was appreciably improved.
And, except for a lucky suggestion that he should make an after-dinner
speech, he would almost certainly have been killed on board.

It was at Greenhithe that he joined the ship. In the train from
London he had travelled with Dickens and John Hollingshead, afterwards the well-known manager of the Gaiety Theatre, but at this time
little more than a promising journalist—another of Dickens's Young
Men—who had also tried his hand at dramatic work. Dickens was
on his way to Gadshill, but Hollingshead was to accompany the party
on behalf of *All the Year Round*, the successor to *Household Words*.
Once aboard, they found that they were to share a cabin with Vizetelly,
a large one on the "first lower deck" which had been built round the
base of one of the ship's huge funnels.

That first day all went well. To the cheers of the multitudes lining
both banks of the river the *Great Eastern* was successfully piloted to
sea, and once she was in the Channel all were loud in their praises of the
colossus's behaviour. Then, late the next afternoon, came disaster.

It was about half-past six. Dinner was over, and the palatial saloon
almost deserted. Most of the visitors had returned to the deck for
exercise or a smoke. At one of the tables, however, a dozen or more
men, mostly journalists, were still sitting over their coffee. Sala, with
work to be done, had intended to return to his cabin, but he had been
persuaded to stay. Amongst those at the table was Herbert Ingram,
just then negotiating for the purchase of the *Illustrated Times* and a
director, I fancy, of the company owning the ship, and somebody
suggested that his health should be drunk. There were cries of "Speech!"
and "Sala!", and the man who was soon to be widely known as one
of the most successful after-dinner speakers in the country rose to his
feet. He was in the midst of paying Ingram the usual compliments
when there was a deafening report. The whole vessel shook, and the
saloon was littered with broken glass. The journalists rushed on deck
to find everything in a state of the wildest confusion, with one of the
funnels lying on its side. The "steam jacket" encasing it had burst.
Sala and Hollingshead managed to reach their cabin only to discover
that it had been completely destroyed: it was the one built round the

funnel which had fallen. "The flooring," Sala wrote, "had been blown up and everything smashed to atoms." There were dense clouds of smoke and dust about, and as they climbed over the wreckage they heard for the first time the pitiful cries coming from below, where about a dozen stokers had been caught by the blast of escaping steam and been fearfully scalded. There were shouts for cotton-wool and oil, but although the oil was immediately forthcoming no cotton-wool could be found. Luckily one of the party, Lord Stafford, afterwards the Duke of Sutherland and a good friend to Sala, had noticed the thickness of the curtains in the saloon. "There must be wool there!" he exclaimed, and the next moment the woollen lining of these curtains was being ripped out by the yard and soaked in oil. But although the unfortunate victims were lovingly tended all through the night the shock had been too great, and few survived the ordeal. There were the ghastliest sights. One poor wretch, Sala records, rolled in his agony off a hurriedly-prepared couch on to the floor. One of the guests tried to help him up. To his horror the flesh of the man's hands "came bodily off" in his own, and "the bones of the stoker's hands were revealed in skeleton nakedness." Hardly less pathetic in their way were the scenes witnessed next day. For all the confusion on board there had been no panic amongst the officers, and there was never a moment when the great ship did not keep to her course. No news, of course, of the disaster had reached England, and there were cheering crowds on shore to greet her arrival at Weymouth. In addition, a whole fleet of pleasure-boats, each with its party of revellers, had come out, and on all sides bands were playing gay marches. Then it was seen that the *Great Eastern's* colours were at half-mast, and when it was learnt what had happened there came an "awful silence" as moving as it was impressive. Truly a dreadful business, and, as it happened, only the first of many misfortunes which were to beset the ill-fated ship.

For Sala it was to be a never-to-be-forgotten experience. Again and again he was to recall the horrors of that night on board. "I have seen many harrowing spectacles both in war and in peace in my time," he wrote more than thirty years later, "but never, perhaps, have I witnessed a spectacle ghastlier and more pitiable than that which presented itself when the wounded firemen were brought up out of the hideous chasm made by the explosion, and laid out in the saloon." As a good journalist, however, he realised his responsibilities, and, once ashore, with an overcoat borrowed from Lord Stafford—he had lost all his luggage which had fallen through the floor and been burnt—

he telegraphed to his wife and rushed up to London to write what was probably the most vivid and intimate account of the tragedy that appeared in any of the newspapers.

Only a few months later he was given another opportunity to show what he could do in the way of picturesque reporting. In June, 1860, there came the Great Volunteer Review in Hyde Park. It was the first of the kind to be held in this country, the Queen herself was present, and the greatest interest had been aroused, not least because from so many quarters the whole Volunteer movement had been either violently opposed or greeted with amused contempt. Napoleon III. might have ambitions which one of these days would have to be curbed, but what use, it was asked, did these amateurs, some of them well past middle age, expect to be were England really to be invaded? The *Daily Telegraph*, however, had never taken that view. All its influence, indeed, had been exerted in favour of the movement, and when the Review was announced to take place there seems to have been no doubt in Edward Levy's mind as to which member of his ever-growing staff should be given first place amongst the special correspondents and "commissioners." Sala was obviously the man for the job, and he made the most of it. In the course of the nine or ten columns for which he was responsible he not only succeeded in giving a most spirited account of the entire pageant, but also managed to convey to the man in the street unable to be present, a very good idea of the real significance of the occasion.

His work, too, brought him an unexpectedly large sum of money. A day or two after his articles had appeared, a young man named Edward Tinsley, who had recently set up as a publisher in partnership with his brother William, came to see Sala. So graphic a description of the Review, he thought, could be used as the basis for a shilling pamphlet which would command a large sale. Generous terms were offered, and a delighted Sala sought Levy's permission for his work to be reprinted. This was at once given—it was to be given many times during the next twenty years—and, as Tinsley expected, *A Narrative of the Grand Volunteer Review* sold in its thousands.

2

Meanwhile his marriage had been having a beneficial effect. In due course there was to come a recurrence of those regrettable bouts. Soon enough, if the story be true, Edward Levy would often be obliged to keep him locked up in a bare room until such work as was required

from his pen for the next morning's issue had been completed. At
the moment, however, he seemed determined to make the most of
his opportunities, and in spite of financial troubles which obstinately
refused to become any less serious he worked as he had rarely worked
before. Once the last chapter of *Make Your Game* was off his hands,
he prepared himself to accept almost every commission which should
be offered him. As a result, during the next year or two he not only
managed to write two long and two short novels, a book upon Hogarth,
and a volume of imaginary letters, but also a score or more of short
stories and nearly a hundred essays, to say nothing of the innumerable
reports on art-exhibitions, theatrical criticisms, and lengthy book-
reviews which more than one editor was now asking him to undertake.
And this output was all the more extraordinary in view of the fact that,
except on Saturdays, there was work which required the greatest care
and often kept him in Fleet Street until a late hour, for the *Daily Telegraph*.
It is difficult to understand how he managed to maintain any standard
at all, yet some of his best work was to be written at this time, when
in addition to all his various commissions he accepted an important
editorial post. And even this was not all, for in the intervals of studying
the classics he was now making a beginning with those subsequently
famous common-place books of his, for all the world as though he
would shortly be required to pass the stiffest of university examinations.

Friendship with Vizetelly had been resumed, but in that autumn of
1859 the *Welcome Guest* passed into other hands. Its purchaser was
John Maxwell, afterwards the well-known publisher and husband of
Miss Braddon. Maxwell was a shrewd man of business who was not
afraid of a little speculation. He had been the chief advertising agent
of the *Illustrated Times*. He had had something to do with the Royal
British Bank, which, by the way, was not the staidly solid corporation
that its name suggested. He had an interest in the firm of Ward and
Lock, where once, I fancy, he had been a mere clerk, and he was
associated with another publishing house recently established under the
name of Houlston and Wright. Already, too, he had tried his hand
at newspaper-proprietorship. In the previous year, and with Edmund
Yates as its editor, he had launched *Town Topics*, a journal still sometimes
remembered today, though it enjoyed no very long life, for its connection with the Garrick Club controversy which led to the estrangement
between Dickens and Thackeray. Maxwell knew that the *Welcome
Guest* had been losing money, but he had his own ideas for its improvement, and amongst its assets there was one which he believed—correctly—
would be of very considerable value. This was the copyright of *Twice*

Round the Clock, which, as we have seen, it was now proposed to republish in book-form. As for the *Welcome Guest* itself, Maxwell altered its shape, size and price, installed Robert Brough as editor in Vizetelly's place, and widely advertised the fact that his chief contributor would be "the most picturesque essayist of the day." And for a while it seemed as if his boldness was to be well rewarded. *Twice Round the Clock* was amongst the most successful books of the season, and another series of papers by its author in the *Welcome Guest* caught the popular taste.

Lady Chesterfield's Letters to Her Daughter may not be a work of much distinction, but the little book is not without a pawky interest of its own and it contains one or two useful biographical sidelights. It is not, as it was expected to be, a burlesque, and it suffers from the fact, cheerfully admitted by the author himself, that "although Lady Chesterfield does not talk exactly like a costermonger, she talks a great deal too much like a man": in other words, like Sala himself. Yet, equally in her reminiscences of the 'thirties and 'forties and in her advice to a débutante daughter in London, the forthright old dame can be decidedly piquant. One short passage may be given here. In her last letter she warns her impressionable Louisa against the common belief that "authors resemble their writings." A friend of hers, a Mr. Nedwards, has, it seems, a wide acquaintance amongst the London scribblers. "He tells me," she records, "of another popular literary character, who by the immense amount of work he gets through, and his painfully minute and symmetrical handwriting, might be thought to be the most methodical and the most industrious writer of the day. In his work he tries to be alternately funny and sentimental, from which I was inclined at first to put him down as a poet too; but, according to Mr. Nedwards, he is a brawling, fractious, disorderly, indolent man; he hasn't a grain of sentiment in him; his fun is a perversity of humour —wit with a hump, indeed; that as for his sentiment, there lives not a profounder cynic: one who keeps a common-place book of pathetic phrases; was never touched by anybody's woe, save when, by relieving it, he could administer to his own vanity, and placing the *summum bonum* of his enjoyment in a choice flask of wine and a rare cigar. Oh, for the anomalies, the contradictions, and the sorry reverses to the most brilliant of medals!"

At the same time work had been resumed on the *Illustrated Times*, he was writing for *Everybody's Journal*, and unsigned articles of his in two other periodicals, the *Critic* and the *Leader*, were appearing with sufficient regularity to warrant his including their names on his professional visiting-cards. Now, too, Thackeray was launching his own monthly, the *Cornhill Magazine*, and had not forgotten the "Key of the Street." "About to start new magazine," he wrote. "First-rate bill of fare. Want rich collops from you. Come and see me. W. M. T. P.S. Don't forget Hogarth." Sala called at Onslow Square, and "we agreed that a serious biography would be somewhat too weighty an adventure in a magazine; so it was arranged that my monthly articles were to have the title of *William Hogarth, Painter, Engraver, and Philosopher: Essays on the Man, the Work, and the Time.*"

Those nine essays, "shallow and inconclusive" though their author called them, were not written without a considerable amount of research work conducted almost daily at the British Museum. Modern biographers of Hogarth may not regard them as anything more than a picturesque embroidery, but they were not the least popular contributions to the magazine and brought Sala commendatory letters from, amongst others, Charles Kingsley, Forster, and Lord Sidney Osborne (S. G. O.). Now, indeed, he was being accepted, even in the more scholarly circles, as a man of letters who for all his eccentricities and shortcomings might well be destined to take a high place. George Smith, the *Cornhill's* proprietor, paid him exceedingly well, and at the monthly banquets which he was pleased to give in its honour Sala was introduced to a world which had hitherto hardly been aware of his existence. Monckton Milnes, Leighton, Millais and Landseer, Browning and Anthony Trollope: it was men like these whom he was now meeting. They may not have thought much of his novel, but they must have appreciated his *Twice Round the Clock* and the reprinted essays from *Household Words*, of which the second volume, *Looking at Life*, had now appeared.

Now, too, Ingram invited him to join the staff of the *Illustrated London News*, and in June there appeared the first of his weekly columns of gossipy notes which, beginning as "Literature and Art," were afterwards to become the better-known "Echoes of the Week" and continued to appear in that journal with one long and several short breaks, until 1887. They were probably no better and no worse than similar causeries in half a dozen other periodicals, but they were up-to-date, amusingly personal, and, in contrast to Yates's "Lounger" articles, free from veiled malice. Above all, they subtly flattered the public which was buttonholed in a new kind of way, invited when possible to air its opinions, treated, in fact, as a highly-esteemed collaborator. The time, indeed, was to come when thousands of people who hardly knew of Sala as a writer of books or even as a special correspondent eagerly looked forward each week to his "Echoes." Nor did his severance from the *Illustrated London News* mean their end, for they continued to appear successively in the *Entertainment Gazette*, and, during the last years of his life, in the *Sunday Times*, as well as in various provincial newspapers.

A memorable year, then, this 1860, for Sala, and it is hardly surprising to find him confessing that it was one of the happiest periods of his life. European thrones might seem to be toppling, men spoke of the possibility of an invasion of England (when they were not arguing about the fight for the Championship between Tom Sayers and the Benicia Boy), and there were signs of impending trouble in America; but for Sala, and in spite of private bereavements, all was unusually well. The *Saturday Review* and one or two other journals of the starchier type might continue to attack him on the score of vulgarity and bombast, but recognition had come, and even though the moneylenders were to resort to sterner methods, there would never again be a lack of work so long as he retained his health. It was now that he was able to take his wife to a little house of their own and to indulge his passion for finely-bound books and prints "before letters." Now, too, came the first of those little luncheons and dinners, cooked in part by himself, which in later years were to be so deservedly popular. Yet, as I have said, this year was not without its sorrows for him. On April 10th his mother died in Brighton "in the arms of her two surviving sons." (So ran the obituary notices, though Albert was alive at the other end of the world. But he had not been behaving too well, and he was conveniently forgotten.) Sala has little to say of his feelings at the time. "I brought her remains to London, to lay them by the side of my brother Charles and my sister Augusta at Kensal Green Cemetery, and when the funeral was over, I found, behind a tombstone, our old, old servant Letitia Merriman." Only a month or two later he was to begin his long series entitled "Streets of the World," and his first two essays were devoted to Brighton, but there was no mention of Madame Sala and no hint that for him the town henceforth would be subtly changed. But until his later years, and for all his love of indulging in personal reminiscences on every possible occasion, he rarely spoke of family affairs. The old lady had gone, he wrote, "in happy peace," and perhaps there was nothing more that he could properly say, even though once on a time Madame Sala's name had been at least as well known to the public as was now his own. On the other hand he had much to say when, in rapid succession, he lost his two oldest friends in the literary world. In May he was shocked

to hear of Albert Smith's death. In his time he was to quarrel with
most of his friends, but for Albert Smith he had always retained his
affectionate regard, and, after his death, lost few opportunities of
singing his praises. Then in June Robert Brough's last remnants of
strength—for some time now he had been in the wretchedest health—
ebbed away. Brough was the most lovable and generous of men :
too generous, in fact. All his short life he had worked hard, but he
had saved nothing at all and left a family almost destitute. It is pleasant
to record the fact that Sala, that "profound cynic," immediately set
to work to raise funds. He sent out begging letters by the dozen, he
wrote a memoir for the *Welcome Guest* for which no payment was
taken, he saw through the press the dead man's *Marston Lynch*, the
novel which had been written for the *Train*, and he arranged a theatrical
performance at Drury Lane, at which he read some moving verses
of his own. It was largely due to his efforts, indeed, that an annuity
could be purchased for the widow.

3

During its first year the *Cornhill* enjoyed the greatest success, and it
was only to be expected that rival magazines would appear in the field.
In the early autumn rumours arose that one of these was to be launched
by one of Mr. Thackeray's principal contributors. There had been
the bitterest quarrel, it was said, and the contributor, one of the most
picturesque essayists of the day, had stalked out of the office of Messrs.
Smith and Elder, vowing vengeance. It was suggested, in words which
contained more than a hint of contempt, that with Sala in the editorial
chair neither grace nor scholarship could be looked for. "Light
literature!" quoth the prophets, using a phrase which at the time
seems to have meant little more than conventional jocularity or sentimental rubbish. When, moreover, it was whispered that Edmund
Yates (whose recent expulsion from the Garrick Club on Mr. Thackeray's
account would doubtless be remembered) was to be associated with
the new venture, who could doubt, it was asked, that it was the
promoter's intention to inaugurate an anti-Thackeray campaign ?
There was no truth whatever in the stories of a quarrel, and for the
next two or three years, almost, indeed, to the day of the novelist's
death, "the Reverend Doctor Sala," as he was affectionately called,
remained on the friendliest terms with Thackeray and was regularly
to be found, a most welcome guest, at his house. On the other hand
it was true that he had been approached by the enterprising Mr. Maxwell

"THE FIRST CONDUCTOR OF TEMPLE BAR"

From the *Drawing Room Portrait Gallery*, July—December, 1861.

Office of "TEMPLE BAR",

A LONDON MAGAZINE,

CONDUCTED BY GEORGE AUGUSTUS SALA,

122, FLEET STREET, E.C.

94 Sloane Street, Knightsbridge. S.W

Monday night.

My dear Mr Wills,

Will you be so good as to ask Mr Dickens
if there be any objection to my republishing "Since this old
Cap was new"; "Caliph Haroun alraschid"; "How Coaches" and
"Mynheer Van Rig". The permission would be serviceable to
me to complete a collection I am about.

A line here would oblige. We have not
set the Thames on fire with Temple Bar; but we have sold
excellently well, and No. 2 will I trust be better than No. 1.

You might have asked an old hand for
a tale in the Xmas no. I had such a ghost story

most faithfully yours

George: aug: Sala.

W. H. Wills, Esq

Do you see my col in the I.L.News: the printers this week have made a horrible
hash of a paragraph about no 1 of great expectations

LETTER TO W. H. WILLS, (1860)

asking for permission to reprint certain essays from *Household Words*.

and agreed to "conduct" a new monthly magazine. In view of all
his other work, however, he had felt obliged to insist on the engagement
of a suitable assistant—another W. H. Wills, in fact—for the routine
editorial work. Yates was clearly one of the few men exactly fitted
for the position, and on his acceptance early in October schemes for the
new magazine were put in hand. Annoyed at the ill-natured stories
in circulation Sala took every opportunity to contradict them. There
was no question of rivalling the *Cornhill*; there was surely room for
the billy-boy as well as the three-decker. As for the suggestion that
the new magazine would lack dignity and scholarship, it would "have
scarcely anything to do with 'light literature' usually so called," but be
"as solid and serious" as was "compatible with non-stupidity." As
his letters show, moreover, he set to work with the greatest zeal to
draft his plans and gather about him a staff of contributors either already
well known to the public or promising beginners whose work appealed
to him. He had taken chambers in Clement's Inn, and there day after
day worked on the magazine which under the name of *Temple Bar*
was to enjoy a solid success for a quarter of a century or more—until
the day, in fact, when even the most cultivated Victorian was beginning
to ask for something which he had once on a time despised as "light
literature."

Within a decade Sala was to be in the van of a campaign to be rid
of the real Temple Bar, but at this time he seems to have regarded it
as anything rather than the inconveniently-placed and out-of-date
structure which it undoubtedly was. In a prospectus he paid tribute
to it as a venerable London landmark particularly well suited for his
purpose. Almost, he thought, it might be said to mark the centre of
the literary world. And it was while he was sketching a rude design
for a cover that he had an inspiration for a motto—perhaps the most
widely-quoted sentence he ever wrote though he is rarely credited
with its composition. In one of his *Household Words* essays entitled
"Down Whitechapel Way" he had begun by expressing his admiration
for Dr. Johnson. "'Sir,' said Samuel Johnson to the Scotch gentleman—
'Sir, let us take a walk down Fleet Street.'" His readers had naturally
supposed that the words had been taken from Boswell, but that was
not the case. No doubt the Doctor more than once said something
of the kind, but it is nowhere recorded that he did. Here, however,
was precisely the motto that was wanted for *Temple Bar*. The "Scotch
gentleman" was eliminated, and "*Sir*," *said Dr. Johnson*, "*let us take
a walk down Fleet Street*" duly appeared on the purple covers of the
new magazine.

George Cruikshank was asked to furnish the cover-design—"you will of course have your own terms," wrote Sala—but the old man excused himself and the work was entrusted to the then youthful Percy Macquoid. It had been announced that the Conductor's contributions would be illustrated by his own pen, but this idea was abandoned, and, indeed, any extra work of the kind would have been impossible. "Temple Bar," he wrote to a friend, declining an invitation to dinner, "has to be made up by Saturday next; I have a lot of special commissioning to do for the Illustrated news besides my Literature and Art; and this with a Street of the World for the Welcome Guest, a chapter of a serial story for Weldons Register and my usual two leaders a day for the Telegraph make every hour and moment valuable."

And yet, with all this work on his hands, he had actually begun two new novels!

Frederic Chapman had signed a contract for one of these, to be called *Quite Alone*, which, as it happened, was destined never to be finished by Sala himself, but at the moment another idea was taking hold of him—the story of an "impossibly" bad woman—and he made a valiant though unsuccessful effort to have enough of it ready for that Saturday. Nevertheless, even though it became necessary to postpone the appearance of *The Seven Sons of Mammon*, the first number of *Temple Bar* was not without a contribution from its Conductor, and the first of his "Travels in the County of Middlesex," as gaily picturesque as anything that he had published, lent it a sufficiently Salaesque touch.

The magazine was well received. The Thames, Sala confessed to Wills, had not been set on fire, but 30,000 copies were sold, and even those critics who might have been expected to be scornful, expressed their admiration and spoke of a salad delectably mixed. Such well-established writers as John Oxenford and Blanchard Jerrold were represented, and two of the younger men, Mortimer Collins and Robert Buchanan, contributed short poems which found an appreciative public. When, moreover, in the second number, *The Seven Sons of Mammon* was begun, it attracted instant attention.

To me it is a little astonishing that so much praise was lavished at the time on this undoubtedly exciting but wildly melodramatic romance. As always in his fiction Sala here wandered off almost at random into a discussion about anything that happened to strike his fancy, including his own shortcomings as a novelist; his design, when he remembered its existence, was singularly loose; and although the central figure, the beautiful but quite poisonous Mrs. Armitage, blackmailer, forger, and murderess, was professedly "taken from life," she is rarely much more than a stage puppet. Yet alike during its serialisation in *Temple Bar* and after its publication in volume-form at the end of 1861, the story received the most effusive adulation.

All its scenes, wrote one London critic, were "drawn with a spirit and fidelity which Balzac could not have surpassed." "If," wrote another, "there be any who still entertain a doubt as to Mr. Sala's claim to hold the first rank among living novelists, we would entreat of them to read the chapters describing the race course on Derby Day and . . . the arrest of the 'Fair Widow'." "Had Mr. Sala done nothing else," declared the *Morning Post*, "to establish his claim to literary distinction, *The Seven Sons of Mammon* would alone place him in the foremost rank of modern writers of fiction." And "this," announced the *Spectator*, "is a work of broad and unquestionable genius." All of which, of course, was exceedingly pleasant for the author. Who could doubt that he was now on the crest of the wave?

Now, too, his reputation was growing in another direction: as a fluent speaker and an agreeable conversationalist. The *salon* in this country was dead, but there were fashionable ladies on the look-out for "interesting discoveries," and, no doubt to his secret amusement, Sala found himself in request as a drawing-room celebrity, whose neat autograph was begged for innumerable albums. More important, he was being invited to speak at public banquets, not because he was in any way a great orator but because about his remarks there would invariably be a touch of that personal confession and amusing irrelevancy which informed all his writings. A witty fellow, they would tell you, and all the more welcome because, unlike most of the "real swells," you could never be certain what he would say. Not exactly indiscreet (even when it seemed possible that he had dined, or, rather, wined, a little too well), but blessedly different from the usual dull after-dinner speaker. In the previous autumn he had accepted an invitation to speak at Huddersfield and been delighted to find on the platform with him the aged Lord Brougham, a now almost legendary figure, who had not only been exceedingly gracious but departed from the arranged programme in order publicly to extol his genius. Now London was following Huddersfield's lead, and there were many who, like Brougham, were eager to pay their tribute to him.

It is easy to exaggerate, yet it is hardly too much to say that during 1861 and 1862 Sala held a position in the London literary world which was shared by no more than four or five other writers, all of them considerably his senior. He was, of course, no Dickens or Thackeray, but amongst the younger school he was the one who was most confidently expected to go furthest. When, moreover, it was seen that *Temple Bar* was continuing to follow a dignified course, its Conductor became definitely a figure of importance. He might be the writer of "sensational" articles in the *Daily Telegraph* (though many of those ascribed to him on the grounds of their alleged sensationalism were not his), and his style might be as vulgarly florid as his worst enemies declared, but he had made his mark. Now, indeed, he was something more than the most picturesque essayist of the day : he was given the more highly-prized designation of a man of letters.

4

He signalised his altered status in an unoriginal but understandable manner. Gone, he chose to think, was the day when he must keep his address secret from even the best of friends ; gone the time when a modest house in a Brompton square (with a lodger) would suffice : he was a man of letters making his two thousand a year, and nothing would satisfy him but to turn country gentleman. In the lordliest way, moreover, he chose for his residence no mere cottage but a roomy old manor-house, part of it dating back to the fourteenth century, which stood in extensive grounds.

No doubt the rent asked for Upton Court, Upton-cum-Chalvey, a village in a line between Eton and Stoke Pogis and only a little way out of Slough, was not excessive. For all its finely-timbered front and long and steep-pitched roof, for all its great hall and winding stairways and panelled bedrooms, it had not been "modernised" in the utilitarian if ugly Victorian way. It had its history, and of course it had its ghost. But it needed all manner of repairs, and there were rats about : rats, it would seem, of every known species, rats of incredible size and unimagined ferocity, rats which refused to order their lives behind a decent veil of silence but throughout the night would advertise their presence by a dozen different but all eerie noises, rats, in a word, which might well be collectively responsible for any number of ghosts. Nor was this all, for the owner of the house, a coal-merchant in Windsor, insisted on retaining for himself some of its amenities. On the other hand nobody could fail to be impressed by its baronial air. The hall by itself seemed to confer a patent of nobility on the occupier. There was a lake, too, and a rose garden, and you could wander through well-stocked orchards or, from the courtyard in front of the house, obtain a fine view of an even more baronial structure, Windsor Castle. Obviously the right kind of retreat for a distinguished man of letters

(a) Madame Sala, from a miniature, 1827.

b) Harriett Sala, from a photograph, 1883.   (c) Bessie Sala, from a photograph, 1896.

SALA'S WOMENFOLK

(a) A "Special Correspondent."

Caricature by Frederick Waddy, 1872.

(b) Caricature by Alfred Bryan.

From the *Entr'acte Almanack*, 1876.

TWO CARICATURES.

about to startle and delight the world with more novels of broad and unquestionable genius and more essays of astonishing picturesqueness. Obviously the right setting for an important editor wishing to dispense hospitality to celebrities who might be persuaded to number themselves amongst his contributors. And I have not the least doubt that Sala, who all his life recalled with pleasure the days when he had been able to wander through orchards and woods or across wide meadows without having to open his front gates, looked forward to the time when Upton Court would be his own freehold property.

Why not? Already another volume of essays—*Dutch Pictures*— had been issued and added not a little to his laurels. Then at the beginning of 1862 *The Strange Adventures of Captain Dangerous*, another novel in an entirely different manner, made its first appearance in *Temple Bar* and was received, if not with the enthusiasm which had greeted *The Seven Sons of Mammon*, at least with the respectful admiration due to a bold innovation carried out with immense gusto. Ambitious plans, too, for the future were not lacking. A brief visit to Italy with his wife had given Sala the material for a series of the liveliest despatches home, and Thackeray's publishers were suggesting their reissue in book-form. More, they were talking of an elaboration of the Hogarth papers into two large and lavishly-illustrated volumes. Nor was this all, for in the summer of 1862 Sala turned professional reader, and an agreeable voice combined with his knowledge of the actor's craft enabled him to delight large audiences; and in spite of his wife's "horror" at any such public appearances, he must have looked forward to pleasant additions from that source to his already large income. He read from yet another collection of his essays—*Accepted Addresses*—the sales of which by no means suffered because this or that story had been orally delivered and widely commented upon in the press. Finally there came his election to that least Bohemian of London Clubs, the Reform. It was Charles Mackay, then editor of the *Illustrated London News*, who proposed him for membership, but it was his seconder, Thackeray, who by waylaying each member as he came in and asking for his vote as a personal favour to himself secured his election. True, no less than twelve black balls found their way into the receptacle for such unfriendly tokens, but that was to be expected. In some matters the members of the Reform Club, even at that date, were as conservatively-minded as any of their neighbours at the Carlton, and it was enough for a man of any reputation whose father was not a member or whose lineage was not noble to present himself for election for black balls to be freely used. But—they had elected him, the man who, not so many years before, had looked up with envy at the Club windows as he wandered along Pall Mall, unknown and poverty-stricken, forced to be satisfied with the savour of somebody else's cigar.

Yet it was just at this time that he took the decision which for all its wisdom so greatly surprised his friends and admirers. There was still a novel or two to be written, and in the course of the next twenty years he was to publish close on a hundred short stories as well as a dozen fat volumes, but "literature," as he understood the term, was no longer for him.

They might lavish compliments upon him, but he was good enough critic to realise and accept his own limitations. "I knew perfectly well," he records, "that I was altogether destitute of a particle of that genius without which I could never excel or become famous in pure letters, but," he adds, "I was fully cognisant of the fact that I had learned my trade as a journalist and that I could earn a handsome income by it." As an imaginative writer he *might* be able to produce a novel which would not only repeat the success of *The Seven Sons of Mammon* but even carry his name down the ages, but—was it likely? Calmly he admitted to himself that it was not. He was not a man to be frightened away by unfriendly and possibly envious critics, but it was more than possible that that infernal *Saturday Review* was right. On the other hand he knew now that a position in the journalistic world could be his which need not be below that occupied by the then king of correspondents, William Howard Russell, and might even be above it. Already the Levys were hinting at commissions of far greater importance than any that had hitherto come his way, and they had never disguised their high opinion of what he had done for the *Daily Telegraph*. Why, then, not concentrate his attention on the one branch of writing at which he really did excel and might become supreme?

5

How far, if at all, his decision was accelerated by the appearance of yet another financial crisis, it is difficult to say, but it did so happen that in the summer of 1862 he was brought, as it were, almost to the portals of the bankruptcy court. In the previous year great changes for the better had been made in the laws relating to defaulters, but the position of the bankrupt remained, as was only right, exceedingly unpleasant, and the consequences of public examination in Sala's case might well have been serious. The determination on the moneylenders' part to put forward at this juncture an ultimatum is not altogether surprising, and yet until the last moment Sala does not seem to have worried himself much about it. He was probably paying away a monthly or quarterly sum and supposed that everybody would continue to grumble but remain fairly well satisfied with the arrangement. His creditors, however, must have come to the conclusion that a country gentleman who could freely dispense hospitality to his friends, the editor of a popular magazine, a man of letters who published a new book every few months and was a highly-paid member of the *Daily Telegraph's* staff, could, and should be made to, do very much more than that. What exact threats were made I do not know, but that they could not be ignored is obvious from his correspondence at the time. A large sum of money was required, and required at once. How was it to be obtained?

There was a fair amount to be squeezed from the publishers. It was unfortunate that the copyright of *The Seven Sons of Mammon* had been sold outright for no more than £350, but he managed to sell a fifth and final collection of his *Household Words* essays, and from the well-satisfied Tinsley he secured a pleasantly large advance for *Captain Dangerous*. Wills, too, came to his rescue and paid for articles to be written for *All the Year Round*. I fancy, moreover, that Smith and Elder now advanced money for the Hogarth book, though three or four years were to pass before it was published, and in their generous way the Levys almost certainly helped. At the same time the sternest efforts were made to cut down expenses. Upton Court, of course, was given up and lodgings were taken in Guilford Street, Bloomsbury. Even so, however, the required sum could not be found and by the end of August when several hundred pounds were still required, Sala was desperate: desperate enough to beg from one who was almost a stranger to him. I would hesitate to give details of so private a matter were it not that in the two letters which he wrote about it at the time the harassed man has so much of interest to say about himself. Incidentally, too, there is an additional piquancy about the business in view of the fact that the man whom he approached was none other than the proprietor of his particular bugbear, the *Saturday Review*!

They had met, it is true, once or twice, and in sufficiently curious circumstances. Mr. A. J. Beresford Hope, then in his forty-second year and temporarily out of Parliament, was a wealthy politician and landowner well known for his charitable undertakings and the warm interest he took in the Church Union movement. In the previous May public meeting had been held in the Chapter House of Westminster

Abbey with the object of restoring it to its former glories.   Many
bishops and other high dignitaries of the Church were present, and to
his great surprise Sala had been invited to attend.   More, on coming
into the building he was introduced to Beresford Hope who asked
him to speak.   No doubt the fact that he was not only known as a
ready speaker but also as a man who in the columns of the *Daily Telegraph*
could address a much larger audience than any hall would hold, was
responsible for the unexpected invitation, but it is to be noted that on
this occasion he was asked to come in his private and not his professional
capacity.   He spoke, in his usual unconventional way, and must have
made an impression, for he was forthwith invited to sit on the Committee
of Restoration, which naturally included Beresford Hope.   He did
so, and attended one or two meetings.   That, however, was the extent
of their acquaintanceship when on August 7th he boldly asked "the
Lord of Deepdene" for assistance.

He would as soon have thought of addressing the Grand Lama of
Tibet, he wrote, but for the "kind and courteous conduct" which he
had received from one whom, he admitted, he had been at first inclined
to regard with hostility.   The usual honeyed compliments followed,
after which he asked leave to speak of his public career.   *Was* the
Saturday Review right in calling him a snob and a fool, ignorant and
stupid?   It might be so, and yet was he a fool to continue to plead
the cause of the weak against the powerful, as he was endeavouring to
do every day in the *Daily Telegraph*?   He *must* go on, and he would
go on—if only he could free himself from his shackles.   He was earning
between £1200 and £1500 a year, but was being "eaten up by usurers
and creditors of long standing" whose demands never diminished.   He
wanted the loan of £500 for two years.   An insurance company might
accommodate him, but he shrank from possible medical refusal.   With
such a sum, he might, he thought, without vanity look forward to the
day when he would be able to help the people with his tongue as well
as with his pen.   Yes, a seat in Parliament was not beyond the bounds
of possibility.

There were to be several occasions when Sala's name as a Liberal
Candidate for Parliamentary honours was to be placed before the
Committees or Associations which dealt with such matters, and although
he never actually fought a seat there were times when his name was
prominently before the public in such a connection.   His private
letters, too, right on until the middle of the 'eighties, frequently make
mention of his political ambitions.   That they were always to be
frustrated did not occasion much surprise, for at such times rumours of

those "disappearances" of his would take a most sinister turn, but it was only in his sixties, a tired old man well aware of his waning influence, that he seems to have abandoned them. In 1862, however, he had little reason to suppose that the way would be so persistently blocked, and an allusion to his hopes was well calculated to appeal to a man like Beresford Hope.

He was not long kept in suspense. Only four days later he was writing again to the proprietor of the *Saturday Review*. It was some consolation to him, he said, in his terrible and, as he now found, "irretrievable embarrassments," that his correspondent was not mortally offended, and "I can but sadly acquiesce in the sufficiency of the reasons you give for saying nay to me. Yes; I know them all—to what a deluge of petitions every rich man . . . is exposed—how often his confidence is abused—how often he finds that he has cast away his bounty on unworthy objects—how at last he is compelled to make a stern resolve to lend no more. If I was mad enough to hope that an exception might perhaps be made in my favour—the cause of my delusion was founded on the impression that you might perhaps recognise the exceptional nature of my position. . . . By my own unaided efforts, I have risen from the low estate of a scene painter in a theatre, of a hack engraver, of a draughtsman on wood to the position I now occupy. I have forced myself on the public. I have dragged myself up. I have *compelled* the world to listen to me. And now," he continued, "when the recognition of which I have spoken has come :—when I am known if not celebrated, when I am popular if not esteemed, when I can command Power if not Love—all this only finds a man drowning in bankruptcy. I have made large sums, and each succeeding work commands a higher price than its predecessor, but I declare that I have not for years enjoyed such a quiet competence as is the lot of a government clerk with three hundred a year. I have had to keep up an incessant and exhausting combat with the liabilities of youth—to stave them off—to buy time as though it were diamond dust—and at last has come a period when ruin can no longer be averted. . . . To me Bankruptcy is not only financial but social ruin—loss of position, destruction of any prospect of succeeding in public life, expulsion from clubs—exposure to the astonishment and censure of the well-to-do who will lift up their hands and say 'Here is a man who admits having made an average income of fifteen hundred a year and who becomes bankrupt for less than five hundred!' . . . What I am to do I know not."

6

Was the situation really so terrible?

At such critical moments a little exaggeration is to be expected. There was just a chance, too, that a second, judiciously-worded letter might cause Beresford Hope to change his mind. That he did was extremely improbable. Other letters were to pass between the two men at intervals during the next fifteen years, but they contained no hint of any financial transaction of the past. No; help, I think, was not forthcoming from that quarter. Yet the well-to-do did not raise their hands in astonishment, there was no expulsion from the Reform Club, and there was certainly no loss of position. Sala was not made bankrupt, and only a very few people knew of the real state of his affairs. Precisely how the moneylenders were appeased it is impossible to say, but Maxwell, in spite of some money troubles of his own, agreed to publish in book-form a series of papers which its Conductor had begun for *Temple Bar*, and Chapman and Hall advanced money for the unwritten novel. It may be, however, that his creditors saw the hopelessness of pursuing their claims further at this time, for in September their victim became very seriously ill and was more or less confined to his room until the end of the year. "Liver and head both wrong," he was informing E. M. Ward, the painter, in the following January. "I have been burning the candle at both ends, and those who adopt that mode of illumination usually die in the dark." But by the end of the month he was well again, writing *Quite Alone*, and, what was of more importance, being given work by the Levys which allowed him a freedom of expression not always permissible in a leading article.

The year 1863, indeed, marked his emergence as the *Daily Telegraph's* principal special correspondent. Luckily for him there were exceptionally good opportunities for "picturesque" reporting. There was the grand ceremonial opening of the Metropolitan Railway, that daring underground innovation at which *Punch* and its imitators never seemed to tire of making fun; there was the welcome to the "sea-king's daughter from over the sea" and the Prince of Wales's marriage with all the celebrations that followed; there was the inauguration of the Albert Memorial which, at any rate at the time of its unveiling, seems to have been regarded as the world's eighth wonder; and there was the Congress of Sovereigns at Frankfort which provided a whole series of agreeable "sensations." And it was then that the Levys, after some hesitation, made their, to Sala, memorable offer: would he be prepared to pay a

long visit to the United States for the purpose of describing "America
in the Midst of War"?

It was not a mission to be easily refused—two articles a week for
a period of six months, and an inclusive fee of £1000—but on the
other hand it was not one to be lightly undertaken. Almost without
exception British correspondents in the States had succeeded in making
themselves exceedingly unpopular, no matter where their personal
sympathies happened to lie, nor what the declared policy of their newspapers might be. Even the great William Howard Russell had come
to grief. As representative of the *Times*, itself a strong supporter of
the South, he had been unable to disguise his hatred of slavery, but he
had, very rightly, deemed it his duty to describe in some detail the
disorderly retreat of the Federal troops at the first battle of Bull Run,
and so roused the fiery indignation of the North. Lesser men had gone
out and endeavoured to maintain a more or less neutral attitude, but had
similarly incurred American displeasure. It seemed almost impossible
for a British correspondent to remain *persona grata* in the United States
for any length of time.

In Sala's case there were additional reasons for caution. He was
the grandson of a West Indian slave-owner; he had never disguised
his Southern sympathies; and he would not be going out as an unknown
man. Already a majority of his books had appeared in American
editions for which, in those days when international copyright was
little more than an author's dream, he had received little or nothing.
Time and again, too, he had spoken his mind on the subject and in
words as blunt as any that Dickens himself had used. And the Levys
themselves were fully aware of the risks they would be running. But
they believed that, given a free hand, Sala might very well provide
the world with a picture livelier and more intimate than, while as
accurate and informative as, any that had yet appeared; and here they
were right, for the letters which he was to send home caused such
widespread interest and were so warmly acclaimed in this country
(though bitterly attacked in the States) that the proposed six months
were doubled before he was summoned back to England.

As to Sala himself, he admits that he was cock-a-hoop. True, his
wife did her utmost to dissuade him from so dangerous a venture.
(But how like a woman! he thought. There would be no danger at
all, and when he had acclimatised himself she would be invited to join
him.) True, there was his conductorship of *Temple Bar*; but was not
Edmund Yates ready and willing to step into his shoes? True, there
was his novel, *Quite Alone*, no more than half-finished, and by this

time Dickens was interested and spoke of purchasing the serial rights for *All the Year Round*. But what a grand opportunity! What a book he would be able to make of his letters home! On his return Tinsley would pay him hundreds of pounds for the copyright. Pond, too, or one of his other friends, would assuredly be able to fix up a lecturing tour. Why, if he only kept his head, there was a fortune to be made, and at long last he would be in a position to pay off every one of his creditors. Of course he must go, and it was in a state of the wildest excitement that he made his preparations.

Good wishes and letter of introduction poured in upon him; there were one or two farewell dinners; Dickens gave him some sterling advice in the matter of abstaining from public speeches; Robert Brough's widow came to Guilford Street to stay with Mrs. Sala; and on Saturday, November 14th, Sala stepped on board S.S. *Arabia* bound for Boston, U.S.A.

CHAPTER ELEVEN

SPECIAL CORRESPONDENT

I

"It may perhaps be news to you," wrote Edward Dicey from Magdeburg in June, 1866, "to learn how fearfully hard you work your correspondents abroad." His words were addressed to the *Daily Telegraph* at the moment when the Seven Weeks' War was about to begin. "The world," he continued, "at least the Prussian world, is informed upon the authority of the London correspondent of the *Kreuz Zeitung*, that your 'Special Commissioner,' the first feuilletonist and newspaper satirist of the age, a Spaniard by descent, but *Anglais renforcé* in all his feelings, has been sent by the *Daily Telegraph* to Austria and Italy at the same time. This ubiquitous gentleman, who clearly beats Sir Boyle Roche's famous bird hollow, being in no fewer than three places at once, is said to supply you with concurrent articles on 'The European Crisis,' 'The State of Affairs in Austria,' and 'The War Feeling in Italy.' But then he is evidently used to that kind of work, having in the course of the last fifteen months, had to write special letters for the *Daily Telegraph* from all parts of the compass, including the United States and Mexico, Berlin and Seville, and divers other places, including," he added jocosely, remembering Thackeray's ballad, "Jerusalem and Madagascar."

The special commissioner, of course, was Sala, who, within a year or two of his decision to eschew "literature," had managed to secure for himself a position in the journalistic world which it is hardly an exaggeration to call unique. The picturesque essayist had transformed himself into an international figure, and a generation was to pass before he had any real rival in his own particular field.

It was the ninety-two despatches sent home from America in the course of 1864 which definitely established his reputation as a special correspondent of the highest order. From that time, indeed, the Levys rightly regarded him as their "star" performer, and did a political crisis arise abroad or some great national celebration was announced to take place in any part of the civilised world, their first reaction would almost always be the same: Sala must go. For a variety of reasons this was not always possible, but during the next twenty years he was sent hither and thither, often at no more than a few hours' notice, and he gratefully acknowledged the fact that on all occasions he was given "the salary of an ambassador."

The great success of his American letters is not difficult to understand. Nothing quite so blunt about the New World had been printed in this country since the days of the last Anglo-American war. It may be admitted—long afterwards he admitted it himself—that there were passages in his letters which were "tinted" and "even distorted." There was some very hard hitting, and no doubt Mr. (or Colonel) Simon's grandson now and then failed to give due prominence to the appalling difficulties against which the Lincoln Administration had to contend. At times, too, there was a touch of malice in what he wrote, as, for instance, in his description, widely quoted at the time but suppressed when his *Diary in America in the Midst of War* was published, of his interview with the President's wife. Today, perhaps, it may be reprinted without causing any offence.

"I think," he wrote, "I can give almost a shorthand writer's report of my conversation with Mrs. Lincoln. After the first salutation she said :

"'Do you keep your health, sir ?'

"I replied that I was happy and thankful to say that I enjoyed tolerable health.

"'How long have you been in this country, sir ?' she asked.

"I said that I had been seven weeks on the American continent.

"'How long do you conclude to remain, sir ?' she went on.

"I replied that I hoped to remain about seven months longer.

"The President's wife was then good enough to ask 'how I liked the country.' I replied diplomatically, that it was very large and very wonderful. Now ensued a deep and, to me, embarrassing silence. I didn't know what was to come next, and I don't think Mrs. Lincoln did. At last she spoke again, and once more in interrogatory form :

"'And you keep your health, sir ?'

"I answered this kind enquiry as best I could . . . and gave Mrs. Lincoln a series of bows."

It was a little unkind, no doubt, but it amused England. So did his sprightly pictures of less exalted circles. The South was closed to him, but alike in the Northern States and in Canada, Mexico, and Cuba, he wandered freely about, following that inquisitive nose of his, answering questions about Thackeray, whose sudden death shortly after his departure from England had deeply shocked him, and accumulating and passing on a mass of curious if not always valuable information of a kind not often to be found in the despatches of other correspondents. So little was known by the man in the street about "these Yankees"; so many odd stories were current about them : what was the truth ? From Sala's lively letters it was possible to obtain at least a clear enough impression of the *kind* of folk they must be. If, moreover, his criticisms at times were uncomfortably forthright, he did not neglect the more amiable sides of Northern character and social life.

In the main his accusations were directed against their boastful self-assurance and pitiful self-deception which, to him, seemed almost ubiquitous. These Northerners declared that they had the best government in all the world, but he had found it to be "practically a despotism." They demanded British sympathy for a war undertaken for the purpose of liberating the blacks, yet so far from conducting a crusade for human freedom they were exercising the most detestable cruelty and oppression over white men, and showing no real sympathy for the negroes who were treated with general contempt. How, then, could they expect British support ? And what was one to say of a "free" people who would not permit the truth to be told in their own newspapers and attacked as "traitors" and "spies" those bold enough to uphold it ? No, they did not want the truth told, and in that fact lay the explanation, he thought, of his own great unpopularity and the uproar occasioned by his despatches.

The American campaign of abuse, indeed, had begun even before he was across the Atlantic. Another Britisher in search of lies, of course, and probably a Secesh spy : they would know what to expect. When, moreover, it became known what monstrous libels his newspaper was printing, there arose a howl of rage which did not die down until long after his departure. As the months passed it did not matter with what pains he endeavoured to make Britain understand and appreciate the Northern point of view ; it made no difference that his books had given pleasure to thousands : this "bloated miscreant," "fat cockney," and "venal hack" was the enemy of the country and deserved a lynching. Such, too, was the general indignation that although the North itself was far from being politically united, to no section was he other than a shameless and heavily-bribed "traitor." "The Copperhead," wrote an English critic, "would have none of him ; the Black Republican eyed him askance ; the Democrat reviled him ; and the Rev. Henry Ward Beecher and his connection passed by him on the other side." He did make one protest in print shortly after his arrival, but it only helped to fan the flames, and henceforth he followed Dickens's advice and remained silent, refusing all invitations to speak in public and maintaining that "poker-face" upon the possession of which the Yankees were so pleased to pride themselves. Once or twice it was privately suggested to him that all press-attacks could easily be stopped, and with considerable advantage to himself, by a change of attitude, but Sala only smiled. "They will give their heads," he told Hepworth Dixon, then editing the *Athenaeum*, "for powerful advocacy, and if I had chosen to be dishonest and to sell my employers I might have left the country with five and twenty thousand dollars in my pocket."

If, however, the press campaign against him was waged with ever more violence as one or another side of Northern life and character became the subject of not too favourable comment, Sala in his private capacity was warmly welcomed by many distinguished Americans and paid repeated tribute to their lavish hospitality. He found himself in "a whirl of excitement." The war might be raging, but in Washington and New York there was no lack of gaiety. The theatres were crowded, there were balls most nights, and every fashionable club seemed eager to meet the author of *The Seven Sons of Mammon*. The press might vilify him, but he had come to the country well sponsored. The Prime Minister himself had given him a letter to the British Ambassador, and Lord Lyons went out of his way to be kind. He personally introduced the visitor to the Hon. William H. Seward, the Secretary of State, and it was the hardly less prominent Senator Charles Sumner—almost a Macready in appearance, Sala thought—who took him one morning into the President's sanctum. Contrary to his expectations, Mr. Lincoln had no whimsical stories to tell him and his visit to the White House was in the nature of a disappointment. He was happier in bookish circles. He met the well-known James Gordon Bennett who admitted that even he with all his experience had never really understood the American character, and he renewed his acquaintance with Horace Greeley, possibly the most forceful journalist of the day and a future nominee for Presidential honours, and with Nathaniel P. Willis, "now turned," he recorded, "into an elderly imitation of Count D'Orsay, with perhaps a slight dash of Mr. Mantalini." Willis, it would seem, could talk of little but the great European houses which he had been privileged to visit: a fact which gave point to Sala's somewhat acid remark that the American's own rather shabby residence might well be called Willis's Rooms. In all probability the man in whose company he enjoyed himself most was Phineas T. Barnum. They had met in England, and Sala was fully aware of his questionable reputation. "A colossal fraud" he might be, but—what a jolly bluff fraud! What fun to be taken behind the scenes and allowed to become on friendly terms with the weirdest freaks ever born to be publicly exhibited! But there was a side to Barnum, he knew, of which his thousands of patrons knew nothing: in private life he was the most delightful companion and a very real friend in need.

Only one of his letters of introduction seems to have led to trouble. The Rothschilds had warmly recommended him to the attention of the well-known New York banker, August Belmont. For some reason Mr. Belmont maintained a noticeably unfriendly attitude towards him, and the day came when there was a "scene." This was not to be the only "scene" of the kind which was seriously to embarrass his friends, but it was the only occasion in America when he temporarily forgot himself and gave those who were in the habit of hinting that his private life was not all it should be some grounds for their assertions.

Amongst those Americans whose hospitality he most enjoyed was a prominent lawyer and bibliophile by name Samuel Barlow. He possessed a splendid library of books, and Sala was a frequent guest at his house. One Sunday evening Mr. Belmont was present at a small reception given by Mrs. Barlow, and there were "words" and almost what Artemus Ward would have called "a fite." From a letter of apology which Sala sent next day to his host, we can imagine more or less what happened. "It would be a sorry requital," he wrote, "for the constant kindness and hospitality I have received during many months in your house were I to omit to express to you my very sincere regret that I should have been compelled to let Mr. August Belmont know my opinion of him under the circumstances of last night. But no other course was open to me. The rudeness and insolence with which I have been treated came, as I conceive, to a culmination in the . . . abrupt manner in which he acknowledged a very civil salute on my part." The banker, he contended, had repeatedly treated him with contemptuous indifference, and matters had come to a head when he had been heard to mutter, in Mrs. Barlow's drawing-room, that he, Sala, did not know how to behave himself. That had been too much, and had the words not been uttered where they were and in the presence of his hostess, he would "at once have knocked Mr. Belmont down."

"There are times," he concluded, "when the modestest man cannot help being a little self-conscious and . . . a moderate amount of self-assertion becomes not only a relief but a necessity. I am not given to bragging or boasting, but I feel it due to myself to remind those who perhaps ignore or are indifferent to the fact that I am a man of letters occupying no second rate position, and that by my own unaided efforts I have established a position not only in literature, but in European society to which Mr. August Belmont with all his millions would with difficulty obtain admission, and that my name will live, for good or evil, long after that of Mr. August Belmont is extant only on a few cancelled bills of exchange."

Well, well, the language used on that occasion was no doubt forthright enough.

2

Meanwhile the letters home had been so greatly to the taste of the
Daily Telegraph's readers that its proprietors had suggested a further stay
of six months, on the same agreeably high terms.   At once Sala sent for
his wife.   She joined him in New Jersey, but, like Mrs. Dickens a quarter
of a century before, soon found that a life of incessant movement, with
strange food and an almost daily ceremony of fresh introductions, was
too much for her shy and retiring disposition.   Together they visited the
chief cities of Canada, and stayed for a while at Saratoga, but she took the
first opportunity to return home, after making sure that her husband's
wardrobe had been suitably, if expensively, replenished.

Her going coincided with yet another of Sala's failures to complete
a literary commission.   At the time of his sailing from England about
half of his novel *Quite Alone* had been written.   This story, possibly the
best that he wrote, contains the adventures of an ill-used little girl, the
daughter of a tempestuous actress, who deserts her except at such times
when her presence will be useful; it has some really good scenes in Paris
and one or two diverting portraits.   Dickens, admiring, no doubt, the
sympathetic delineation of the poor little waif, had broken a rule of his
by accepting the book for serialisation without having the completed
manuscript in his hands.   For some months the chapters had been punctu-
ally forthcoming, but in August, 1864, ominous announcements in *All
the Year Round* began to appear, and after a week or two's delay its
Conductor took the bold but justifiable step of inviting Andrew Halliday
to complete the story.   Halliday, who had no means of knowing in what
way Sala had intended to finish it, did his work exceedingly well, not
only gathering up the various threads in the most skilful way but also
managing to reproduce Sala's peculiar style.   Sala himself was a little sore
when Frederic Chapman insisted on using Halliday's conclusion when
he issued the book in the following year although an offer to give it its
rightful ending had been made.   Like Dickens, however, Chapman was
not unaware of what had happened over *Make Your Game*, and he preferred not to wait for something which might never be forthcoming.

"I am sure I did my best," bewailed the "distressed author," "but I
signally failed."   This was hardly surprising.   At the Brevoort House on
Fifth Avenue he could work in comparative comfort, but in Mexico and
Havana, or with the Army of the Potomac, it became more and more
difficult for him to turn his attention away from American affairs.   "Page

after page," he wrote, "like so many drops of blood, about two hundred slips of manuscript, oozed from me between spring and summer. They were written with a hard pencil on slips of carbonised paper placed upon tissue. I was obliged to 'manifold' the manuscript, to guard against the uncertainties of the post. They were written in a hammock in Cuba, on board steamers, in railway cars, in hotel verandahs, in the midst of noise, confusion, smoke, cursing and swearing, battle, murder, and sudden death. In the month of August I broke down altogether, and the mail went without any more of my tissue paper. I had lost the thread of my narrative. I had forgotten the very names of my *dramatis personae*. I was in a new country—a new world . . . badgered and baited and hated, always abused, often in peril of my life, and under all hazard compelled to send home every week from six to eight columns of matter."

This possibly excusable lapse, however, was forgiven, and when in November he came home it was to a London very ready to fête him. "His house in Guilford Street," says Vizetelly, "became the favourite resort of his many literary and journalistic friends," and it was now that the "swells" as well as the Bohemians began to come. Men like Richard Burton, the explorer, George Alfred Lawrence, of *Guy Livingstone* fame, the Mayhews and Hepworth Dixon, were regularly to be found there together with the smart "sprigs of nobility"—was *that* one of Sala's inventions ?—who had apparently been told what exceptionally amusing parties he gave and managed to secure an invitation. Edward Tinsley, too, was a very frequent visitor at this time and urged on his host the importance of preparing the American letters for immediate publication in book-form. A fortnight, he thought, ought to suffice for all the necessary rearrangement and the addition of a 15,000 word "justificatory" address to "an intelligent American," and in the second week in December he applied an agreeable spur in the shape of a cheque for £350. Actually it was six weeks before the two volumes had been passed for press, but, as Sala pointed out with some truth, "six weeks considering what I have had to do verges on the superhuman."

The volumes were published towards the end of January, and such was their success that a second edition was required at the beginning of April. From the historical point of view the *Diary* may be without much value : as a record of personal experience during days of unusual excitement it can be read with pleasure even today.

Incidentally, there was a curious little sequel to the American visit. In the summer of 1865 there was published a book called *Belle Boyd, in Camp and Prison*. Miss Boyd was a Southerner who had been arrested as a spy, imprisoned, and treated with considerable harshness before she managed to escape to Europe. Her story had created no little interest, more particularly because during her adventures she had managed to persuade an impressionable lieutenant in the Federal Army to adopt her own views. The two of them had been married in London. The book was of no literary or historical importance, but Miss Boyd's name was well known and her story, whether "embroidered" or not, created a mild sensation at the time.

Now in both British and American editions there was a lengthy introduction, but whereas in the London edition its writer was merely described as "a Friend of the South" the New York edition boldly stated that the introducer was "George Augusta (*sic*) Sala." Some years later Sala hotly denied that he had ever written a word of it, but he was undoubtedly interested in Belle's story, wrote about it just before the publication of the book in his "Echoes," and is said to have sung or rather recited to music her favourite song "Maryland, my Maryland," at that time wholly unknown in England, on more than one occasion to gatherings of friends. Undoubtedly he knew both her and her husband, and may have been present at their wedding.

In England, of course, the book was speedily forgotten, but in America there were those who took offence at some words used by the introducer, and amongst them was the young Bret Harte who in 1867 began his literary career in a Californian newspaper with some amusing travesties of well-known works of fiction. Included amongst these *Condensed Novels* was one entitled "Mary McGillup. After Belle Boyd. With an Introduction by G. A. S–la." It was not until the *Condensed Novels* appeared in book-form in England that Sala took any action, but he was fully justified in insisting that the offending item be omitted from future editions, for it was distinctly malicious. Bret Harte, however, had not been writing, it would seem, merely for fun: he believed that Sala had not only written the introduction but to a certain extent had been responsible for the book, and, according to one account, had sworn to shoot him at sight. Shortly after his arrival in England there was a scene in the house of W. P. Frith, the painter. There was a dinner-party at which Bret Harte was to be the guest of honour, and the Salas had been invited. The American was announced. Frith was about to introduce the two men when Bret Harte shocked the company by announcing his refusal to shake hands with "that scoundrel."

It was an awkward moment, and once again, had not ladies been present, there might have been "a fite." But Sala, who, according to one eye-witness, seemed to be "startled," left hurriedly with his wife before dinner. There is no reason to suppose that he actually *wrote* anything that appeared in the American book, but I cannot think that he was wholly uninterested in its production. I mention the incident at Frith's house more particularly because a perverted version of it in which Sala was made to appear the aggressor was afterwards current—the two men never did meet on friendly terms—and used to illustrate his alleged "bad manners" in society.

3

It will hardly be necessary to give in any detail the story of Sala's wanderings over Europe during the next few years. Such of his despatches as he considered worthy of preservation—only a small proportion of those which appeared in the *Daily Telegraph*—were incorporated into one or other of his books. Much that he did not write was attributed, both at home and abroad, to his pen. At times his wife joined him for a month or two. He was handsomely paid, but was frequently in financial difficulties, and on one occasion was obliged to sell all his furniture and the small but valuable library of books and prints which he had collected. Attacks upon him continued to come from several quarters, but his reputation steadily increased, and on that memorable day in 1870 when he narrowly escaped being shot as a Prussian spy in Paris, his name was as well known as any other special correspondent then writing.

He has some amusing things to say of his responsibilities and anxieties in an article he wrote for Miss Braddon's *Belgravia* in 1871.

"Let the Special be a crass donkey, or a blockhead, or a mere respectable mediocrity, and his letters will pass without much comment. . . . But let the Special only be so unfortunate as to have a style of his own—let him have a capacity for minute observation, or a gift for picturesque and vivid description; let him be endowed with the power of thinking, and of expressing his thoughts in vigorous language—and the whole of Hampstead Heath will be upon him at once, kicking and braying with all the intensity of its hairy-hoofed, long-eared, hoarse-voiced energy. He must expect to be called a scribbler and a penny-a-liner. . . . To assume that the Special Correspondent is a Cockney, an ignoramus, an emancipated tailor, or a drunken Irishman; to accuse him, if he happens to mention that he has dined with a duke or conversed with a general, of being a flunkey, a toady, a Jenkins, and a lickspittle; to insinuate, if he happens to advocate the claims of this or that political party, of being bribed by them; and in particular, when he is doing his best to tell the truth, to brand him as an impudent and deliberate liar;—these are among the amenities to which every Special Correspondent who has attained eminence in his vocation must look forward as his continuous and inevitable portion."

Yet if "the Reverend Brainworm Babble" might maunder over "the morbid feelings awakened by constant perusal of highly-spiced suffusions of a sensational press"—apparently an actual quotation from a letter printed in the *Times* or the *Saturday Review*—or "Major-General Sir Barabbas Whitefeather" might fulminate on the steps of the Praetorian Club against "those damn writing fellows," Sala had the satisfaction of knowing that his work was being widely appreciated. It may be admitted that he was not at his best when describing military operations, but behind the lines there was nobody to touch him.

In this article, too, he gives us the qualities most useful to a man forced, as he now was, to "follow the footprints of history."

"It would be better for him to speak half a dozen different languages with tolerable fluency; to have visited or resided in most parts of the habitable globe . . .; to be a good cook, a facile musician, a first-rate whist-player, a practised horseman, a tolerable shot, a ready conversationalist, a freemason, a philosopher, a moderate smoker . . . and a perfect master of the art of packing."

I cannot believe that Sala was ever comfortable on a horse, and he was certainly no musician, but most of the other accomplishments were his. As for the luggage which demanded such expert packing, his list of necessities includes a passport (a more ornate document in those days than it is today), a large number of visiting-cards, a revolver, "a little huswife full of pins, needles, buttons, and thread," an umbrella, a corkscrew, and a dress-suit. The special correspondent must be able to write his despatches "on a drum, on the deck of a steamer during a gale, on horseback, in the garret of a house on fire, on the top of an omnibus, or on the top of Mont Blanc." Finally, "when there is no war afoot, he must be prepared to 'do' funerals as well as marriages, state-banquets, Volunteer reviews, Great Exhibitions, remarkable trials, christenings, coronations, ship-launches, agricultural shows, Royal progresses, picture shows, first-stone layings, horse-races, and hangings." He must, in fact, be "Jack of all trades, and master of all—that are journalistic."

In the earlier part of 1865 there were one or two important funerals to "do," but Sala was eager for further adventures abroad, and the Levys were equally eager for him to go. An Exhibition was due to be held in Dublin, but he wished for something "less cut-and-dried." He could have accompanied the *Great Eastern* on her Atlantic Cable voyage, but frankly admitted that he had had enough of that "marvel of naval architecture." Then it was announced that the Emperor Napoleon was about to visit some of his African possessions.

Algiers! Yes, that sounded distinctly better, more particularly as the Royal progress was not, it seemed, to be "covered" by any other London correspondent. And so, barely five months after his return from America, Sala was off again. He was in Paris dining with William Howard Russell when the news of Lincoln's assassination reached him; he was kept waiting a considerable time in Marseilles; but at the beginning of May he was in Africa, and in the course of the next few weeks, travelling hither and thither, sometimes in the greatest discomfort, interviewing the Emperor, and in general enjoying himself hugely, he succeeded in producing a picture of Algerian life which if fragmentary was at least high-spirited and pleasantly informative.

"This Algeria," he wrote to Horace Mayhew, typically amusing himself by using white ink on a black shiny paper, "is a very jolly place, and *very cheap*. . . . There is an immense amount of fun to be had, for little or nothing. I mean to bring Mrs. Sala in September." Any such plan, however, proved impossible, for in the early autumn he was busily engaged in lecturing to Scottish and Irish audiences on his American experiences, and in November he was bidden to make an extended tour of Europe.

It was in June that he said good-bye to Algeria, and, taking his annual holiday earlier than usual, went by way of Nice, Paris, and Strasburg to his favourite Homburg. And here, as almost invariably happened, he speedily won large sums of money: so large this time that an immediate investment seemed essential. In the circumstances he chose wisely, purchasing a number of valuable jewels for his wife, all enclosed in their appropriate leather-cases. Alas! further visits to the tables proved progressively disastrous, and all that poor Mrs. Sala received on his return was a charming assortment of empty cases. What she said on that occasion is not recorded, but she seems to have given expression to her natural indignation during the lecture tour that followed. In spite of her "horror" at seeing her husband on any platform she boldly accompanied him North, and in Edinburgh was unable to resist the fascinations of the Princes Street shops. She insisted, Sala told George Hodder, who, I fancy, had been largely instrumental in arranging the tour, on purchasing, at his expense, "the most wonderful bonnet and at the most wonderful price ever known." The lectures themselves seem to have been a fair financial success, though in Belfast he was momentarily annoyed to find that he was expected "to give a free show" to more than 3000 people, all of whom, he thought, would have been well pleased to pay their

three or five shillings for a seat. On the other hand, in Ireland there were
no expenses, which in Scotland had been high, for they were entertained
at Clandeboye by Lord and Lady Dufferin, who on many occasions in
the future were to show Sala the greatest kindness.

4

The continental commission which almost immediately followed
seems to have been of the most elastic nature. "Go abroad; take your
wife; look about you; and let us have two or three letters each week."
Such, I imagine, was about the extent of the Levys' instructions. Sala
tells us that he proposed to begin his explorations at Brussels and end
them in Moscow, and there is little doubt that he was in no hurry to
return to England. His departure, indeed, came at a moment when he
was particularly glad to be out of reach of those who, however greatly
they might admire his work, were no more eager than before to remain
his creditors. There had been new difficulties with the Income Tax
Commissioners, he had been "dunned" by a dozen or more tradespeople,
and the usurers were demanding even more than their usual hundred-
weight of flesh. Only the sale of his "sticks" in the Guilford Street house
saved him from legal proceedings, and then only after his solicitors,
Messrs. Lewis and Lewis, had worked exceedingly hard on his behalf.
All his most valuable books and most of his fine prints were thus lost to
him—they fetched £400, he told Shirley Brooks, which was "more
than I expected, as they had cost me (only) three times as much"—and
the few family possessions from which he could not bring himself to
part were taken care of either by an old fellow-lodger of his, Rudolf
Glover, or by one or other of his good friends the Mayhews.

And so, dispossessed and homeless and not yet out of debt, though he
had agreed to set aside a portion of his earnings which (in theory) would
free him by June, 1867, Sala began his "long exile." He took Mrs. Sala
—"my one remaining treasure"—with him, and prepared for a task for
which he knew himself to be well qualified and one which was certainly
not being ill-paid. He knew, moreover, that Tinsley was very willing
to reprint anything that he chose to write—the Barbary book had just
appeared and been well received—and if he had no particular "address,"
it would not be for the first time. There were some responsibilities, as
he had discovered long ago, with which he could very well dispense.

Only a few months had passed, however, before his plans were being
hurriedly changed. He had left an England about to be torn in dissension
over a Reform Bill almost as drastic in its way as that of 1832, and he was

to come into a Europe on the eve of yet another series of international squabbles. He had sauntered with his wife through Holland and Belgium, spent Christmas at Homburg and New Year's Day in Berlin, and was preparing to continue his leisurely progress eastwards when a telegram from London caused a long-continued postponement of a second visit to Russia. There was serious trouble, it seemed, in Spain. There often was serious trouble in Spain those days, and, after leaving his wife in Paris, Sala hurried south to Madrid expecting to find himself in the midst of civil war again. To his surprise he found that an attempted military rising had speedily been suppressed, and all was quiet on the Spanish front. So peaceful explorations were continued, and for the next few months readers of the *Daily Telegraph* were regaled with pictures of Spanish life in Sala's cheeriest vein. Then for the second time came a rude interruption. Trouble was brewing over the Venetian question between Austria and Italy, and Prussia was showing signs of that military arrogance which was to become her most notorious characteristic. War, in fact, was imminent, and Sala was ordered to Vienna.

Once again Mrs. Sala joined him, and at the end of April they were in Vienna, in a hotel which was "dark, disagreeable, infamously mismanaged, and even more infamously dear." It might be very nice, he informed Shirley Brooks, at this time almost the only one of his friends to whom he was writing with any regularity, "to be staying in the same house with the Prince of Rumpelstiltkin, the Hospidar of Hungulia, the Waywode of Enguaria, the Caissiacan of Kagmagawissel, and the Ban of Dogstein," but, he added, "when your board costs you a florin a mouthful and your bed fifty kreutzers a feather, you are apt to grumble." He was inclined, too, to grumble at the more political turn which his despatches were now required to take. "Drat Austrian politics : I long to be out of this stew." A month later, however, while at Trieste only a few days before war was declared, he was better pleased with his lot. "Not precisely in the midst of war," he wrote, "but on the very threshold thereof. My agreeable instructions are to get as near to the scene of action as ever I possibly can directly the first shot is fired. The Austrians," he continued, "who are good-natured folk will give tourists a few days' grace . . . so Mrs. Sala can get away to Switzerland or somewhere else safe and leave me to wrestle with wild beasts at Ephesus." And for the next few weeks he was wrestling with them as best he could and in considerable discomfort, now in the Tyrol at Garibaldi's headquarters, now with other British correspondents like G. A. Henty, Edward Dicey, and Henry Hyndman, at Padua or Milan, where, by the way, he was amused to meet no less than three gentlemen of his name—a tinsmith, a

baker, and a rich carriage-builder—and finally in Venice, whither Mrs.
Sala managed to make her way, and where he was to stay on and off
until the triumphant entry of the Italians in the late autumn. It was here,
too, that there occurred an "ugly scene" between Sala and George
Meredith, then the *Morning Post's* representative and as yet hardly known
to the public as a writer. Meredith, according to Hyndman, was not finding
his work too congenial, and he seems to have got on Sala's nerves. His
"keen and at that period rather sardonic and satirical intelligence grated
on Sala's ebullience." The quarrel, it seems, "arose out of a petty matter,
which, when all was said, only amounted to the fact that Meredith,
though just in all his dealings and hospitable in his way, was by no means
liberal, while Sala, though extremely liberal, and hospitable as well, was
by no means always just." Matters came to a head at the dinner-table,
Sala lost his temper, and "most grossly insulted" his colleague. Blows,
in fact, seem to have been averted only by Meredith's quiet departure.

His despatches to the *Daily Telegraph* sufficiently reveal the nature of
Sala's activities at the time. Transport he found troublesome, but
generally managed to obtain a conveyance of some kind by assuming the
haughty demeanour proper (in native eyes) to a Field Marshal. Food
was sometimes a difficulty, but valiantly he played cook, and not only
for his own delectation. There was, of course, an almost continuous
shortage of cash, but here he was singularly lucky, for the manager of
his Venice hotel, Herr Robert Etzensberger (afterwards well known in
London as the manager of the Midland Hotel and always a good friend
to Sala) was delighted to play banker to so convivial and "unrepresenta-
tive" an Englishman. He seems to have impressed Austrians and Italians
alike with a sense of his unusual importance, and his despatches were
widely quoted in newspapers abroad.

From his letters to Shirley Brooks, one gathers that for all his grumbles
he was not dissatisfied with his lot. "I have dogged about a good deal,"
he was writing two days after the war was officially at an end, "seem to
have lived twelve years in as many months, and feel immensely old."
Nevertheless, he was by no means tired of his "exile." He still hoped, he
said, "to put in a brief appearance in London in May next to let those
who hate me know that I am still alive and am strong and can bite and
have eightpence three farthings," but he was planning further peaceful
explorations. Of late the first Napoleon had been constantly in his mind,
and he thought that his next book might well be an account of the great
man's captivity and last days in St. Helena, to which island he would
be willing and even eager to go so soon as Dame Europa and her unruly
pupils permitted. Mrs. Sala—"the only Englishwoman in Venice during

the war"—would be required to go with him, apparently in order that her continuing passion for new and expensive bonnets might be temporarily curbed. As for his immediate plans, he was "going to be lurching up and down Italy in search of prey" during the winter. He was losing, he concluded, many of his illusions about the Italians—"a damned set of macaroni-gorging, lemonade-swilling, bragging, screeching, yelling, and cowardly curs: always excepting Garibaldi who is a Trump and more than half crazy"—but there would be much to enjoy in Rome, he thought, and, as later letters were to show, this was certainly the case.

He did not visit St. Helena, and he did not show himself to his enemies in London in May. In 1867 Paris had her second Great Exhibition, and early in the year Sala settled down at the Hôtel Windsor in the Rue de Rivoli, sent home some dozen columns each week, and remained there until the late autumn.

5

Back in England, the wolves descended upon him at once.

Hitherto, it seems, they had been satisfied with punctual payments of the interest on the various sums of money which he had borrowed: now they insisted (though Sala preferred to have it believed that it was his own suggestion) on a gradual repayment of the principal—a matter of some £3000. What this meant he explained in a letter he wrote about this time to Mr. John Bertrand Payne, then manager of the publishing firm of Edward Moxon and Company. "I get a thousand a year from the Telegraph and pick up another thou by miscellanising; but every week of my life the vampires drain me of between twenty-five and thirty pounds, before the domestic mutton chop can be thought of." It was a large sum to find and all the more difficult to secure in view of the fact that after a few weeks in Brompton lodgings the lease of a small furnished house in Putney—with the "sticks at a valuation"—had been taken. There was but one way to find it, and valorously Sala set to work to increase his "miscellanising" output.

"My dear Hepworth Dixon," he wrote, only a week or two after his return, "you have become most deservedly famous and prosperous. Poor old George Augustus has fallen, at forty years, on evil days. He is bankrupt and beggared. Can you give him some work on the Athenaeum? Every pound he can earn will help him." That, I imagine, was not very different from a number of other letters from the same source which found their way into editorial and publishing offices at the time. Yet Sala was already committed to an amount of work, outside Peterborough Court, which most men would have found far in excess of what they could conveniently undertake. There were his monthly articles for *Belgravia* (which delighted one admirer so much that he had every one of them separately bound) and occasional essays for *All the Year Round*. He had begun his association with John Dicks, one of the pioneers of the cheap reprint, whose *Bow Bells* was in process of becoming one of the more popular "family weeklies," and he had commissions for two or three Christmas Annuals. In addition, there was Tinsley, for whom his Paris Exhibition book was being prepared, while Moxon had invited him to edit a new and complete edition of Charles Lamb's Works. (It may be admitted that he was not particularly well fitted for this last-mentioned task, and, as it happened, it was soon to be given up, though not before Vol. I. with a long introductory essay had appeared.) There were also fairly regular contributions to *Notes and Queries*, though for these, I presume, he received no remuneration. Nevertheless, if the vampires were to be satisfied, other commissions were necessary, and he now allowed it to be known that he would undertake work of a kind at which men of letters had hitherto looked askance.

The trade pamphlet—that is to say, an advertisement of a particular firm's goods written in the form of a semi-historical, not too technical essay intended for the lay public—was, if rare, not unknown at the time. So far as I know, however, few if any such publications had borne their author's name, and almost certainly no well-known writer had as yet allowed himself to acknowledge a connection with any such work. True, there was an enterprising firm of London tailors who advertised their wares in doggerel verses, and there was another firm which at intervals issued a kind of House Annual in which the work of fairly popular writers would appear. But so much was permissible, for these writers had merely been invited, on agreeably high terms, to make a literary contribution. It would have been a very different matter had they been required to prepare, say, an outline of the firm's history or to descant on the superlative merits of their new winter suitings. At all costs the Dignity of Letters must be preserved, though what exactly the phrase meant it would not be too easy to say. Dickens, it will be remembered, had been widely attacked when he announced his intention to give Readings for his own profit, though nobody, I believe, raised his voice in alarm when Thackeray began to give his "lectures." But at least no man of letters had so far "demeaned" himself as to *puff* without disguise this or that commodity on the market, and when it became known that Sala's clever pen could be "bought" in this way, there was the expected growl of protest (but was it perhaps tinged with envy?) which culminated in an unwise attack in print, and this, as we shall see, brought its author into the Law Courts. Yet was not "poor old George Augustus" fully justified in accepting any such commission when it increased his chances of being finally free from all the vampires? He was paid fifty guineas—sometimes a little more—for a single short essay which at least had the merit of being interesting, no matter whether its subject was the history of hats, the evolution of the sewing-machine, the manufacture of whisky, or the seemingly philanthropic methods of a large insurance company. There was certainly no question of any of his employers being dissatisfied, he made no attempt to disguise the nature of the work he was doing, and the money he received was honestly earned. And when read today the dozen or more trade pamphlets for which he was responsible during the next year or two not only make up a most amusing little collection but are not without their value for the social historian.

One other venture of his at this juncture remains to be mentioned, though here, I am afraid, my information is scanty. On September 2nd, 1867, there appeared the first number of a penny serio-comic weekly called *Banter*. There was little to distinguish it from any of its predecessors: it seemed to be just one more would-be rival to *Punch*. Advertisements, however, were soon appearing which announced that "George Augustus Sala's Life and Adventures in Many Countries" would be found in the fifth number, and be continued weekly. These statements were distinctly misleading, suggesting as they did that Sala had chosen to entrust his autobiography to this as yet obscure periodical. In point of fact they referred to a new novel of his, *The Bargraves: a Romance of Many Countries*, which, with a further series of London vignettes called "On a Bus; or, Philosophy on a Knife-Board," did become a regular feature and was continued until December 20th, when it was broken off never to be completed. *Banter* itself, with Augustus Mayhew's *Mrs. Letts' Diary* as its principal contribution, dragged on for another month and then quietly disappeared.

Now when its twenty-one numbers were subsequently reissued as a slim volume Sala's name appeared as its Conductor, and so, presumably, he had acted in an editorial or at least an advisory capacity; but who its proprietors may have been I do not know, and what was the quarrel, hinted at in one of his letters, with a firm of paper-manufacturers which seems to have led to his sudden withdrawal, has likewise eluded me. *Fun* had now firmly established itself, and earlier in the year *Judy* had appeared and was already showing signs of a healthy youth: there seemed a good chance, no doubt, for *Banter*, which, so far, at any rate, as its political cartoons went, maintained much the same standard as theirs.

But it was not to be, and more than twenty years were to pass before Sala, with hardly more satisfactory results, was once again conducting a periodical of his own.

Meanwhile there was more work for him than ever before on the *Daily Telegraph*. This was the time when the Fenians were making their uncomfortable presence felt in this country, when the public's bewildered attention was first being directed to the Alabama claims, and when the name of Tichborne was beginning to be vaguely familiar to the man in the street. In December, 1867, there occurred the great Clerkenwell explosion—after a madcap attempt on the part of some Fenians to liberate two of their friends then confined in the House of Detention— and Sala, hurrying from Putney to the scene, was able, in spite of the extraordinary confusion, to produce a most vivid account of the tragedy. Only one of the accused men, Michael Barrett, was found guilty and sentenced to death, and, as it happened, his execution at the end of May was to be the last public hanging in England. Sala was present at that melancholy spectacle—he drew attention to the vast changes since the days of the Mannings and Palmer in the behaviour of the public gathered in front of Newgate—and he was also present in Maidstone Gaol, sorely against his will, a few months later, at the first private hanging. Here there was nothing about the condemned man's crime which called for any particular comment—a Dover stationmaster had been foully struck down by one of his porters—but the occasion was not without its social importance. Yet although it was his duty to describe the ceremonies in considerable detail, his own feelings could not be altogether hidden, and then and there he determined that in no circumstances whatever would he witness another execution. "Thus much detail," he concluded his report, "would not have been bestowed on a most appalling and sickening transaction but for the fact that this, the first private execution in England, marks the beginning of a new and most important chapter in the history of English civilisation, and that record of what was actually done on the 13th of August, 1868, will, in process of time, become of moment to those who study the manners and the customs of a nation. May God grant that when the time comes for this page to be cited by students still perhaps unborn as evidence of what has been, it shall be no more possible in England to hang a man, be he a murderer as vile as he who suffered yesterday in the hole at Maidstone."

Fortunately not all a special correspondent's duties at home took him to scenes of tragedy. Great men like Brougham might die, and their funerals would have to be described in a detail which seems strange today ; but there were Art Exhibitions to be visited—by this time Sala had become the *Daily Telegraph's* chief art critic—as well as Volunteer Reviews, and ceremonial Openings of public institutions, and, at holiday times, the amenities of this or that fashionable watering-place would be the subject of lively sketches. There was also the Boat Race—of more than professional importance to Sala in 1868, for his house provided an excellent grand stand: amongst his guests was J. L. Toole, who was recognised by the crowds and persuaded to make a speech from the balcony—and it is amusing to read his account of a horse-flesh dinner at the Langham Hotel. Week followed week, and, except for the usual month's holiday, he was kept hard at it, in or out of the newspaper office, more than once being responsible for *three* leading articles in a single number. If, however, the record of his activities at this time must take on a soberer aspect than usual, that is not to say that he was receding in any way from the public view. On the contrary, his influence, direct and indirect, was almost daily increasing. Were a new periodical to be called into existence Sala's name was amongst those most eagerly canvassed for inclusion in its list of contributors. Did some semi-public body, celebrating an anniversary, decide to give a huge banquet, Sala would be amongst the first of those invited to speak. He had, in fact, become an institution. There might be curious stories about him, even rather sinister stories, but what did that matter? What public man escaped them? There might still be unkind references to slipshod writing and the "George Augustan" period of English literature, but who could doubt that he had carved out his own niche? There was nobody just like him. And it was now that he was paid the compliment usually reserved for celebrities who have obtained the public's affections: no longer was he "the most picturesque essayist of the day"; he had become the one and only G. A. S.

For the next twenty-five years there was probably no more familiar combination of initials throughout the British Empire.

6

Yet another financial crisis presented itself at the beginning of 1869, though details are not forthcoming. Sala took his wife to lodgings in Great College Street, Camden Town, and for a while "lay as low" as he conveniently could. In March he was attacked for the first and only time in the House of Commons—one of the Irish Members complained of the harm that his American book had done—and for some days he was angrily set on a counter-attack: fortunately Dickens was able to dissuade him. Otherwise the months passed uneventfully. Articles continued to pour from his pen, and by July he had overworked himself to such an extent that an immediate holiday became imperative.

As usual he went to Homburg, and as usual the tables proved unkind. Luckily for him he met John Hollingshead in Frankfort, and Hollingshead, now manager of the recently-erected Gaiety Theatre, made a proposal which effectively improved Sala's financial position. A Christmas burlesque was wanted : would George write it ? For a subject, why not a new Wat Tyler's Rebellion directed against some of the taxes which Robert Lowe, the Chancellor of the Exchequer, had imposed a few months before ? Sala agreed, and in December his "operatic extravaganza" was produced with Toole and Nellie Farren in the principal parts.

It was hardly a work of genius. Reading it today, in fact, one is surprised to hear that it was received with any favour at all. Its rhymed couplets suggest a provincial pantomime, even though once or twice there comes a really happy quip or a clever jest. But the little piece was superbly mounted, the music was tuneful, Toole was at the height of his popularity, and the public was curious to see what a man like Sala would write for the stage. *Wat Tyler, M.P.*, ran for more than seventy nights, and its author was able to leave Camden Town and take the lease of a house in Alexandra Square, Brompton.

He had hardly settled in, and written a few columns of gossip for the newly established *Graphic*, when he was ordered abroad.

7

That January, all France, sublimely unconscious of the greater tragedies which were so quickly to follow, was whipped up into a state of angry excitement by a sensational trial for murder, in which the accused man was a member of the Imperial family. For some considerable time a political storm had been brewing, with that most aristocratic of firebrands, Henri Rochefort, at the head of the malcontents : now there came a moment when even a Revolution as widespread as that which was to come in the following year would not have been altogether surprising.

On January 10th two journalists, a Jew named Yvan Salmon who was better known as Victor Noir, and a young man called Ulric de Fonveille, called at the house of Prince Pierre Lucien Bonaparte in order to convey to him a challenge from a colleague of theirs, M. Pascal Grousset, who considered that he had been grossly insulted in a newspaper article printed under the Prince's name. As it happened, Prince

Pierre, who after a stormy career was supposed to be living in retirement but had recently amused himself by attacking "the rebels" in print, was expecting a challenge from his chief victim, Rochefort, and his first words to his visitors, whom he supposed to be Rochefort's representatives, were not too politely couched. There was an angry scene, and the Prince raised his revolver and fired—twice. Victor Noir staggered to the front door but collapsed on the steps, and died a few minutes later. De Fonveille who had hidden behind a chair and not been hit, then rushed out shouting Murder! and brandishing a revolver which, it seems, he had been too unskilful or too frightened to fire. During the investigation which followed the Prince admitted that he had fired the fatal shot, but pleaded that he had acted only in self-defence: Victor Noir had struck him a violent blow on the cheek, the while de Fonveille had threatened him with his own weapon.

Almost at once there were political reverberations which by no means died down when it was learned that the Prince (long known to be the black sheep of the family) had been arrested and would stand his trial like any commoner. Rochefort fulminated even more vitriolically than usual in his newspaper—the Bonapartes were now openly termed "bandit-assassins"—and he received a sentence of imprisonment. At Victor Noir's funeral there were disgraceful scenes—"ghoul-like orgies" as well as the expected clashes with the police—and the excitement spread to this country which was not ignorant of the exceedingly delicate state of French politics at the time.

The trial was staged—that, surely, in this case, is *le mot juste*—at Tours towards the end of March. The most elaborate precautions had been taken against further riots; mystery surrounded the whereabouts of the prisoner and some of the chief witnesses; and almost hourly a new rumour, each more surprising than the last, came to increase the general excitement. Almost as much interest, too, was directed at Rochefort as at the Prince himself, for until the last moment it was not known whether he would be brought from prison to give evidence and so provide fresh "sensations." Blood-curdling revelations, of course, were promised. Tours became temporarily the centre of the civilised world, and amongst the army of international journalists who converged on the town was Sala.

He soon showed what he could do with a *cause célèbre*. The letters he sent home not only described in brilliant fashion this "extraordinary trial" which for seven astonishing days held the world's attention, but also and possibly for the first time enabled the ordinary Englishman to understand the considerable differences in the matter of procedure in a

French and a British Court of Justice. And today when the trial has been completely forgotten and not one Englishman in a thousand could recall the verdict Sala's letters read like an exciting detective-story, and it is a little curious to find that, unlike other small collections of articles which he was writing about this time, they were never reprinted in pamphlet form.

Who was to be believed? Indisputably Victor Noir was dead and could not speak for himself, but even some of his friends were forced to admit that he had not enjoyed too savoury a reputation: he was shown to be a man in the habit of making friends in the servants' hall in the hopes of hearing scandal. Was it, then, to be wondered at that the Prince had not been too polite when he learnt his visitor's identity? And what was one to think of de Fonveille's story that it was the Prince who had delivered the first blow, when he was in such a state of bewilderment or distress that he could not fire the revolver which, on his own admission, he had raised? On the other hand, this was not the first occasion on which the Prince had killed his man, and he was known to be a fellow of almost maniacal violence: where, then, lay the truth? In the course of the trial Sala confessed that had he himself been empanelled on the jury he would have moved heaven and earth to get his discharge before being called on to give a verdict. He did not mince his words about the Prince, but at the same time he did not disguise his contempt for most of his opponents and accusers, the not over-valiant de Fonveille coming in for his harshest condemnation. Day followed day, and the fiercest insults were bandied in Court, as disgraceful incidents in the Prince's life were gleefully recalled or words written by Rochefort or his colleagues were declaimed. "Every virulent form of oratorical disease manifested itself," recorded Sala, and he was hardly guilty of exaggeration. Sensation followed sensation, and the only disappointment was provided by Rochefort himself, who, except for a veiled hint that the Emperor's parentage was not quite so imperial as it might have been, was singularly restrained. Almost to the last, too, the issue remained in doubt. Then, on a Sunday afternoon, came a verdict of complete acquittal, though the Prince was ordered to pay compensation to Victor Noir's family, and Sala, little dreaming of what was in store for him on his next visit to France, hurried to London to write his last despatch.

8

Almost immediately he was being invited to play a prominent, indeed the principal, part in what was intended to be about the most ambitious journalistic scheme of the century but actually proved to be the least successful of them all.

Between the 'forties and the 'eighties there must have been hundreds of new periodicals, from the solidest of quarterly reviews to the feeblest of weekly "comics," which flickered into life and died within a month or two of their birth. A few, like Sala's own *Conservative Magazine*, did not survive the first number. But, so far as I know, this was the only occasion when after large sums of money had been expended, a band of contributors gathered together of whom any editor might be proud, and a complete number, with elaborate illustrations, set up and printed, the proprietor refused to allow even the first number to appear on the bookstalls. Yet this happened with the magnificent but ill-fated *England in the Nineteenth Century*, which, if a proof-copy be still in existence, must be about the rarest of Victorian journalistic curiosities.

It was the elder James Willing, founder of the well-known firm of advertisers, who inaugurated the scheme. He visualised a vast encyclopaedia of England, to be issued in monthly parts, which would cover every possible aspect of the country's activities: literature, all the professions and trades, politics, railways, theatres, sports, crime, everything. All the best writers and artists were to be engaged, and no expense was to be spared to make it the most splendid production ever launched. William Tinsley was approached and agreed to act as publisher, and Sala, unable to resist the bait of an exceptionally handsome salary, accepted the editorship. Mr. Willing gave a great banquet at which a hundred and fifty more or less distinguished people were present. Sala was in the chair, and at the feast many speeches were made, all of which enlarged on the (ostensible) reasons for the new monthly. England, of course, was the greatest and most prosperous country in the world. That prosperity, however, ought to be increased, and by every legitimate method. In other words, England's greatness must be advertised to the world as never before.

And so Sala set to work, in a lordly office, with lordly notepaper and a lordly staff. Did he have any doubts? Yes: the whole scheme, he saw, was just a little too lordly to be true. He was given the free hand for which he had asked, but—it speedily became clear to him that in advertising England Mr. Willing was primarily intent upon advertising his own firm. Even so all might have been well—for a time, for by the exercise of the greatest ingenuity the name of the firm, while prominently displayed wherever possible, never *seemed* to be markedly out of place. Was a picture of Regent Street, for instance, required (to illustrate an article by the editor himself), what more natural than to show a crowded omnibus bearing the well-known name on its body? At any rate when Sala was able to show a proof of his first number, he had no cause to be ashamed of it. Excellent, said Mr. Willing, and—what about the advertisements?

Alas, even with Mr. Willing's great flair for publicity, even with a small company of enthusiastic agents, even with the admitted value of Sala's name, other advertisers proved lamentably shy. Right, said Mr. Willing, who seems to have been a man of remarkably quick decisions, pay off everybody; the scheme is abandoned. And abandoned it was there and then, though with such financial advantage to everybody except its originator that not a single voice was raised in protest.

What Sala thought is not recorded, but the loss of his editorial chair at that moment did not mean any lack of work. Only a few days later all England was mourning the death of Charles Dickens, and not the least moving tribute paid on that occasion came from the pen of the erstwhile commercial engraver who, nearly twenty years before, had nervously deposited his "Key of the Street" at the offices of *Household Words*. In his memorial essay in the *Daily Telegraph* Sala naturally made no mention of his personal relations with the dead man, but when at Routledge's suggestion he revised and expanded it for publication in pamphlet-form, he spoke out about himself in a preface, and freely admitted that he, with his "evil" temper, had been to blame for their quarrel. He had hardly completed his task of revision, however, before the news of impending war between France and Prussia sent him hurrying across the Channel again.

He had been commissioned to ascertain the state of opinion in Paris, and, if possible, make his way to Metz. A special military correspondent was to have accompanied him, but the French authorities put so many difficulties in the way that Sala, in the white waistcoat and red tie which by this time were beginning to assume almost passport value, travelled alone.

He found a Paris eager for war though showing few signs of warlike preparations, given to occasional bursts of hysterical excitement, and, of course, full of the most astonishing and generally contradictory rumours. War had been declared on July 15th, and for the next ten days Sala remained in the capital, roving about in his inquisitive way, listening to casual conversations in theatres and cafés, and meeting with no restrictions at all. It was a different matter when, after an unsuccessful endeavour to find the Imperial Guard at Nancy, he reached Metz. Here were the Imperial Headquarters, and here the natives had come to look upon all foreign visitors with the deepest suspicion. There was, indeed, a sharp

attack of spy-fever, in the course of which more than one British correspondent was temporarily detained. Sala as usual managed to make his
despatches entertaining and instructive, although he had little but rumours
to record, and with his excellent French to help him had little difficulty
in remaining *persona grata* with the harassed officials of the town. Then
at the beginning of August came the disasters at Worth and Forbach, and
with Metz in a state of panic the correspondents were politely requested
to return to Paris, where, it was ironically suggested, there would be no
lack of exciting news for them. At the moment the railway services
were completely disorganised, but Sala, with one of the Mayhews,
managed to find a carriage-and-pair, and after an exceedingly uncomfortable journey reached Paris, to find it more or less in a state of
siege and even more ready than Metz to regard every stranger as a
Prussian spy.

That fatal month passed, and although there were frequent reports of
astonishing victories, it became increasingly difficult for the authorities
to hide from the public the true state of affairs. On August 9th the
Ministry fell; on the 10th Strasburg was occupied by the Germans. A
few days later its evacuation was confirmed, and with it came the news
of the defeat at Courcelles. And then at the beginning of September
came Sedan, and the Revolution, and for Sala, whose despatches continued to be amongst the fullest to reach England, yet another escape
from death. Indeed, as in Russian days, his death was widely presumed,
for a report, which was copied into many of the newspapers, announced
the news that he had "ended a noisy and not unknown career by being
shot dead in the streets of Metz."

It was not quite so bad as that. On the evening of Saturday, September 3rd, he was sitting in a Paris café when with loud shouts two men
unknown to him suddenly denounced him as a Prussian spy. He was
immediately seized by an angry crowd and hustled to the guardhouse in
the Rue de Richelieu. Unfortunately he had left his passport and papers
at his hotel, and his application to send a messenger for them was contemptuously refused. At the guardhouse he was well treated, but "at
about five o'clock in the morning a squad of sergeants de ville made
their appearance, and, to my astonishment, I was placed in the midst of
them, and dragged violently through the streets to the Central Poste of
the Boulevard Bonne Nouvelle," and there after terrible insults had been
hurled at him from every policeman on duty, he was "thrust into a
horrible dungeon, which, at the most, perhaps, would have adequately
accommodated six persons standing upright. In this abominable den,
however, no less than seventeen persons were crammed; and this number,

by seven o'clock, was increased to twenty-two. This Cave of Despair was lit by one small circular orifice high up in the wall, heavily grated, and communicating not with the open air, but with a lobby. Two boys in blouses had contrived, by hoisting themselves on to the shoulders of their elders, to hang on to the bars of the window, whence they shrieked unremittingly for air and water. . . . My companions in captivity were ruffians accused of crimes of violence, thieves, and vagabonds of the lowest description. The heat of the place was suffocating, the stench insupportable, the filth simply Malebolgian; and consequently, in common language, indescribable. I fainted away, but no efforts were made to succour me. On the contrary, when I recovered consciousness —under the impetus of a kick from a wooden shoe which has cut a triangular piece out of one of my ankles—I found that I had been thrust under the long wooden bench running along one side of the cell, and that my pockets had been carefully turned out. . . . Then," he told his *Daily Telegraph* readers, "commenced a series of outrages which I shall not forget until my dying day, which I shudder to recall, and some of which I cannot recall. . . . One cannibal bit me severely on the back of the hand. . . ."

It was ten o'clock in the morning before he was taken out of "this den of wild beasts' and marched through the streets "so dazed and stupefied" that he could not afterwards remember his destination. The Commissary before whom he was taken, himself in a state of frightened bewilderment, for the news of the Emperor's surrender had just reached him, ultimately decided that he must be sent to the Préfecture de Police. He allowed him under guard to fetch his papers from the hotel, though a request to be permitted to call on the way at the British Embassy was refused. At the hotel he managed to scribble a few lines to one of the secretaries, but his troubles were not yet over. At the Préfecture they refused to deal with him, and for a third time he was escorted away, this time to a prison considerably less disagreeable, where he was placed *à la pistole*, in solitary confinement. Here, too, a warder, possibly impressed by so unspylike a garment as a white waistcoat even when covered, as it now was, with blood, listened sympathetically to his story and made him as comfortable as he could. He even fetched materials for writing, but no further letter was necessary, for Lord Lyons had taken immediate action, a secretary arrived at the prison, and within an hour or two the unfortunate man was in the safe hands of the Embassy physician.

He was badly shocked. The bitten hand, which, in point of fact, had not wholly healed three or four months later, was in a dreadful condition and was giving him the greatest pain. For the next week he was confined to his bed. He did manage to send a short letter or two to his newspaper, describing the death-agonies of the Empire, but he was obviously in no condition for regular work. At the end of the month he was in London for a day or two—*Fun* had an amusing drawing of the returned correspondent with his hand in a sling—but he was far from being fully recovered, and when the Levys suggested another mission to Rome where there was trouble between King and Pope, it was tacitly understood that there would be no hurry for him to return home. A winter holiday in the South, they considered, had been very well earned.

CHAPTER TWELVE

INTERLUDE: THE "ROWDY PHILISTINE" LIBELLED

I

In *Friendship's Garland*, his wittiest book, Matthew Arnold kills off his outspoken friend Arminius, Baron von Thunder-Ten-Tronckh, in the course of the Franco-Prussian war. The poor fellow, you may remember, is discovered in a dying condition on the road between Rueil and Bougival by "a young lion" of the *Daily Telegraph*. Leo Adolescens receives his last words, obtains help to bury the corpse, and, considerably shaken by so melancholy a scene, looks about him for sympathy. He is lucky enough to meet Sala in a Versailles hotel, and tells him the sad tale. " 'The old story,' says Sala; '*life a dream!* Take a glass of brandy.' " And in the course of the conversation that follows the imaginary Sala is made to say to his young colleague: " 'Old Russell's guns are getting a little honeycombed . . . and why should not you succeed him ?' "

Young Leo is clearly taken with the idea. "I cannot, without a thrill of excitement," he informs the world, "think of inoculating the respectable but somewhat ponderous *Times* and its readers with the divine madness of our new style,—the style we have formed upon Sala. The world, *mon cher*, knows that man but imperfectly. I do not class him with the great masters of human thought and human literature,—Plato, Shakespeare, Confucius, Charles Dickens. Sala, like us his disciples, has studied in the book of the world even more than in the world of books. But his career and genius have given him somehow the secret of a literary mixture novel and fascinating in the last degree; he blends the airy epicureanism of the *salons* of Augustus with the full-blooded gaiety of our English cider-cellar. With our people and country, *mon cher*, this mixture, you may rely upon it, is now the very thing to go down; there arises every day a larger public for it; and we, Sala's disciples, may be trusted not willingly to let it die."

This gently satiric passage formed part of Matthew Arnold's long-continued onslaught on "the Philistines": those increasingly influential but dunderheaded folk of the Middle Classes who, in his opinion, were so ill prepared to play their part in the country's intellectual and political development. That he should repeatedly have chosen out Sala, moreover, that "rowdy Philistine," as he called him, for his barbs is significant. The world in which scholarly poets like himself were accustomed to

move recognised Sala's great verbal dexterity; a few of them were
even pleased to call him their friend; but—they were suspicious of him
and, more particularly, of his undoubted influence, direct or indirect,
on the masses. He was giving the Philistines something that they
wanted but ought not to want. In his work, they considered, it was
only the world of the flesh-pots that was being mirrored: the finer
touches were lamentably lacking, and without them, without the
application of more spiritual standards, how could any country hope
to escape slow degeneration?

That was the substance of many attacks, some of them grossly
unfair, which about this time were launched against those, Sala and
Hepworth Dixon at their head, who were held to be the chief spokesmen
of the Middle Classes. A superficial brilliance, a parade of learning,
but beneath the façade—what? A deliberate pandering to man's baser
instincts. As Arminius is made to say of the *Daily Telegraph*, and it
is Sala who is chiefly in his mind, it "foments our worse faults," and,
adds his inventor, I am "fond of applying to it Dryden's dictum of
Elkanah Settle, that its style is boisterous and its prose incorrigibly lewd."
Lewd, even in the older sense of the word? One wonders what he would
have said about some of our modern "tabloids"! But even the very
versatility which Sala had shown was condemned. Of what value, it
was asked, could the work be of a man who was never given the
opportunity to study any particular question but must needs shift his whole
attention every hour of the day? This, of course, was absurd—what
writer of leading articles could do otherwise?—but it was freely made.

So, too, in the satirical epics of the day Sala as a kind of evil enchanter,
waving a detestable wand over the entire newspaper kingdom, began
to be pilloried, and even his liveliest despatches, never composed without
the most careful preparation, were dubbed mere plagiarisms. "And is
this Sala," asked the author of the *Obliviad*:

> "... once reputed hack,
> With all this luggage at his back?
> Alas! so changed, who, when on earth of yore,
> Toss'd high in air the cap and bells he wore;
> Set wide his heels, a slav'ring tongue held out,
> Gaz'd, grinn'd, and jabber'd, and then frisk'd about:
> Ne'er by such bulk agility such shewn,
> And Sala nimble as a Logan stone:
> As work'd Galvanic battery in his brain,
> Flung himself down, and straight jump'd up again;
> Spasmodic laugh'd, and next, with changed grimace,
> Made sad the merry-andrew in his face;

To sudden clamour with crack'd accent broke,
And rasp'd his throttle, as when Touchstone spoke;
Whose language, to match the motley of his coat,
Of languages a patchwork got by rote;
French, German, Russian, but whose English such
As seem'd a cross 'twixt Portuguese and Dutch.
In former days, in a fantastic guise,
Have wits by covert introduced the wise;
But Sala soon whoever reads detects,
Who fool affecting, is what he affects,
Illogical in all, from method free,
His ev'ry art of impropriety;
How what least fitting, best to introduce,
And how of reason to reject the use;
Describe anew whate'er in guide-book shown,
And by distorting make it all his own."

At the same time there were subtler attacks which did not get into print: a whispering campaign. For all his good-fellowship and amusing conversation, was there not something *wrong* with the man? What was the real truth about those periodic disappearances of his? Mere drunken bouts or—something more vicious? They *did* say that he had been seen slinking into an East End den of the vilest description, and what about those pornographic verses of his which were sometimes circulated in masculine haunts of the less particular kind? Everybody "knew," of course, that he was rarely sober, even at important social functions. Why, moreover, when he was paid so handsomely (and sometimes for commissions accepted but never carried out) was he so frequently in financial straits? A case of long-continued blackmail, peradventure? Certainly he was a brilliant man, and to be found these days in some of the best houses, but there was an uglier side which—— No, better be exceedingly careful: not a good man to quarrel with, George Augustus.

As it happened, there was a man who at this time was not too careful, and he came to grief.

2

James Hain Friswell, a man of Sala's own generation, had been intended for his father's profession of the law, but for financial reasons was obliged to adopt an uncongenial commercial career. For some years he had been connected with a firm of metal engravers, but all his spare time was given to literature, and from the early 'fifties there had been a steady output of articles and books, not a few of them educational or semi-religious in character. A story for boys called

Out and About had given him some small reputation, but it was *The Gentle Life*—"Essays in Aid of the Formation of Character"—published in 1864 which introduced him to a really wide public. I do not know whether this decorous lucubration is still read today, but in Victorian times edition followed edition—the Queen herself accepted the dedication of one of them—and henceforth he was able to live modestly on his literary earnings. Of the volumes of essays, novels, and translations which followed, none was in the front rank, but all showed dignity and a grace of expression and helped to endear him to a fairly wide circle of readers. A puritan, and not without some of the puritan's usual prejudices, unhumorous in spite of an occasional quip, and by no means a great scholar, but a painstaking and wholly sincere man who hated the vulgar shams of his day and a warm friend to all those who "sought to improve their minds." And the last man in the world, you would have thought, who would ever get himself into serious trouble in the law courts.

He and Sala had known one another for twenty years or more without ever becoming intimate. Except, indeed, for an appreciation of fine literature the two men had little if anything in common. Once or twice in his letters Sala speaks of "Mr. Frizzle" and in a not too laudatory manner, but the nickname was not his invention and its use implied no particular contempt. On the contrary, when one of Friswell's books, obviously written in a hurry and without sufficient preparation, had called for his private condemnation, he refrained from attacking it in print because he was aware of its author's narrow purse. More than once they had been contributors to the same periodical, and it was Friswell who had been chosen—Sala himself takes credit for the choice— to write the weekly "Echoes" in the *Illustrated London News* during their usual compiler's absences from England.

And then, in the course of 1870, roused to indignation by what he considered the dreadful degeneration of contemporary literary criticism, this champion of orthodoxy entered the lists in the role of a man determined at all costs to be honest. "We are getting wary," he wrote, "of false friendships and false animosities in literature; it is time to call a spade a spade." Some twenty essays of his on prominent writers of the day which had appeared in various journals were revised and enlarged, and, well aware of their author's reputation in the most respectable and even august quarters, Messrs. Hodder and Stoughton, then as now a firm of the highest standing, were delighted to publish his new book. If, moreover, they despatched the manuscript to the printer without a very careful examination, were they greatly to blame?

A libel, even an impropriety, from the author of *The Gentle Life*? It was surely a ridiculous notion.   And so, in the late autumn, *Modern Men of Letters Honestly Criticised* duly appeared, and if it failed to create any great sensation with the general public, it undoubtedly caused what Sala might have called an agreeable fluttering in the literary dovecotes. Old Frizzle letting himself go in this fashion!   Who would ever have thought it?   Yet there was little in the book which those who knew the author's work might not have expected to find.   Plain speaking there certainly was, but in general the judgment shown was sound. At times a touch of petulance appeared when the author under consideration happened to be of aristocratic birth, but in a sturdy democrat like Friswell so much need have occasioned no surprise.   And, of course, the heaviest artillery was reserved for those who had dared to speak "against the moral code."   Yet there was one article which might well have caused eyebrows to be raised, for although it said little more than many men were thinking, it was expressed in such a manner that from the beginning its malice was clear.

Today the little book is by no means without an interest of its own, and not only because it must be included in the category of books which have been "suppressed."   Oddly enough, Friswell pays an almost Lombroso-like attention to the *faces* of his various authors : a fact which was to play its part in the legal proceedings that followed.   As for his verdicts, not many of them have been reversed.   Dickens, it is to be noted, is acquitted of the repeated charge of vulgarity and dubbed genius for all the ages.   Tennyson is "sugar-sweet," and not a great poet; Browning is great though "seldom clear."   In Ruskin he finds a writer after his own heart, and Carlyle is a man whose words will live.   Trollope is little more than a fashionable photographer, Charles Kingsley and Grote are "noble," and Disraeli brilliant but "unreal."   The "young, godless" Swinburne is allowed to be "a poet of a rare order—forcible, free, salt, and buoyant as the sea," but naturally receives some very hard knocks for those "mocking songs" of his which, Friswell thinks, might well have been sung by choirs in Sodom and Gomorrah.   Even more violent is his attack on Harrison Ainsworth, whose very existence "is an event to be deplored."   Nothing, it is declared, can undo the evil for which "this unhappy man" with his "open applause of robbery and brutality" must be held responsible.   Poor Ainsworth !   He was now long past his best work, though forced to write on.   Like all his fellow-victims except one, however, he could afford to ignore any such outburst, for there was no attack on his private character.   But what of the essay sandwiched in between the two devoted to Tennyson and Charles Lever?

Perhaps it is a little odd to find Sala there at all, but there he is, and from the opening sentence the reader is made aware that in his case Friswell is out to wound. It was all very well for him to praise Sala's great industry and picturesqueness, and to admit that it was no crime to give the "virtuous publicans and intelligent greengrocers"—in other words the readers of the *Daily Telegraph*—the "trifle and whipt cream" that they wanted; but it was less legitimate to speak of him as "a driveller of tipsy, high-flown, and high-falutin' nonsense." Doubtless, too, Friswell was not alone in holding the view that a man who could "sell his pen to describe a Jew clothier's, an advertising furniture dealer's, a Liverpool draper's, a Manchester hatter's, or a St. Paul's Churchyard bonnet-shop" was "utterly careless" of his own reputation and of the dignity of letters. But what followed surely went beyond the bounds of "honest" criticism.

"In ninety cases out of the hundred G. A. S. will bring up his copy with the accurate regard to time which newspapers require, but at the last number in every decennial he will have failed. This has gained him respect with the dullards who generally conduct and start papers, who believe that a man of genius cannot but be irregular and eccentric. If the 'Genius' gets into the hands of the Jews, is often drunk, always in debt, sometimes in prison, and is totally disreputable, living *à tort et à travers* the rules of society, these newspaper proprietors think more and more of him, and go down on their knees and bribe him to write.

> 'Great wits to madness sure are near allied,
> And thin partitions do their bounds divide.'

When the 'great wit' writes a novel, draws all the money, gets in a mess with it, and asks somebody else to finish it whom he is unwilling to pay; or when he starts on his travels, leaving a proprietor of a periodical with a half finished serial on hand, the admiration of Bohemia, printer, and public, is enormous. The recalcitrant author is afterwards pardoned, and received with open arms."

At this point Friswell must have felt that he was going rather too far, for he hastens to add: "Like this has been the reasoning with regard to Mr. Sala, of whom we, of course, do not relate all these little fables." The fact, however, that every one of the little fables could be traced back to Sala and nobody else was immediately patent to anybody who knew him, and the "honest" critic was not to save himself by so paltry a subterfuge. But there was more to come. There was Sala's personal appearance, by this time fairly well known to the general public from the cartoons and caricatures of him which were now so regularly appearing. That unfortunate nose, of course, could not be omitted, and, as we have seen, his face was held to be an index to his style if seen in a photograph which had been coloured. But the duffer eye was pilloried too, and in a manner which afterwards "caused amusement in Court." Sala in the flesh, it seemed, was *goguenard*, whatever that peculiar word might mean. Finally came the unwisest accusation of all, and one, as it happens, which has not been forgotten today when not a few publications of the Penny Dreadful type are alleged (without a shred of evidence) to be Sala's work.

"It is whispered," wrote Friswell, "that he wrote at one time for the excelling Mr. Lloyd . . . certain romances . . . such as 'Adah, the Betrayed ; or, the Murder at the Old Smithy,' 'Julia, the Deserted,' and the like. These penny romances were not vicious, though morbidly exciting; one called 'Sweeny Todd ; or, the String of Pearls,' related how a certain barber in Fleet Street cut the throats of his customers, and then sunk them down a trap to the kitchen, where they were made into, and whence they issued, as mutton-pies !" Here, of course, he was curiously wide of the mark, and once again hardly helped himself by expressing his doubts as to whether "our eccentric genius wrote such stories." If he was in doubt, why mention them at all ?

Well, no doubt some of Sala's colleagues thought that it might have been considerably worse than it was. At least they could laugh at the allusion to "sometimes in prison." G. A. S. might periodically "disappear," but so far nobody else had advanced the theory that at such times he was behind prison-bars. Libellous ? Possibly it was, but with a man like Frizzle was it worth while worrying yourself overmuch ? And that seems to have been Sala's own view at first when he was shown the book. Was it much worse than what the *Saturday Review* was accustomed to say of him ? There was, however, an old friend of his—I think that it must have been Shirley Brooks—who took a more serious view. This, he thought, would not do ; there were innuendoes which could not be allowed to stand; Sala must go to his solicitors at once.

So to George Lewis he went, and that astute lawyer agreed that there was a case. Forthwith he issued a writ, not against Friswell with his meagre purse but against his much wealthier publishers.

Friswell seems to have been badly frightened, but he behaved well. He immediately instructed his publishers to withdraw the book, offered to write any apology which might be considered necessary, and insisted, in the event of the case being taken into the Courts, that any damages or costs there might be should fall on himself. On Lewis's advice, however, the offer of an apology was rejected, and on February 17th, 1871, in the Court of Queen's Bench the case of Sala v. Hodder and Another was tried before Lord Chief Justice Cockburn and a special jury.

3

Considerable interest had been aroused. In more than one quarter the spiciest revelations were confidently expected. Sala under cross-examination in the matter of his private peccadilloes, about which, of course, a fresh crop of rumours had arisen, should be well worth hearing. Many of those, however, who drove down to the City that morning and found seats in Guildhall—the new Law Courts were not to be completed for some years to come—must have been disappointed, for although the plaintiff was duly cross-examined it was in the most perfunctory way, and from the beginning the defence made it clear that so far from pleading justification they proposed to say nothing which could in any way aggravate the situation. Nevertheless, the day was not without its entertaining moments and even its small excitements, and the newspapers reported the proceedings at unusual length.

It was Mr. Serjeant Parry who opened the plaintiff's case, and he worked himself up into a fine state of indignation, almost as though he was being called on to defend the entire British Genius from the most scabrous attack ever launched against it. Was it honest criticism, he thundered, when the libeller resorted to "tomahawk and scalping-knife" methods, venomously pursuing a hard-working and justly celebrated public figure into the innermost privacy of his home? Was it honest criticism when a man's very nose was made the subject of contemptuous attack? (He had been informed about the unfortunate Panton Street affair, but preferred to ascribe the obvious peculiarities of the organ injured on that occasion to the effects of long-continued travels in strange and presumably nasal-affecting countries.) Why, he continued, Mr. Friswell had not even hesitated to apply the word goguenard—surely the vilest of Parisian importations—to his client!

There was an expectant hush in Court as he paused.

Cockburn, L.C.J., looked up in some surprise. The word, he thought, merely meant jolly.

"Jovial," supplied Mr. Digby Seymour, Q.C., who, with the future Sir Edward Clarke, was appearing for the defendants.

But Mr. Serjeant Parry would not have that. The word, he allowed, might bear that innocuous interpretation, but more usually it meant "goggle-eyed." "I looked in the dictionary this morning, my lord," he explained.

"You have the advantage of me in that, brother."

"Your lordship is a dictionary in yourself," rejoined the Serjeant in his best manner, but continued to press his point that the use of this particular word must be held to be cruel and malicious, when, as the jury would see for themselves, his client had had the misfortune to lose the use of one eye. He was complaining, however, of something much worse than mere malice and shameful innuendoes : there were monstrous charges which were wholly and demonstrably false. That his client was the author of various pestilential publications most likely, as he himself would be the first to admit, to debauch the minds of the young. That he had dishonourable dealings with his editors. That he was repeatedly in prison, a confirmed drunkard, and for ever verging on the edge of bankruptcy. In other words, Mr. Friswell's words, a "totally disreputable" person. What more truculent libel could well be imagined ? But the Court would hear from Mr. Sala's own lips a complete denial to every one of these charges, and it only remained for him to ask for damages of an "exemplary" nature.

Whereupon, after publication had been proved, Sala, resplendent in red tie and white waistcoat, stepped into the witness-box, took the oath, and proceeded to give a very good account of himself. He had little to fear—word, I fancy, had reached him that all awkward questions would be avoided—and he was entirely at his ease. He might have been making one of his after-dinner speeches : a modest, urbane gentleman, distressed at being obliged to proceed against another gentleman of his own profession, but forced, of course, to defend his reputation.

Troubles with editors ? Novels unfinished ? But such little matters were easily explained, and explained they were, with frequent mention of the kindness he had received from Dickens and Thackeray. Penny romances for Mr. Lloyd ? But he had never *written* such things in his life. Selling his pen to manufacturers ?—in other words, writing advertisements for them ? Well, it was true that in some old *Household Words* articles of his he might well have described in some detail this or that great industrial venture—at Mr. Dickens's suggestion. (And the trade pamphlets bearing his name, which could so easily have been produced ? The learned disquisitions on hats and sewing-machines and eiderdown quilts and somebody's wine-vaults ? They were not mentioned at all.)

Then came the crucial questions. Often in prison ? A "tipsy writer " ? Always in debt ?

The plaintiff took Friswell's book in his hands, and sonorously read out the whole of the offending passage. Then he looked up. "I am not," said he, "in the hands of the Jews. I am not drunken. I am not always in debt. I am not sometimes in prison. And as regards my being totally disreputable"—he paused and smiled—"I must leave it to the public at large and my own particular friends to be the best judges."

The Court laughed, and Mr. Digby Seymour rose to cross-examine. But he had little to say. There was more argument about the word *goguenard*; there was a short passage of arms over the phrase "tipsy writer"; Sala agreed that Friswell had done what he could to minimise the effects of his words; and the ordeal, if ordeal it can be called, was over. A few of his friends spoke of his good character, and the defence offered no evidence at all. The Lord Chief Justice summed up, and the jury retired.

"£150 at the least," whispered George Lewis.

"£250," said Maxwell.

Could it possibly be more?

The jury filed in after an absence of three-quarters of an hour.

Damages: £500, which meant rather more in those days than it does today.

4

He may not have been in the hands of the Jews, but there were apparently numerous gentlemen of other persuasions who, on the announcement of the verdict, took immediate steps to ensure their own participation in the plunder. Every tradesman in London with whom Sala had ever had dealings seemed able to produce an account, until then "overlooked." One of them, a furniture-dealer, even declared that some of the "sticks" which had been sold, as we have seen, at the time of Sala's "exile," had not been paid for, and collected almost £100 at one horrible swoop. There was also another firm of solicitors who now sent in their account for services rendered some years back, though of what nature their services had been I have been unable to discover. And, of course, there were numerous friends who, rightly from their own point of view, judged this to be the best time to exhibit I.O.U.s, many of them bearing dates of almost prehistoric antiquity. The public, too, stepped in, and sacks of letters arrived, all expressing their writers' great admiration for the genius of G. A. S. and all giving excellent reasons why such admiration should be rewarded with gifts, or loans, of money.

There were those who said at the time that Sala had been badly advised not to accept the apology which had been offered him. That, they thought, would have been the more dignified course to take. There were others who thought that he might well have listened to the representations made privately on Friswell's behalf—he had agreed to pay what he could to his publishers—for smaller damages. Rightly or wrongly Sala refused, and as a result one worry followed another.

"Five hundred pounds damages!" he wrote. "Confound them! They never did me the slightest amount of good." On the contrary, no long time elapsed before his health was being seriously affected. Worse, from that day he was rarely free for any long time from one distressing ailment or another.

He had still, however, an astonishingly large amount of work to do.

G. A. Sala

UNPUBLISHED (AND UNFINISHED) CARICATURE BY "SEM," 1872.

"JOURNALISM"

The inevitable cartoon in *Vanity Fair,* September 25th, 1875.

CHAPTER THIRTEEN

ON THE TREADMILL

I

Soon after this not too fortunate lawsuit the Levys sent him to Berlin, ostensibly for the purpose of describing the ceremonies at the opening of the new German Parliament, but primarily to get him away from importunate creditors and others who were continuing to criticise his demeanour in the witness-box. As it happened, this was to be Sala's last commission abroad until the beginning of 1875, and the story of his activities during the intervening years may be summed up in a sentence or two. For him, indeed, it was a period of hard routine work, with frequent interruptions—one of considerable length—owing to illness: so many columns to be turned out every week for the *Daily Telegraph*, so many stories and sketches for other journals, a book or two to be prepared for the press, and a steadily growing stream of social engagements. It was the least adventurous period in his life.

After fifteen years' hard labour on the *Daily Telegraph*, he was telling his friend Charles Leland of "Hans Breitmann" fame, early in 1872, "I can pretty well choose my own subjects," and as year followed year and his commonplace books were assuming encyclopaedic proportions, the range and variety of his leading articles became greater than ever. Now, too, as some of his friends were quick to notice, much of his attention was being given to questions of more than ephemeral interest. The unusual crime, or some new and juicy revelation of night-house life in London regularly continued to provide him with material for that "fourth leader" to which so many readers would eagerly turn on opening their newspaper; but at this time and henceforth it frequently happened that the graver lucubrations which preceded it were also his work. He was still silent about home politics (unless, perchance, a new Licensing Bill or a measure for curbing the activities of financial sharks was before Parliament), but, with his now considerable experience of the world outside Britain, his ability to read the newspapers of half a dozen foreign countries, and his desire—not yet abandoned—to prepare himself for a political career, he felt, with some justice, that he was fully equipped to reflect and even guide public opinion on matters of international importance.

O

So it was, as a scrap-book of his proves clearly enough, that when in the course of 1872 the vexed question of the Alabama claims brought this country and the United States to within a measurable distance of war, Sala set himself to make a comprehensive study of the whole unfortunate business, and, day after day, as he expounded each point in the controversy, ever counselled a moderate policy, no less so after the Geneva Commissioners, with one dissentient in the person of the British representative, had awarded huge damages against this country.

"I don't think," he wrote to Leland, himself an American, "that we shall be idiots enough to go to war. . . . You folks," he added, and it is amusing to find him writing with such frankness of his political leaders though his own radicalism is made abundantly clear, "do not appear to be abnormally blood-thirsty; and there is no probability of *our* going to war with anybody while a shop-keeping, psalm-singing government (such as the existing one) is in power. There is unfortunately a chance of this parliament and government going speedily to Hell—the collapse may be from social rather than political causes: licensing Bill, contagious diseases, sanitary bill, or something of that sort—and of a Tory government coming in. Tory governments fight. . . . War to them is subsistence, honour, advancement, emolument, and command. So, if you see Gladstone go out and Salisbury come in you had best send a special train to Rouse's Point, and annexe Canada at once. You may have it, and Lake Memphremagog to boot for anything that nine out of ten Englishmen care." And jocosely he concluded with a suggestion of his own, should the negotiations fail. "Suppose each nation subscribed $100,000,000 apiece, and then tossed up—two out of three—which should have the lump $200,000,000? To satisfy the 'innate desire for blood' suppose you agreed to slaughter a given number of rowdies, Irishmen, Tombs lawyers, Christy Minstrels, 'interviewing' reporters, Mormons, and Broadway stage drivers, while we consented to massacre a corresponding quota of roughs, garrotters, special correspondents, Brighton tradesmen, theatrical boxkeepers, makers of bad half-crowns, Commissioners of Income Tax, quack doctors, and Lords of the Admiralty. Contracts might be made with the railway companies for effecting the necessary bloodshed with the utmost regularity and despatch."

Mr. Gladstone, however, did not leave office until 1874, and for the man in the street the excitement over the Alabama claims soon subsided in favour of the more theatrical thrills of the great Tichborne case.

2

Now although today, at any rate to the younger generation, "the Claimant" will suggest no particular person and it may be difficult for it to realise to what an astonishing extent this peculiar drama captured the attention of the entire kingdom from May, 1871, when the civil action began in the Courts, to March, 1874, when the Claimant was found guilty of perjury and sentenced to fourteen years' penal servitude, so much has been written about the case that any detailed description would be out of place here. Yet it cannot be wholly passed over, if only because Sala, who saw much of the Claimant during his "glory," and not always in his professional capacity, was the author of enough articles and papers about him—two at least of real historical interest— to make a fair-sized book, all of which were informed by sterling good sense and in marked contrast to the hysterical outbursts to be found even in journals professing to despise the sensationalism of the *Daily Telegraph*.

What, then, were the main facts ? In 1854 Roger Tichborne, heir to a baronetcy and large estates, sails from Rio in the *Bella*: a slim, weakly young man who speaks French in preference to English, and is bound for New York where £1000 is waiting for him. He has £1000 a year settled on him and is heir to about £24,000 a year. The *Bella* is lost at sea, apparently without survivors. For eleven years there is silence; then on a sudden "there steps out of a Wagga-Wagga slaughter-house a big, fat, burly, uncouth man who declares himself to be the long-lost man," rescued with eight others from the *Bella* and taken to Melbourne, and now, on the death of the reigning baronet, Sir Roger Tichborne. On the face of it his claim seems to be wholly absurd. He never applied for the £1000 and he has sent no word to the family. He has been satisfied to spend eleven years of his life in the name of Castro as a journeyman butcher at a pound a week. When, moreover, he has raised the money to return to Europe, a great barrel of a man who is illiterate and knows no word of French, many of Roger's old friends at once repudiate him, which is hardly surprising in view of the fact that he can remember so little about "himself" as a young man and makes the most ludicrous mistakes. The Tichborne trustees launch their enquiries, necessarily on the most elaborate scale, are forced to the conclusion that the Claimant is one Arthur Orton, the son of a Wapping butcher, and prepare to fight.

Unfortunately for them, there were also those who were ready to swear that they recognised him for the Roger they had known—amongst them several military officers with whom the missing man had served, old tenants and servants and one of the family's solicitors, above all Lady Tichborne herself, who for years had been advertising for news of the son she refused to believe was dead.   Even so, "it seems at first sight wonderful that the Tichborne Claimant should ever have found a single adherent or follower.   And yet, gross and palpable as the imposture was from the very first, there was always a certain *per contra* account in its favour.   From the moment that the man first appeared he was surrounded by financial agents, lawyers, moneylenders and others who made his claim known in all directions, and left no stone unturned to win over the thoughtless to his side.   The undoubted facts of the case were ignored.   It was the old story of 'credo quia absurdum.'   The very improbabilities of the man's tale were accepted as conclusive proofs of its truth.   It pleased the vulgar mind to find that a baronet had turned butcher.   More than this, the fat man himself was a species of Jack Cade, able to measure exactly the credulity of his dupes, and to fool them to the top of their bent.   He was full of a certain bonhomie of his own, which told irresistibly in his behalf.   He was a jovial fellow, an attender of races and pigeon matches, a user of strong words, and a drinker of strong drink.   His very bulk told in his favour.   He was 'Sir Roger' in short . . . and 'I hope, my dear mama,' says he, referring to some witnesses to be brought against him, 'God will forgive them wicked people as has persuaded them pore sailors to pergur themselves for a fue pounds.'"

Thus wrote Sala after the Claimant's conviction, and I am persuaded that he had never altered his private opinion that the man was an impostor. Previously, of course, it had been necessary to adopt in public a more careful attitude, and even in his more personal articles he wrote as one who for the time being is reserving judgment.   As long ago as 1868 he had met some of the Claimant's supporters in a neighbour's house in Thistle Grove, but it was only in the following year that he had found himself face to face with the Claimant at Henry Labouchere's dining-table.   At once he had been aware of the man's strange fascination and begun to realise the gigantic nature of the fight ahead.   And he was not surprised when the whole country was whipped up into a state of "tichbornitis," with those in almost every town and even village who not only "swore by the Claimant" but were also willing to risk their money on the chance of his ultimate success.

For Sala, however, the one point of paramount interest was not the identity of the Claimant but his real character.   What manner of human being was this who could accept the public's frantic acclamation with the same dignity and apparent unconcern with which, in the Courts, he gave utterance to the most astounding admissions of ignorance ?   A man

who could hardly write his own name correctly and yet one whose
mellifluous voice could sway thousands. A man who could confess that
he had seduced his own cousin with the same nonchalance with which he
asserted that in spite of a public-school education he could not remember
whether Caesar had written in Latin or Greek. (He was inclined to
think that it was in Greek.) Sala found himself utterly baffled. The
details of the case might weary and bore him—so much he admitted,
even in print—but the novelist in him never tired of attempting to probe
that mountain of flesh in the hope of finding what was beneath. Baronet
or butcher: that was the one question which was exciting the public;
to Sala, who liked to think that he was a fairly good judge of a man,
the Claimant remained an enigma. Years ago they had accused him of
putting "impossible" people into his novels, but would any novelist
have *dared* to invent so unlikely a creature as this imperturbable hippo-
potamus? And it was this desire to uncover the man's true personality
which caused him to follow every phrase in the long-drawn-out business
with even closer attention than his professional duties required. He was
"in the very thick of it," he told an importunate editor: legitimate
excuse, it seemed, for articles repeatedly promised and never delivered.
I fancy, too, that more than once he played with the idea of compiling
an elaborate record of the whole business, and even as late as 1881 he was
sufficiently interested to have a copy of another alleged Roger Tichborne's
"private notes" made for him by a legal firm.

At the civil trial which lasted for several months it was Serjeant
Ballantyne who led for the Claimant, but it was Hardinge Giffard, the
future Lord Halsbury, whose examination-in-chief, a classic of its kind,
did most to hearten the romantics who had subscribed their guineas to
the Cause. Giffard at first believed wholeheartedly in his client and
refused many valuable briefs on that account, but as Sir John Coleridge's
deadly cross-examination proceeded—it was reported almost verbatim
in many of the newspapers—and one damaging reply followed another,
he gradually lost faith, and when in his temporary absence from London
Ballantyne consented to a non-suit and the inevitable arrest for perjury
followed he refused to undertake the Claimant's defence, purposely
asking an impossibly high fee.

It was the fact that Orton could not give his supposed mother's
Christian names correctly which finally caused Giffard's change of view,
but it was the absence of tattoo marks on the Claimant's body—the real
Roger was known to have borne them—which decided the sorely-tried
jury that they had heard enough. This was at the beginning of March,
1872, when, as it happened, Sala was already sickening for his most

serious illness. "I am suffering from an acute attack of bronchitis," he had written in the previous November, "and have been supporting nature for the last fortnight principally on prussic acid and morphia," and in January he had been confined to his room again, but he was well enough to undertake the task of writing a Special Thanksgiving Number of the *Graphic* in celebration of the Prince of Wales's recovery from typhoid fever, and he was able to accept an invitation to attend a meeting of the Claimant's "friends and supporters" at the Waterloo Hotel in Jermyn Street on March 4th.

It must have been a weird gathering, and its details remained clearly in Sala's mind almost to the day of his death. He described it in a lengthy article in the *Daily Telegraph* called "The Claimant Collapsing" which even today reads excitingly enough. The scene, he wrote, as the friends and supporters waited for the chief figure to arrive was the oddest mixture of the board meeting of a company in difficulties, a committee summoned to a nobleman's house to discuss the wrongs of Poland, and "an assemblage of friends and relatives of somebody who had become nobody and was being screwed down upstairs." There were drinks provided, and solemn waiters moved noiselessly about. Somebody was bold enough to hand on a rumour that the great case had been stopped. The supporters laughed the tale to scorn and drank a little sherry. A moment later the Claimant came in "very cool, very collected, very slow and soft in his gait and looking rather like an affable seal." He had a piece of paper in his podgy hand and after glancing round in his courteous way announced the startling news. His case, he said, "seemed to be stopped." And once again Sala, standing next to a supporter who, he thought, would have torn his hair had he not remembered in time that he was completely bald, was baffled and bewildered, not at the news, which he had been expecting, but at the Claimant's demeanour. He might have been announcing the fact that for the time of year the weather was remarkably mild. Later, too, when he had been summoned to Court to consult with his solicitors and returned after an hour's absence with the certain knowledge that his arrest was imminent, he merely assured the company that if his counsel advised him not to produce the twenty-five witnesses who would swear that Roger Tichborne bore no tattoo marks, he must submit to a non-suit.

"This was all," wrote Sala. "The shadows had been lengthening and deepening still; the friends and supporters had been dropping off by one, by twos, and by threes; they still, of course, believed in him as Sir Roger Tichborne, but they preferred just then to believe in him somewhere else. It was getting near dinner time. I began at last to contemplate the possibility of being left alone with the Claimant, and of his suddenly becoming confidential, and making astounding revelations about Wagga-Wagga, or Melipilla, or the Cordilleras, or the Kangaroos, or something dreadful of that kind. At this thought the hair of my head stood up; and so I wished the Claimant good-evening, and left him sitting in the gloom, like a large sphinx, affable but inscrutable. Everything, he said, would be settled on Wednesday morning. By Wednesday afternoon he was in Newgate. So, going my way, I saw him no more, and I suppose I shall not see him again."

3

More than a year was to pass before the trial for perjury was to open in the Court of Queen's Bench, and by that time Sala had been struck down. For months he struggled valiantly to maintain his regular output for the *Daily Telegraph*. He had managed, in addition, to prepare two books for the press, written "Imaginary London" for *Belgravia*— a "derisive directory" in fifteen entertaining chapters—and invented for *Fun* an explosive figure called Colonel Guido Vaux, who contributed various pyrotechnical papers on the events of the day couched in language which Sala's friends gleefully recognised to be a neat parody of his own florid style. Again and again, however, he had been forced to retire to his bed, all the more worried because as yet his doctor could give no name to the malady which was so obviously creeping upon him. His chest had become better, but his legs had begun to swell. There seemed to be aches and pains in every part of his body, and at nights he was unable to sleep. A second doctor advised a change of scene and complete rest from his daily labours in Fleet Street, and during the late summer and autumn he wandered with his wife, now seriously worried, from one seaside town or inland spa to another. Some work he could do, and from such resorts as Brighton, Ramsgate, Tunbridge Wells, Leamington, and Scarborough, he sent to Peterborough Court a long series of sketches which "local" historians eager for a vivid peep at the past will do well to consult.

It was the long and elaborate funeral service of the ex-Emperor of the French in January, 1873, which brought matters to a head. With his colleague Edward Dicey, Sala had driven down in a brougham to Chislehurst, spent a most strenuous day at Camden Place, and arrived home exceedingly late and in a state of exhaustion. The next day he was in bed with a chill; within a week he was dangerously ill. Thighs as well as legs had swollen most monstrously, and now he "turned from head to foot a reddish purple"—erythema in one of its most virulent forms. He was utterly helpless, in the greatest pain, and, from lack of sleep and worry about his financial position, a nervous wreck. Other physicians were called into consultation, but for some months they were able to do little to alleviate his condition. His limbs were "toasted and broiled and boiled," but the sick leopard, as he described himself, refused to mend. The months passed, and he was obliged to miss the Royal Academy Exhibition—the only occasion for nearly thirty years—and the closing scenes of the Alabama business. He fretted so badly about his absence from Fleet Street that the Levys sent a shorthand reporter to his bedside; but he was unable to dictate much more than a literary review. His wife nursed him with the greatest devotion—at one time she succumbed to the strain, and it was fortunate that Frederick Sala's daughter was living with them at the time—and his friends rallied round him. Shirley Brooks, now editor of *Punch*, kept him amused with his gossipy letters which gave no hint of his own rapidly failing health. Watts Phillips, the dramatist, a near neighbour, looked in almost daily, and when unable to do so would scribble one of those much-prized letters of his which were enriched with the quaintest caricatures. "Labby" came to tell him the latest developments of the Tichborne case—during one of its many adjournments the Claimant, now on bail, nearly broke his leg on a Leeds platform—and Augustus Mayhew facetiously suggested that the wretched Friswell be "coaxed" into another libel and so made to pay the alarmingly high medical bills. Consolatory letters, indeed, poured in, and Sala must have been particularly pleased by one, from Mortimer Collins and written in verse, which showed that his own "Caviar and Rudesheimer" had not been forgotten. The invalid, too, was cheered by the news that at a public reading by a well-known elocutionist by far the most popular item had been his "Conversion of Colonel Quagg."

His tortured body, however, mutinously refused to mend. They sent him to Hastings, but his skin, instead of assuming a decent tan, continued to show a Tyrian hue, while his legs obstinately declined to shrink to normal proportions. Weary months passed, and at one time it almost seemed as if Fleet Street would know him no more. But he fought on valorously, and in the late summer, though by no means fully recovered, was in harness again.

A warm welcome awaited him. Leo Adolescens and his colleagues might be modelling themselves upon him, but the peculiar Salaesque sparkle could rarely be found in their work. Now, too, the position which he had won for himself was being acknowledged in new ways.

He was invited to write his autobiography, and so far complied with the request as to publish a short series of papers on his schooldays. From this time, moreover, his name would rarely be omitted from the popular satirical Annuals which in rhyming couplets would pillory, in the slightest of disguises, the most prominent political and literary celebrities of the day. Sala was not always allowed to escape criticism of the severer type, but at the same time it would be made clear that there was only one G. A. S. in the world, for whom, it was assumed, most people held a kind of amused affection : a privileged personage, in fact, who in his own way was adding to the gaiety of the nation.

So it was with the anonymous authors of *The Coming K——* which in the previous year had achieved a quite astonishing success. This winter they produced *The Siliad*, which, though it dealt hardly at all with literature or journalism, could not ignore the "rowdy Philistine" or his peculiar style. Mercury was appealed to for his approval and invited to

> ". . . bid Salaneos through the Kosmos rove,
> To aid us with encyclopaedic lore,
> To write as poets never wrote before ;
> Too superfine, our native tongue to use,
> Unless adorned with epithets profuse ;
> And our high muse instruct the chiefs to lot,
> In bastard Greek or limping Polyglot !"

A barbed compliment, no doubt, but he was almost the only journalist to be mentioned. In later years he was to be given a much more prominent position in these up-to-date satires (which were occasionally accompanied by elaborate "keys"), but his appearance in *The Siliad*, like the *Vanity Fair* cartoon that was to follow in the next year, was not without its significance.

Incidentally, that winter saw the appearance of his first volume of short stories. Originally contributed to *Bow Bells*, they were now reissued as its Christmas Annual under the needlessly alarming title of *Terrible Tales*. They may be bracketed with his novels : interesting more for their biographical digressions than for their miniature melodramas.

4

He was not to "rove the Kosmos" again until the beginning of 1875, when Spanish affairs were engaging the world's attention, but in the meantime he was far from idle. He was not considered fit enough to be sent to Russia for the Duke of Edinburgh's marriage, and so was in

London during Shirley Brooks's last illness. They had quarrelled, of course, in their time, but for many years now they had been the closest friends. The two men had a great deal in common, and no matter how busy they might be seldom let a week pass without a piquant letter or two about current events. Could their complete correspondence be recovered, it would furnish the prettiest commentary on social as well as literary affairs during the mid-Victorian period. And, as it happened, Brooks's death, a week before the Claimant disappeared involuntarily from the public view, was to add considerably to his friend's labours at home. For some years he had been editing a weekly newspaper called *The Home News* which circulated in India, China, and the Colonies, and gave a summary of European intelligence. This, for the editor, seems to have entailed little more than a few columns each week of the "Echoes" type, and no doubt the proprietors were well advised to invite Sala to take the dead man's place. That he accepted was in all probability due rather to a laudable determination to pay off the £800 which his long illness had cost him than to any desire to address India or the Colonies. I cannot think that it was a congenial job—readers of *The Home News* seem to have demanded a "loftier" tone than came natural to him—and he must have been delighted when one of the Ingram brothers, meeting him casually later in the same year, suggested that he continue the "Echoes" in the *Illustrated London News*. Here, he knew very well, he would be entirely at home. His place had never been filled, though one or two writers, including Shirley Brooks himself, had contributed weekly notes. The "Echoes," however, were something peculiar to himself, and, after resigning from *The Home News*, he set himself out to transform what had been a few paragraphs of gossip into the whole-page "feature" which for the next twelve years was to remain without a rival in English journalism.

"Unimportant" and egotistical it may have been, but it suited the great public—all except those who looked for the scholarly wit of a Sydney Smith or the amusing impertinences of an Edmund Yates. What today would be called his "fan-mail" grew to almost unmanageable proportions, and there might be two or three hundred letters from strangers within the week. They would ask him to procure jobs for them, how to make good soup, when pins were invented, or who the Man in the Iron Mask had been. They particularly enjoyed themselves when they could point out one of those careless mistakes which Sala himself was always very willing to acknowledge. Now and again he would complain, in print, about his vast correspondence, but his words were not meant to be taken too seriously: like most public men he keenly appreciated his ever-growing popularity. And, as one woman wrote to him: "You are at the top of the tree and must expect to be poked at by the umbrellas of those beneath." Yet it is to be noted that, contrary to the general belief, these "Echoes" were not "dashed off" within a light-hearted half-hour. "That little column of mine (which I love very dearly)," he told Percy Fitzgerald, "is very difficult to write. You have to address an audience among whom clergymen, old maids, and people who live in country houses preponderate. They all want gossip, and are not averse from scandal; but woe to you if you tread on one of the corns of their prejudices; and nearly all your readers are centipedes." It meant, indeed, much extra reading, though on the other hand it helped, substantially, to secure that second thousand pounds a year which by this time he was finding indispensable.

Unfortunately for him, as I have said, the *Daily Telegraph* had first call on his services, and although he made several attempts to write "Echoes from Abroad" the experiment seldom lasted for any long time, and he was wise to make no effort of the kind when he paid his second visit to Spain in 1875.

"In his hands," wrote "Jehu Junior" that year in *Vanity Fair*, "the most trivial journey or the most imposing function becomes equally interesting, and invariably leaves the impression on the mind of the reader that he himself was actually present, and was more amused and tickled than ever before in his life." There you have the truth, and it is well illustrated in the letters which he sent home from Spain at this time. Queen Isabella had abdicated, the young Alphonso XII, so recently a Sandhurst cadet, had been proclaimed King and was about to make his entry into Madrid, and the Carlists were giving serious trouble in the North. In the Capital Sala found an old friend of his, Antonio Gallenga of the *Times*, and forthwith many important doors were open to him. Neither of them possessed any uniform, but both had brought dress-clothes with them, and thus uncomfortably attired were not only presented to the King but invited to accompany the Royal party in their journey by train to Saragossa. And it was just here that Sala surpassed himself. He had described the King's entry (on a white horse with an indigo tail: surely an equine rarity?) and the rather lazy enthusiasm of the *Madrileños* in his usual intimate way, but had not disguised the fact that there were dangers ahead, and one in particular, the Carlist railway "terror," now engaged his attention. The Carlists, indeed, were playing at train-bandits throughout the northern provinces, and he was prepared both for the loss of his despatches home and for trouble to himself. "Imagine," he wrote, "a Jacobite force at Derby, a Fenian army at Crewe, a Fifth Monarchy host at Swindon, and a Red Republican rabblement at Peterborough, all offering £5000 for the heads of the Postmaster-General and the editor of *Bradshaw*, and you may form an idea—a very faint one—of the state of things postal and telegraphic in this interesting but improvable country." Luckily the Royal train was well guarded and the two Englishmen were able to enjoy a luncheon of a truly regal kind on board at the King's own table. It was, perhaps, a little unfortunate that a lack of soap and water had reduced them to clean their begrimed faces with *candles*—Gallenga had heard that they made a most admirable substitute if rubbed on with sufficient zeal—for the wax melted into tears of almost Hollywood intensity as cigars and liqueurs were being handed round. If, however, any Grandee noticed anything unusual, he was too polite to say so. It was only after they had taken their leave of Majesty that the Carlists appeared and held up their train. Then, indeed, there was confusion, with nearly all the passengers in a state of panic; but Sala, though still, I imagine, in his dress-clothes and not wholly free from wax, seems to have been more than a match for the doubtlessly important "official" who, after extracting "fines" from his own countrymen, brandished a revolver and demanded to see his papers. He explained that his own monarch was neither Carlos nor Alphonso but Victoria Regina, Defender of the Faith, and at the mention of Her Majesty's name he swept off his hat, stood rigidly to attention, and in sternly ambassadorial tones, called out in English, "GOD BLESS HER!" And he must have glared so intently that the Spanish gentleman was hypnotised into attempting to pay a similar tribute. After which he bowed himself out of the carriage and gave no further trouble. I mention this incident, admittedly of no great moment, because in his account of it Sala not only entertained his readers with the liveliest record of a personal adventure but at the same time succeeded in giving them a very good idea of what the Carlist rising meant to the Spaniards in general. It was just his ability to do this, in fact, which largely explains how Sala as a special correspondent came to stand by himself. Trivialities about a passport and a bandit could become of significance because in his hands they were skilfully used to lift the veil from the things of real importance in the background.

It was much the same, too, when after a visit to Gibraltar and a short holiday in Algiers, he was sent to Venice for the Meeting of the Sovereigns, Franz Josef and Victor Emmanuel. There was the expected chatter about beggars and cabs and food; there were the usual glittering vignettes of Court functions; and there were some typical auto-

biographical reminiscences which, at a first glance, would seem to have
no connection whatever with Austro-Italian relations; but in the
background there was a commentary on the real significance of the
Meeting the shrewdness of which could not but be very generally
acknowledged.

The peregrinations of 1875, however, were not without their effect
on Sala's health. Back in London, in a Gower Street house, he managed
to find time to write a lengthy dissertation on the Prince of Wales's
forthcoming visit to India, and to play an active part in raising the Byron
Memorial Fund, in addition to his usual journalistic work; but by the
end of the year he was seriously ill again: eczema, gout, rheumatism,
almost everything in the way of depressing complaints, and until the
summer of 1876 he was obliged to be a "half-timer." Even so, he was
able to get through an amount of work which to most men would have
seemed excessive. He might be, as he occasionally complained, a tired
man, but there were as yet no signs of fatigue in his daily columns. On
the contrary, it was now that there could be found in his leading articles
a new keenness and a more marked assurance, particularly in those which
dealt with the radical reforms nearest his heart. There must be further
changes in the Bankruptcy laws, and a licensing system which would
put an end to the existing chaos. Shop assistants must be given greater
leisure, and museums and cafés must be opened on Sundays for the
working man. Above all, the appalling slums which disfigured the
greatest city in the world must be ruthlessly swept away. It was on such
matters as these, I believe, that he was eager to speak in the most uncom-
promising terms should they ever return him to Parliament; in the
meantime the Levys were permitting him to write very much what he
pleased in the *Daily Telegraph*.

It was now, too, that, almost single-handed, he achieved a minor
triumph by forcing the authorities to pull down Temple Bar. Week
after week, in words which were alternatively bellicose and bitterly
sarcastic, he challenged the City Fathers to produce a single good
argument for the retention of what to him had once marked the centre
of the literary world but was now a "crazy old nuisance," a "grimy
architrave," and a "cracking and dangerous obstruction." There were
sentimentalists, of course, who as warmly opposed its destruction or
removal, and called on the shade of Sir Christopher Wren to rise up and
smite the would-be vandals, but Sala brought the man in the street
round to his own way of thinking, and in the autumn of 1876 had the
satisfaction of watching a demolition squad at work. (In later years he
was to deplore the unlovely memorial which was to rise on its site—

if a dragon, or a griffin, or whatever the winged monster might be, was necessary, he pertinently enquired, why not a mock turtle as well?—but even so he continued to take pride in the success of his anti-Bar campaign.)

The part that he played in the matter was freely acknowledged at the time by his colleagues in Fleet Street, and when a month or two later the authors of *The Coming K——* produced their new satire, a mock-Shakespearean drama called *Edward the Seventh*, Sala was given a prominent place in its impertinent but amusing pages. This pastiche, with its attack on the Queen for preventing the Prince of Wales from taking any part in affairs of state, was considered so scurrilous that some of the newspapers refused to insert any advertisement of it and the largest firm of newsagents declined to allow it upon their stalls: two facts which, when they became generally known, naturally whetted public curiosity. It was certainly the authors' most outspoken production, and even today it is not wholly without interest. Here it will be enough to say that in the course of it Prince Guelpho is shown various aspects of London life with not all of which, it is to be presumed, his prototype was familiar, and Sala, in the thin disguise of Scala, comes to "Malborrow House" from

> ". . . distant Fleet Street
> where I work the Levigraph"

to play "Virgilian cicerone." His various speeches and songs are not particularly Salaesque, but his importance in the general scheme of things soon becomes obvious. As for the "blackguardly" book itself, it sold so well that a "Key" was printed. Here the fun was distinctly crude at times, but the biography of the Virgilian cicerone, whose motto, of course, was *cum grano salis*, ended prettily enough with the words: "Town Residence—Temple Bar."

By this time, however, Sala himself was in St. Petersburg on another roving commission, this time with what was then rather loosely called the Eastern Question.

At home official attention was being directed almost hourly to the unhappy Balkans and their two powerful neighbours. There had been the alleged "atrocities" in Bulgaria and crisis after crisis in Turkey, with three Sultans in as many months and Ministers living in constant peril of assassination. There was also Servia, which strongly objected to a Turkish army at her borders. Her Prince, Milan, with Russia at his back, had rattled his sword and declared war, and now, after both sides had had their successes and failures, an armistice was in being. But what of the future, and what would Russia do? British sympathies were divided, but daily an anti-Russian feeling was growing stronger owing to the belief that the Czar, in spite of repeated assurances to the contrary, was bent on seizing Constantinople: an eventuality which we could not permit. This, indeed, was the celebrated moment in English history when we didn't want to fight, but by Jingo if we did . . .! But would it come to war? Sala, who privately admitted that, unlike the newspaper which he represented, he was not a Turkophil, never wavered in his opinion: a major war there might be, but if the Czar was to fight it would not be against us.

He found, at any rate in St. Petersburg, little enough anti-British feeling, and his earlier despatches, which, of course, had much to say of the differences between the "unknown" country he had so eagerly explored twenty years ago and the Russia of 1876, were calculated to allay the increasing uneasiness at home. Lord Augustus Loftus, the British Ambassador, was kind to him, and he made many new friends, not only in diplomatic circles. He had, however, forgotten most of the little Russian that he had learnt, and, outside the Embassy, spoke in French, a fact which, though he did not know it at the time, helped to rouse much suspicion against him and in more than one quarter. An English journalist with an Italian or Spanish name who did not talk English? Was he really the Briton he pretended to be? No; he was a Turkish subject, or, if not, a man whom Turkey had been employing for many years. When, moreover, the inclement weather caused a sudden change in his itinerary, and it was learnt that he was going to Constantinople, who, it was asked, could doubt that he was a Turkish spy? Luckily for him, there was to be no repetition of his Paris misadventures. No newspaper ventured to speak of the suspicions until after his departure from Russia, and by that time the authorities were well aware that he had been mistaken for that Count Sala, a Turk, whom I have already mentioned.

Moscow, Warsaw, Odessa, Constantinople: as the weeks passed, each with its crop of disquieting rumours, Sala was bidden to go this way and that, and saw no reason to change his views. Moscow might be "in a hurry" for war, Odessa "uneasy" at the prospect, and Constantinople under her latest Sultan in process of accepting what was euphemistically described as a Constitution; but for a while Sala remained undisturbed, and whenever he could conveniently do so forgot all political crises, wandered into cafés or bazaars, described any eccentric figure who crossed his path, made exhaustive enquiries into the peculiarities of Turkish cooking, and in general seemed to be enjoying himself in his own particular way. Russia and Turkey would probably fight, but how much more interesting to investigate the Dancing Dervishes, or listen to the talk of men like Hobart Pasha and Colonel Fred. Burnaby! And on this occasion the Levys seem to have been less delighted than usual with their prince of correspondents. At the time of Lord Salisbury's coming, in an attempt to prevent war, they were fully justified in sending out a "political" correspondent to Turkey; but it is to be noted that they did not print all the despatches which Sala sent home, and by the end of January the roving commission seems to have been gradually transforming itself into a holiday. Precisely what further instructions had reached him I do not know, but from an outspoken essay of his called "The Grand Turk at Home" which was printed a few months later in the *Gentleman's Magazine*, it is difficult to resist the conclusion that in Peterborough Court they were becoming afraid of his steadily increasing Turkophobia. He might be enjoying "the polite society of Pera," where, indeed, the British and American colonies exerted themselves to entertain him, but even there every visitor was expected to take political sides, and, Russophil though he remained, Sala was now minded to echo Mercutio's words and cry "a plague o' both your houses"! He was, to say truth, working himself up into a temper, which was not assuaged when his skin misbehaved again and the Turkish chemist to whom Dr. Benjamin Richardson's prescription for a lotion had been entrusted, apparently used vitriol in place of the more amiable zinc. He showed his feelings when in writing of Swinburne's pamphlet on the "Muscovite Crusade" he besought the poet to "leave the loathsome age of special correspondence, diplomatic lying, and windy leading-article-writing, and the more loathsome stage of the Eastern Question, to their own abominable devices." He was heartily tired of the Turk and nearly all his oriental ways, and, no doubt, in those final despatches of his he was a little too forthright.

So, at the beginning of March, he slipped away from the now hateful Pera, amused himself in Athens for a while, and then in search of more familiar excitements, journeyed westwards to Nice, which is no great distance from the gaming-tables at Monte Carlo.

5

There was now to follow, for Sala, a time of even greater renown, a time, indeed, when that twenty-year-old ambition of his to become "a popular author" (the soberer Victorian equivalent of our twentieth-century "best-seller") was fulfilled, though not quite in the manner that he had then envisaged.

Hitherto his books of travel, with the single exception of his American war-diary, had not sold in any great numbers. The publishers had been satisfied enough to ask for more, but nobody's fortune had been made. Now, however, in quick succession there were to come two books of much the same intimate and gossipy type, reprints of his *Daily Telegraph* despatches, and both were to achieve a success which he could not have dared to expect. He went to Paris for the 1878 Exhibition, and his *Paris Herself Again* ran to no less than ten substantial editions, and in the following year he crossed the Atlantic for the second time, and his *America Revisited* almost repeated the huge success of his Paris book. Before their publication he had made himself fairly well known; after their appearance (which was followed by reprints of some of his earlier books), his name was on everybody's lips, long articles about him appeared in the reviews and magazines, and those who had the arranging of semi-public banquets eagerly sought his services as chairman. Now, indeed, as he tells us, he was able to "mingle again in that society in which, through the position of my dear mother, I had mixed in my boyhood."

He came home from Nice in the late spring of 1877, and there were few signs of the coming blaze of popularity. Nobody seems to have suggested that the Russo-Turkish despatches should be reprinted, though they were quite as entertaining as any that he had written, and he settled down to routine work in Fleet Street, with "extras" in the way of a series of theatrical reminiscences for a short-lived weekly called *Touchstone* and more "terrible" tales for John Dicks's *Bow Bells*. He was in poor health—"I cannot ever be in good health again," he was bewailing in a little while, "and half at least of my days are spent in the acutest pain"—but this did not prevent him from accepting a great number of invitations to dine out or from playing host frequently in the roomier house in Mecklenburgh Square to which he had moved from Gower Street at the end of the year. (It was "under the friendly wing of the Governors of the Foundling Hospital," he informed a friend, "north-west corner, *no thoroughfare*, nice garden in rear, one of the oldest and greenest of full-bottom-wigged squares in front, and a shilling cab-fare to one's offices and one's club.") And when, after a spring rendered wretched by the unexpected arrival of yet another distressing ailment in the shape of spasmodic asthma, though made memorable to him by his occupation of the chair at the Savage Club's coming-of-age dinner, he took his wife to Paris, he was hardly prepared for what was to follow.

It would be the third Exhibition in Paris to claim his professional attention, and he did not expect to remain abroad for more than a

P

fortnight. Why, indeed, should he? There were rather too many Exhibitions these days, and surely there would be nothing to say that he had not said scores of time before? On the other hand, Paris had changed considerably since the fall of the Empire, and it might be possible to construct a fairly lively panorama of the city, with the Exhibition not always in the foreground. He set to work on these lines, and Edward Lawson—the name had now been changed—bade him stay on.

Carefully he hid himself and his wife from all English acquaintances, and was satisfied with "a little box of a salon and sleeping cabinet" in a quarter to which few foreigners came. He was not too comfortable, and his health did not improve. In addition, he was greatly worried by a financial matter which at one moment threatened to have serious consequences to himself. (In the previous February he had had the melancholy privilege of acting as a pall-bearer at George Cruikshank's funeral, and, apparently at the widow's request, he had been rash enough to stand security for a relative of the artist who was now in Holloway Gaol.) Nevertheless, he continued to send home the gayest of letters, and Edward Lawson continued to ask for more. Four months passed, and only after the Exhibition had closed its doors did the Salas return to England. Even then, and popular though his "Paris after the Peace" despatches had been, there was little enough reason to suppose that their republication in book-form would meet with anything more than a fair "library" sale. On the contrary, none of his previous publishers seemed interested, and a whole year was to pass before the book was printed. Meanwhile there were more banquets to preside over, more private dinners in the highest circles—"I have been dined half to death this season," he declared—much hard work in the background with Lord Rosebery for the newly-formed Greek Committee, and, in the late summer, what seemed at long last to be a chance for Parliamentary honours.

Now, a few months before, T. H. S. Escott, a journalist of high standing who was to write more than one sound book about the Britain of his day, had contributed to one of the newer reviews a long and appreciative essay upon Sala and his work. In the course of it he had not hesitated to say that never before had a journalist "so thoroughly mastered the tastes and requirements of the colossal circle of readers" to whom he appealed. But, he had added, it was not only as a writer that he excelled: as a public speaker he was also in the front rank, and there followed a passage which many readers must have read with particular interest for it expressed what they were feeling themselves

"Enriched with all these accomplishments," wrote Escott, "George Augustus Sala, it may be thought, has never filled the place in life for which nature may be supposed to have destined him." This, as it happened, was not Escott's own view, but it was one which was held by many shrewd judges, Anthony Trollope amongst them. A man, moreover, they said, who had shown himself to be deeply interested in so many of the social questions of the day was surely entitled to hope that one day he might be allowed to air his views in Parliament. But— those odd stories about him? Nonsense: he had lived them down. Today he was being received everywhere. And for some little while a few of his friends had been working quietly on his behalf. There was, for instance, Labouchere, "as fast and true a friend as any I have in the world"; there was Lord Rosebery, who delighted in his company and was inviting him ever more frequently to his house; and there was a Master in Chancery named Charles Skirrow—his wife must surely have been twin-sister to Mrs. Leo Hunter—who was "lobbying" most industriously in the background. Unfortunately there was an obstacle in their way which Sala himself did nothing to remove. He was no "Party" man. He had always called himself a Liberal, but of recent years his views on a number of questions had widely diverged from the orthodox Gladstonian standpoint: in other words, he was what a Tory colleague of his called "the flamingest of Radicals." Nevertheless, friends continued to work on his behalf, particularly at Brighton. M.P. for Brighton! The chances were not great perhaps, but there were shrewd judges who were prophesying a Liberal landslide, and the Brightonians had known him for the past forty years. Many no doubt would give him their vote on personal grounds. Already, too, there was a nucleus of an "advanced" Liberal Party in the town, and he was making it his business to be in Brighton as often as possible.

It was then that the news came of a "split" in the Liberal Party at Lambeth. It was complained that one of the sitting members, a man named M'Arthur, had not only neglected his duties but was "shutting out" some of the local Liberals; it was declared that a more Radical policy was wanted; it was proposed to form a new Association in the very near future; and—within a few days' time—the rumour that Sala had been invited to stand was general.

It was a piquant bit of news for the gossip-writers, though the staider journals were wary in mentioning his name in this connection. Stray paragraphs, however, appeared, and, so far as I know, they were not contradicted. One of the popular comic weeklies even celebrated the news in a set of verses which, I do not doubt, fitly reflected what the unpolitically-minded man in the street thought about it. Here are the last two stanzas :

> "When Sala sits for Lambeth, each unmitigated bore,
> Whose rhetoric but ranges from the snarl unto the snore,
> Will, improved by sensate passion, have a quite impressive fit:
> 'Why, by Jove, the land's demented! Here, they've sent us in a Wit!'
> Towering Tories on back benches wax a weird and woeful white:
> 'What the dickens *is* occurring? Here's a fellah who can write!'
> Perennial rays will melt e'en bold Obstruction's cold cuirass,
> When Sala sits for Lambeth and they ne'er turn out their G.A.S.
>
> "When Sala sits for Lambeth, then what can't the House discuss?
> He has coffee'd with the Moslem, he has tea'd it with the Russ;
> He can analyze the natives from Granada to New York;
> He has tasted pumpkin squashes! he can speak the tongue of Cork.
> On high art as on good cooking he can put his colleagues right,
> And the leaders of the morrow shall instruct them overnight.
> Then some rather wiser speeches might some more respect command
> When Sala sits for Lambeth—which is when he likes to stand."

When, however, at a stormy meeting the Lambeth Radical Association came into existence, the all-important resolution expressing dissatisfaction with M'Arthur was not carried, and Sala wisely retired. But he was not dismayed, for other constituencies now wanted to hear what he had to say. In October he addressed a political audience at Peterborough, and only a few days later he was in another part of Lincolnshire, speaking on behalf of William Ingram. Brighton, however, remained the borough of his choice, and almost every week-end was spent there. And then at a moment when it seemed that his candidature might at last be formally endorsed, all political ideas had to be temporarily thrust aside : marching orders had been received once again, and he was off to America with his wife.

Since the earlier part of the year there had been some talk of his going. He wanted to go; in particular, he wanted to visit the South and if possible go west to San Francisco. Now, rather suddenly, I fancy, Edward Lawson came to a decision, and plans were hurriedly made.

It was for Sala an exciting, but also a worrying, time. In the first place his departure was more than once postponed owing to the (to him) extremely unwelcome fact that Edward Lawson had brought an action for libel against Henry Labouchere, and it was believed that his evidence would be required. Both men were friends of his of long standing— more than once both had come, financially, to his rescue—and he hated the idea of having to speak, however briefly, in the witness-box on such an occasion. (Luckily in the end he was not called upon.) In the second place there was some disagreement in Peterborough Court over his proposed itinerary, and in point of fact the last four or five of his letters home never appeared in the *Daily Telegraph* though they were duly printed in his American book. Now, too, the political prophets were hinting at an early general election. On the other hand for the first time in his life he was the guest of honour at a widely-attended Farewell Banquet, and there was the Paris book, which to his great astonishment not only pleased those critics who had consistently attacked his previous books, but was selling so well that a second edition (with a new preface) was in hand within a few days of publication.

What was it about this Paris book which captured the great public's interest and caused it to remain a popular favourite on the book-stalls for the next ten years? It was not as if the Exhibition were still luring thousands of visitors to France. True, there was much in it about Paris outside the Exhibition, and the two volumes made a handsome enough present. Had the title something to do with it? It was certainly an attractive one. I think, however, that the four hundred illustrations, the work of well-known French artists, must have done not a little to help it to popularity. Sala in sending a copy of the book to his friend Lady Lindsay of Balcarres apologised for the "rubbishy" illustrations with which the publisher had insisted on "cramming" it, but to most English people of the time they must have seemed gay and up-to-date and amusingly varied—a fitting accompaniment to the author's pleasantly discursive chapters. But, whatever the reason may have been, the book continued to sell, and not only in this country: already the Americans were appreciating its intimate pictures of what had come to be their favourite European city.

It is possible, indeed, that *Paris Herself Again* proved to be as useful a letter of introduction to its author as any that he carried in his pocket. From the moment when he stepped ashore at Boston he was royally treated. Not now did politician and pressman alike fulminate against him: both welcomed him as an unofficial ambassador from Britain, as in a way he was.

North or South, Middle West or California—it did not matter where he went: it was one long triumph for him. "We are overwhelmed," he told Mrs. Skirrow, always his fervid admirer and just now his most regular correspondent, "with invitations and courtesies of all kinds, and, indeed, our progress has been a great deal more brilliant than I ever dreamt it would be or than I deserve." Perhaps it was not altogether surprising. Not yet was the time when a British celebrity would visit America almost as a matter of course, collect his dollars in assembly-room or lecture-hall, and return with all speed to offer the world his "impressions": such expeditions were comparatively rare, and for Americans there was still something excitingly novel about them. And so Sala was regally entertained by State Governors, men of letters, famous actors, and millionaires. In Richmond there was a gubernatorial party for Mrs. Sala (who by this time had overcome a little of her old shyness and remained "smilingly serene"), and the Confederate Generals who turned out in force to greet her husband were no more enthusiastic than was the Irish journalist at a New York Press Club banquet who in slyly reminding his audience of their honoured guest's aforetime Copperhead tendencies excused them neatly as the sympathies naturally and properly extended to the underdog!

He met few of his own countrymen, but he was delighted to discover in San Francisco the Frederick Marriott who so many years before had given him the editorship of *Chat*, and Americans like Joseph Jefferson of *Rip Van Winkle* fame and "Dundreary" Sothern whom he had known in England went out of their way to make him at home. The visitor, too, was careful to make no mistake this time. He was enjoying himself, and let everybody know it. His speeches were just the witty and pawkily appreciative addresses which the Americans had always enjoyed. In this new and mellowed G. A. S., indeed, they found a jovial and not unimpressive figure very much to their liking and asked him to come again.

His success with the Americans was reflected in his despatches home. "I have not seen any of my letters to the D.T. in print," he was writing at the beginning of February, "and am worrying myself with the apprehension that they are futile and stupid." But he need not have worried. In England the letters were being widely enjoyed and seemed to be adding to his popularity and, incidentally, to the sales of *Paris Herself Again*. When, moreover, he described with even more than his usual gusto the celebrations at Philadelphia in connection with ex-President Grant's return from his world-tour and introduced the word BOOM to the British public, the wits amused themselves by prophesying what further importations of the same nature he was likely to produce—quips which though not always so witty as they might have been helped to keep his name prominently before the public.

There was only one matter which occasionally marred his enjoyment of his "triumph." Would he be able to reach home in time to take part in the General Election which was obviously so near? He seems to have had little doubt that he would be able to secure nomination in Brighton, if he were on the spot, and almost to the last moment was

writing home with suggestions and appeals for help. In particular there
was Charles Skirrow, who was more than once urged to lose no opportunity to press his claims. "You would materially assist me," wrote
Sala on one occasion, "first by getting hold of the Brighton lawyers on
the Liberal side, and next by conferring with Labouchere, with whose
libel crazes I have nothing to do, but who is otherwise a thorough
gentleman. . . . Mr. Willing," he added, and must have thought of those
few but glorious days when *England in the Nineteenth Century* was to have
startled the world, "the famous bill-sticker who has a house in Brighton
where he spends oceans of money would also do anything for me, and
has great influence. Unfortunately," he could not resist adding, "he has
a habit of going temporarily off his head, and I am not quite sure whether
just now he is in full sail or laid up in dock." But if Mr. Willing
happened not to be in the best of health, there were others whom the
ever-helpful Mr. Skirrow was exhorted to see without delay, whether
they were Liberals or not.

But it was not to be. The General Election was in full swing by the
end of March. It was on Monday, April 6th, before the Salas reached
England, to hear that the Brighton election had been fought two days
before. Result—two Liberal gains.

I do not suggest that Sala would undoubtedly have secured nomination
had he not gone to America, nor, in that event, that he would necessarily
have been elected. It is more than possible that some of the old stories
were still persisting, and quite on the cards that owing to Skirrow's
exertions his name was put forward but rejected. That his disappointment, however, was acute can hardly be doubted, and, although in 1888
he did, on request, allow his name to be submitted to a London Association, he seems after that date to have expressed no further desire to
obtain Parliamentary honours.

For all that, it was a decidedly Eminent Victorian who returned in
1880 to the house in Mecklenburgh Square.

CHAPTER FOURTEEN
THE TOPMOST RUNG

I

"Who," Sala was asking Mrs. Skirrow some little time after his return from America, "who do you think put in an appearance here last Sunday? Great excitement in the Square. The Baroness Burdett-Coutts and her 'sposo' in a mail-phaeton!! She spent an hour inspecting the 'curios,' but Mrs. Sala (who was peeling potatoes) would not show."

Actually there was nothing remarkable in the fact that the Baroness should call on the Salas in Mecklenburgh Square and bring her young husband with her. She had known and liked them both for some years, and the "curios"—a miscellaneous collection of objects gathered together by Sala on his travels and a library of handsomely-bound books, original drawings, and fine prints—were well worth a visit. It was not, moreover, as if Sala were boasting of a new lioness he had secured to such an expert in that curious pastime as Mrs. Charles Skirrow. It was well enough known now that Society (with the largest of capital S's) delighted in Sala's entertaining chatter at the dinner-table, just as it was accepted as very natural that on such occasions Mrs. Sala preferred to remain at home. Recently, too, that inquisitive and talkative "little bird" which the Victorian gossips found so useful had been whispering that H.R.H. himself had "taken him up." And it was true that, in common with the great majority of lesser mortals, the Prince of Wales enjoyed his company. (It was at a Rothschild wedding early in 1881 that Sala had been presented to the Heir Apparent by Lord Rosebery, and only a few weeks later Mr. Oscar Clayton, a fashionable surgeon of the day who was to be knighted in the following year, invited him to a small private dinner-party to meet the Prince—at the Prince's request: the first, as it was to happen, of many such meetings.) No, there was no boasting on Sala's part, and I quote his words only because they illustrate to some small extent what I believe to have been his real feelings at the time about his own great success. Of course he was delighted, for it had been fairly earned, but he was also, I cannot doubt, immensely "tickled" at the idea of himself as a social lion.

Here he was, the son of an unsuccessful dancing-master, a popular author, asked almost nightly to speak, a man who was earning his £2000 a year or more, and one who was to be found in the most exclusive

SALA.

From a photograph by Elliott and Fry, 1887.

and with their permission.

"A Missy" of Fire and Twenty years ago.

G. A. Sala
1881

(a) " A Missy of five and twenty years ago."

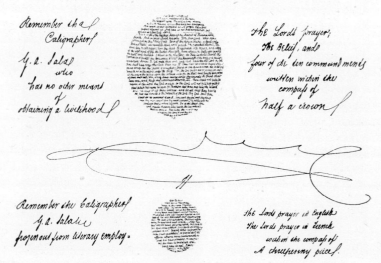

Remember the Caligrapher G. A. Sala who has no other means of obtaining a livelihood

The Lord's prayer; The Belief, and four of the ten commandments written within the compass of half a crown

Remember the Caligrapher G. A. Sala frozen out from literary employ.

The Lord's prayer in English The Lord's prayer in French within the compass of A threepenny piece.

(b) The Lord's Prayer on a half crown and a sixpence.
Contribution to a Charity Fair by the Distressed Compiler of the
" Echoes of the Week."

ARTIST AND CALLIGRAPHER.

circles; and—it could be the greatest fun. He was genuinely fond of the kind-hearted Baroness and Lady Lindsay of Balcarres and the octogenarian Lady Combermere, the Field-Marshal's widow, at whose house he lunched or dined almost every week; he enjoyed going to Mentmore to browse in its library with Lord Rosebery; and the coroneted envelopes which the postman brought to his house every few days were not unwelcome; but—he was decidedly not of their world. On the contrary, like his next-door neighbour and friend, the Hon. Lewis Wingfield, who dabbled in most of the arts, deplored the accident of his lordly birth, and was happiest in the green-room of a theatre or the roughest saloon of a public-house, he belonged to Bohemia and nowhere else. It was not that he was conscious of any strain outside its borders—by this time he was sufficiently cosmopolitan to make himself at home in any kind of gathering—but rather, I fancy, that when, in contrast to his present magnificence, he thought of the old penniless days, of the few other Salas who were still alive (and doing none too well), of cousins who were tradesmen and old friends who did not speak the King's English, a chuckle would be born somewhere in his throat and have to be hurriedly suppressed, for a lion, of course, must not chuckle to himself while on exhibition. That chuckle, however, would change to a great roar of laughter when, after rushing away from a great City banquet or ducal party, he found himself in a smoke-filled supper-room or cigardivan, describing in his own inimitable way for the benefit of those, like himself, of commoner clay, some whimsicality of the evening's entertainment which had particularly amused him.

It was only in such masculine company that he could relax and become the real Sala: the bluff, warm-hearted, and sometimes Rabelaisian figure who might so fittingly have belonged to Falstaff's immediate entourage. In the presence of ladies, as his friend Francis Burnand is careful to point out, he would always be "the very quintessence of courtliness," and his letters to them were invariably models of propriety, but he was of the people, and away from the mansions of the great ones, unworried by nice points of etiquette. And here he was not unlike another and greater celebrity of the day, Henry Irving, now his very good friend, who was far from being the schoolmasterish ascetic that many of those who knew him only in his stage-roles so mistakenly imagined him to be. With Dickens himself, too, he had in this respect not a little in common: to both men good manners came naturally, but neither of them relished the thick crust of conventionality within which the politer Victorians were at such pains to confine themselves.

Unfortunately that abnormally thin skin of his still occasionally led

to trouble. All Bohemia knew about it. His prickliness, it is true, had
not grown worse with his success, but it had hardly become much better.
He could be extraordinarily kind and sympathetic, particularly to younger
men in his profession who sought his advice, and nobody was more
generous than he while playing host, but he could also be brusque and
bearish, and a snub from him would not easily be forgotten. It is
recorded that a very young man who had shown himself a little too
eager to exhibit his anecdotal powers in the presence of his elders and
presumably betters was reduced to silence by one of Sala's unceremonious
interruptions. The fatal words "And that reminds me of a rather good
story" had just been uttered, when "Enough!" snapped Sala. "No
good your telling us *that* yarn. If it's proper we don't want to hear it,
and if it isn't we've heard it fifty times before." Yes, there often came
rather difficult moments. In his cups, too, and he often was in his cups,
sometimes very deeply, he was not the right man against whom to
measure your wits. He *might* be amused, but more probably he would
rise (or lurch) in his wrath and embarrass everybody about him. Even
in Peterborough Court they were sometimes at a loss to know how best
to deal with him. A year or two ago, on his fiftieth birthday, they had
fitly celebrated the occasion and presented him with a handsome piece
of plate. They were proud of their "prince" of contributors, and had
no little affection for him, but—all was not always smooth. With
Edward Lawson there were certainly some sharp passages of arms, and
the story goes that on one occasion of the kind the Editor-in-Chief was
goaded into hinting at something like instant dismissal. Whereupon
Sala stared stonily at him for a moment or two, and then without a
word retired to less respectable quarters, where, some hours later, he
was loudly informing the world, or, rather, that portion of it within
hearing distance, that Levy the Jew was no prophet. He might have
changed his trade ; he might have changed his name ; he might even
have changed his religion ; but if he thought he was going to change
his chief leader-writer he was making the biggest mistake of his life.
After which, in the small hours of the morning, he returned to Peterborough Court and composed a most admirable leading-article on the
manifold blessings of temperance.

With the staff in general he was on good terms. He liked and
admired Edwin Arnold, whose *Light of Asia* had appeared a year or two
back and who was now more or less the *Daily Telegraph's* editor. He
rejoiced in the close friendship of Edward Leman Blanchard, that most
diligent pantomime-writer, who was now one of its dramatic critics.
So far as I know, too, there was never a quarrel between Sala and Godfrey

Turner, whose leaders, particularly those on culinary matters, were so often mistaken for his colleague's work, or, indeed, with "Jeff" Prowse who, had he lived, might have written as many leading-articles as did Sala himself. Towards Clement Scott he was rather less amicably disposed, though there is no record of any battle royal between them. As it happened, they were colleagues on the *Illustrated London News* as well, and here, too, there was sometimes trouble with the editor, John Latey, if, as was very often the case, the "Echoes" were not delivered in time. Sala, however, would produce such piquant excuses and apologies and behave so munificently to the printers who were kept working overtime on account of his dilatory methods that Latey could not but forgive him. Indeed, it was just now that his best-known contributor was offered other work for the paper, and for some years provided a weekly article on "The Playhouses" in addition to the ever more popular "Echoes."

It may be admitted that as a dramatic critic Sala was not at his best. He brought with him an expert knowledge of the theatre both before and behind the curtain, and the stage reminiscences with which his critiques were so freely interspersed were lively enough; but he was a little too effusive and a little too chary of hurting people's feelings. With the managers he was naturally popular, but too often, it was said, his notices read like a discreet "puff" by the management. There was some justification for this statement, though he was far from being a mere log-roller, writing with his tongue in his cheek. The truth, I imagine, was this: he genuinely enjoyed this new freedom of the theatres (rather different from that accorded him in the old *Chat* days), and it was far from being disagreeable to be recognised as he sat in his stall or box; but what he wrote the next day was more liable to reflect the pleasure of an evening's entertainment than to provide the public with a critical opinion of the play's merits.

His new position, however, in the theatrical world was not without its significance. The public, it seemed, could not be given too much G. A. S. these days.

So you are to figure him just now standing sturdily on the topmost rung of the ladder, free (more or less) of his financial embarrassments, and with as much highly-paid work as he could conveniently manage to do. He was well aware of the enviable heights to which he had reached, but saw no reason to assume an air of Olympian aloofness on that account. There was no repetition of the swollenheadedness of the 'fifties, and even his worst enemies never accused him of "side." In his public speeches he had much to say about the dignity of his profession, and his

words were sincere, but that did not mean to say that he was incapable
of appreciating a joke at its expense or of laughing, on occasion, at himself. And thereby hangs a "terrible" tale of this particular time which
was often retold in later years. It concerned G. A. S. and his old enemy
Punch.

From 1870 to his death in 1874 Shirley Brooks had been *Punch's*
editor, but although the two men were such intimate friends, Bunn's
Word with Punch could not, it seemed, be forgotten, and Sala's name
was never mentioned. Tom Taylor had followed him in the editorial
chair, and for the next four or five years Mr. Punch might never have
heard of G. A. S.'s existence, though rarely a week passed without one
or other of the comic weeklies having something pert or amusing to
say about him. In 1879, however, when Taylor's health was so poor
that Burnand was assuming most of his editorial duties, there came a
change. Burnand was determined to put an end to what he regarded as
the silliest vendetta, and in the course of his *Injiyable Injia* he made play
on the name of a well-known Indian statesman and introduced to the
public Sir Jarge Orghustus Salar Jung, a jovial personage whose portrait
by Linley Sambourne left nobody in any doubt about his identity. In
the following year he was again mentioned as "the celebrated Jarge
Orgustus Salamander," and it was very generally understood that henceforth Mr. Punch and Sala were to be the best of friends.

To everybody's surprise, Burnand had been installed in the editor's
chair for no more than a few months when a cruel parody of the "Echoes"
entitled "Egoes of the Week" appeared in *Punch*.

Now Sala, of course, had been parodied a score of times and in a score
of places, and in several journals, as we have seen, he had been persistently and maliciously attacked. Of recent years a rather scurrilous
weekly called the *Hornet* had taken the lead in pillorying him and his
work for the "Daily Twaddlegraph" and only ceased to do so when
its editor retired to a prison cell; but with this one exception there had
been little malice in such travesties and burlesques, and Sala had rightly
regarded them as a tribute to his growing popularity. But that Mr.
Punch should turn on him in this way so soon after their apparent
reconciliation seemed to Burnand's friends not a little astonishing.

They spoke to him about it. Was it not rather a mistake to attack
Sala of all people?

Burnand was ready to admit that it might be, though surely, he suggested, Sala must by this time be well inured to such harmless quips?
He also pointed out that so far as he knew George and he remained on
the best of terms. And could they deny that the "Egoes" were really

very funny? They could not, but gloomily prophesied trouble if there was anything more of the kind. To their amazement there were more and even crueller "Egoes" in the next number of *Punch*, and they waited uneasily for the inevitable quarrel.

Matters came to a head at one of the Friday night suppers at the Beefsteak Club. Both Sala and Burnand happened to be present. Somebody introduced the one subject—parody—which, it had been hoped, would be left severely alone. Sala seized the opportunity to demand in his loud clear tones who the writer of the "Egoes" might be. Burnand pleaded editorial privilege and declined to say.

"But," growled Sala, "it's a personal attack on me!"

Somebody else, scenting serious trouble, endeavoured to play peacemaker by turning the conversation on to more general lines, but Sala would not have it, and Burnand seemed only to be making matters worse when in slightly apologetic tones he asked how he was expected to reject an article which he considered exceedingly clever.

There was an ominous rumble from Sala, and it was followed by signs of increasing excitement. "When I was younger," said he, "I'd have pulled the nose of any man who'd attacked me in that way, and no matter who he was."

"Then," retorted Burnand coolly, "you'd better pull mine. I'm the responsible party."

Another would-be peacemaker now urged that the matter had gone far enough and might conveniently be dropped, but Burnand would not be silent. It was a petty matter, he admitted, and hardly worth fighting a duel about, but, he added, staring bellicosely round, "if George Sala really wishes to carry out his threat, he can easily take the affair entirely into his own hands."

"I can," shouted Sala, springing up from his seat, "and I will!"

"Everyone," records Burnand, "jumped to their feet. It seemed as though he were going to assault me there and then! What was their surprise at seeing George, first with one hand, then with the other, *wring his own nose*, and, murmuring humbly 'I apologise,' drop down abashed into his seat. They all stared. George burst into one of his shoulder-shaking fits of laughter. All were puzzled, and looked from one to the other for enlightenment.

"'At my request,' I explained, 'George wrote that article himself.'"

In his *Fifty Years of Fleet Street* Mr. Frederick Moy Thomas mentions another occasion when Sala's zeal for the dignity of his profession did not prevent him from hoaxing an audience in his impish way. A banquet was being given in London to a party of distinguished French journalists, and Sala, of course, was asked to speak. He began his remarks in the most dreadful French ever heard. "'Mossoo le Presidong. Nous avong monjay ung tray bong dinay. Noo somm tray obleejay pour voter bontay,' and so forth, through a lot of most absurd compliments to his worthy hosts. The foreigners, being very polite men, looked perfectly serious, although they wondered no doubt why a man who spoke such execrable French did not stick to his own language. All of a sudden, however, Sala began to warm up to his subject. He talked of international good-feeling, of the miseries caused by jealousies between neighbouring countries, and as he went on, his accent, his language, became transformed, and he addressed his hearers in the purest Parisian. The change was so sudden that for a second—not more—they looked puzzled, and then they burst into such a shout of laughter that the orator's eloquence for the moment was sadly spoiled."

I cannot help thinking that this was the Sala who, for all his faults, endeared himself to so many of his contemporaries in every class.

2

On Sunday, March 13th, 1881, Sala was dining in Cavendish Square with the Earl of Fife, who was frequently his host these days. The beautiful Lady Lonsdale was present—she was eager to make his acquaintance—and among the guests was to have been the Russian Ambassador. That afternoon, however, news had reached London that bombs had been thrown at the Czar who was badly wounded, and His Excellency had been obliged to remain at Chesham House. Then in the middle of dinner came the news of the Emperor's death, and for Sala the evening was spoilt. He knew what would be in store for him. On the hall-table in Mecklenburgh Square there would be a message from Peterborough Court with instructions to leave at once for Russia.

Very definitely he did not want to go. His engagement-book was crowded; he was becoming rather tired of writing about funerals, however magnificent they might be; and with fresh diseases ever seeking a temporary resting-place in his body he had no wish whatever to undertake a third Journey Due North in March. But there was another reason why he was anxious to remain in London just now, for, most unexpectedly, he had turned novelist again, and within the next week or two the opening chapters of *A Party in the City* would be required by the printer.

In the previous January yet another sixpenny illustrated journal had been launched with even louder fanfares than usual. Its editor and part-proprietor was an old friend of Sala's and one of those men who would probably have made a big name for himself had he not attempted, like Lewis Wingfield, to shine in so many different roles. Alfred Thompson had begun his career as a subaltern in a cavalry regiment, but a neat turn for caricature and a ready pen had brought him to Fleet Street. So long ago as 1868 he had edited the *Mask*, a monthly magazine, which, incidentally, had published an admirably comic portrait of Sala, and since that time he had been special correspondent, political cartoonist, playwright, and designer of stage-costumes. Now with *Pan*—"Music, the Drama, Money, Books, Sport, and Gossip"—he hoped to consolidate his position, and he had certainly gathered round him an attractive band of contributors. There was music from the future Sir Frederic Cowen and there were drawings by Leighton. Sala headed the list of writers, but others whose work had appeared included Jules Verne, Palgrave Simpson, Oscar Wilde, and, for sport, Captain Hawley Smart, whose racy stories were already becoming widely popular.

The first three or four numbers, indeed, promised well, but Thompson was not satisfied. He wanted some new feature which would mark off *Pan* from its rivals. And—why not a serial story, not by one of the regular feuilletonists but by Sala himself? After all, he had written novels in the old days. One of them had recently been reissued, with gratifying results to the publisher, though, as Thompson happened to know, not a halfpenny had come its author's way. Yes, such a story was almost bound to be "a winner." So Sala was approached, and at first was dubious. He was a poor hand at fiction : besides, he had too much to do as it was. Thompson, however, had been prepared for a refusal and was ready with an offer which could hardly be refused. Apparently he had seen a publisher who agreed with him in thinking that a new Sala novel would be well worth a high price, and £1300 for serial and book-rights was suggested. It was a pleasantly large sum of money—far larger than any he had yet received for a novel—and Sala agreed to have the opening chapters ready by the beginning of April.

By that Sunday in March, however, when the Nihilists threw their bombs, little enough of the novel had been written, and a sojourn in Russia, even though it were to last no more than a fortnight, would interfere very seriously with his plans. Which was why, after bidding Lord Fife good-night, Sala most irrationally but understandably postponed his return home until the early hours of the morning : he wandered from club to club, and could not bring himself to face the inevitable message.

He breakfasted in peace, for no message had come, but it arrived very soon, and Sala never forgot its laconic contents. "Please write a leader," it ran, "on Billingsgate and the price of fish, and start for St. Petersburg this evening."

So the Billingsgate article was hurriedly written and bags were as hurriedly packed, and at 8.30 that evening Sala was at Charing Cross Station in a very poor temper. It had not improved when on the Thursday afternoon he stepped out of the train at St. Petersburg into a blinding snow-storm. It was intensely cold, he had brought insufficient furs with him, and he could think only of *A Party in the City*. Nor was he better pleased with the world or himself when, after viewing the Lying-in-State "in the preposterous inky magpie gear known as evening dress," he was on a sudden struck down by the sharpest attack of lumbago. At all costs it must be vanquished, and in time for the funeral some thirty-six hours later. Everything had been arranged. His old friend, Lord Dufferin, now our Ambassador, had introduced him to an English merchant from whose drawing-room windows the finest possible view of the various processions could be obtained. But how was he to get to that delectable window when the slightest movement was agony? Lumbago, as its victims well know, comes and goes at its own not very sweet will, and not all the remedies in the world will ordinarily affect its decision. The Russians, however, then as now, have their own heroic methods of dealing with an enemy, and on the orders of a Russian doctor no less than four gigantic Amazons arrived, bared their brawny arms, and proceeded to buffet and batter the unfortunate man into something like insensibility, after which the medical man calmly painted every inch of his body with successive coats of iodine in its most concentrated form. It is satisfactory to record the fact that the lumbago was not proof against such inhuman treatment, and, shaken though once again upright, Sala was able to send home as picturesque a record of the funeral ceremonies as any that he had ever penned.

His troubles unfortunately were not at an end. From the first, indeed, the Fates seem to have frowned down on *A Party in the City* and the £1300. On his return to London Sala was invited by Edward Lawson to supplement his despatches in the shape of six long articles on the Russians as he had found them. He did not like to refuse, and set to work. Somehow he managed to write enough of his novel to fill several numbers of *Pan*, and the first three instalments were duly printed. Then the blow fell. Alfred Thompson's finances were misbehaving; there was an action in the Courts; and, almost without warning, *Pan* expired.

"I had hoped," Sala was writing in a little while, "to invest the £1300 in the elegant simplicity of the Three per Cents for my wife when I am

SALA

Unpublished Caricature by Alfred Bryan, *circ*. 1888.

(b) Harry Furniss's Revenge. Caricature of the Prosecutor in
Sala *v.* Furniss, 1890. From *Confessions of a Caricaturist.*

TWO MORE CARICATURES.

(a) First Sketch for " Punch's Fancy Portrait
No. 46" by Linley Sambourne, August, 1881.

By kind permission of the proprietors of Punch.

under the daisies ; but I shall never have the heart to finish the story now."
Perhaps, however, it was just as well, for only a few months later he was
abroad "on the prowl" again, and, even had *Pan* survived, I can hardly
imagine that the "Party" would have been very regular in his appearances.

On this occasion he travelled Due South, and seemed in no mood to
hurry back. (Henceforth a winter in England was for him an eventuality
to be avoided if possible.) He took his wife to Marseilles, fulfilled an old
desire of his to visit Corsica, where, incidentally, he was charmed to find
that the "dear old diligence" of his childhood was still surviving, and
wandered on to Venice and Rome. Miraculously, his letters home continued to be both piquant and picturesque.

No new (or old) bacillus seems to have experimented upon him at
this juncture, and, back in London, he was able almost without interruption
and for a whole year to add, day by day, to his incredible output of words.
You may obtain a fair idea of his multiple activities during 1882 by
glancing through his *Living London*, a volume of excerpts from his
"Echoes," but to understand the real extent of his labours it is necessary
to scrutinise the *Daily Telegraph*, hardly an issue of which at this time
fails to exhibit clear signs of his untiring pen. This was the time when the
proposed sale of Jumbo, the Zoo's largest elephant, to Barnum was
exciting half England, when Cetawayo with his retinue was exacting the
admiration of thousands, and when Arabi Pasha was becoming rather
more than a mere nuisance in Egypt, and about each of these alien curiosities Sala, of course, had his own views to air. There was a new play
produced every few days, and no dearth of celebrities who chose to be
buried on days when Sala had hoped to make progress with a short
story—he could command a high price for them now—or had intended
to enjoy a few hours by the sea. It was now that the London Press Club
was launched, and naturally Sala was invited to become its first chairman.
It was now that the Falstaff Club sprang into existence, and naturally
Sala was elected to its committee. His *America Revisited* was published,
and more and more powerful dowagers or professional beauties desired
to make its author's acquaintance. There came the great libel case of
Belt *v.* Lawes—Mr. Belt was a fashionable sculptor who was alleged to
pay "ghosts" to do all his best work—and Sala in the witness-box scoring
heavily over learned counsel ignorant of his technical knowledge or
practical experience of the plastic arts, was not the least of its attractions
for the public. And many people reading what he wrote or the reports
of the speeches he made, seeing him, moreover, mentioned as being
present every other day at this or that fashionable function, wrote to
ask him "how the thing was done." He attempted to give a reply in

one of his "Echoes," but his "sketch of how a hardworking writer for the newspapers really does dispose of the twenty-four hours diurnally at his disposal" was hardly satisfactory, for the industrious day which he outlined only uncovered a part of the truth. It was necessary for him to work very hard, but the strain was beginning to tell. Life had become exciting, but he must ever have more excitement, and this was not always to be found at respectable houses or at reasonable hours.

They sent him again to Russia in 1883, and it is interesting to find him again unwilling to go, on this occasion for a less selfish reason. By this time he knew the Russians well enough to know the importance which they placed on a uniform. On his previous visit, indeed, it had been only Lord Dufferin's personal "protection" which had saved him from endless troubles with the police. He was still not entitled to wear uniform, and, as Hall Richardson, then newly appointed to the *Daily Telegraph*, relates in his *From the City to Fleet Street*, he always took the view that *his* newspaper ought not to play second fiddle to any other journal. "And that second fiddle," he wrote, "I shall undoubtedly play. I know," he added, "that Alfred Thompson, who is going for the *Daily News*, will take his old Carabineer's uniform with him, and I know the Russians too well not to feel assured that the great Russian official who is to select the one or two correspondents privileged to be present in the cathedral will select Monsieur le Capitaine Thompson in the gold-laced tunic with sabretache and spurs, however tarnished they may be, in preference to a correspondent in plain clothes. The other papers will send correspondents who are either officers in the active service or retired, or those who have been presented at Court. The only court of which I have any cognisance is Peterborough Court."

What ultimately happened was that Le Sage, afterwards editor of the *Daily Telegraph*, who was entitled to wear the uniform of a Deputy Lieutenant of the City of London, went to Russia with Sala, who, on condition that he was "presented" on his return, was, by the Lord Chamberlain's special permission, allowed to wear Court Dress. And in this way the *Daily Telegraph* in Russian eyes assumed its rightful importance.

At home throughout the remainder of the year and the greater part of the next there was for Sala much the same hectic programme. When the cold weather came he continued his "travels in search of sunshine," and his letters were afterwards incorporated into *A Journey Due South*, another of his books which sold well. When, moreover, the Reform Club lost the services of its head chef, who but Sala (now, I need hardly say, a member of its committee) could be entrusted with the delicate

task of securing in Paris the right man to follow in Soyer's footsteps?
But otherwise there was little enough to mark one day off from another,
and what, he was beginning to ask himself, of the future?

It was good to be at the top of one's profession, even though to stay
there meant constant hard work, and it was pleasant to be on intimate
terms with half the celebrities of London; but was he expected to slave
on in this way to the end of his days? He had saved little or nothing,
and these were not the days when great commercial firms pensioned off
their old servants as a matter of course. He was aware that a small legacy
would be forthcoming when his cousin, Miss Sarah Ashley, now a very
old lady and still a warm admirer of his, were to die, but it would be
insufficient to set him up as a gentleman of leisure. He would never
starve: there was enough material in those commonplace books of his
to provide him with good material for the rest of his life, and half the
publishers in London were keen to have him on their lists, but how in
this rush could he find time for the books he was keenest to write? There
was that History of Cooking promised long ago to Messrs. Chatto and
Windus. There was the Autobiography which Mr. Bentley wanted him
to write. And there were one or two other ideas for books at the back
of his head. But would they ever be written? It seemed very doubtful.
Even so, he need never starve *if* he remained well enough to write or
dictate. But suppose that ill-health forced him to retire? It might
happen: it had happened to many of his friends. Retirement! Yes, he
would be glad enough to retire, at any rate from a good portion of his
labours, but only if some scheme were forthcoming which would make
him financially secure.

Along some such lines, as I judge from his letters, his thoughts were
now running, but it was not until his return (with a chef) from Paris in
May, 1884, that he seems to have come to any decision.

There was to be an Australian tour, with G. A. S. "presenting" himself
on the lecture platform. He had long wished to make such a trip, and,
according to friends of his, there was a great deal of money to be made.
Why, Archibald Forbes, the war correspondent whom he had known
and liked for years, was supposed to have brought back with him something like £12,000!

Of course he must go.

3

"Yes, my dear cousin," he was writing that July to Miss Ashley on
the back of a letter from Lady Rosebery asking him to supper to meet
the Prince of Wales, "*ça marche* . . . and my wife and myself laugh, and

think it's a very funny world, and we work harder than ever; and we don't want to be knighted, and if we make enough money in Australia to be able to say farewell to 'the bustle and the raree-show that occupy mankind below' we will retire to a cottage in a vale, and grow cabbages, and thank God for all things.''

But—just how much money was he likely to make? At least his reputation had gone before him. They liked his books in Australia and New Zealand, and wrote to him to say so. Lord Rosebery, moreover, had assured him that so far as official hospitality went he had nothing to fear: letters of introduction from himself would open every important door. On the other hand, he was not, he knew, a very good lecturer. A light-hearted after-dinner speech before an audience comfortably replete and prepared to regard the simplest quip as wit of the highest order is one thing; a lecture, however entertaining or instructive, is quite another, requiring a technique that is peculiar to itself. Sala in the chairman's seat at a banquet was exactly in place, but on the platform he was less at home. He could not cure himself, he admitted, of the bad habit of "cruising about" with his hands in his pockets, with the inevitable result that he was not always as audible as he might have been. Nevertheless, with careful rehearsals he saw no reason why he should not repeat Archibald Forbes's great success, and preparations were put in hand.

There was a slight setback when Forbes's Australian agent declined to act for him until he had heard him lecture—a matter of some difficulty as he was in Victoria at the time and unwilling to come to England except at Sala's expense. Luckily Lewis Wingfield was able to come to his rescue. A great friend of his, George Rignold, the well-known actor who was also part-lessee of the Theatre Royal, Melbourne, was in England at the time. He was returning to Australia shortly and offered his services as advance-agent on terms which Sala would have been unwise to refuse. At the same time Edward Lawson agreed to print a long series of Australian despatches. There remained the route to be taken, and here, too, it seemed, the Fates were being kind. Sala was in need of a long rest from all journalistic work, and for this reason he was proposing to cross America at his leisure, and visit Honolulu before resuming his labours in New Zealand or Australia. His decision to do so reached the ears of an entrepreneur named Frank Bowden, who suggested that a short series of lectures under his management in the larger cities of the States might add very considerably to the financial success of the tour. He was prepared, he said, to pay £500 in advance, and promised to defray all reasonable expenses between New York and Chicago. It was a good offer, and Sala gleefully accepted it.

And while the man in the street was discussing Mr. Gladstone's Midlothian campaign or (more probably) the future of the Claimant who was just now released from prison with a figure considerably less bulky than that which had pleased the caricaturists so much, Sala was rushing hither and thither, making and remaking his plans, and working feverishly hard in an endeavour to leave his affairs in some kind of order. He would be away for at least a year, and there was much to be done outside Fleet Street. The house in Mecklenburgh Square was to be shut up, though a faithful Annie was to look after the "curios," and a temporary home had to be found for Mrs. Sala until the time came for her to sail direct to Melbourne. There were his two agents to be constantly consulted, and financial adjustments to be made. He was determined to write his daily leader and the "Echoes" until the last possible moment, and this was no easy matter in view of the great amount of work necessary in the preparation of his lectures. He was leaving nothing to chance: his addresses on Russia, Shows and Pageants, Wars and Revolutions, British Statesmen, and Dickens and Thackeray, must be made as good, as picturesque, as Salaesque as he could make them, and that was only possible if he were alone. "I shall go to Venice," he told William Howard Russell, and "take a gondola every day and spout them on the Lido," but he was obliged to be content with a quiet Brussels hotel. Rightly he intended, if he could, to speak and not read on the platform, but it was as well to be prepared for a possible break-down. So he set to work to write out in enormous letters and on huge sheets of paper the four or five lectures which he proposed to deliver. (His eyes were troubling him these days, and he used glasses to read; but they were not to appear on the platform.) When, however, he had filled three or four pages with this Brobdingnagian script he grew tired of his task and had the rest printed off in a fount almost equally large. The volume—for the pages were sewn together—must be one of the oddest of lesser Victorian relics.

So the days passed, and his house was closed and his wife sent into the country. Invitations continued to pour in upon him, but few of them could be accepted. He was bidden to Dunrobin by that Duke of Sutherland who, as Lord Stafford, had been with him in the *Great Eastern* and torn down the curtains for wool. He was asked to Invercauld, to Mentmore, and to Blenheim Palace. But as the day of his departure drew near he left London only once, to say good-bye to his much-loved Lady Combermere down in her St. Leonard's retreat, and only once dined out—with Lady Burdett-Coutts, who gave him a letter of introduction to Royalty: in this case the King of the Sandwich Islands. He was hugely excited, for this was to be no roving commission of the usual type : it might perhaps be the biggest venture of his life. With luck he would return with a fortune. He was not yet an old man—no more than fifty-six—but he was tired, and the word retirement was ever before his eyes : a delectable word.

There came the final farewells, and he sailed in the *Gallia* with Mr. Bowden. All the lectures had been written and rehearsed. He was in excellent spirits. The best part of a year, and no printer waiting for copy ! He was going to the Land of the Golden Fleece, and it might well turn out to be the Land of a Golden Harvest for himself.

Yet it had been better for him, I think, had he never sailed at all.

4

"My lectures have all been, oratorically, brilliant successes ; but towards the close of the course I was scandalously treated by an incompetent and unscrupulous agent who broke his agreement with me ; and at length, at Cincinnati left me wholly in the lurch, vanishing with his booty. By his malfeasance I have lost £170, but as I took the precaution to put a couple of Hundred pounds Bank of England notes in my pocketbook before starting, I shall take no more harm than the consequences of having been 'done' by a fellow, half idiot and half rascal."

So wrote Sala to Mrs. Skirrow from Chicago on the first day of February, and no doubt he had good reason for feeling more than a little sore with Mr. Bowden. Yet in later years he was inclined to modify his opinion of the "recreant manager" and spoke of him as an unwise optimist who had been more or less forced to bow before such a storm as he could never have anticipated. The worst of ill-luck, indeed, attended both of them throughout the nine lectures under Bowden's management, and the tenth at Chicago, which Sala staged for himself, was about the least satisfactory of them all. Oratorically they may well have been brilliant successes, but in almost every other respect they were lamentable failures.

Yet the little tour began well enough. At New York an army of reporters met him, and Sala had no cause to be displeased with the newspapers next morning, for they were full of him and his plans. When, moreover, no less a celebrity than Oliver Wendell Holmes took the chair for him at the first of the three lectures which he was to deliver in Boston, the omens remained good. The hall was comfortably full and he himself in fine form. Unfortunately on the second night Patti was singing and proved to be the greater attraction : Sala's audience was small. And

then there began a "Week of Prayer" which seems to have scared
Bostonians away from any pursuit of culture, and the third lecture was
given to almost empty benches. He was heartened on his return to New
York by a banquet in his honour at the Lotus Club, but his addresses at
the Chickering Hall and in Brooklyn were only sparsely attended.
Something was wrong, though who, if anybody, was to blame it is
difficult to say. The fall of Khartoum and Gordon's death, announced
at this time, can hardly have caused many Americans to mope in their
own parlours, and Sala himself was not unduly affected by the fact that
one of his oldest friends, Edmund Yates, had been sent to prison for
libelling Lord Lonsdale. Yates had taken the blame for a contributor's
indiscretions, and, as Sala told Mrs. Skirrow, he was satisfied that the
visiting justices and the prison doctor between them would make his
"first-class" sojourn in Holloway more than tolerable. No, it just
seemed that some feature was lacking which the Americans demanded
in their lectures. Affairs improved in Philadelphia, where on his previous
visit he had made many good friends, but in Washington an astonishing
snow-storm chose the evening of his lecture to exhibit its ability to keep
good folk indoors, while in Baltimore it was as though the City Fathers
had passed a bye-law forbidding the natives to listen to any alien address.
Then came Cincinnati, and Mr. Bowden admitted himself beaten.
There remained only Chicago, where Sala was determined at all costs
to have a success. Henry Irving was there and gave what assistance he
could. Free tickets were handed to two or three hundred people. Even
so the lecture was doomed, for at the very same hour and in a much
larger hall Mark Twain, then at the height of his popularity, was lecturing
himself! For poor Sala this was the last straw.

Nevertheless, though no fortune had been made, he was far from
being out of pocket, and once out of Chicago his luck took a surprising
turn for the better. In the train to Sacramento, it is true, he was robbed
of £20, but on the other hand he was travelling free, and in the city
itself an Italian Jew came forward with exciting proposals for the immediate future. San Francisco, it seemed, was the one city of all others
to appreciate lectures. San Francisco regarded George Augustus Sala as
one of the world's greatest figures. San Francisco's theatres and halls
were the most spacious ever built, and if he were to agree to appear in
them for, say, six nights, the whole population would be fighting to
secure seats. Sala explained that he would not be staying in this celestial
city for more than eight or nine days, and felt bound to add that he had
not hitherto met with much success as a lecturer, but the Jew only smiled
and shrugged his shoulders. What could you expect from those cold

Eastern States? Here in California (with himself in charge) there would be a very different story to tell.

He was right. Sala delivered the six lectures, on successive nights, and each brought him in some £70 or £80. In addition, he was fêted as never before in his life. "I have made a pot of money," he told Mrs. Skirrow, "by my speechifyings, and my manager (an Italian and for once an honest man) is in ecstasies, having cleared even more than I have by the transaction. Very probably I shall deliver a lecture at Honolulu while the steamer waits for the mails—another $500 perhaps. Don't think me mercenary when I talk about dollars. You know *why* and for whose dear sake I am working the mine of my capacity to the last vein of the ore." And it was in keeping with his high spirits that he was able to add: "no bronchitis, no asthma; in magnificent health."

There followed the visit to Honolulu, where unfortunately for him there was no time for a lecture. For four hours only could he remain ashore, and there was the visit to the King to be paid. His Majesty was gracious—they discovered that they were fellow-Masons—and sent his private band to play Sala off the island; that was about all. But one little piece of family news which was given him as he was driven away from the Palace must have brought a rather wry smile to his face. Long years ago his brother Albert had cut himself off, though at least twice there had come appeals for help. Originally, according to Sala, Albert had been "in the piratical line of business at Key West," and then turned missionary in Polynesia. His appeals for help had on both occasions followed on the death of a Mrs. Albert. Now, his brother learnt, there had not only been two further Mrs. Alberts, presumably buried at somebody else's expense, but also a fifth who was still alive—a native lady with the slightly alarming name of House on Fire.

So to Auckland, for another four hours only—but he was to return to New Zealand later—and on to Sydney, to receive his first taste of real Australian hospitality, and from there to "marvellous" Melbourne, where a happy Mrs. Sala, with George Rignold and his wife, were waiting to greet him.

From that moment he was projected into the "dream-like rush" in which he was to live until the end of the year.

5

It is hardly necessary to speak of his Australian tour in any great detail—there are the columns of the *Daily Telegraph* to be consulted by those who may like to know how the Land of the Golden Fleece appeared

to a much-travelled and highly inquisitive Englishman in the 'eighties—
but there are one or two facts to be recorded, and a glance here and there
at his private letters reveals interesting sidelights. Financially speaking,
he had no cause to grumble. The considerable fortune which Archibald
Forbes had secured did not come Sala's way, but he must have returned
to England with some £3000 or more in his pocket. His lectures were
not always so well appreciated as they might have been, and if his share
of the proceeds from the first of them, delivered in the Town Hall,
Melbourne, was £300, he had often to be content with a bare £10 or
£20. On the other hand his despatches home, for which he was receiving
£20 a week, were also being printed in several of the Australian papers
whose proprietors were paying him £100 a week for the privilege. In
addition, his expenses were being materially reduced by the courtesy of
railway-officials and the kindness of private admirers, and on one occasion,
in New Zealand, he received a fee of £100 for formally opening some
baths in the Hot Lakes district. It was hard work, and tiring work, and
if hospitality was showered upon him and his wife he was frequently
expected to sing for his supper. There would be sudden changes, too,
in his itinerary, as this or that remote township woke up to the fact of
his presence in Australia and wanted to hear him, and not seldom this
would mean a long train journey at a time when he had hoped for a day
or two's complete rest. Moreover, he was finding it necessary to recast
some of his lectures and compose new ones. Australian audiences, as
others besides Sala have discovered for themselves, are not slow to express
their feelings, and although most of what he had to say was received
with applause, there had been awkward moments in the shape of forthright interruptions when he gave his opinion of certain great statesmen
whom he had met, moments which he had no desire to see repeated.

There are some gossipy details of his wife and himself in his letters to
the ever-faithful Mrs. Skirrow. At the beginning of July he is in Sydney
after a three months' scamper up and down Queensland. Mrs. Sala is in
"awfully" good health and "feels only seventeen although she is going
on for seventy." She is only fifty-two, but no matter. They have been
handed along, rather like the parcels-post, over an irregular route of
some three thousand miles, but are not yet hopeless cripples. They have
seen sugar-canes, bananas, arrowroot, and alligators, as well as every
variety of climate, and so many abominations in the shape of mosquitoes,
dust clouds, snakes, floods, and poor cooking that he feels obliged to
lapse into the Italian of his forefathers to describe them with a sufficiency
of passion. They have been to Dubbo, and they have been to Mudgee.
"Shades of my ancestors!" he cries. "That I should have been to

Mudgee!" Nor is he likely to forget that doubtlessly salubrious spot, for it was there that an ancient dame after listening to his account of Queen Victoria's coronation and obviously finding his recollections of that august ceremony strangely at variance with her own, had shouted out "Rubbish!" and reduced him for a whole minute to silence. But his skin is thickening, and he is now prepared for anything in the way of a snub. They are off again on the morrow to Wagga-Wagga, and, maybe, he will have something to say of a gentleman who, at their last meeting in a Jermyn Street hotel, had reminded him so strongly of an affable seal. He goes there, and does have something to say of the Claimant, though not on the platform. The Assizes are on, and he dines with the Bar Mess and makes a speech and is shown a row of new houses called Tichborne Buildings on the site of the historic butcher's shop. As for the daily round, it is hard, he thinks, but "intensely amusing." "Imagine (at my age, if you please,) having to tumble out of bed in the dark at 6 a.m., travel all day, arrive in the lecturing town (often only a few hovels in the bush) at 7 p.m. and with nothing more in the way of refreshment than three raw eggs beaten up in a glass of sherry, stand up in a barn lighted by kerosene lamps, and talk for two mortal hours! Australian audiences detest lecturers who *read*, so I never look at my notes, but 'spout' extempore," and, he adds, "if all goes well we shall after touring in South Australia, Tasmania, and New Zealand . . . bid farewell to Australia at the end of November and go via Ceylon to India. After 'doing' Hindostan we shall make our way homewards. Mrs. Sala will drop us at Brindisi and come straight to London and I shall go on to Rome to dodge the winter. . . . Mais l'homme propose . . ." he finishes, and it is almost as though he were vaguely conscious of the tragedy to come.

In the course of the next month he is writing from Adelaide in the highest spirits. All is very well indeed, with halls overflowing and enthusiastic reports in the newspapers. He is particularly amused at a description of himself in the *Christian Colonist* which draws attention to one or two of his mannerisms on the platform. Mrs. Skirrow is asked to show the cutting he sends to Labby. "The winking of the left eye will make him laugh. Curiously enough," he adds, and a memory of the Friswell trial must have passed through his mind, "the Paris *Figaro* made a similar remark in describing me at the trial of Pierre Bonaparte fifteen years ago. '*Avec un sourire goguenard il dignait l'oeil en regardant l'accuse.*'" He is looking forward to New Zealand and not less to India where his old friend Lord Dufferin is Viceroy. And in New Zealand, at any rate, he is not disappointed: all is "bright success." In Auckland

and Wellington there is a repetition of his Californian experiences, and after his tour in the provinces one of the newspapers does not hesitate to say that few if any of his predecessors have enjoyed so triumphal a progress. "It has been reserved for G. A. S.," it finishes, "to fix the standard by which the success will be measured of all future visits of European celebrities." The Tasmanians, it is true, are less enthusiastic, but even there there is money to be made. And then, with appalling suddenness, tragedy engulfs him.

Mrs. Sala leaves him at Hobart : she is to go straight to Melbourne, but he has business with one of the banks in Sydney. He spends his Christmas there, and an evening or two later is bidden to dinner with Lord Carrington, the Governor. The Queen's health is drunk. Usually it is the only toast, but tonight His Excellency proposes another : "Mrs. Sala !" Afterwards the visitor is taken into the gardens, and Lord Carrington exclaims : "What a beautiful country this is, and what a happy time you must have had here !" The next day Sala returns to Melbourne—in time to hold his wife's hand during her last few hours on earth.

"You will have read," he is telling Mrs. Skirrow a week later, "in the London papers the brief but to me awful telegram which I sent to Edward Lawson on Dec. 31. At 3 a.m. on that day my beloved wife died. At 5 p.m. on the same day . . . she was buried in the General Cemetery. Her illness only lasted thirty-six hours, but her agonies were dreadful. . . . I found her in horrible pain, but she recognised me. They had so drugged her with narcotics and belladonna that she was more or less in a state of stupefaction during most of the afternoon and evening, but on three occasions she murmured kind and loving words to me and long after she was speechless she continued to hold my hand. . . . I am completely stunned and overwhelmed. All my plans are shattered. All my joys in the past, my hopes in the future lie in that grave. The money which I have made for her dear sake—of what good is it to me, now ? I have not the heart to write any more. I leave this accursed place on the 14th by the *Massilia* for India. . . . God bless you, my dearest friend. . . . How often we used to talk about you both ! What famous schemes we formed for little dinners in Mecklenburgh Square when we returned ! . . ."

The poor little woman must have been suffering from cancer for a considerable time, and said nothing at all. It is hardly an exaggeration to say that after her death Sala was never the same man again.

BOOK III: THE CURTAIN FALLS

CHAPTER FIFTEEN

A FLAT IN VICTORIA STREET

I

"I HAVE made my money and more than I hoped to make, and I am a miserable and desolate old man."

So wrote Sala to Francis Burnand from Calcutta at the end of February, 1886, and there was no exaggeration in his words. Yet everybody had been extraordinarily kind to him. The directors of the P. and O. line were "franking" him home and had been "simply noble" in their efforts to make him comfortable. Lord Dufferin had been in Burmah at the time of his arrival, but he had left detailed instructions about the visitor, and on his return had done what he could to make the Indian programme as interesting as possible. He insisted on Sala meeting all the most prominent men in the Capital, and although there could be no complimentary banquets saw to it that there was no lack of private hospitality. Consolatory letters were reaching the bereaved man from all quarters, and Miss Braddon was only voicing the general view when she wrote of Mrs. Sala as the perfect wife who had been loved and admired by all who knew her. The visitor, however, was finding it very difficult to attune himself to the new conditions, and any long spell of work was impossible. He found solace, he tells us, in trying to translate the gossip-columns of the society papers into the Greek of Thucydides, and, mindful, no doubt, of the work to be done on the still active Greek Committee, was attempting to teach himself the modern tongue. Yet the shock persisted. Even an unexpected meeting in Colombo with Edwin Arnold and his family had been in the nature of a further ordeal, for, as he told Mrs. Skirrow, the poet-editor had not heard of Mrs. Sala's death, and "with his wife and daughter, came to ask *us* to dinner." The old, miserable story had had to be told once again, and "I dread," he wrote to an Australian friend, "returning to England."

Yet he did try to pull himself together, and in the one or two despatches which he sent home from India there was nothing to suggest that their writer was a desperately unhappy man. Unfortunately at a time when his pen showed signs of an increasing activity he caught a severe chill while witnessing at night some religious ceremony on the river, and what he afterwards described as "some kind of jungle-fever"

attacked him. On his recovery the doctors forbade any further expeditions inland and advised a speedy return to England. So, after a few
days spent with Lord and Lady Reay at Government House, Bombay,
Sala stepped aboard the *Ballarat* and sailed (in a luxurious cabin by
himself) to Europe.

Back in London, as he had feared, he felt his loss more keenly than
ever. Friends gathered about him, Labouchere prominently amongst
them, but they could do little to comfort him. The faithful Annie
had the house in Mecklenburgh Square all ready for him, and "Mrs.
Cook" was there, professing her willingness to be instructed in all
manner of Eastern dishes. His books and papers were in order, and the
piles of newspaper-cuttings sent home via Mrs. Skirrow together with
a mountain of accumulated letters were neatly arranged on his desk.
All, indeed, was prepared for him to take up the reins again. But the
house itself, he thought, had changed: it had become curiously
unfriendly and far too large. Even the "curios" seemed to be mocking
him, for so many of them brought back memories which he would have
preferred to forget. Idleness, however, was not to be thought of, and
doggedly he set to work to carry out something like the old routine.
Almost at once ideas for leading articles were being sent, as of old, every
morning by messenger to Peterborough Court and in the afternoon
the chosen subjects would be dealt with in his usual sprightly fashion.
But he was less eager to resume his *Illustrated London News* work. What
was there to write about in the "Echoes" when he was refusing to see
anybody except his closest friends? As for the "Playhouses" he
could not bring himself, even in a professional capacity, to visit a
theatre. Soon enough, too, he was understanding to the full what his
wife's assistance had meant to him. Into the great world she had rarely
ventured, but at home, he saw now, he had been depending upon her
to a far greater extent than he had realised. A link had snapped, and he
was conscious of an unfamiliar helplessness. There was work to be
done, and in a fashion he could do it, but sooner or later he would be
needing help. There were friends upon whom he could have called
and Fleet Street men who would have been glad to "devil" for him;
but for a while he shrank from anything like a new regime. Then, on
a sudden, he took his decision, and in the early summer was advertising
for an amanuensis, preferably one who had been a governess and so,
presumably, able to spell. Over four hundred applications reached him
from highly-accomplished ladies, who, he was interested to discover,
demanded anything from six to twenty-five shillings a week for their
services.

He was considering what to do when Antonio Gallenga came to his rescue and by giving a letter of introduction to the wife of a Greek friend of his unwittingly altered the whole course of Sala's remaining years.

This Mrs. Caralampi was an Englishwoman by birth. Her father was the still-surviving Robert Stannard who had worked with George Stephenson when the Manchester and Liverpool Railway was under construction. She herself had been born at Upwey in Dorset in 1855, and her sister-in-law was the Mrs. Arthur Stannard who under the pen-name of John Strange Winter was a popular novelist of the day. Who or what her husband may have been I have been unable to discover, but Bessie Caralampi was a clever and ambitious woman who, after a short-lived career on the stage with one of her sisters some four years back, now wished to make her way in the world of journalism and was seeking Sala's advice.

Now, whether Gallenga in sending this "tall, comely lady" to Mecklenburgh Square had any idea that she might be engaged as an amanuensis, or whether Sala, after making Mr. Caralampi's acquaintance and airing such modern Greek as he possessed, made the suggestion that as his secretary she would probably obtain as good a training as she was likely to receive elsewhere, I do not know; but within a very short time she was in daily attendance, taking down from dictation almost all his leading articles, and before the end of the year his private as well as his professional affairs were more or less in her charge.

Her arrival was opportune, for she provided the necessary spur. She was bright and energetic, and she had ideas of her own. Sala was not the first celebrity she had met, and she knew how to treat him. In domestic affairs, too, she was of the greatest assistance, and with Annie as a willing helper she saw to it that the widower was not allowed to mope by himself. A Pomeranian was secured, and given the name of Hobson-Jobson, and washed clean every few days, and generally made free of the house. Little luncheons and even dinners were inaugurated for particular friends. Gradually the signs of deep mourning disappeared, and Sala became aware that the new regime was considerably less upsetting than he had feared. There were to be no more roving commissions abroad, but he was beginning to feel the desire to be "on the prowl" again, and when it was suggested at Peterborough Court that he might find something of interest to say about Royal Ascot, he seized the opportunity to play special correspondent at home.

As it happened, he was to have an unusual experience. He had arrived at a very early hour on the course, in order to view the preparations, and few people were about except attendants and policemen. It was hot, and he was thirsty, and there was a lemonade-stall in one of the less aristocratic corners. He drained his glass, and found himself without any small change. The proprietor obligingly offered to fetch what was requisite if his customer would be good enough to attend to business during his absence. And for the next ten minutes the great G. A. S. dispensed lemonade to all comers at a penny a glass. The little incident seems to have amused him hugely. More important, it gave him an idea for an "Echo," and the next week the familiar initials were to be found in the *Illustrated London News*.

He was, it seemed, his old self again. *The Land of the Golden Fleece* was taken out of the manuscript drawer, and one or two further instalments were written and printed in *Tinsley's Magazine*. John Dicks asked for more stories, and at least one reached him in time for his Christmas Annual. A preface was required for a translation of Melmonti's *Dogaressa*, and Sala supplied it. Bentley signed an agreement for his *Autobiography*, and optimistically announced that it would appear in the following spring. "Mrs. Cook" produced some surprising curries, and friends like the Skirrows, Mrs. Jopling the painter, and the Laboucheres persuaded him to come to their parties. All seemed to be going very well. And then in the old way his bronchitis returned, bringing in its trail some peculiar Indian complications, and almost to the coming of winter there was "relapse after relapse." For weeks at a time he would be unable to leave his room, but Mrs. Caralampi attended to all his newspaper work, and Annie proved herself to be a most efficient nurse. He was ordered to Folkestone, and there was some talk of a long sea-voyage and a second visit to India; but there were good reasons for his remaining in England just now. There was some worrying business connected with the lease of his house—he had decided to move into a flat as soon as it was settled—and his lawyer wanted him in London. The Australian book was "hanging fire," and he was worrying about it. Worst of all, however, and perhaps not very surprisingly, for he ever remained ignorant about "the City" and all its ways, the best part of the money from his lectures had been invested in one of Mr. Horatio Bottomley's concerns. There had been a nasty "crash," which meant at any rate some retrenchment. Even his usual winter in Rome was postponed. But by the spring he was pining to go, and by this time Mrs. Caralampi's services and Annie's nursing had become so indispensable that he refused to travel without them.

It was on his return from Italy that a second link snapped.

2

On May 11th he gave a lecture in St. James's Hall on his Australian experiences. It was in aid of one of the hospitals, and half the dowagers in London were there. Three days later his admirers were delighted to see that at long last he had resumed his dramatic criticism in the *Illustrated London News*. In the following week both "Playhouses" and "Echoes" appeared, and there was nothing about them to suggest that anything was amiss. To the public's astonishment, however, in the course of the next few days advertisements were appearing in various newspapers to the effect that Mr. Sala had "transferred" his "Echoes" to the *Entertainment Gazette*, a fortnightly journal launched at the beginning of the year, of which, it is safe to say, not one in a hundred among his readers had ever heard.

What had happened? Rumour was immediately busy, and all manner of explanations were put forward, some of the wildest of which came from those who might have been expected to know the truth. "Readers of the *Illustrated London News*," declared a writer in *Land and Water*, "have for some time been noting the evidence of somewhat strained relations between the writer of the 'Echoes' and his *confrères*." I can find no such evidence myself, but paragraphs of this kind appeared in several journals. In the clubs and the green-rooms it was freely said that Sala had demanded an unheard-of salary and, on Ingram's refusal to pay it, threatened him with physical violence. It was whispered that Clement Scott, who for more than a year had regularly been writing the "Playhouses," was on the war-path and would shortly be in the law courts—it would not be for the first time—as prosecutor, or it might be defendant, in a libel-case of the most sensational kind. And in less responsible quarters there were hints of a more sinister nature which showed that the old stories had not been entirely forgotten.

It was left to Labouchere in the columns of *Truth* to acquaint the world with the real facts. Sala, he said, on his return from India, had "reluctantly consented" to resume the "Echoes" and the "Playhouses" at a salary of fifteen guineas a week. It had been agreed that Clement Scott should continue *pro tem.* to write the "Playhouses" at a salary (apparently five guineas a week) to be paid him by Sala. This arrangement had been in force until Sala's return from Rome when he had resumed his theatrical work. Ingram had disapproved of the change and insisted on the "Playhouses" being written by Scott. And "on this," wrote Labby in his stiff and most careful manner, almost, indeed, as though he expected to hear his words being quoted against him in

the Courts, "Mr. Sala informed Mr. Ingram that he was at full liberty
to have them written by whom he liked, but that he (Mr. Sala) must
in this case have fifteen guineas for the 'Echoes,' adding that he did not
wish to put undue pressure on Mr. Ingram, and that if that gentleman
considered the terms exorbitant or wished to discontinue the 'Echoes,'
he (Mr. Sala) would acquiesce in their discontinuance. Mr. Ingram at
once decided that they should be discontinued."

Neither side, I suppose, can be blamed overmuch. Sala was fully
entitled to resume the "Playhouses" when he chose; Ingram had every
right to appoint his own dramatic critic, and there is little doubt that
in Clement Scott he had the better man. Labouchere spoke of the affair
as the result of an unfortunate misunderstanding, and that may well
have been so. Ingram's curt decision may have followed on nothing
more than acute annoyance, and in that case there is nothing more to
be said. It occurs to me, however, as a possibility that for some little
time the proprietor of the *Illustrated London News* had been considering
a change, so far as the "Echoes" were concerned, and if this be so the
affair may not be without its significance.

Now, it is true that in other journals the "Echoes" continued to be
an apparently popular feature until the day when Sala was able to write
no more of them. It is also true that so long as he was working for
Ingram the number of letters from the public with which the "distressed
compiler" was called on each week to deal, showed no signs of
diminishing. Yet it may well be that Ingram, in common with other
shrewd men in the newspaper world, was becoming aware of new forces
at work in Fleet Street, forces with which sooner or later he and his
fellow-proprietors would have to reckon. For it was just about this
time that a new type of journalist was making his presence felt: the
public school or university man who was bringing to his work something besides accurate observation and the old-time "picturesqueness."
Like Andrew Lang or H. D. Traill, he combined no mean scholarship
with a new delicacy and a new kind of charm. There had, of course,
been scholars in Fleet Street long before now, but in place of the cheery
gusto of the 'sixties there were growing signs of the literary graces of
the 'nineties. I may be wrong, but it is to be noticed that almost from
the moment of Sala's departure, the *Illustrated London News* underwent
a subtle change in the matter of its literary tone.

As for Sala himself, I can find no record of his feelings at the time.
Within the next fortnight he made two speeches in London, in both
of which he spoke at some length of the journalist's responsibilities, but
there was no allusion, even of the playful kind that might perhaps have

been expected, to the recent change in his own affairs. The *Entertainment Gazette* had announced its intention of appearing henceforth every Saturday, and on June 18th, three days before the Jubilee celebrations, the "Echoes" reappeared, and, except that there were no "Answers to Correspondents," it was as though there had been no break at all.

The weeks passed, and London was *en fête*, and once again Sala had cause to recall what he could remember of Queen Victoria's coronation as he described the Abbey ceremony fifty years on. In August, and most unexpectedly, he was induced by the Laboucheres to take part in some theatricals in aid of the Charing Cross Hospital. There was to be an open-air performance of *A Midsummer Night's Dream*, with both amateurs and professionals in the cast, at Pope's Villa, Twickenham. Lewis Wingfield was the producer, and he set to work on the most lavish scale. Two of the best-known actresses of the day, Miss Fortescue and Kate Vaughan, were to appear as Hermia and Titania, Lady Archibald Campbell was to be Oberon, and Sala undertook the uncomfortable part of Bottom. He had his own distinctly unorthodox views as to how the part should be played—there was an allusion to Bottom's performance by "a bogus kinsman" in the "Echoes"—and it seems to have pleased a large audience. So much, at any rate, is to be gathered from the pages of the *Entertainment Gazette* which reviewed the production as a major theatrical event. It was almost the only London newspaper to do so, and there is little doubt that its editor was now falling into the mistake of believing that Sala by himself was a big enough figure to bring success to any periodical. He went so far, indeed, as to change the cover of his paper. It remained the *Entertainment Gazette*, it is true, but the words were now printed in small type while below them in huge letters appeared *Echoes of the Week* which became its real title. Not content with this, he gave to his chief contributor the prominence which is proper, no doubt, to the Head of a State, and wholly neglected to give him any reasonable support. There could be only one result, and it was not long in coming. The sales dropped in the most alarming way, the correspondents who had written in their thousands to the offices of the *Illustrated London News* were seemingly unaware that their admired G. A. S. was still very willing to answer their queries, and at the beginning of October Sala discreetly retired. The *Entertainment Gazette* continued its struggle for existence until the end of the year, and then in the usual way was incorporated into another gossipy weekly which was not to be much more successful than itself.

After which, for some little time, it seemed unlikely that the "Echoes" would be heard of again. I do not imagine that Sala was altogether sorry, in spite of the financial loss to himself, for at this time he was homeless and cut off from his books. He had at last succeeded in getting rid of the lease of his house, but the new flat in Victoria Street, Westminster, which he had chosen required extensive alterations, and he was obliged to resign himself to the unwelcome fact that for the next six months he would be a "wandering Christian" with a considerable amount of work to be done besides his daily leader. He was still attempting to complete his *Land of the Golden Fleece*, he had begun to make rough notes for his autobiography, and in addition—I fancy at Mrs. Caralampi's suggestion—he had agreed to write a series of articles for a monthly magazine for ladies called *Myra's Journal of Dress and Fashion*.

"Pity the sorrows," he was writing in November in mock-lugubrious fashion, "of a poor old man with five addresses," none of which, it seemed, was really suited to a poverty-stricken penny-a-liner like himself. He had been staying at the Orleans Club, Brighton, which was comfortable but too draughty for a man who might at any moment be struck down simultaneously by a score or more of hideously painful diseases. Then there was the Reform Club, where he liked to forgather at luncheon with James Payn, William Black, Wemyss Reid, and one or two others—they were known as the Press Gang—but the Reform Club had selfishly closed its doors for some alleged repairs, and in the more radically-minded institution which was giving its members temporary hospitality he missed the usual faces. The house in Mecklenburgh Square was shut up, which was no more than what was to be expected in view of the enormous sums of money which the landlord required before his tenant would be permitted to take his final departure, and a battalion if not a brigade of workmen apparently intended to remain in residence at the Victoria Street flat until the end of their days. And so he was reduced to lodgings in Montagu Street, Russell Square—lodgings suited to a Rothschild, though in justice to the landlady it was only right to proclaim to the world that "bath" and "cruets" were provided without extra charge.

The financial situation, however, was to ease a little now, for Miss Sarah Ashley died and left her cousin £1000 or more which at least helped to pay the wages of the workmen's brigade. But it was not until the late spring that he was able to move into his new home, and then, almost at once, he was struck down again, though with what particular alloy of diseases I do not know. He went to Brighton, but the weather was unkind and the Orleans Club draughtier than ever. In September, though not yet out of the doctor's hands, he was able to "go out a little in a closed brougham," but in the following month, with Mrs. Caralampi and Annie in attendance, he was well enough to go to Rome and write the last despatches of any importance from abroad which he was to send to the *Daily Telegraph*. And then, only a few weeks after his return, he was once again in the public eye, being unexpectedly called upon to play a tiny but by no means uninteresting part in one of the biggest political sensations of the century.

3

There is no need to speak in any detail of the Phoenix Park murders and their political reverberations. It had been in May, 1882, that Lord Frederick Cavendish, the newly-appointed Irish Secretary, and Mr. Burke, the Under-Secretary, had been done to death in Phoenix Park, Dublin, and the Irish Party, with Parnell at their head, had immediately issued a statement expressing their horror at the crime and lamenting the unfortunate effect which it was bound to have in their country. Five years later, at a time when Mr. Balfour's Coercion Bill was before Parliament, the *Times* had printed a series of articles entitled "Parnellism and Crime," and on April 18th, 1887, the day when a vote was to be taken on the second reading, it had published in facsimile a letter purporting to be signed by Parnell at the time of the murders and declaring that although his Party had denounced the crime as "the only course open" to them, it was his opinion that Mr. Burke had "got no more than his deserts."

At once there was the greatest excitement, and not only in official circles. The letter became the one topic of conversation throughout the country. Was it genuine or the cruellest of forgeries? The *Times* hinted at further revelations, and the excitement increased. Parnell himself, however, seemed disposed to take no notice of what, according to those who knew him best, could only be regarded as the most obvious forgery; but the Irish Members insisted on the charges being investigated, and after a series of the most bitter debates a Special Commission was appointed. Its first meeting was held on October 12th, 1888, the day upon which, as it happened, old Mr. Levy of the *Daily Telegraph* died, and for some weeks the public remained unimpressed: it was rather more interested in the mysterious Whitechapel murders which were soon to make "Jack the Ripper" a bogey known, at any rate by name, to all the world. On a sudden, however, the Special Commission drew all eyes to itself. This was when it became known that the *Times* had received the letter which it had facsimiled, together with others in a similar handwriting, from the secretary of an Irish patriotic society, who had had them from a Mr. Richard Pigott. On Wednesday, February 20th, 1889, Mr. Pigott went into the witness-box: a most venerable figure, with the domed forehead and white beard which suggested scholarship of the highest order, though the monocle which from time to time would be raised to his eye and a suit too "careless" for anybody except a millionaire held a hint, perhaps, of an ex-Colonial Governor with at least three dukes amongst his forefathers. Unfortunately for himself Mr. Pigott hardly shone under cross-examination by Sir Charles Russell, M.P. He was so far from shining that when the Commission adjourned on the Friday evening, with Mr. Pigott still in the box, it had not only been established that the witness's past was extraordinarily murky but also that he had himself written letters with reference to Parnell's complicity with the murders which could bear only one construction: they were blackmailing letters. Furthermore, and most damning point of all, on being asked to write down two words which had been misspelt in the facsimiled letter, Mr. Pigott had misspelt them in the same way.

The Court reassembled on the following Tuesday, when it was hoped that Mr. Pigott's cross-examination would be concluded. The gentleman with the white beard, however, did not appear, and on the Wednesday morning the circulation of the *Daily Telegraph* was appreciably larger than usual, for in the most prominent position there was printed a long letter, signed in full by Sala, which gave details of a curious interview at which he had been present on the previous Saturday.

It was Sala in his most Salaesque vein; a Sala conscious that the world would be taking very particular notice of what he had to say and determined to be meticulously accurate, but also a puckish Sala to whom life even at its more tragic moments could show a decidedly comic streak.

"Saturday," he began, "is popularly supposed to be the sabbath of the daily journalist, and . . . I always do my best to keep the last day of the week as a whole holiday." This might mean "running down to Brighton, dusting one's china, striving to reconcile the odd volumes in one's library," or, most pleasant of all, falling into "a gentle slumber in your easy chair between breakfast and luncheon." He left it to his readers to imagine in which of these ways he had been enjoying himself when a note reached him from Labouchere: "Can you leave everything, and come here at once. Most important business. H. L."

Within a quarter of an hour he had reached Labby's house in

Grosvenor Gardens, and there in the library found his old friend obviously in a state of excitement and, in a large arm-chair, a gentleman with a white beard whom he immediately recognised. "The individual," he wrote, "had an eyeglass screwed into one eye, and he was using this optical aid most assiduously, for he was poring over a copy of that morning's *Times*, going right down one column and apparently up it again; then taking column after column in succession; then harking back as though he had omitted some choice paragraph; and then resuming the sequence of his lecture," all the while either tapping his forehead with a little silver pencil-case or twiddling it between his fingers. There was no necessity for the introduction which Labouchere was beginning to make; it was not even a moment for "Mr. Pigott, I presume?": Sala knew his man, and when he was told that Mr. Pigott had come "unsolicited, to make a full confession," and that he, Labouchere, had refused to listen to it except in the presence of a witness, he just stared and waited.

"It has been my lot," he continued, "during a long and diversified career, to have to listen to a large number of very queer statements from very queer people; and, by dint of experience, you reach at last a stage of stoicism when little, if anything, that is imparted to you excites surprise. Thus, if Mr. Labouchere had told me that Mr. Pigott proposed to avow that he had discovered the philosopher's stone or found a four-leaved shamrock, that he had formulated a Universal Theorem, or that he was the murderer of Eliza Grimwood, I should have been fully prepared to hear what he had got to say, without indulging in any unseemly exhibitions of astonishment. It was one thing, however, to be told that Mr. Pigott intended to confess and quite another to get the confession from his lips. As in the case of the gentleman at Tyburn who 'oft fitted the halter, oft traversed the cart, and often took leave, but seemed loth to depart,' so it did appear that Mr. Pigott, although he had screwed his courage to the sticking-place of saying that he was going to confess, manifested considerable tardiness in orally 'owning up.' Conscience, we were justified in assuming, had 'gnawed' to an extent sufficient to make him willing to relieve his soul from a dreadful burden; but conscience, to all seeming, had to gnaw a little longer and a little more sharply ere he absolutely gave tongue. . . . Perhaps conscience was gnawing like gout in his toes."

At last, however, he began his confession, at first in a low muttering, but afterwards in louder tones and a more fluent diction. All the Parnell letters were his work, and he explained just how they had been forged. "It was to my mind as frank, free, and full a confession as that of the

CHAPTER SIXTEEN
LAST VENTURES

I

ABOUT his domestic affairs Sala, very properly, had little enough to say in print. True, he made frequent mention of his mother and his brother Charles, but both of them had claims to be considered public figures. On the other hand he had nothing to say of Frederick, the music-master at Southampton who fell upon evil days and for whom he was obliged to provide until his death at Erith in 1880; nothing of Frederick's two children, one of whom gave him a great deal of trouble; and nothing of the ex-pirate with rather more than the usual number of wives. He had made a mystery, moreover, about his first marriage, and when on January 25th, 1890, he married his secretary at St. Margaret's, Westminster, not even his closest friends were invited to the wedding, and it is doubtful whether more than two or three of them had the least idea of his intention.

Curiously enough, too, there is also a little mystery attached to this second marriage of his. I had imagined that at some time between 1887 (when Sala speaks of his "Greek friend," the husband of his secretary, coming to dinner) and 1889, Mr. Caralampi had been gathered to his fathers, and I expected to find his widow so described in the marriage certificate. Instead, the bride's name is given as Bessie Stannard, with, incidentally, a wrong age. But there is abundant evidence that it was "Mrs. Caralampi" whom he married. What, then, had happened? The certificate provides something in the nature of a clue, for the bride's "condition" is not given as "spinster" but as the oddly tautological "single and unmarried." A divorce? It certainly suggests itself, though I should have thought that in that case the words "divorced wife of," or something of the kind, would have been used. (But perhaps the Victorian registrars were more chivalrous than their successors?) And if there had been a divorce, who was the guilty party? I have my own views, but they may be wrong, and it is only fair to say that all search for Court proceedings has failed. As for the wedding itself, the newspapers which recorded it had nothing to say except that the bride was Robert Stannard's daughter and related by marriage to "John Strange Winter."

Now it would be wrong to suggest that this second marriage was the terrible mistake which some of those who knew Sala well during the last years of his life have not hesitated to call it. There is abundant proof that Bessie Sala not only looked after her husband with the greatest devotion until the day of his death, but did her best to lighten the ever-increasing burdens which he was called on to bear. Without her active assistance he would not have been able to continue his work for the *Daily Telegraph* with almost the old-time regularity. Without her to preside at his table the little luncheons and dinners which he delighted to give to his friends would have lacked a lively hostess who enjoyed all such functions as much as he did himself and saw to it that others enjoyed them too. Unfortunately, she was herself largely responsible for the increasing burdens which I have mentioned.

Almost at once she showed her hand. There were two goals to be aimed at: at all costs George Augustus must be kept securely on the highest rung of the ladder, and Mrs. George Augustus must be given the opportunity to show the world that she was rather more than a celebrity's wife. She was, as I have said, a clever woman, and she was in no doubt at all about the means whereby this double goal was to be reached. In those days the value and uses of publicity had been but imperfectly realised, and Bessie Sala had her own ideas about their development. G. A. S. was well enough known—was not a tableau of him at his desk now on view at Madame Tussaud's famous Exhibition, flanked by two others of Lord Tennyson and Charles Dickens?—but hitherto the lime-light had only fitfully been turned upon him: henceforth his (and, of course, his wife's) name must be kept constantly before the public. There might be those, she was aware, who thought that her husband had done his best work, and at times he might be too ready to look upon himself as a tired and sick old man; but with her by his side there was nothing to prevent the return of all his old vigour. Naturally she expected to be introduced to all his distinguished friends, but that was not enough: henceforth they, too, must be made to play, however un-wittingly, their part in the good work. In a word, the bad old Bohemian past must be forgotten (except for the purposes of the forthcoming Auto-biography), and for the future the Salas were to take their "proper" place in Society. This would require money, more, perhaps, than Sala was earning just now—unfortunately Cousin Sarah's legacy had already vanished—but what of that? The money would be found, it would have to be found, and in due course George Augustus would receive the knighthood which he so richly deserved and on which, I have no doubt at all, she had set her heart.

So it happened that before any long time had elapsed the Salas had not only moved into a larger flat in Victoria Street, with three, and after-wards four, servants, but they also had their own house in Brighton,

So, too, at a time when he might well have retired from the greater part of his journalistic work, Sala was induced by his wife to launch a new weekly journal for her and more or less driven to write the greater part of it himself. Nor was this all, for in an endeavour to cope with the increasing expenses of his household, the overworked and ailing man once again made an exploration of the investment market, with disastrous results to himself.

2

The first step under the new regime was highly auspicious.

Since the "Echoes" had ceased to be printed in the *Illustrated London News* Sala had lost a useful pulpit: just such a pulpit as, in Bessie Sala's opinion, would now be most valuable. But where was it to be found? A good London newspaper was essential, but which was it to be? Exactly how the first move was made I do not know, but less than a month after his marriage Sala was in the offices of the *Sunday Times* discussing matters with its editor, Arthur à Beckett, the son of the man whom he had caricatured more than forty years before in *A Word with Punch*. And on March 2nd the "Echoes" were reborn, to be continued, with one or two short intervals, until the summer of 1895.

They received a warm welcome. Many of Sala's anecdotes and vignettes of people must have been printed often enough before; but readers, constant or otherwise, appreciated his views on this or that question of the day—views which were freely quoted in other newspapers—and once again filled his letter-box with their comments and queries. Undoubtedly, too, Sala was well pleased to find himself back in his old role, a possibly distressed, but urbane and judicious compiler, very ready, it seemed, to be friends with all the world.

Yet within a few weeks there came another exhibition of bad temper, when he seemed determined to make a laughing-stock of himself. There came another libel-case, this time against Harry Furniss, the *Punch* artist and well-known caricaturist, and "The Great Six Toes Trial" was staged. It was the absurdest affair, yet "fanned into almost European importance," according to Frank Lockwood, one of the counsel engaged, and I cannot help feeling that had Bessie Sala added her entreaties to those of Labouchere, Burnand, George Lewis, and other old friends of his, he would never have permitted so trumpery a case to be brought into Court. Unfortunately he could not forget the result of the Friswell case. Another £500 would be particularly welcome now that his wife was talking of a Brighton house in addition to the new flat, and he refused to listen to reason.

The ridiculous business had begun with a lecture on portraiture by Furniss, who was fond of appearing on the public platform and added considerably to his income by doing so. A leading article in the *Daily Telegraph* attacked him for some glaring omissions, and its editor refused to print the caricaturist's reply, though this appeared, with a letter of explanation, in the *Pall Mall Gazette*. At the Garrick Club Furniss discovered that Sala, as he suspected, had been his attacker, and at the *Punch* table that evening casually mentioned the affair to Du Maurier, who was immediately reminded of a story he had heard about G. A. S. As an art student, he said, Sala had attempted to enter the Art Schools of the Royal Academy and been rejected because in his drawing of a human foot there had appeared six toes instead of the more usual number. In point of fact Du Maurier afterwards remembered that the story had been told him about somebody else and had nothing whatever to do with Sala, but by that time the mischief had been done. Then Furniss delivered another lecture, this time at Nottingham, and after telling the well-known story of Thackeray as a young man going to Dickens with a view to becoming his illustrator, he passed on to the art critic of the *Daily Telegraph*—Sala himself—as another instance of an artist turning writer, and repeated the tale of the six toes. Unfortunately he was carelessly reported and made to say that it was Sala who had wanted to illustrate Dickens's books and that as a result of his rejection by the Academy Schools he had become the *Daily Telegraph*'s art critic.

It was not much of a joke, but there were reports of the lecture in various London and provincial papers, and some of these included facetious remarks at Sala's expense. The story of the six toes became widely known in London, and although the three leading comic weeklies preferred to ignore it, an unsigned cartoon—the work of Carruthers Gould—appeared in the *Westminster Gazette* showing a six-toed Sala threatening a diminutive Furniss. Soon enough, however, the journalists who had indulged in any comment realised that they might have gone too far. Apologies to Sala were hurriedly inserted, though not always hurriedly enough, for, according to Furniss, in some cases money was paid to Sala's solicitor—not on this occasion George Lewis—"to avoid actions-at-law." Meanwhile the unlucky lecturer had been doing his best to put matters right. There had been more explanatory letters to the press, and at a London banquet at which both he and Sala were amongst the speakers he endeavoured to make the *amende honorable*. Sala, however, would have none of it : he chose to believe, or pretended to believe, that the "offensive" cartoon in the *Westminster Gazette* was Furniss's own work, demanded an apology so abject that nobody could have been expected to make it, and on Furniss's refusal, prepared for battle.

So the silly action came on. Frank Lockwood, for Furniss, proposed to laugh the whole affair out of Court. "Don't worry about facts," he told his client in effect; "don't deny anything. We'll take the view that the whole thing is too trivial for serious consideration." And in Court he treated every point in the airiest manner, did not even trouble to distinguish between what Furniss had said and what he was reported to have said, took no steps to show that the "offensive" cartoon was the work of Gould, and made no serious attempt at cross-examination when Sala was in the box. The judge, however, was in no mood for light-hearted quips: the prosecutor was taking himself seriously, and the Court was no theatre. He summed up very strongly in Sala's favour, and the £500 seemed to be delectably near.

But the jury had seen the joke of the thing. They did their duty, and found for the prosecutor. They awarded him £5 damages, which, when the unhappy Sala had paid his share of the costs, meant a loss of rather more than £75.

And then, of course, the wags became busy. "Out of the Furniss into the fire," wrote one of them, "for of a surety five pounds will hardly repay Mr. Sala for the roasting he will receive from his good-natured friends." The music-halls, too, found the six toes much to their taste. As for Furniss he took his revenge by sending an illustrated report of the trial to the *Daily Graphic*; but it was in a private letter to Du Maurier that he perpetrated his best joke. "Sala," he wrote, "has no sole for humour—you have made me put my foot in it," and, in place of his signature, he sent this exceedingly clever sketch. Sala never forgave him—the sketch was afterwards reproduced in Furniss's own weekly *Lika-Joko* — but he had learnt his lesson, and when another and severer attack came from W. E. Henley's *National Observer*, it was answered not by a summons but, more fittingly, in the pages of his wife's weekly.

3

So I come to the rather sorry story of *Sala's Journal*.

It may be said to have begun in July, 1890, when a new ladies' weekly called the *Gentlewoman* first made its appearance. It was destined to enjoy a long and prosperous career, with the *Lady's Pictorial* its only serious rival, during the 'nineties; and on learning that it was about to appear Bessie Sala seems to have applied for the position of art critic and also suggested a series of articles by herself to be entitled "Famous People I Have Met": in other words, friends of her husband. Only three weeks before the first number was due to be published the editor wrote to say that she might consider herself the *Gentlewoman's* art critic and that he was willing to print the proposed series "by Mrs. George Augustus Sala." The remuneration would be at the rate of a guinea a column— "a better price," she was informed, "than the other ladies' journals pay" —and it was suggested that Miss Dorothy Tennant, whose forthcoming marriage to Henry M. Stanley was arousing the greatest interest, would make a capital subject for the first article of the series. In a delightfully modest letter, however, the future Lady Stanley begged to be excused. She might, she said, have made some small name for herself as a painter, but "famous" she was not, and she hated anything in the nature of publicity.

In the circumstances Bessie Sala was probably wise to begin her series with a sketch of Stanley himself. His arrival in England after the successful Emin Relief Expedition had led to such a reception as had rarely if ever been accorded to any man, whether reigning monarch or all-conquering hero, and the most trivial details of his private life were eagerly welcomed. She had met him for the first time only a few weeks before at Lady Burdett-Coutts's house; she had sat opposite to him at a City banquet a week later; and he had brought Dorothy Tennant to dinner one evening at the Victoria Street flat. That was the extent of their acquaintance, but it was made to do. One or two remarks of his uttered in private conversation were recorded, and the article was described as "interesting" in one of those welcoming paragraphs which a new periodical can generally expect from established contemporaries. It will not, I am afraid, be read with any particular interest today, and the same is true of the twenty or thirty other vignettes which followed it. They were no worse, it may be admitted, than much contemporary stuff of the same rather snobbish kind, but they were certainly no better. The trouble, of course, lay in the fact that with few if any of her famous people could she claim anything like a close friendship. She knew little or nothing about them except what her husband had told her or what she had found in the reference books. But she sang their praises neatly enough, admitted very cheerfully her own pleasure in being allowed to meet them, and, when the time came for the articles to be republished in book-form, managed to persuade a number of them to write to her, so that their letters could be printed in facsimile. Let us say of the series that it had its clever touches, particularly in the manner in which her husband and herself were brought into the picture, but in general was naive and second-rate. It is perhaps significant that although the publisher of the book had proposed to print a second volume he found it convenient not to do so.

As a result, however, of her work for the *Gentlewoman* Bessie Sala began to take herself seriously as a journalist, and it must be allowed that on questions of interest to women she could write easily and with shrewdness. Letters of hers began to appear in the newspapers. Two or three of them were printed in the *Daily Graphic*. All of them, it may be noted, had something to say about the Sala *ménage*. The much-debated question, for instance, of Flat *v*. House enabled her to inform the world that Mr. and Mrs. Sala now had their Brighton house as well as their London flat, and that a house was better suited to four servants than a flat. But such contributions were few and far between; the *Gentlewoman* series was nearing its end and there was little opportunity for art criticisms; and it was only as "Mrs. George Augustus Sala" that she seemed able to interest London editors. If, then, she was to create a position for herself, there would have to be a decided step forward, and it must have been some time in the spring of 1891, after a visit to Rome (whence, by the way, the Salas returned with an Italian man-servant) that the idea of a weekly periodical of her own began to fill her thoughts. G. A. S., of course, would have to be its Conductor as well as its chief contributor, but much could be their joint work, and the woman's side would be wholly hers. It would be her property, she would be its manager, and to all intents and purposes she would be its editor as well. Was it, she wondered, a possibility?

What her husband thought about the scheme when it was first mooted I do not know, but I can make a guess. He was still writing his six leaders a week as well as the "Echoes," which, greatly to his advantage, were about to be syndicated in various provincial papers in the North. He was gathering materials for his autobiography and planning an introductory series of reminiscences for the *Daily Telegraph*: enough work, surely, for a man of sixty-three in poor health. If, moreover, he were to undertake further work *The Land of the Golden Fleece* must come first. As his letters show, he still intended to complete it. And what about the capital? True, at the time he had one or two little ventures on hand which were promising well. There was the Berners Hotel Company of which he was chairman. Hotels had always interested him, and he had his own ideas for their improvement. There was also some talk about transforming the London Opera House in Cambridge Circus into a

Theatre of Varieties. Sir Augustus Harris was interested and intended
him to sit on the Board should the proposed company be formed. But
how much capital could he himself find? Not a great deal. No, he had
seen too many periodicals launched with insufficient capital and fated
to perish miserably within the year.

Very soon, however, it must have become clear to him that his wife,
like the infant in the bath stretching out for his cake of Pears' Soap—
perhaps the most popular advertisement of the day—would not be happy
till she got it. Nothing would damp her enthusiasm. The time was ripe
for a really "bright" penny weekly: everybody was saying so. Not
another *Tit-Bits* or *Answers*: rather an elaboration of the "Echoes."
She had a hundred ideas. Why should not G. A. S. write an up-to-date
version of *Twice Round the Clock*? Why should he not make a feature
of "Answers to Correspondents"? Why not a weekly column about
cookery, with G. A. S.'s own recipes? It might be well, too, to have a
series of those "competitions" which were now becoming so popular.
There must be a page or two of gossip, and why should it not be their
joint work? By "Self and Partner," perhaps. Why, with G. A. S. still
at the top of the tree, there was a fortune to be made! Already George
Newnes was a very rich man; so was young Alfred Harmsworth:
neither of them had had a name to begin with. Thus I imagine her
speaking, and by the summer of that year Sala had allowed himself to be
persuaded. Plans, in fact, for *Sala's Journal* were in active preparation,
and it may well be that for some little time he found her enthusiasm in-
fectious, more particularly after one or two of his friends had agreed to
help, either with money or as guarantors.

Yet it was Bessie Sala who undertook all, or nearly all, the business
arrangements. Throughout that winter she was indefatigable. Her
capital was small, but it was not proposed to move into sumptuous offices
or engage a large staff. She had the fullest confidence in her own abilities,
and, indeed, seems to have taken on the duties of manager, publisher, and
distributing agent as well as those of editor-in-chief. "How ought I to
manage the newsvendors of the North?" she was writing in February,
1892, to the well-known antiquary William Andrews of Hull. "Would
it be advisable to make Hull a centre and let someone from that town
supply the districts for many miles round or settle with various small
vendors myself?" And that was but one of numerous similar letters sent
alike to commercial firms and private friends which, you would have
thought, might well have been entrusted to some more experienced
person to write. Yet this semi-private approach to the trade seems to
have succeeded fairly well, and when on April 30th that year the first

number of *Sala's Journal*—a Weekly Magazine for All—in its buff-coloured cover was on sale throughout the kingdom, it met with a heartening success : more than 200,000 copies were sold.

This was not surprising, for, apart from the curiosity which the public will generally show in any new periodical, the contents were piquant enough. There was a generous measure of G. A. S., and, indeed, at a first glance, it might well have seemed that with his Topic of the Week, the first instalment of his "London Up To Date"—the name given to the new Twice Round the Clock series—Reviews of Books, Cooking Recipes, Answers to Correspondents, and Sala-d of Anecdotes, Sala himself had written most of the twenty-four pages. But the other contributors included T. P. O'Connor, with some reminiscences of his early days in London, and Mrs. Campbell Praed, a popular novelist of the time, with the first chapters of her new story. Incidentally, it is to be noticed that Bessie Sala confined herself to some paragraphs of gossip signed, as she had suggested, "Self and Partner," though her recently published book was reviewed and advertised with much prominence.

It was certainly "bright," but even in that first number, so warmly acclaimed by the press, there were signs, as Henley did not hesitate to point out, of something not exactly second-rate, not exactly vulgar, but wholly without distinction. It was not so much Sala's own contributions, which, though they might lack a little of the old-time sparkle and have too much to say of what G. A. S. could remember of olden days, were interesting enough, but, rather, an atmosphere of self-advertisement which hung heavily over the whole magazine. This was particularly noticeable in the gossipy notes, printed under the title of "You Don't Say So !" and for which Bessie Sala was largely responsible : again and again they seemed to have been printed only in order to include some not over-important fact about G. A. S.'s triumphs in the past.

Unluckily the advertisers remained shy, and before the end of the year it had become clear that all was not well. Not unnaturally Sala was feeling the effect of all the extra work he had undertaken, and was off on a longer holiday than usual, this time alone. He went to Brussels, Rome, Venice, and Paris, and although he sent to the *Journal* a series of eight long articles on his adventures (which included a bomb explosion near to his hotel in Rome and his presentation to the Queen of Italy), there were signs that some, at least, of his old "picturesqueness" was deserting him. A publisher was easily found for his *London Up To Date*—it sold well—but this "most unsentimental journey" was commonplace stuff. Perhaps it was that the financial situation was once again not too satisfactory. The Palace Theatre of Varieties had duly opened its doors, but there had been repeated trouble with the authorities, and such money as he had been able to invest in the new company was in serious jeopardy. (He was soon to resign his directorship and sell his shares at a very considerable loss.) With his reminiscences and autobiography in print he would be in a better position, for he was now employing Mr. A. P. Watt, the first of the literary agents, who had obtained for him generous terms, but unfortunately with all the work for *Sala's Journal* they were not progressing at any great speed. Bessie Sala, too, was already in financial difficulties, trying in a hundred different quarters to sell a quarter-share of the *Journal*—for this optimistically she asked £3000—or raise a mortgage upon it. The weekly profits, she said, were "from £11 to £25," but some of her statements about the revenue from advertisements were more than merely rosy, and it was obvious that without a great deal of new capital the whole venture would collapse. Sala, too, seems to have "struck" against writing so much of the magazine himself, and nobody can blame him. As a result Bessie Sala endeavoured to take his place, and filled pages with her "Table Talk," a causerie of personal doings, the domesticities, and advice to young people. It was innocuous prattle, but hardly exciting, and even when Arthur à Beckett anonymously took G. A. S.'s place, as he occasionally did, with the "Topic of the Week," the *Journal* seemed to be in danger of losing what personality it had ever possessed.

4

Nevertheless, it was not yet moribund, and on his return Sala worked valorously on its behalf. At the end of May a new company—Sala's Journal, Limited—was formed, with William Howard Russell and B. L. Farjeon the novelist on the directorate, and for a few months, under less amateurish management, there was a marked increase in the sales, more particularly as Sala himself dictated a new novel (published after his death as *Margaret Forster*), the opening chapters of which appeared in the *Journal* at the beginning of July.

It was a last flicker of the old-time vivacity and sprightly invention : a fantasy embracing the startlingly different worlds of the "rich" and the "poor." It had good scenes in it, and the mystery of the girl who at one moment seemed to be a rich heiress and at the next an adventuress from the slums whom the police regarded with the deepest suspicion was well kept. For some considerable time, it seems, Sala had had the theme in his mind, and he made dexterous use of his knowledge of Belgravian mansions and the poverty-stricken hovels in their near vicinity. The apparent ease, moreover, with which the story was dictated seems to

have had the effect of spurring him on to complete his two autobio-
graphical books.

As a result of "advanced payments" for these books and the "brilliant
success" which had attended Mr. Watt's negotiations in the matter of
other copyrights of his, there was a fair amount of money banked just
now in his name, and in his impulsive way he rid himself of the Victoria
flat—Bessie Sala had never liked it—and purchased the freehold of a yet
larger Brighton house in Eastern Terrace. Here, during the early months
of 1894, the Salas entertained on a scale which must have satisfied even so
ambitious a hostess as Bessie, and G. A. S. seems to have decided that now
at long last the old financial worries could be finally forgotten. With
his business affairs in the safe hands of Mr. Watt, his wife's magazine
apparently round the corner, and his health much better than it had been
for some time past, he could, he hoped, cheerfully settle down to a not
too strenuous old age. He had no idea of retirement—to the end he
would remain in harness—but he had said good-bye to the garish lights
of London and proposed to enjoy the last years of his life by the sea,
surrounded by his beloved books and curios, welcoming his friends,
comfortably serene. There were ideas in his head for new books; there
would be reprints of old ones; and if the proposed volume of his leading
articles upon which his wife was already at work were to be a success
and others demanded, why, then, the future would be rosy indeed.

We are given glimpses of him at the time by various old friends who
were glad to run down to Brighton to enjoy a beautifully-cooked meal
and some excellent conversation. One or two of the visitors were not
ignorant of the financial crises of the past and, recalling the recent frantic
endeavours to find money for *Sala's Journal*, were not a little surprised
at the splendours of the house and the lavish nature of their entertainment;
but all agreed that G. A. S. was in his best form. Lord Ronald Gower,
a brother of the Duke of Sutherland and for long years one of Sala's
warmest admirers, records a visit he paid to Eastern Terrace at the
beginning of February. "A most comfortable house," he writes, "where,
I think, it may be said that G. A. Sala is enjoying a kind of apotheosis, for,
surrounded as he is by fifteen thousand books and collections of all sorts,
he seems to be supremely happy."

Happy he remained for the next two months. Every day there
would be sent up to London the leading article for tomorrow's *Daily
Telegraph*; the "Echoes" were being despatched with the greatest
regularity; and *Sala's Journal* continued to receive its fair share of G. A. S.
Happy he was, too, on the receipt of an unexpected letter from "Sir
Roger Tichborne" bewailing the evil days upon which he had fallen,

to send a representative to the Claimant's humble lodgings and see to it that he was not allowed to starve. (Luckily for his purse in the following week Charles Morritt the eminent illusionist engaged the old man to appear at the Prince's Hall in his latest "vanishing" trick.) And he was happiest of all when at the beginning of March, after Mr. Gladstone's resignation, he learnt that Lord Rosebery had been summoned to Windsor and kissed hands as Prime Minister.

Then the blow fell.

5

Precisely what happened I have been unable to discover, but it was while its Conductor was correcting the proofs of his *Things I Have Seen and People I Have Known* during the second week in April that the news reached him of the abrupt stoppage of *Sala's Journal*. At the time three instalments of a revised version of his thirty-year-old *Seven Sons of Mammon* had appeared "by request" in its pages, and there had been no falling off in the number of correspondents waiting to be answered; but in the previous week's issue there had been an ominous drop in advertisements, and, to the trade at any rate, this sudden decision to close down can have come as no surprise. Debts must have been accumulating for some time and salaries ruthlessly cut if they had never actually been suspended. There must have been a final desperate appeal from Bessie Sala, and on its failure the printers presumably refused to continue.

Was Sala himself expecting anything of the kind? I fancy not. I believe that he had been content to leave all business matters to his wife and the managing director of the company. I believe that he suffered no small shock which was only mitigated by the fact that his wife had secured for herself some kind of position on the *Daily Telegraph's* regular staff. There is no doubt whatever that he worried himself into a state of nervous exhaustion which brought on yet another form of acute dermatitis. Every available penny was needed to stave off proceedings in the Courts, and I imagine that it was only by agreeing to set aside a substantial portion of his earnings that he was able to persuade the company's creditors to take no legal action. He had been additionally shocked, moreover, to hear of the sudden death in London of Edmund Yates, for some time past a Brighton neighbour of his, but must have smiled rather wryly when he learnt of the considerable fortune which the proprietor of the *World* had left. Once on a time, and not so long ago, he had thought to leave some such sum of money himself. . . .

To the outer world, however, there was little to show that the final crash was so near. The Eastern Terrace house still retained its four servants, and Sala's bookbinder was no less busily engaged on his behalf than he had been for years past. There was no sign in the "Echoes" that G. A. S. was not his cheeriest self, and when in June a letter from Lord Randolph Churchill was printed in the *Times* deploring the "foul" condition of the London streets, he took up the matter with all his old-time enthusiasm in the *Daily Telegraph* as well as his *Sunday Times* columns and received Lord Randolph's thanks in a letter of which any journalist might have been proud. The book of reminiscences appeared and was widely reviewed, and the *Daily Telegraph* printed a further series of early Victorian memories. In August he slipped away to Brussels and Paris, and in the late autumn he and his wife stayed at the newly-erected Royal Palace Hotel in Kensington. The dermatitis had refused to disappear, but with the first proofs of his *Life and Adventures* in his hands he had regained some of his usual good spirits. "We have let our house," he told Burnand, "to a swell who has been fool enough to pay us £25 a week for it; so we are living here in riotous luxury on the proceeds. . . . Come and see us. Like a gent who is 'doing time' I am always in."

Yet he was so far from well that even a visit from very old friends was something of a strain. In their presence he would make an effort to be his old self, speaking of the new books and the latest plays, and even fulminating in the old forthright way against "enemies" like Furniss; but those who came to his hotel left it with the feeling that they would probably not see him again. When, too, he had seen his big book through the press, the only one, incidentally, of all he had written which had not previously appeared in the form of newspaper articles, he found it difficult to settle down to the old routine. It was as though he recognised that his life's work was done. Even the "Echoes" were not always ready for the printer, and more than once, she tells us, Bessie Sala was obliged to finish them herself. It was becoming increasingly clear, indeed, that the day when a leading article by Sala appeared as a matter of course had gone for ever, and when at Christmas, after an attack of influenza, he set off as usual for Rome he had definitely ceased all regular work for Peterborough Court.

CHAPTER SEVENTEEN
THE END OF THE STORY

I

A VIOLENT gale was blowing that December day as the packet-boat left Dover harbour, and in mid-channel Sala fell heavily on deck, injuring a "false" rib, round which, he told a friend, one of his "interior arrangements had got twisted." He stayed in Paris for a little while and could eat nothing solid. At Marseilles he was snowed up for four days, and when at last he found himself in his usual rooms at the Hôtel d'Angleterre, Rome, he was a very sick man. Both the Prime Minister and Lord Dufferin had given him letters to the new British Ambassador, Sir Francis Ford, and he called at once at the Embassy. He was saying good-bye when he fell down in a swoon, and it was some days before he could be driven back to his hotel. Bessie Sala was unable to join him until the early spring, and there was no faithful Annie to nurse him. In spite of the sun the doctor forbade him to go out, and he felt unable to write more than the merest skeleton of the "Echoes." Even the Greek studies which had come to be his chief relaxation had to be given up. Fortunately several old friends of his were in Rome at the time, and they did their best to cheer up the invalid. He was heartened, too, to hear that his book was selling well and to receive letters from those to whom special copies of the *Life and Adventures* had been sent. The Prince of Wales and the Prime Minister were amongst them, and Mr. Gladstone, whose acquaintance he had recently made, wrote from Cap Martin to say that he was reading the volumes "with great interest; an interest all the greater because the absorbing nature of my own profession sadly starved my social knowledge in all departments outside of it."

Probably, however, it was a new friend who did as much as anybody else to brighten these "miserable" days. It happened that Cardinal Vaughan was in Rome at the time. Hitherto the two men had not met, except, perchance, to shake hands at a reception, but the Cardinal wrote to him, offering privileged tickets for some ceremony at St. Peter's, and subsequently came to know and like him. From his first letter, moreover, it seems probable that a mutual friend of theirs—it may have been Burnand—had spoken of Sala's Catholic ancestry and of some vague desire of his to be reconciled to the Church of his fathers before his death.

278

Now, although he seldom entered a church he was not an irreligious man. For all his shortcomings, his evil temper, his intemperance and uglier vices, he was essentially a *kind* man, and one, be it noted, who never wished to be thanked for any little favour he might be able to do. Again and again you may find stories of help given surreptitiously to those in misfortune, even when he was in financial difficulties himself. For his own part, he had never hidden his simple Christian beliefs. But he had been brought up in the Protestant faith, and it will be remembered that at the time of the "Papal Aggression" outcry he had shouted even more loudly than most people, in his two panoramas. Admittedly that had been in his callow days, and since then he had come to number many Catholics amongst his friends, including the Sisters of Nazareth in Bayswater about whose good work he had repeatedly written in the *Daily Telegraph*. Yet although nowhere in his letters is the slightest hint given of any wish to join the Roman Church, there can be little doubt that for some time he had been seriously considering the matter, and if his talks with Cardinal Vaughan produced no immediate result—his next address, he was jokingly writing to a friend a few weeks later, would probably be the *Protestant* cemetery in Rome—they were not without their ultimate effect. And it was now that the Cardinal promised to come, if humanly possible, to his bedside at any time that he should be summoned: a promise which he was to fulfil within the year.

This was in February, 1895. On the last day of the month Sala was sufficiently recovered to accept an invitation to dinner. His host was Lord Ronald Gower, and two other guests were bidden to meet him. One of these, Sir George Arthur, knew Sala well; the other was the future Lord Milner. G. A. S., records his host, was in excellent form and enjoyed his dinner. That night the Coliseum was to be illuminated with Bengal lights, and the four of them sallied forth. It was bitterly cold, and Sala soon excused himself and was driven home. The next day he was laid up with a chill, and few of his friends in Rome ever saw him again.

In a rather pathetic little note he tells us how, unable to write and unwilling to read, he sent for some clay and the requisite tools, and for a fortnight or so amused himself modelling the right arm and hand of the Venus de Medicis and a life-sized mask. Yet notes for the "Echoes" continued to reach England, and if ever there came an uneasy moment about the state of his finances, it was speedily ignored, for a second edition of the *Life and Adventures* was selling, a third had been ordered, and Mr. Watt had forwarded on an agreeably large cheque.

It was only in Paris that he realised what a drastic change in his manner of living might be necessary in the very near future. He had gone to the Grand Hotel and engaged its most palatial suite of rooms, and it was there that Hall Richardson, who at the time was stationed in Paris, found him, "obviously a physical wreck." He had called in response to a telegram from Peterborough Court. "Find Sala and get him to write on anything he likes." "I told him my mission," he relates, and gives Sala's reply. "I'm ready to write on anything from the price of beef to a coronation." But although at Richardson's suggestion he did manage to complete a leading article on the Place Royale and its literary associations, it was the last that was to come from his pen. True, in the course of the next two months some half-dozen signed essays of his were to appear in the *Daily Telegraph*—they were intended for a further volume of *Things I Have Seen*—but henceforth that "fourth leader" which for nearly forty years had been his particular province was to be the work of other hands.

It may be that the telegram sent to Richardson had been inspired by Bessie Sala, who was still a member of the *Daily Telegraph* staff. Perhaps she hoped that it might act as a spur. Soon enough, too, he would be in need of money, and her own affairs were in the sorriest state. The "swell" who had paid £25 a week for the Brighton house had departed, and no philanthropist had been found to take his place. Feverishly she had been endeavouring to arrange for further reprints of her husband's writings, but her efforts had come to little enough. Cassells had agreed to issue a collection of cookery articles and recipes from *Sala's Journal*, but that was all. Her own salary was not large, expenses were still heavy, and her old creditors were becoming pressing. She seems to have been at some pains to keep her worries from her husband, about whose state of health she was under no illusions; and I am almost sure that at this time he was in ignorance of her desperate appeal to Sir Edward Lawson in the previous December. She had asked for a loan of £500, and £300 was sent her. Inexcusably she chose to take offence at "so cruel and unfriendly" a response to her appeal—it had by no means been the first of the kind—and the sharp terms in which her employer thought fit to reply were not, I think, undeserved. Now, some four months later, the position was worse than it had ever been, and when she was able to snatch a holiday and join her husband, it was with the conviction that only the immediate sale of Sala's books and collections could prevent disaster.

She must have been shocked at the change in him—a pale shadow of his old burly self—and I can only guess in what way she made him understand that the palatial suite must be given up and expenses at home cut to a minimum. Not yet was his mind failing, but it was clear that the time had gone when he could hope to be in harness again. He was a very tired man, gentle and apathetic, and unwilling, it seemed, to think about anything except the old Bohemian days and his recent conversations with Cardinal Vaughan. Mr. Watt's cheque was almost exhausted, and it was obviously only a matter of weeks before the "Echoes" must cease. For the last time Sala crossed the Channel, and once back in Eastern Terrace watched with a dismay which could not be hidden while his finest books and best-loved "curios" were packed up for the sales-room.

The ordeal was all the more painful because it was by no means certain that, even if his "sticks" fetched their full value at auction, he and his wife would be free of debt. There was the house, but of course it was heavily mortgaged, and without it where would they live? Years ago there had come a moment when bankruptcy had seemed inevitable. Somehow it had been staved off. Now the position was very much worse because he could no longer sit down at his desk to work. Once the "Echoes" were to stop, and that must be very soon now, he knew that he would write no more.

It may be wondered why wealthy friends like the Baroness Burdett-Coutts or the Dukes of Sutherland and Fife were not approached. Perhaps they were; perhaps they helped; but although a year or two later Bessie Sala was writing most bitterly of the way in which her husband's friends had deserted him at the end, the majority of them knew nothing about these new troubles and were astonished when the news became public. In addition, I fancy, she herself was now chary of making further appeals. Too often in the past she had sought assistance for one or other of her schemes from well-known folk whom her husband knew, and when the schemes went awry written again in not too tactful a way, and been politely snubbed. Perhaps, too, for the last time in his life Sala put his foot firmly down. It is not easy for a dethroned monarch to beg for alms.

Yet he did write to one old friend, and not in vain. On May 20th Lord Rosebery, still Prime Minister though his Government was near to defeat, had returned from a short cruise after his recent illness. On the 29th he had the satisfaction of seeing a horse of his win the Derby for the second year in succession. Two days later he was "more shocked and grieved" than he could say to have news from Sala "so absolutely unexpected and so sad." At once, he promised, he would see what could be done, and twenty-four hours later he was writing again. "I am recommending you to the Queen for a Civil List pension of £100 per annum which I hope will be agreeable to you. I only wish I could do more for you."

So he need not starve, this prince of correspondents who had earned an Ambassador's salary. He received his dole—in the same week, as it happened, that William Howard Russell, his one-time rival and very old friend, was knighted.

2

Little more remains to be told.

In the last week in June there was a not too successful sale of his works of art, and a month later the greater portion of his library was sold at Sotheby's. Sala himself was in no great pain or even discomfort, though his medical attendant, Dr. William Thistle, feared a tumour on the liver: only dreadfully tired. Yet he was able to dictate an article or two, and one morning even insisted on sitting down at his desk in the sadly dismantled study. Bessie Sala suggested that he dictate to her as usual, but with a touch of his old-time obstinacy he told her that he wished to feel a pen in his hand once again. It was for the last time. "Bedrooms on Wheels," I presume, was intended for one of the magazines: it was never finished. He had reached his third page (and his script was as neat and precise as ever it had been) when, in the middle of a sentence, he was obliged to put down his pen; and that was the end of the Sala whom the world had applauded.

A few days later the doctor permitted him to take a drive, and he stopped the carriage at the Orleans Club. He saw few enough people these days, and an hour or so in company would come as a pleasant break. He walked into the Club, and there was struck down. They brought him back in a semi-conscious condition, and Bessie Sala sent for a priest. The next day she went to London and returned with Cardinal Vaughan. Sala had rallied, and was duly received into the Roman Catholic Church.

A month passed, and he lay in his bed, very feeble and hardly speaking at all, though not yet wholly immersed in a confused dream of the past. More of his books were sold and fetched little enough—the treasured "Mrs. Glasse" cost its new owner no more than a ten-pound note—and it became necessary to arrange for the sale of the house. Then, some time in October, when a purchaser had been found and Bessie Sala's work was keeping her in London, the invalid was moved into Dr. Thistle's house in Norton Road, very near to the Church of the Sacred Heart. Here he was nursed by a nun from the Bayswater convent whose work had pleased him so much, and here it was that one or two old friends, distressed to hear of his troubles, called and were permitted to see him, and knew that they were saying good-bye. But soon enough all such visits were useless, for Sala's fine brain was succumbing, and although he spoke affectionately to the doctor of old friends like the Mayhews, Vizetelly, Shirley Brooks, and Labouchere, he recognised none of his visitors, not even his wife. He would shed a few tears now and then, Dr. Thistle wrote, and be pleased when some letter of sympathy was read out to him; but mercifully all knowledge of his last troubles was being blotted out, and during the last weeks of his life—he lingered on until the morning of Sunday, December 9th— he was in the world of long ago, doing odd jobs for that masterful mother of his in the Snargate Street theatre at Dover, watching Beverley at work in the painting-room at the Princess's, hearing Dickens's hearty greetings at Gadshill, and listening to the excellent advice that Thackeray chose to give to his Reverend Doctor Sala.

APPENDIX

CHECK LIST OF SEPARATE PUBLICATIONS

A. *WORKS WHOLLY BY SALA*

(Those which have not been seen are starred. The publisher's name is given in brackets. No mention is made of American editions except when there is no English edition. Binding is cloth except where otherwise stated.)

1850

HAIL, RAIN, STEAM & SPEED. By an Old Stoker.
> Panorama; text and plates. Plain and coloured copies. Boards. (Ackermann)

GRAND PROCESSION AGAINST PAPAL AGGRESSION TO PRESENT THE ADDRESS AND OBTAIN REDRESS IN ORDER THAT WE MAY HEAR LESS OF HIS HOLINESS.
> Panorama; text and plates. Plain and coloured copies. Boards. (Ackermann)

NO POPERY! A PROTESTANT ROLAND FOR A POPISH OLIVER. By Anti-Guy.
> Panorama; text and plates. Plain and coloured copies. Boards. (Ackermann)

THE GREAT EXHIBITION WOT IS TO BE, OR PROBABLE RESULTS OF THE INDUSTRY OF ALL NATIONS IN THE YEAR '51. By Vates Secundus.
> Panorama; text and plates. Plain and coloured copies. Boards. (Ackermann)

> Several etchings and lithographs by Sala were issued separately during this and the next two or three years. Two were included in the sale of Sala's works of art, 1895; a series of designs illustrating the "Bloomer" costume is mentioned in his *Life and Adventures.*

"ALL THE WORLD'S A CHEESE!" A GASEOUS COSMOS OF CARICATURES AND CHARACTER.
> Panorama; text and plates. Plain and coloured copies. Boards. (Ackermann)

An Invitation to attend the private view of the Great Exhibition on April 1st.
> Spoof admission ticket at the head of a letter signed Hookey Hoaxem. Lithograph.

THE BOOK OF THE SYMPOSIUM; OR SOYER AT GORE HOUSE. A CATALOGUE RAISONNÉ, ARTISTIC, HISTORIC, TOPOGRAPHIC, AND PICTURESQUE OF THAT UNIQUE AND GIGANTIC ESTABLISHMENT.
> Text only. Illustrations not by Sala. Wrappers. (Soyer)
> Only one copy is known.

THE GREAT GLASS HOUSE OPEND (*sic*); OR THE EXHIBITION WOT IS!!
> Panorama; text and plates. Plain and coloured copies. Boards. (Ackermann)

THE HOUSE THAT PAXTON BUILT.
    Panorama ; text and plates. Plain and coloured copies. Boards. (Acker-
mann)

1855

GRAND NATIONAL, HISTORICAL, AND CHIVALRIC PANTOMIME YE BELLE ALLIANCE ;
    OR HARLEQUIN GOOD HUMOUR AND YE FIELDE OF YE CLOTHE OF GOLDE, BEING
    A LEGEND OF THE MONARCHS.
    (*Dec.*) "The words by George Augustus Sala." Wrappers. (Francis)
    N.B.—Copies in *pale yellow* covers have an unsigned illustration apparently
    by Sala ; others have none.

1858

A JOURNEY DUE NORTH. BEING NOTES OF A RESIDENCE IN RUSSIA IN THE SUMMER
    OF 1856.
    (*Aug.*) (Bentley)

1859

HOW I TAMED MRS. CRUISER.
    Pictorial boards. (Blackwood)
    n.d., possibly published towards the end of 1858.

GASLIGHT AND DAYLIGHT, WITH SOME LONDON SCENES THEY SHINE UPON.
    (*Apr.*) (Chapman & Hall)

TWICE ROUND THE CLOCK ; OR THE HOURS OF THE DAY AND NIGHT IN LONDON.
    (*Oct.*) n.d. (Houlston & Wright)
    Portrait of Sala (see text) and illustrations by M'Connell.

1860

LOOKING AT LIFE ; OR, THOUGHTS AND THINGS.
    (Routledge)

THE BADDINGTON PEERAGE : WHO WON, AND WHO WORE IT. A STORY OF THE
    BEST AND THE WORST SOCIETY.
    (*May*) 3 vols. (Skeet)

A NARRATIVE OF THE GRAND VOLUNTEER REVIEW IN HYDE PARK, ON SATURDAY
    THE TWENTY-THIRD OF JUNE.
    (*July*) Wrappers. (Tinsley)

★A NARRATIVE OF THE TARGET SHOOTING AT WIMBLEDON, IN THE WEEK COMMENCING
    JULY 2, AND THE DISTRIBUTION OF THE PRIZES AT THE CRYSTAL PALACE, JULY 9,
    1860.
    (*Aug.*) Wrappers. (Dean)
    N.B.—This also contains the Volunteer Review, but is not the same as
    Tinsley's second edition, though that includes a report of the Wimbledon
    shooting.

MAKE YOUR GAME ; OR, THE ADVENTURE OF THE STOUT GENTLEMAN, THE SLIM
    GENTLEMAN, AND THE MAN WITH THE IRON CHEST : A NARRATIVE OF THE RHINE
    AND THEREABOUTS.
    (*Sept.*) Pictorial boards. Some of the illustrations are by Sala. (Ward
    & Lock)

LADY CHESTERFIELD'S LETTERS TO HER DAUGHTER.
   Illustrated by "Phiz." (Houlston & Wright)
PROSPECTUS OF "TEMPLE BAR."
   (*Oct.*) Two varieties, each 2 pp.

1861

DUTCH PICTURES; WITH SOME SKETCHES IN THE FLEMISH MANNER.
   (*Oct.*) (Tinsley)

1862

THE SEVEN SONS OF MAMMON.
   (*Dec.* 1861) 3 vols. (Tinsley)

THE TWO PRIMA DONNAS, AND THE DUMB DOOR PORTER.
   (*Jan.*) (Tinsley)

THE SHIP CHANDLER AND OTHER TALES.
   (*May*) Pale blue paper covers. (Ward & Lock: No. 17 The Shilling Library)

ACCEPTED ADDRESSES.
   (*July*) (Tinsley)
   N.B.—The first issue appeared in *purple* cloth, with the publisher's name at the foot of the spine.

1863

THE STRANGE ADVENTURES OF CAPTAIN DANGEROUS: WHO WAS A SOLDIER, A SAILOR, A MERCHANT, A SPY, A SLAVE AMONG THE MOORS, A BASHAW IN THE SERVICE OF THE GRAND TURK, AND DIED AT LAST IN HIS OWN HOUSE IN HANOVER SQUARE.
   (*Apr.*) 3 vols. (Tinsley)

BREAKFAST IN BED OR PHILOSOPHY BETWEEN THE SHEETS. A SERIES OF INDIGESTIBLE DISCOURSES.
   (*Sept.*) (Maxwell)

THE PERFIDY OF CAPTAIN SLYBOOTS AND OTHER TALES.
   (*Nov.*) Pictorial wrappers. (Ward & Lock: Shilling Volume Library)

1864

AFTER BREAKFAST; OR, PICTURES DONE WITH A QUILL.
   (*June*) 2 vols. (Tinsley)

ROBSON: A SKETCH.
   (*Sept.*) Wrappers. (Hotten)
   Hotten's introduction is almost as long as Sala's essay and so perhaps this little pamphlet ought to be included in B.

QUITE ALONE.
   (*Nov.*) 3 vols. (Chapman & Hall)
   This also should go, I suppose, into B., as the novel is not wholly by Sala. The concluding chapters were the work of Andrew Halliday. See text.

1865

MY DIARY IN AMERICA IN THE MIDST OF WAR.
   (*Jan.*) 2 vols. (Tinsley)

1866

A TRIP TO BARBARY BY A ROUNDABOUT ROUTE.
   (*Nov.* 1865) (Tinsley)

WILLIAM HOGARTH : PAINTER, ENGRAVER, AND PHILOSOPHER. ESSAYS ON THE MAN,
THE WORK, AND THE TIME.
   Frontispiece by Sala. (Smith, Elder)

1867

FROM WATERLOO TO THE PENINSULA. FOUR MONTHS' HARD LABOUR IN BELGIUM,
HOLLAND, GERMANY, AND SPAIN.
   (*Dec.* 1866) 2 vols. (Tinsley)

★ALL THE FUN OF THE FAIR. A SERIO-COMIC, POLITICO-ECONOMIC, INDUSTRIO-
AESTHETIC, GRAPHICO-GASTRONOMIC REVIEW OF THE UNIVERSAL PARIS EXHIBI-
TION OF 1867.
   Panorama. Advertised in *Belgravia* for Nov. 1867 as a forthcoming Christ-
mas book, but I greatly doubt whether it was ever issued.

1868

NOTES & SKETCHES OF THE PARIS EXHIBITION.
   (*Feb.*) (Tinsley)

INSURANCE AND ASSURANCE. AN ESSAY . . . REPRINTED FROM "BELGRAVIA" OF
JUNE 1868.
   n.d. Wrappers. (Liverpool)

THE BATTLE OF THE SAFES.
   Wrappers. (Tinsley)
   An edition was issued in French and English.

THE HATS OF HUMANITY, HISTORICALLY, HUMOROUSLY, AND AESTHETICALLY CON-
SIDERED : A HOMILY.
   n.d. Wrappers. (Gee, Manchester)

COMPTON HOUSE, LIVERPOOL.
   n.d. Wrappers. (Grant)

LISSON GROVE.
   n.d. Wrappers. (Grant)

1869

NEEDLE MAGIC. AN ANECDOTAL HISTORY OF THE SEWING MACHINE.
   n.d. Wrappers. (Bradbury, Oldham)

ROME AND VENICE, WITH OTHER WANDERINGS IN ITALY, IN 1866-7.
   (Tinsley)

THE LATE MR. D—— AND OTHER TALES.
     Wrappers. (Ward & Lock)
     Previously included in *The Ship Chandler*.

WAT TYLER, M.P., AN OPERATIC EXTRAVAGANZA.
     (*Dec.*) Wrappers. (Gaiety Theatre)
     Two versions.

1870

CHARLES DICKENS.
     (*July*) Wrappers. (Routledge)
     In America this essay was included in Harper's edition of the *Speeches,
     Letters, and Sayings of Charles Dickens*.

1871

DOWN CLOTHING.
     n.d. Wrappers. (McLintock, Barnsley)

1872

THANKSGIVING NUMBER OF THE GRAPHIC.
     (*Mar.*) Wrappers.

UNDER THE SUN. ESSAYS MAINLY WRITTEN IN HOT COUNTRIES.
     (*June*) (Tinsley)

PAPERS HUMOROUS AND PATHETIC: BEING SELECTIONS FROM THE WORKS OF
     GEORGE AUGUSTUS SALA. REVISED AND ABRIDGED BY THE AUTHOR FOR PUBLIC
     READING.
     (Tinsley)

*THE PHILOSOPHY OF EAU DE VIE.
     n.d. Wrappers. (Brett)

1873

THE STORY OF THE COMTE DE CHAMBORD: A TRILOGY.
     Pictorial boards. (Routledge)

TERRIBLE TALES.
     (*Dec.*) n.d. Pictorial wrappers. (Dicks: Bow Bells Annual)

1879

PARIS HERSELF AGAIN IN 1878-9.
     (*Oct.*) 2 vols. (Remington)

1881

IN A WINE CELLAR IN STORE STREET.
     n.d. Wrappers. (Robt. James)

1882

AMERICA REVISITED: FROM THE BAY OF NEW YORK TO THE GULF OF MEXICO, AND
     FROM LAKE MICHIGAN TO THE PACIFIC.
     (*Aug.*) 2 vols. (Vizetelly)

1883

LIVING LONDON. BEING "ECHOES" RE-ECHOED.
    (*June*) (Remington)
    N.B.—In this year publication was begun of "The Choicer Works of
George Augustus Sala."

1884

ECHOES OF THE YEAR EIGHTEEN HUNDRED AND EIGHTY-THREE.
    (*May*) (Remington)
DEAD MEN TELL NO TALES; BUT LIVE MEN DO.
    (*Nov.*) Pictorial wrappers. (Dicks: Bow Bells Annual)

1885

A JOURNEY DUE SOUTH. TRAVELS IN SEARCH OF SUNSHINE.
    (Vizetelly)

1888

THE OLD HUMMUMS MADE NEW AGAIN. A RETROSPECT & DESCRIPTION OF THE
    MOST HISTORICAL HOSTELRY IN COVENT GARDEN.
    (Sutton Sharpe)
DUBLIN WHISKEY: AN ESSAY.
    n.d. Wrappers. (Roe, Dublin)

1892

MADAME TUSSAUD: EXHIBITION CATALOGUE.
    Pictorial wrappers.
    "Is entirely rewritten by George Augustus Sala." The word "entirely,"
however, is to be taken in its Pickwickian sense.
    Reprinted, with alterations, additions, and subtractions, almost monthly
until 1916 or later.

1894

LONDON UP TO DATE.
    (Black)
THINGS I HAVE SEEN AND PEOPLE I HAVE KNOWN.
    (*June*) 2 vols. (Cassell)

1895

THE LIFE AND ADVENTURES OF GEORGE AUGUSTUS SALA. WRITTEN BY HIMSELF.
    (*Jan.*) 2 vols. (Cassell)
BRIGHTON AS I HAVE KNOWN IT.
    (*Sept.*) Stiff wrappers. (Black)
THE THOROUGH GOOD COOK. A SERIES OF CHATS ON THE CULINARY ART AND
    NINE HUNDRED RECIPES.
    (Cassell)

T

? 1896

MRS. MELLOR'S DIAMONDS.
"Issued by Mossant, Vallon & Co." (U.S.A.).
n.d. Embossed wrappers.
The story was first published in *Belgravia*, June, 1871.

1897

MARGARET FORSTER. A DREAM WITHIN A DREAM.
Preface by Mrs. Sala. (Fisher Unwin)

B. *WORKS PARTIALLY BY SALA*

(It has not been easy to decide where a line should be drawn, but in general
it may be taken that only those publications which bear Sala's name on the
title-page, or those in which he was responsible for more than isolated
contributions, have been included.)

1847

A WORD WITH PUNCH. BY ALFRED BUNN.
No covers. (Johnson)
Title and illustrations by Sala, who may also have assisted with the text.
★Some copies coloured.

1848

A BOWL OF PUNCH. BY ALBERT SMITH.
Wrappers. (Bogue)
"Illustrated by Hemming, Hine, and Sala."

1849

THE MAN IN THE MOON.
5 vols. In the original issue in monthly parts, Sala's name as an illustrator
does not appear on the covers until vol. 5.

THE BATTLE OF LONDON LIFE, OR BOZ AND HIS SECRETARY. BY "MORNA" [Capt.
Thomas O'Keefe].
(*Feb.*) Pink boards. (Pierce)
"With six designs on stone by George Sala."

★THE APRIL FOOL BOOK: FOR THE WISE MEN OF THE WEST. BY "MORNA."
(Pierce)
"Illustrated by George Sala."
Doubtful, but advertised in the preceding.

1851

★A panorama of the Great Exhibition designed by Alfred Crowquill.
Title not known to me. Plates etched by Sala.

HARLEQUIN BILLY TAYLOR; OR, THE FLYING DUTCHMAN, AND THE KING OF RARI-
TONGO. INVENTED AND WRITTEN BY MR. GEORGE ELLIS AND THE BROTHERS SALA.
Wrappers. (Lacy)

1852

FUNERAL PROCESSION OF THE DUKE OF WELLINGTON.   BY HENRY ALKEN AND GEORGE
AUGUSTUS SALA.
Panorama in colour.   (Ackermann)

*THE CORSICANS.   BY THE BROTHERS SALA.
I have been informed that their version of the play was printed.

1859

THE BOYS' BIRTHDAY BOOK.   BY MRS. S. C. HALL, WILLIAM HOWITT, AUGUSTUS
MAYHEW, THOMAS MILLER, AND GEORGE AUGUSTUS SALA.
(*Sept.*)   n.d.   (Houlston & Wright)
Later editions have "By George Augustus Sala and Other Eminent Writers."

1860

MARSTON LYNCH.   A PERSONAL BIOGRAPHY BY ROBERT B. BROUGH.   WITH A
MEMOIR OF THE AUTHOR BY GEORGE AUGUSTUS SALA.
(*July*)   Pictorial Boards.   (Ward & Lock)

1861-2

TEMPLE BAR.   A LONDON MAGAZINE FOR TOWN AND COUNTRY READERS.   CON-
DUCTED BY GEORGE AUGUSTUS SALA.
Vols. I-VI.   (Ward & Lock)

1865

THE CORNHILL GALLERY, CONTAINING ONE HUNDRED ENGRAVINGS FROM DRAWINGS
ON WOOD.
(Smith, Elder)
"Designs for the illustration of *The Cornhill Magazine*."   Contains Sala's
"Mr. Gamble's Apprentice" and his name on title-page.

[BELLE BOYD, IN CAMP AND PRISON.   WRITTEN BY HERSELF.   WITH AN INTRODUCTION
BY GEORGE AUGUSTA (*sic*) SALA.]
(New York : Blelock)
English edition does not bear Sala's name and is in two vols.   See text.

THE BIGLOW PAPERS.   BY JAMES R. LOWELL.   [PART I.]   WITH AN INTRODUCTION BY
GEORGE AUGUSTUS SALA.
(*Oct.*)   Pictorial wrappers.   (Ward, Lock & Tyler)

*THE AUTOCRAT OF THE BREAKFAST TABLE.   BY OLIVER WENDELL HOLMES.
(*Oct.*)   Pictorial wrappers.   (Ward, Lock & Tyler)
With a preface by George Augustus Sala.   An edition of 1866 has been seen.

★ARTEMUS WARD : HIS BOOK. WITH AN INTRODUCTION BY GEORGE AUGUSTUS SALA.
(*Oct.*) Pictorial wrappers. (Ward, Lock & Tyler)

★MAJOR JACK DOWNING. WITH AN INTRODUCTION BY GEORGE AUGUSTUS SALA.
(*Oct.*) Pictorial wrappers. (Ward, Lock & Tyler)

★THE NASBY PAPERS. WITH AN INTRODUCTION BY GEORGE AUGUSTUS SALA.
(*Oct.*) Pictorial wrappers. (Ward, Lock & Tyler)

★ARTEMUS WARD : HIS TRAVELS. WITH AN INTRODUCTION BY GEORGE AUGUSTUS
SALA.
(*Nov.*) Pictorial wrappers. (Ward, Lock & Tyler)

★THE ORPHEUS C. KERR PAPERS. WITH AN INTRODUCTION BY GEORGE AUGUSTUS
SALA.
? date. Pictorial wrappers. (Ward, Lock & Tyler)

1866

YANKEE DROLLERIES. THE MOST CELEBRATED WORKS OF THE BEST AMERICAN
HUMORISTS. COMPLETE EDITIONS, WITH INTRODUCTIONS BY GEORGE AUGUSTUS
SALA.
(Ward, Lock & Tyler)
Numerous editions, with varying contents as different publishers purchased
old sheets and printed their own title-pages.

1868

THE NINE CHRISTMAS NUMBERS OF ALL THE YEAR ROUND. CONDUCTED BY CHARLES
DICKENS.
? date. Sala's name is on the cover of the edition in green boards.

JAMES SPENCE & CO. : ST. PAUL'S CATHEDRAL AND ITS CHURCHYARD.
Wrappers. (Grant)
Sala's is the only essay in this trade pamphlet, but other (anonymous)
items are included.

THE COMPLETE CORRESPONDENCE AND WORKS OF CHARLES LAMB. WITH AN ESSAY
ON HIS LIFE AND GENIUS BY GEORGE AUGUSTUS SALA. VOL. I.
(Moxon)
Suppressed.

FIRST CLASS : FARE ONE SHILLING
Pictorial wrappers. (Routledge : Christmas Annual)
Sala is amongst the list of passengers on the title-page and his portrait is
included with others on the cover.

THE POOR PRISONERS. EDITED BY GEORGE AUGUSTUS SALA.
Wrappers. (Dicks : Bow Bells Annual)

BANTER. CONDUCTED BY GEORGE AUGUSTUS SALA.
Boards.
The complete run—Sept. 2, 1867 to Jan. 30, 1868—is not always to be
found in bound copies.

1869

MORE YANKEE DROLLERIES. A SECOND SERIES OF CELEBRATED WORKS BY THE BEST AMERICAN HUMORISTS. WITH AN INTRODUCTION BY GEORGE AUGUSTUS SALA.
? date. (Hotten)

1870

A THIRD SUPPLY OF YANKEE DROLLERIES . . . WITH AN INTRODUCTION BY GEORGE AUGUSTUS SALA.
? date. (Hotten)

1874

CRYSTAL PALACE FIRST MULE AND DONKEY SHOW. CATALOGUE & PRIZE LIST, WITH A DISSERTATION ON DONKEYS BY GEORGE AUGUSTUS SALA.
Yellow wrappers. (Crystal Palace)

1875

MORNINGS AT BOW STREET. BY J. WIGHT. . . . WITH AN ESSAY ON BOW STREET BY GEORGE AUGUSTUS SALA.
Pictorial boards. (Routledge)

1878

*FANMAKERS COMPANY. CATALOGUE OF COMPETITIVE EXHIBITION OF FANS HELD AT DRAPERS HALL—2-11 July, 1878. WITH AN ESSAY ON FANS BY GEORGE AUGUSTUS SALA.

1880

*THE SHOWMAN'S PANORAMA. BY CODLIN AND SHORT. [John Latey, jun.] WITH AN INTRODUCTION BY GEORGE AUGUSTUS SALA.
(Fox)

1882

STORIES WITH A VENGEANCE. BY GEORGE AUGUSTUS SALA, AND OTHERS.
n.d. Wrappers. (Dicks: Bow Bells Annual)

1886

MRS. GENERAL MUCKLESTRAP'S FOUR TALL DAUGHTERS. A CULINARY ROMANCE, BY GEORGE AUGUSTUS SALA, AND OTHER STORIES.
n.d. Wrappers. (Dicks: Bow Bells Annual)

1887

THE DOGARESSA. BY W. G. MELMONTÍ. TRANSLATED BY CLARE BRUNE. WITH PREFACE BY GEORGE AUGUSTUS SALA.
(*Nov.* 1886) (Remington)

RIGHT ROUND THE WORLD, WITH SOME STORIES I FOUND ON IT. BY GEORGE AUGUSTUS SALA.
n.d. Pictorial wrappers. (Dicks: Bow Bells Annual)
Contains two stories not by Sala.

1888

NOT A FRIEND IN THE WORLD. A STORY OF A CHRISTMAS DINNER, BY GEORGE
AUGUSTUS SALA, AND OTHER STORIES.
   ? date. Pictorial wrappers. (Dicks: Bow Bells Annual)

1893

SALA'S JOURNAL. A MAGAZINE FOR ALL. CONDUCTED BY GEORGE AUGUSTUS SALA.
VOL. I.
   (Offices of the Journal)
   I fancy that none of the succeeding volumes was officially issued with title-
page and index, though the numbers are often found bound into volumes.

INDEX

A

À Beckett, Arthur, 267, 274
——, Gilbert, 58, 60, 267
Abingdon, Earl of, 3
Accepted Addresses. See Sala, G. A.
Ackermann, Adolphus, 75, 82, 83, 91, 93, 104
Adah the Betrayed, 204
Adelaide, 250
——, Queen, 14
Adventures of Mr. Ledbury, The, 52, 53
Africa, 181
After Breakfast. See Sala, G. A.
Ainsworth, W. H., 5, 202
Aix-la-Chapelle, 82
Alabama Claims, 188, 210, 216
Albany. See London.
Albert, Prince, 83
—— Memorial. See London
Alexander II. of Russia, 115, 121, 223, 238
Alexandra Square. See London
Algiers, 181, 220
Alice's Adventures in Wonderland, 111
Alken, Henry, jun., 104
—— ——, sen., 104
All the Year Round, 151, 165, 170, 176, 186
Alphonso XII. of Spain, 219, 220
Altai Mountains, 121
America, 157, 171, 181, 228, 231, 232
America Revisited. See Sala, G. A.
Anderson, James, 40
Andrews, William, 272
Anne, Queen, 121
" Annie," 245, 253-255, 260, 278
Answers, 272
Arabia, S.S., 170
Arabi Pasha, 241
Arnold, (Sir) Edwin, 234, 252; his *Light of Asia,* 234
——, Matthew, 1, 29, 198; his *Friendship's Garland,* 198, 199
Art of Dancing, The, 3
Arthur, Sir George, 279
Ascot, 254
Ashley, Sarah, 25, 28, 31, 39, 44, 243, 259, 266
Asia, 76
Astley's Theatre. See London
Athenaeum, 174, 185
Athens, 224
Auckland, 248, 250
Australia, 243, 244, 249, 250
Austria, 32, 150, 171, 183

B

Baddington Peerage, The. See Sala, G. A.
Balfe, M. W., 39
Balfour, Rt. Hon. A. J., 260
Ballantyne, Mr. Serjt., 213
Ballarat, S.S., 253
Baltimore, 247
Balzac, 161
Banter, 187
Barbary, 182
Bargraves, The. See Sala, G. A.
Barlow, Samuel, 175
Barnard Braddlescrogs. See Sala, G. A.
Barnett, Benjamin, 146
——, Morris, 146
Barnum, Phineas T., 174, 241
Barrett, Michael, 188
Bath, 73
Battle of London Life, The. See O'Keefe, Thomas
" Battle of Monte Cristo." See Sala, G. A.
Bavaria, 73
Bayswater. See London
Bede, Cuthbert. See Bradley, Rev. E.
Bedford, 109
" Bedrooms on Wheels." See Sala, G. A.
Beecher, Henry Ward, 173
Beefsteak Club. See London
Belfast, 181
Belgium, 183
Belgravia, 97, 179, 186, 215
Bella, S.S., 211
Belle Boyd in Camp, 177, 178
Belmont, August, 175
Belt, Richard, 241
Benicia Boy, The, 157
Bennett, Charles H., 110
——, J. Gordon, 174
Bentley, George, 243, 255
——, Richard, 135, 136
Berlin, 62, 75, 118, 171, 183, 209
Bermondsey. See London
Berners Hotel. See London
Bertie, Lady Elizabeth, 3
Beverley, William Roxby, 48-50, 283
Bewick, Thomas, 55
Beyrout, 33
Billingsgate. See London
Bishop, (Sir) Henry, 10
Bishop of London's Office. See London
Black, William, 259
Blackstone, Sir William, 119
Blanchard, Edward Leman, 65, 234
Blenheim Palace, 245

Printed in Great Britain by T. and A. CONSTABLE LTD.
at the University Press, Edinburgh